United States Income, Wealth, Consumption, and Inequality

International Policy Exchange Series

Published in collaboration with the
Center for International Policy Exchanges
University of Maryland

Series Editors
Douglas J. Besharov
Neil Gilbert

Reconciling Work and Poverty Reduction:
How Successful Are European Welfare States?
Edited by Bea Cantillon and Frank Vandenbroucke

University Adaptation in Difficult Economic Times
Edited by Paola Mattei

Activation or Workfare? Governance and the Neo-Liberal Convergence
Edited by Ivar Lødemel and Amílcar Moreira

Child Welfare Systems and Migrant Children:
A Cross Country Study of Policies and Practice
Edited by Marit Skivenes, Ravinder Barn, Katrin Kriz, and Tarja Pösö

Adjusting to a World in Motion:
Trends in Global Migration and Migration Policy
Edited by Douglas J. Besharov and Mark H. Lopez

Caring for a Living:
Migrant Women, Aging Citizens, and Italian Families
Francesca Degiuli

Child Welfare Removals by the State:
A Cross-Country Analysis of Decision-Making Systems
Edited by Kenneth Burns, Tarja Pösö, and Marit Skivenes

Improving Public Services:
International Experiences in Using Evaluation Tools to Measure Program Performance
Edited by Douglas J. Besharov, Karen J. Baehler, and Jacob Alex Klerman

Welfare, Work, and Poverty:
Social Assistance in China
Qin Gao

Youth Labor in Transition:
Inequalities, Mobility, and Policies in Europe
Edited by Jacqueline O'Reilly, Janine Leschke, Renate Ortlieb,
Martin Seeleib-Kaiser, and Paola Villa

Decent Incomes for All:
Improving Policies in Europe
Edited by Bea Cantillon, Tim Goedemé, and John Hills

Social Exclusion in Cross National Perspective:
Actors, Actions, and Impacts from Above and Below
Edited by Robert J. Chaskin, Bong Joo Lee, and Surinder Jaswal

The "Population Problem" in Pacific Asia
Stuart Gietel-Basten

United States Income, Wealth, Consumption, and Inequality
Edited by Diana Furchtgott-Roth

SCHOOL of
PUBLIC POLICY

UNITED STATES INCOME, WEALTH, CONSUMPTION, AND INEQUALITY

Edited by

DIANA FURCHTGOTT-ROTH

Washington, DC

OXFORD
UNIVERSITY PRESS

OXFORD
UNIVERSITY PRESS

Oxford University Press is a department of the University of Oxford. It furthers the University's objective of excellence in research, scholarship, and education by publishing worldwide. Oxford is a registered trade mark of Oxford University Press in the UK and certain other countries.

Published in the United States of America by Oxford University Press
198 Madison Avenue, New York, NY 10016, United States of America.

© Oxford University Press 2021

Library of Congress Cataloging-in-Publication Data
Names: Furchtgott-Roth, Diana, editor.
Title: United States Income, Wealth, Consumption, and Inequality /
edited by Diana Furchtgott-Roth.
Description: New York : Oxford University Press, 2021. |
Series: International policy exchange series |
Includes bibliographical references and index.
Identifiers: LCCN 2020014716 (print) | LCCN 2020014717 (ebook) |
ISBN 9780197518199 (hardback) | ISBN 9780197518229 |
ISBN 9780197518212 (epub)
Subjects: LCSH: Equality—United States. | Wealth—United States. |
Quality of life—United States.
Classification: LCC HN90.S6 U55 2020 (print) | LCC HN90.S6 (ebook) |
DDC 305.50973—dc23
LC record available at https://lccn.loc.gov/2020014716
LC ebook record available at https://lccn.loc.gov/2020014717

9 8 7 6 5 4 3 2 1

Printed by Integrated Books International, United States of America

CONTENTS

ABOUT THE AUTHORS

Gerald Auten is Senior Research Economist in the Office of Tax Analysis, US Treasury Department, where he has served for more than 30 years. Prior positions include Professor of Economics at Bowling Green State University, Senior Economist at the Council of Economic Advisors, and Brookings Economic Policy Fellow. He received a PhD in economics from the University of Michigan in 1972. His research and publications have focused on federal tax policy, behavioral effects of taxes, charitable contributions, capital gains, and, more recently, measuring economic income for examining mobility and distribution.

Jared Bernstein joined the Center on Budget and Policy Priorities in May 2011 as Senior Fellow. From 2009 to 2011, Bernstein was the Chief Economist and Economic Adviser to Vice President Joe Biden, Executive Director of the White House Task Force on the Middle Class, and a member of President Obama's economic team. He holds a PhD in Social Welfare from Columbia University.

Karlyn Bowman is Senior Fellow at the American Enterprise Institute, a nonpartisan, nonprofit think tank in Washington, DC. She compiles and analyzes American public opinion using available polling data on a variety of subjects, including the economy, taxes, the state of workers in America, environment and global warming, attitudes about homosexuality and gay marriage, NAFTA and free trade, the war in Iraq, and women's attitudes. In addition, Ms. Bowman has studied and spoken about the evolution of American politics because of key demographic and geographic changes. She has often lectured on the role of think tanks in the United States, and writes a column for Forbes.com.

Richard V. Burkhauser is Emeritus Sarah Gibson Blanding Professor of Public Policy in the Department of Policy Analysis and Management at Cornell University, having previously held tenured positions at Vanderbilt University, Syracuse University, and Cornell University (1979–2017). In September 2017 he was appointed a member of President Trump's Council of Economic Advisors, a position he held until May 2019. His professional career has focused on how public policies affect the employment and well-being of vulnerable populations. Most recently his research has focused on how government tax and transfer policy ameliorate poverty and market income inequality.

Edward Conard is an American Enterprise Institute Adjunct Fellow, a former Bain Capital Managing Director, and the author of two *New York Times* top-10 best-selling books on the economy: *The Upside of Inequality: How Good Intentions Undermine the Middle Class* (2016) and *Unintended Consequences: Why Everything You've Been Told About the Economy Is Wrong* (2012).

Kevin Corinth is Chief Economist for Domestic Policy at the Council of Economic Advisers in the Executive Office of the President. Previously, he was a Research Fellow at the American Enterprise Institute. His research focuses on poverty and homelessness. He obtained a PhD in economics from the University of Chicago and a BA in economics and political science from Boston College.

James Elwell is an economist at the Joint Committee on Taxation, where he started in 2019. He previously attended Cornell University, receiving his PhD in May 2019. His graduate research focused on the relationships between various tax and transfer programs, labor supply, and measurement of poverty and income inequality. Prior to completing his PhD, he served as a staff economist on the Council of Economic Advisers from June 2016 until July 2017. He received his undergraduate degree in Economics from Lewis and Clark College in 2010.

Diana Furchtgott-Roth is an economist and author or coauthor of five books on economic policy. She has been Senior Fellow and Director of Economics21 at the Manhattan Institute for Policy Research, Adjunct Professor of Economics at George Washington University, Chief Economist of the US Department of Labor, Chief of Staff of the President's Council of Economic Advisers, and Deputy Executive Secretary of the Domestic Policy Council. She holds a BA in Economics from Swarthmore College and an M.Phil. in Economics from Oxford University. She served as Acting Assistant Secretary for Economic Policy at the US Department of the Treasury, and she currently serves as Deputy Assistant Secretary for Research and Technology at the US Department of Transportation.

Beila Leboeuf is a Senior Economist in the United States Congress in Washington, DC. Previously, she was a research fellow at Baruch College and an adjunct professor of economics at Hunter College in New York City. She has a BA in mathematics from Queens College and a PhD in economics from the Graduate Center of the City University of New York. Her research focuses on women in the workforce, and she examines policies that enable mothers to be successful at work and at home.

Eleanor O'Neil is Program Manager for public opinion research at the American Enterprise Institute (AEI), where she coordinates survey projects with the research team, analyzes and writes about public opinion, and is an editor of AEI's *Political Report*, a monthly compilation of polling on current topics. She earned a BA in political science from Southwestern University in Georgetown, Texas.

Dave O'Neill received his PhD from Columbia University, where he was a student of Gary Becker and Jacob Mincer. He taught economics at the University of Pennsylvania, Pace University, and Baruch College/CUNY. In the early 1970s, Dr. O'Neill and his family moved to Washington, and he joined the Center for Naval Analyses. He went on to hold positions at the American Enterprise Institute, the General Accounting Office, and the Bureau of the Census. In 1988, he joined the New York Federal Reserve. He later worked at the Nathan Klein Institute and then returned to teaching at Pace University and Baruch College. He served in the US Army during the Korean War, stationed in Japan. He died in 2016 and is survived by his wife, June O'Neill.

June O'Neill served as Director of the Congressional Budget Office from 1995 to 1999. Prior to that, she held positions as Director of Policy and Research at the US Commission on Civil Rights, Senior Economist on the President's Council of Economic Advisers, Senior Research Associate at the Urban Institute, and Research Associate at the Brookings Institution. She was elected Vice President of the American Economics Association in 1998. She served as the Director of the Center for the Study of Business and Government at Baruch College, CUNY, and she was an Adjunct Scholar at the American Enterprise Institute. She was married to the late Dave O'Neill.

Stephen Rose is Nonresident Fellow in the Income and Benefits Policy Center at the Urban Institute and Research Professor at George Washington University. He is a nationally recognized labor economist and has spent the past 40 years researching and writing about the interactions between formal education, training, career movements, incomes, and earnings. His book, *Social Stratification in the United States*, was originally published by New Press in 1978, and the seventh edition was released in 2014. His book, *Rebound: Why America Will Emerge Stronger from the Financial Crisis* (St. Martin's Press, 2010), addresses the causes of the financial crisis and the evolving structure of the US economy over the past three decades. Currently, he is working on a new book on the growing size and economic impact of the upper middle class. Rose has held senior positions at the Georgetown University Center on Education and the Workforce, the

Educational Testing Service, the US Department of Labor, the Joint Economic Committee of Congress, the National Commission for Employment Policy, and the Washington State Senate. His commentaries have appeared in the *New York Times, Washington Post, Wall Street Journal,* and other print and broadcast media. He has a BA from Princeton University and an MA and PhD in economics from the City University of New York.

Emmanuel Saez is Professor of Economics at the University of California Berkeley. He received his PhD in Economics from MIT in 1999. His research focuses on inequality and tax policy. Jointly with Thomas Piketty, he created the top income share series that show a dramatic increase in US inequality since 1980. The data have been widely discussed in the public debate. His most recent book, *The Triumph of Injustice* (W. W. Norton, 2019), co-authored with his colleague Gabriel Zucman, narrates the demise of US progressive taxation and how to reinvent it in the 21st century. He received numerous academic awards, including the John Bates Clark medal of the American Economic Association in 2009, a MacArthur "Genius" Fellowship in 2010, and a honorary degree from Harvard University in 2019.

David Splinter is an Economist at the nonpartisan Joint Committee on Taxation, US Congress, where he analyses tax proposals. He received his PhD in economics from Rice University. His research on income inequality, income mobility, and tax policy is available at davidsplinter.com.

John C. Weicher is Director of the Center for Housing and Financial Markets at Hudson Institute. He has served at the US Department of Housing and Urban Development as Assistant Secretary for Housing and FHA Commissioner, Assistant Secretary for Policy Development and Research, and Chief Economist. He was President of the American Real Estate and Urban Economics Association and received the Association's award for Lifetime Achievement. He has chaired the Committee to Evaluate HUD's Research Program of the National Academies and served on the Committee on Urban Policy of the National Academy of Sciences. His research on wealth has appeared in numerous scholarly and popular journals and newspapers, including the *Review of the Federal Reserve Bank of St. Louis, Housing Finance Review, The Wall Street Journal,* and *The Public Interest.* His most recent book is *The Long-Term Dynamics of Affordable Rental Housing* (Hudson Institute, 2018, co-authored with Frederick J. Eggers and Fouad Moumen). He holds an AB in English from the University of Michigan and a PhD in economics from the University of Chicago.

INTRODUCTION AND SUMMARY

Diana Furchtgott-Roth

The global pandemic that emerged in early 2020 in the form of Covid-19, the novel coronavirus, has had a dramatic effect on the world economy, incomes, wealth, and income distribution. In the United States, the subject of this volume, the initial flash of data for April 2020, the first full month of the country's shutdown, gave new meaning to the description of economics as "the dismal science." As this volume was going to press, the economy lost over 20 million jobs in one month, the unemployment rate rose from 4.4 percent to 14.7 percent, and 23 million people were receiving unemployment benefits.

Average weekly and hourly earnings, however, both increased by 5 percent in just one month. If this trend continued for the entire year, this would be approximately an 80 percent increase. If average earnings were a measure of well-being, the country would be better off. But the increase in earnings came about because the individuals who lost jobs were primarily low skilled. Their restaurants, retail stores, and personal service establishments were closed to stop the spread of Covid-19. In June 2020, protests against inequality and the treatment of minorities convulsed cities in the United States and elsewhere. Addressing inequality is not merely an academic pursuit; it captures imaginations of people globally.

This book's examination of income trends, consumption, wealth, and inequality provides a framework for analysis both in times of crisis as well as in other times. For instance, should incomes of those who lose their jobs be measured including the expanded unemployment and healthcare benefits, or without? What are the effects by race and gender, and why? As asset prices change, including pension holdings for blue-collar workers, what are the effects on the distribution of wealth?

Diana Furchtgott-Roth, *Introduction and Summary* In: *United States Income, Wealth, Consumption, and Inequality*. Edited by: Diana Furchtgott-Roth, Oxford University Press (2021). © Oxford University Press.
DOI: 10.1093/oso/9780197518199.003.0001.

Do those with a greater appetite for risk, perhaps those who are trading in much-needed equipment or who are investing in new technologies, get a larger share of the income gains?

LACK OF CONSENSUS ABOUT APPROACHES TO INCOME DISTRIBUTION

Economists have long been concerned with the distribution of income. In the *Wealth of Nations*, Adam Smith discusses the effects of taxes on the "labouring poor" and explains that various members of society ought to oppose "all direct taxes upon the wages of labour" because such taxes harm not only labour but other parts of society as well.[1] Economists since Smith who have written directly or indirectly about income distribution have sharply differing views about topics ranging from how to measure income distribution to whether and how governments can alter it.

Unlike issues of economic efficiency for the theory of consumer behavior or firm behavior, where there is a broad consensus among economists about both methodological approaches and theoretical outcomes, no broad consensus exists among economists on either the theory or outcomes of income distribution. Nor is there consensus on the curriculum for teaching income distribution. Sections on income distribution may be taught in graduate courses on macroeconomics, labor economics, public finance, or in separate classes on income distribution.

Some books by economists that have addressed the topic of income distribution have become best-sellers. Aside from the *Wealth of Nations*, other examples include the works of Karl Marx, Milton Friedman's *Capitalism and Freedom*, Lester Thurow's *Zero-Sum Society*, and *Capital in the Twenty-First Century* by Thomas Piketty—whose coauthor, Emmanuel Saez, is featured in Chapter 2 of this volume.

The public's interest in income distribution is reflected in wide political discussion. Governments since Biblical times have had programs for the poor and the needy. Political campaigns in 2020 address issues of income distribution with concern both for supporting those with little or no income and for providing for catastrophic expenses related to Covid-19, and for equitably raising taxes from those with substantial incomes. Politicians have found no consensus about how to address income distribution, although many constituents want it to be addressed.

Economists have differing views on whether income inequality is a social ill in search of a cure or simply an unpleasant but necessary byproduct of a competitive economy. The former view proposes taxes and government redistribution programs to lead to more balanced incomes across individuals or households. The latter approach sees differences in income partly as a natural outcome of income patterns over the life-cycle and partly as a necessary incentive to encourage individuals to invest in human capital, to work hard, and to save.

CHALLENGES OF MEASURING INCOME INEQUALITY

Consensus on how income should be measured has proved elusive for several reasons. Every alternative measure features technical hurdles in measurement, cross-sectional and longitudinal comparisons, and interpretation. For instance, household income surveys suffer from misreporting and a high level of both random error and bias. Compared to primary sources such as tax returns, respondents tend to underreport their wage and capital incomes in surveys, as well as income from government transfers. Even though some studies show the net bias toward underreporting is small, it can be problematic when reporting bias affects some types of households more than others.

The prevalent use of wages and capital gains as a standard compound measure has tended to overlook their flaws as a proxy for well-being. Individuals and households can call on government transfers, savings, and physical assets to smooth out consumption through spells of unemployment, as many did during the global pandemic, making comparisons across income groups complicated. Some studies use so-called *market income*—wages, pension annuities, and returns on financial assets—while others include taxes, government transfers, and social insurance programs, which lead to lower measures of inequality.

Some income measures have included home ownership and other forms of wealth, as well as in-kind benefits such as Medicare and Medicaid. But many studies have yet to account for the entirety of benefits enjoyed by most Americans, which would include the value of public goods. The disparate yardsticks used across different studies point to a legitimate research quandary: If scholars are trying to capture the gaps between different strata in society, should they not aim for the most comprehensive measure of well-being? Transit systems, national defense, and public schools may one day be included—but what about clean air and the free flow of knowledge?

In a break from the narrow concept of income, some recent studies have measured consumption in an attempt to capture better a household's fulfillment of basic needs, and have found much less inequality than is suggested by more income-based metrics. The reader is encouraged to read Chapter 1 and Chapter 4 of this volume for details.

INCOME INEQUALITY AND THE AMERICAN DREAM

One of the paradoxes of income distribution is that societies with high levels of income often have higher measures of inequality. Although Japan and some European countries have both high incomes and low inequality, other countries such as the United States have high incomes and more inequality.

Individuals and households from impoverished countries around the world seek to migrate to wealthier countries, and the American Dream of hard work leading to economic and social success is often portrayed as a magnet drawing people to the United States. In recent decades, however, studies have questioned the persistence of income mobility.

Some economists see portending challenges to the American Dream. Uniquely premised on the ideal of equal opportunity, the American social compact seems at risk when the road to prosperity is mired by a deepening divide between high- and low-income groups. The problem is compounded by observations that income gaps persist along racial lines.

SOURCES OF CHANGES IN INCOME DISTRIBUTION

This volume is more than just a survey of methodologies to measure income and income distribution in the United States. It also seeks to track some of the root causes of income growth and inequality that are equally difficult to measure.

Though surely part of the picture, demographic changes among women in the labor force and in society seem to fall equally short of a comprehensive rationale. These changes can sometimes pull in different directions, and they need to be understood in the broader context of cultural and societal shifts, as well as increases in labor-saving household technology. Granted, the movement of women into higher education and the labor force has multiplied the number of two-earner households at the top of the income scale. But the decline of the family, the rise in divorce rates, and other societal shifts, on the other hand, have made single-mother households prevalent among those at the lower end of the income scale.

International trade is a major factor affecting income distribution in the United States. When displaced by trade with low-wage countries or automation, high-paid manufacturing workers may end up with substantially reduced earnings, while the rest of society reaps the benefits of lower prices and expanded choice. Policy may alleviate some or all of the shocks to income distribution, but leaving the market to allocate the benefits of trade and technological disruption augurs no certain outcome even when the overall effect is a net benefit to most people.

International migration is a major issue closely related to income distribution in the United States but is not addressed in detail in this volume. Over the past few decades, tens of millions of people have migrated to the United States, both through formal legal channels as well as through other, undocumented avenues. These immigrants have affected income in the United States both at the lower end, in the form of unskilled workers, as well as at the high end, through the immigration and employment of skilled engineers, doctors, and scientists. Politically, low-skilled immigrants are sometimes blamed for wage stagnation in the United States, yet, in the global market for low-skilled workers, wages in the United States remain well above much of the rest of the world.

Evidence-based answers to questions about income may guide how governments influence the distribution of income. But beyond any number of positive propositions on the scope, origins, and trajectory of inequality lie normative questions that economists have trouble answering. Is income equality in itself a policy goal worth pursuing, or should our goalposts encompass equality of opportunity and social mobility as well? Is inequality always negative, or may it be the byproduct of attaining other desired social objectives, such as a meritocratic labor market, a better international division of labor, or innovation?

Any set of policies seeking to modify the distribution of income should be informed by evidence but also by the ultimate value judgments over what it is that society should pursue. This volume makes no pretense to address the latter, but does seek to reflect academic consensus where it exists and findings that have stemmed from years of research into the levels and trends of inequality in the United States. These findings are more timely than ever.

OUTLINE OF THIS VOLUME

The book opens with an examination of the complexity of income measurements by Stephen Rose of the Urban Institute. Chapter 1, "The Ins and Outs of Measuring Income Inequality in the United States," discusses the fluid definition of income and the need to adjust household income by size, as well as the statistical maze produced by uncoordinated agencies and disparate inflation figures and corresponding price deflators that make the job of researchers more difficult. He also succinctly summarizes the vastly dissonant inequality measures arrived at by scholars in the past and explores cultural, political, and racial perceptions of inequality. Rose concludes that, contrary to popular belief, real median incomes have grown since 1979 between 30 percent and 51 percent and that the best estimate is that they have grown by 42 percent.

Chapter 2, "Income and Wealth Inequality: Evidence and Policy Implications," a survey of US income trends since the 1970s, is written by Emmanuel Saez of the University of California at Berkeley. Saez is one of the leading contributors to the literature on inequality, one of the architects of the World Inequality Database, and the 2009 recipient of the John Bates Clark Medal. Saez's chapter describes income trends since the 1970s and the government's role in reducing pre-tax inequality through taxation and transfers. The chapter's conclusions are that income inequality has substantially increased in the past 50 years and that income growth has diverged since the 1970s, with the income growth of the bottom 90 percent of earners substantially decreasing, unlike that of the top 10 percent. As a consequence of increased income inequality, wealth inequality has grown as well. Saez says that greatly increased capital income for those at the top of the wealth distribution has further increased income inequality.

The main subject of his policy analysis is the relationship between top marginal income tax rates and the share of pre-tax income that goes to different income groups in several developed nations. He concludes that higher top marginal income tax rates reduce inequality without having a clear effect on economic growth.

Chapter 3, "Improving Economic Opportunity in the United States," by Jared Bernstein, Senior Fellow at the Center on Budget and Policy Priorities, discusses why high levels of income inequality reduce economic opportunity and mobility and what the government can do about it. He cites evidence that shows how the recovery from the Great Recession has been uneven across income groups and geographic areas. Among the factors he cites that limit people's economic opportunity are their past income and education, regional and racial segregation, a greater debt burden, and inadequate investments in childcare.

What to do? Bernstein suggests two types of solutions: those that cover short-term barriers to opportunity and those that cover long-term barriers. A key short-term policy goal is a tighter labor market since it tends to overwhelmingly benefit low-wage and disadvantaged workers—and the tight labor market before the pandemic indeed led to the lowest recorded unemployment rates for African Americans and Hispanics, as well as to greater wage growth for lower paid workers. Bernstein suggests that ways to achieve this goal are by increasing investment in infrastructure; direct government job creation, especially for high-unemployment areas; government support for healthcare; expansion of the Earned Income Tax Credit (EITC); investments in renewable energy; and help for manufacturers competing in the global economy. His long-term solutions to inequality and low economic mobility include raising the value of the EITC for childless adults, strengthening the child tax credit, providing more generous housing vouchers, and expanding Medicaid, as well as criminal justice reforms that could reduce racial inequality and increase economic opportunity.

James Elwell, Kevin Corinth, and Richard V. Burkhauser show in Chapter 4, "Income Growth and Its Distribution from Eisenhower to Obama: The Growing Importance of In-Kind Transfers (1959–2016)," that when accounting for the market value of in-kind transfers such as Medicare, Medicaid, employer-provided health insurance, and others, inequality appears to decline from 1969 to 2016. When leaving such benefits out, the median market income in the United States appears to fall through the 1960s, and inequality grows before both trends reverse in the 1970s. When more fully accounting for government's role by measuring the taxes and transfers stemming from the New Frontier and Great Society programs, median market income increases and inequality declines through both decades. Elwell, Corinth, and Burkhauser conclude that conventional measures of inequality that exclude government and private in-kind transfers substantially understate the effect of government policies and workplace changes, such as employer-provided insurance, and overstate actual income inequality.

Chapter 5, "Top Income Shares and the Difficulties of Using Tax Data," by Gerald Auten and David Splinter, uses tax data to show that the top 1 percent share of national income has increased slightly between 1962 and 2014. However, the increase in tax rates for upper income earners and increases in transfers for lower income earners have almost completely offset that increase. Hence, the top 1 percent share of income after-taxes and transfers has remained nearly the same over the period. They adjust their data to account for declines in marriage rates and increases in the number of young people who are dependent on their parents. Although incomes of the top 1 percent have grown, transfers have kept up. Transfers have grown from 5 to 17 percent of national income, and the tax system has become more progressive due to tax cuts for lower income households. In addition, the data show a substantial turnover in the income distribution at both the top and bottom ends. The authors conclude that economic growth has not disproportionately benefitted top earners since most earners in the top 1 percent have lower incomes in following years and most earners in the lowest groups see the largest increases in subsequent years. Other methods of estimating income inequality with different datasets produce similar results.

Chapter 6, "The Effects of the Movement of Women into the Workforce on Income Trends," by Diana Furchtgott-Roth and Beila Leboeuf, shows that some of the perceived growth in inequality is owed to women's gradual entry into the workforce and institutions of higher education, along with increasing life expectancy, higher rates of divorce, and other societal shifts. They point to the unwise use of income distribution tables to infer the trend of inequality, given that the composition of income percentiles varies from year to year as incomes and personal circumstances vary. With more higher earning women in the labor force, two-earner couples dominate the top fifth of the income distribution, while the growing numbers of single-parent households, low-income divorcees, and retirees have concentrated at the bottom. These demographic shifts resulting from changes in social norms and women's shattering of the glass ceiling have exacerbated the apparent growth in inequality.

Much of the national conversation on inequality has focused on gaps along racial and gender lines. In Chapter 7, "Explaining Race and Gender Wage Gaps," June O'Neill and Dave O'Neill examine wage gaps between men and women and between blacks and whites. They find that the wage gap between men and women is primarily explained by differences in choice of education, occupation, and hours worked, whereas the wage gap between blacks and whites is largely due to differences in education. In both cases, accounting for occupational choices and demographic and educational characteristics almost entirely closes the earnings gap in the data.

They also find that Asian and Hispanic income gaps with whites are overstated due to the effects of immigration. Hispanic immigrants' incomes are, on average,

lower than those of American-born Hispanics because that immigrant population usually comes to the country with fewer years of work experience, less ability
to speak English, and a lower level of education. The opposite is true for Asians,
whose immigrant population is on average highly educated and geographically concentrated in high-income areas. Consequently, immigration tends to
lower the average Hispanic income and increase the average Asian income,
thus exaggerating the income differences between both groups and whites. The
authors conclude that, after adjusting incomes based on the education, English
proficiency, and geographic location of immigrants within ethnic groups, the gap
between those groups and whites is nearly eliminated.

In Chapter 8, "The Distribution of Wealth in America (1983–2013)," John
C. Weicher of the Hudson Institute depicts the steady rise in households' wealth—
primarily bank accounts, cars, and homes—through the second half of the 20th
century. The trend was halted by a precipitous fall due to the Great Recession
and an ensuing sluggish recovery. He finds that age is the main factor that drives
both wealth and income inequality since adjusting just for this factor greatly
reduces the Gini coefficient of both inequality measures. Older age cohorts have
more work experience and education as well as more wealth than younger ones.
Weicher also finds that the distribution of wealth remained approximately constant until the Great Recession, with wealth growing for all groups. However,
he concludes that the burst of the housing bubble disproportionally affected
middle- and low-income households whose total wealth depends more on the
value of their homes.

In Chapter 9, "Public Opinion on Inequality," Karlyn Bowman and Eleanor
O'Neil of the American Enterprise Institute (AEI) bring public opinion into
the picture. Bowman and O'Neil analyze Americans' survey responses on the
levels and trends of inequality. The results show mixed feelings about whether
more concentration of income at the top is a result of hard work or unfair privi-
lege and about how the government should address the issue. What is clear, the
authors conclude, is that Americans believe inequality should be reduced and
overwhelmingly want more opportunity for all to get ahead.

Finally, in Chapter 10, "The Economics of Inequality in High-Wage
Economies," Edward Conard suggests that inequality is mostly the result of an
increasing premium on returns from risk and high-skilled labor ushered in by
technological disruption and the feedback loop of elite talent working to increase their own productivity—a logical outcome when properly trained talent
constrains growth. The answer, argues Conard, lies increasing the ratio of high-
to low-skilled workers chiefly by training and recruiting more high-scoring
domestic and immigrant workers. Rather than greater income redistribution
slowing growth by dampening high-skilled productivity and incentives to innovate, these alternatives would accelerate growth and narrow income inequality
by relieving constraints on talent and increasing resources devoted to raising
low-skilled productivity.

ACKNOWLEDGMENTS

I gratefully acknowledge the assistance of Professor Douglas Besharov of the University of Maryland, Professor Neil Gilbert of the University of California (Berkeley), and editors at the Oxford University Press, especially Dana Bliss, who conceived of this volume and others in the series. Arlene Holen and Beila LeBoeuf gave valuable comments on the entire manuscript. I would also like to thank anonymous referees for insightful suggestions. I appreciate the work of Daniel Di Martino, who reviewed, collected, and organized the manuscripts, data, and tables for each chapter—but all errors are mine. Deepest thanks go to my husband, Harold, and my six children, Leon, Francesca, Jeremy, Godfrey, Theodore, and Richard, for their advice and encouragement. Finally, the views expressed in this publication are my own and do not necessarily represent the views of the US Department of Transportation or the United States government.

NOTE

1. Adam Smith, *An Inquiry into the Nature and Causes of the Wealth of Nations*, Part II, Article IV, at https://www.econlib.org/library/Smith/smWN.html?chapter_num=36#book-reader

1

THE INS AND OUTS OF MEASURING INCOME INEQUALITY IN THE UNITED STATES

Stephen Rose

Perfect income equality never exists in economically advanced countries; some level of inequality always exists. Furthermore, there is no obvious standard of what level of inequality is acceptable and what level creates social tensions. Psychologist Keith Payne (2017) argues that most people have a natural sense of fairness and will be upset if they perceive the distance between people at different rungs of the income ladder to be too large. For those with a strong sense of social justice, even a low level of inequality is undesirable.[1] If inequality increases to a level that many people are uncomfortable with, then concerns about inequality will be a major social problem.

While inequality is a "relative measure" (i.e., how the rich compare to the middle and the middle compare to the poor), absolute values matter as well. Consider neurosurgeons: their median pay is about $500,000 a year while the highest paid practitioners make more than $1 million and the lowest paid make $200,000. Thus, there is inequality among the pay of neurosurgeons, but no one would consider this a social problem. This is relevant because the rising incomes of the rich may have a different social effect if middle incomes are stagnating versus if middle incomes are rising but not as fast as are upper incomes.

The 2003 publication of the first Piketty and Saez (PS) article combined both a relative and absolute component—the rising share of the very rich and the stagnating income of the bottom 90 percent, because the top 10 percent achieved 91 percent of income growth. This work garnered tremendous attention and would become the most important single work on American income inequality

Stephen Rose, *The Ins and Outs of Measuring Income Inequality in the United States* In: *United States Income, Wealth, Consumption, and Inequality.* Edited by: Diana Furchtgott-Roth, Oxford University Press (2021).
© Oxford University Press. DOI: 10.1093/oso/9780197518199.003.0002.

ever produced. The authors changed the whole focus of inequality and are consistently cited as being leaders in the study of inequality. Their focus was on the very top of the income ladder, and they presented income levels and shares of the top 1 percent, the top 0.1 percent, the top 0.01, and even the top 0.001 percent of tax filers.

The consequences of their continuing research are evident in many ways. First, Appendix A of this chapter lists 20 books on the problems of high-income inequality in the post-PS era. Most of these books liberally cite the PS findings, often with tables and graphics, and have fueled continued coverage of inequality by major newspapers, radio, TV, and cable outlets. Second, the Occupy Wall Street movement began in September 2011 and spread quickly in the ensuing months. Its main slogan was "We are the 99 percent"—a clear echo of PS's findings. Third, public opinion polls show that a majority of the population think income inequality is a problem. Two outsider presidential candidates in 2016, Donald Trump and Bernie Sanders, based their appeals on the lack of middle-class income growth over the past several decades.

While it may seem that measuring inequality should be straightforward and uncontroversial, this is not the case, and the purpose of this chapter is to present the differing ways in which researchers have tried to measure income inequality and how much this inequality has changed over time. Many of the recent studies on trends in income inequality, including the works of Piketty and his collaborators, require tens of pages to explain their methodology. In this chapter, I present the key issues and show the effects of different methodological choices.

As will be shown, the results of various studies differ substantially. For example, the gains in inflation-adjusted median income from 1979 to 2014 range from an 8 percent decline (the original PS methodology) to a 51 percent gain (Congressional Budget Office, 2018). In the end, it is important to remember that income is a proxy for living standards. Changes in the real median are not an inequality measure, but they do tend to move with levels of inequality. Slow median growth usually means that upper-income people are receiving the lion's share of growth. As noted earlier, absolute changes may affect how people react to relative changes.

The first part of this chapter focuses on the methodological choices that various approaches employ: definition of income, dataset used, unit of analysis, use of different income measures (market incomes only, total cash income with government transfers, and post-tax, post-transfers), whether to adjust incomes for different households of varying sizes, and choice of price deflators.

The second part presents the results of various approaches and shows exactly why they vary. In addition to different estimates of the change in median incomes, I present information on four studies showing how much of economic growth went to the top 10 percent and seven studies showing how much income was held by the top 1 percent and how much this share changed over time. All the different results will be tied to the methodological choices made in each study. The high and low outliers will be explained vis-à-vis the international consensus of the best income inequality measuring approach.

METHODOLOGICAL ISSUES

What Constitutes Income?

This basic question determines what we are measuring. It does not have an easy answer. On the one hand, the Haig-Simons classic definition of income is the value of consumption plus change in net wealth. On the other hand, the more common view of income is the cash that you receive during a year. This consists primarily of payments for working—wages, salaries, bonuses, and much of self-employment income. Another component of cash income consists of returns to ownership: dividends, interest payments received, business income, and rental payments. Finally, the elderly receive pensions and Social Security and government provides monetary transfers to those with low incomes.

Economists believe that this list does not cover the value of economic resources that people consume. They argue that employer-provided benefits are part of the earnings of those workers who receive them. Employer contributions for health insurance and retirement directly benefit workers and can be easily seen as important to their standard of living. Employers also pay taxes on their employees—6.2 percent to the Social Security Trust fund, 1.45 percent to the Health Insurance Trust fund, and between 1 and 10 percent for federal and state unemployment insurance.[2] These payments often escape attention, but, from the employer's point of view, total compensation determines a firm's employment decisions. Furthermore, employer payments are significant and growing: in 1979, employer benefits and taxes were 10 percent of total worker compensation and rose to 15 percent in 2014.

Mishel et al. (2012) and others believe that benefits should not be included in income because they are not controlled by the recipients. However, Medicare and Social Security were created for retirees because these services were considered too important to leave to individuals who might short-change their futures. Rather than providing these benefits out of tax revenue, the government could have mandated their purchase by individuals—just as states mandate the purchase of auto insurance for drivers. Instead, the universal governmental provision of retirement and health services subsidizes the retirement income of lower income people.

When the government provides payments for medical services or insurance (Medicare, Medicaid, and public clinics), food stamps, housing vouchers, and other assistance, the insurance value or direct costs of these government services should be considered income for those who receive them. Medicare is available to virtually all elderly people, but other benefits require that the recipients have low incomes.

A thorny issue is how to deal with appreciation of financial assets. On the one hand, capital payments—interest, dividends, and rents—are reported on tax returns and surveys. But the appreciation of stocks, business interests, and home values are not covered. PS (2003) use reported capital gains as a proxy for increasing capital values. They then have two income series, one with capital gains and one without.

Using reported capital gains misses many capital gains because they occur at death or because they come from housing sales, which receive favorable tax treatment. In addition, because capital gains are lumpy, those with big capital gains in specific years can be vaulted into the top 1 percent. When these people drop out of the top 1 percent, they may be replaced by other people with big gains in that year. The movement of individuals into and out of the top 1 percent makes it appear that big investors are continuously reaping large capital gains.

Larrimore et al. (2017) track the gains of all assets (including housing) to get accurate changes in wealth. However, big swings in the stock and housing markets can distort incomes in a given year and may result in some negative incomes. Volatility makes historical comparisons very sensitive to starting and end years.

Another approach allocates retained earnings as a proxy for changes in capital wealth. This approach is used by Piketty, Saez, and Zucman (PSZ, 2018) and Auten and Splinter (2018) and is consistent with the Bureau of Economic Analysis (BEA) national incomes totals. This avoids the problems of using reported capital gains and the volatility of asset prices. Given that most people do not change their capital holdings regularly, individual feelings toward yearly gains and losses may not be strong because they are using these assets for retirement.[3]

Finally, if incomes mean benefits from economic activities, then three possible imputations should be added to personal income. For those who want to allocate all national income, including these sources of income is necessary.

The first imputation deals with home ownership. When renters pay landlords, this is an economic transaction for the consumption of housing services. Since economists do not want the transition from renting to ownership to change economic output, they create an "imputed" transaction—owners pay themselves rent for the consumption of housing services. This imputation represents 6 percent of gross domestic product (GDP) and benefits most in the middle and upper middle classes. Very rich people have expensive houses, but the imputed rent on this asset is a small addition to overall income.

Second, another large imputation is the services that financial institutions and insurance companies provide for their customers who either pay nothing or pay a very reduced rate. An example of this is our free checking accounts and use of ATM machines. Banks provide this service because they use the idle assets to make loans, from which they make profits. The third element of economic activity that does not get paid for directly is the range of government services. While defense, infrastructure, and even public administration are forms of "collective consumption," no collective entity exists, and therefore government services should be allocated as income for each individual income that is offset by the taxes that people pay.

The value of this consumption represents 17 percent of national income, so this can have a big effect on measured income inequality. In 2013, the Congressional Budget Office (CBO) estimated that 40 percent of federal spending was for goods and services that served the entire public (e.g., national defense, judicial and legislative expenses, and administration of all programs). The CBO then allocated the $920 billion in income that would have gone to each of five income quintiles of non-elderly people in two very different ways. One way was to divide it equally among all people such that each income quintile would receive $184 billion dollars of extra income.

The second CBO method divided the value of government goods and services by market income. The logic here is that government services support the economy and that individuals' stakes in the economy are best reflected by their market income. Using this approach, the bottom quintile received $25 billion while the top quintile received $520 billion. So, distributing the value of government services on a per-person basis lowers income inequality because the extra money to the bottom quintile would make a much bigger relative difference than the same dollars for those in the top quintile. On the other hand, distributing the value of government services by income would have little or no effect on income inequality. Finally, a hybrid approach (e.g., 80 percent per person and 20 percent by income decreases inequality) may make the most sense because the protection of life is more important than the protection of property.

It could be that these services should be considered part of citizenship and not part of personal income. If these services are allocated on a per-person basis, it might seem that low-income people no longer have low incomes. If the reason to include them is to have all persons receive all national income, this may put too much emphasis on statistical completeness and not on the task of showing the living standards of people on the different rungs of the income ladder.

Reporting Income with Size Adjustments

Once a total income is determined for each family (including single people as a family of one), those with identical incomes will not have the same standard of living if they have differing numbers of members.[4] Government reporting on poverty is based on separate thresholds for each household depending on the number of people in them. While the adage that "two can live as cheaply as one" is not true, economists have argued that "economies of scale" take place when multiple people share one roof: the rent on an apartment is only marginally higher with two bedrooms rather than one bedroom. Similarly, a larger household still only requires one set of furniture, one set of plates and utensils, one set of cooking pots and pans, etc.

Mishel et al. (2012) and others argue that size adjusting overstates incomes because having fewer children is endogenous in the sense that this decision is driven by the couples' low incomes. While this factor certainly reflects the actions of some people, it is inconsistent with worldwide trends: the birth rate of every country has declined as it has become richer. For poor people around the world, having extra children means extra workers to bring in income once they are capable of working, which outweighs the extra mouths to feed. In addition, children can care for their parents in their old age. Furthermore, many young adults who set up a separate domicile after finishing their education are motivated by wanting to be autonomous rather than by saving money by living at home. When the economy is tight and more young people return to their parents' homes, this is treated as a sign of distress.

Adjusting for size narrows the income gap between single people and married couples. For example, the most widely cited number for the median income in America in 2016 was $59,000. But the median for married couples, independent of age or how many are working, is $87,000. In contrast, the median for non-family households, often with just one single person, is $35,000. While there was some debate on how to best adjust for economies of scale, the most common procedure is to divide by the square root of the number of people in a family to get "size-adjusted" equivalent incomes. (In my work, I have used family-of-three equivalents because the median of family-of-three equivalents is close to the median reported in the Census data).[5] This is not surprising because the average household size today is 2.6 persons. Table 1.1 shows that the three-person equivalent income of $100,000 is less than $58,000 for a single person and more than $115,000 for a family of four.

Using this approach changes the size of the gap between the median incomes of husband-wife couples and the median income of non-family households cited. With the unadjusted numbers, the median of the single-person households is 60 percent less than the median of husband-wife couples. But the gap is narrowed to 30 percent if the single person is compared to the $87,000 of a family of three.

Table 1.1 Income level necessary to equal $100,000

Family of three equivalent

Family size	Actual income
1	$57,735
2	$81,650
3	$100,000
4	$115,470
5	$129,099
6	$141,421
7	$152,753

And the advantage of a family of four with $87,000 over a single person with $35,000 falls to 20 percent.

This issue is important because there has been a shift to more people living alone: from 1979 to 2014, the share of single people with no dependents rose from 16 percent in 1979 to 22 percent in 2014 (Rose, 2015). If incomes were reported in size-adjusted levels, then the reported growth of median income would have been nearly 10 percentage points higher.

Data Sources

The United States has been the world leader in producing publicly available data on individuals. Most of the data consists of surveys that are nationally representative of the population. Using careful sampling techniques and post-data collection analyses, each observation is given a sample weight to ensure that the results are nationally representative. Furthermore, the government contracted with the Population Center at the University of Minnesota to create similar coding for the same questions (www.usa.ipums.org).

Most of the research on inequality has revolved around the Annual Socioeconomic Supplement of the Current Population Survey (CPS) and income tax records. Each of these sources has limitations, and the income series of the CBO links these sources to get the benefits from both surveys. Finally, one set of researchers uses the Survey of Consumer Finances (SCF) as a main data source, while others use it as an aid of added information on capital income, which is often underreported.

Current Population Survey

The Bureau of the Census has a variety of data collections on incomes. The Decennial Census is mandated by the Constitution. Since 1940, long-form questionnaires targeting 1 to 5 percent of respondents have posed questions about earnings, race/ethnicity, education, age, gender, marital state, employment, earnings, hours worked, and incomes from a variety of sources.

To get accurate information in a more timely fashion than the Decennial Census and to produce monthly estimates of labor market conditions, the Census Bureau was instructed to begin the CPS in 1940. Once a year, starting in 1948, surveyors asked detailed questions about family incomes. But it was not until 1968 that the coverage was expanded to include everyone, including non-family households. In 2000, the Census Bureau contracted with the newly formed University of Minnesota Population Center to make all available CPSs and other surveys compatible by creating a consistent set of answers to basic questions. These freely downloadable Integrated Public Use Microdata Series have made historical analyses of income-related questions easier to perform.

The Census relies on the recollection of incomes. Errors occur because the respondents cannot accurately remember the monetary value of different income sources. These mistakes are not just random: one weakness of such data is that the values of some sources of incomes are underreported. While the sum of wages and salaries are close to equal to national totals as reported by the BEA's GDP accounts, the amounts of pensions, capital income, and certain government payments are lower than national estimates, some by as much as half of the known total. Furthermore, the level of underreporting is likely growing.

Two other limitations to using CPS data are as follows. First, Census questions tend to be focused on money that individuals receive. As discussed earlier, economists have a broader definition of income, with elements such as employer benefits not being reflected in these surveys. Second, the Census is concerned about ensuring respondent anonymity. It suppresses the exact income of very high earners, often by setting a "top code" reflecting income at or above that level. Consequently, data on the top 1 percent are not reliable and must be estimated through statistical techniques.

Tax Records

Because of the lack of income information on upper-income people in Census data, PS turned to a public dataset created by the Internal Revenue Service (IRS) that used many anonymized tax returns. This allowed PS to get meaningful data on the top 1 percent and even smaller slices of the top 1 percent, down to one-thousandth of 1 percent. The advantage of tax records is that they contain reasonably accurate (underreporting is relatively low) figures for different kinds of income.

However, disadvantages can be found as well:

- The information on the receipt of Social Security and other government cash payments is inconsistent.
- The non-taxed employer's benefits and taxes paid on the worker's behalf to Social Security and unemployment are not included.
- The number of filers has risen as older children with low earnings have increasingly become tax filers.
- When marginal rates were high (at least 70 percent through 1980), corporate and business owners took reduced salaries to avoid taxes. The Tax Reform Act of 1986 lowered the highest marginal tax rate to 38.5 percent in 1986, to 33 percent in 1987, and to 28 percent in 1988. Along with other changes, business owners and executives increased the share of their compensation as salaries.
- The decrease in the number of married adults meant that there were many more low-income filers because former husband-wire couples would combine incomes in a joint return versus two separate returns.
- It is difficult to do family size adjustments because of the incomplete information on the number of people sharing incomes in families.

Survey of Consumer Finances

The SCF wealth survey was first fielded in 1983 and become a more consistent triennial survey in 1989. (For more information on the distribution of wealth, see Chapter 8 in this volume by John Weicher.) Because of the highly concentrated holdings of wealth, the survey has always oversampled rich people and encouraged respondents to have their tax records and other information about their wealth handy during a survey that could last up to 80 minutes. This means that capital income tends to be much more accurately reported by the respondent. The drawbacks of this survey are small sample size and no information on employer benefits.

Linked Surveys

Many researchers have developed methods to link surveys through "statistical matching." Therefore, the household characteristics available on CPS can be included with the better income numbers of tax filers and/or the greater detail on financial assets of the SCF.

Observation Unit

CPS questions are organized in three nested components: households, families in households, and persons in households. Households consist of every person living in the same residential unit; people who live in group quarters (military bases, long-term care facilities, prisons, and any other group setting are not included). So, household income is the total of every person's income in that unit, while family incomes only include the incomes of the householder, spouse, their children, and other relatives of the householder. It is confusing to have separate series for household and family incomes with the only difference being the 6 percent of people who are not relatives of the householder. To make things easier, for the remainder of this chapter, I will use the terms "households" and "families" interchangeably.

Many researchers organize their data into different "sharing income groups" to represent the 2014 distribution of income:

- In 2014, CPS income figures are reported for 122 million households, and each household counts as one observation no matter how many people are in it. Because larger households have more people and higher incomes, this understates median incomes and income growth as more people move to single-adult families.
- CBO (2018) reports income by aggregating the incomes of each person within 122 million households and then converts this figure into a size-adjusted number. Its income tables are organized into quintiles by having the same number of people in a quintile (i.e., a family of five is one household but appears as five people with the same size-adjusted

incomes). Average quintile incomes are then computed on the basis of non-size incomes of each household.

- PS (2003) documents 165 million tax "filers (estimated as [the] sum of married men, divorced and widowed men and women, and single men and women aged 20"). The incomes of non-filers are imputed, most of the additional 43 million observations over the number of CPS households have low incomes because Social Security and other government cash transfers are excluded and because many low-income children in households file separately.

- PSZ (2018) develop income levels for 234 million persons 20 and older (including people in group quarters). Incomes are not size-adjusted, and husbands and wives equally split all common income while older children, parents, and other relatives in the family only have their own incomes.

- Rose (2014, 2016) tracks 186 million "independent adults": all husbands, wives, single parents, and cohabitors (who are joined with the householder with incomes being pooled), and all roommates are treated as separate single-person families. Incomes are reported in size-adjusted terms, and other family members and their incomes are included.

- Auten and Splinter (2018) use all 232 million people older than 20 years (including non-filers with imputed incomes). They link dependent filers and their incomes to their families and then size-adjust incomes to stratify families and single people into equally sized centiles. As with CBO, average quintile incomes are reported in non–size-adjusted incomes. (In addition, see Auten and Splinter's Chapter 5 in this volume.)

Price Deflators

Price deflators are used to turn nominal dollars into real dollars (usually the dollars of the last year of available data). It is arduous to follow the change in price of the same commodity over time. This task is complex because products may embody new features and improvements that require disentangling the cost of the improvement from the listed price to obtain the "pure" change in price.

Over the past 40 years, the Commerce Department has done two major recalibrations of how it computes its main price series, the Consumer Price Index for All Urban Consumers (CPI-U). Each adjustment has led to showing less inflation and more economic growth. This creates three separate series that can be used to create adjustment factors that translate nominal prices in the past to equivalent prices today.

The CPI-U-RS (the RS stands for research series) corrects the weaknesses of the CPI prior to 2000 such that researchers can do historical analyses reflecting the methodology that was used in 2000. This approach is used in all Bureau of

Labor Statistics and Census reports to report historical series in real prices. Most researchers adopt this approach as well.

The chained CPI (C-CPI)[6] was a belated response to the report of the Boskin Commission in December 1996, which concluded that the CPI overstated inflation by 1.1 percent to 1.3 percent per year.

Starting in the mid-2000s, increasing numbers of researchers began to use the personal consumption expenditures (PCE) deflator from the National Income and Product Accounts prepared by the BEA. This showed less inflation than the CPI-U-RS, was in line with the changes of the C-CPI in the years after 2002 and is available back to 1913.

To show the importance of which price deflator is used, consider the following question: How much real income growth was there if the median husband-wife incomes were $20,000 in 1979 incomes and $80,000 in 2014 (nominal dollars but not the exact figures)? If the official CPI-U is used as the price deflator, real growth is 16 percent. In contrast, using the CPI-U-RS finds 31 percent real growth, while the C-CPI shows 46 percent real growth. This example shows that the choice of a specific price deflator can change the size of real growth by 30 percentage points.

Measures of Income Inequality

Since inequality is a slippery concept, it is not surprising that researchers use a variety of techniques to measure it. On the one hand, the annual CPS report on incomes has six summary measures of income inequality which all tend to move about the same amount when distributions change. The most cited measure is the *Gini coefficient*, which computes the gap between the current income distribution and perfect equality. The other six are the *mean logarithmic deviation of income* (average distance from the income mean), the *Thiel index* (has the advantage of being able to disaggregate the causes of inequality; e.g., urban versus rural, age, or race), and three values of the *Atkinson index*. Since the values of each of these indices do not have an obvious interpretation, what matters is how much they change over time.

A different approach is to compare different points on the income ladder: the most common metrics are the income ratios of the 90th to 50th, 50th to 10th, and 90th to 10th percentiles. This represents the gaps between the rich and the middle, the middle and the bottom, and the rich and the bottom. Again, no obvious level designates when inequality is too large. Instead, historical comparisons show that the gaps are increasing, which is translated into inequality becoming larger and less good for the country.

The third method is to look at shares of total incomes. The Census P-60 report tracks the shares of each of the five income quintiles and of the top 5 percent. PS shifted the focus to the growing share of the top 1 percent. When this was combined with stagnation in the bottom 50 percent, it was a clear signal that inequality had become too high.

Multiyear Incomes, Volatility, and the Life Cycle

Saying that the rich (be it the top 1 percent or the top 10 percent) got richer *does not mean* that a group of rich people in Period 1 had higher incomes in Period 2. While certainly some of the people in the top 1 percent in Period 1 had gains, the comparison that is being made is that the group of rich people in Period 2 had average incomes higher than the group of people in Period 1. If Period 2 occurs decades after Period 1, then few people will be in the top 1 percent in both periods. Even over a shorter 10-year period, as many as 10 percent of the population have at least 1 year in the top 1 percent.

In terms of year-to-year fluctuations at the top, Katherine Abraham (2016) cites unpublished IRS tabulations of the change in incomes between 2011 and 2012 that show the volatility of top incomes ($500,000 or more in 2011): 37 percent reported incomes in 2012 that were 25 percent lower than their 2011 levels, another 24 percent had lower incomes in the second year, 19 percent had gains greater than 25 percent, and 20 percent had smaller gains.

Virtual income inequality studies deal with structural change. Instead of tracking the individuals who start on different rungs of the income ladder, these researchers are comparing "similarly situated people" at different points of time. When the CPS report says that median income stayed steady, it does not mean that the incomes of people in the middle did not change.

In fact, as Figure 1.1 shows, a systematic pattern can be seen in the changing incomes of people over their lifetimes. Incomes rise quickly from ages 20 to 40 as people find higher-paying jobs, get promotions, and get married. From 40 to 50, incomes tend to rise and then reach a plateau and decline. But because children

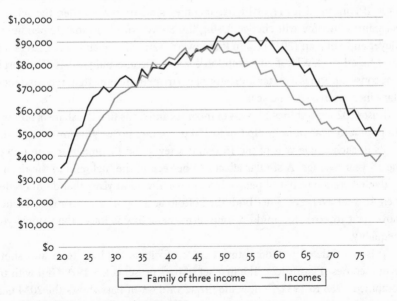

Figure 1.1 Median Income Growth, 1979–2014.

have gone off to lead independent lives, size-adjusted incomes (a better measure of standard of living than just monetary income) stay higher longer and remain higher through the last years of working and through retirement.

A useful image is that of an up escalator in a busy department store. While the escalator continues to be full, every single person has started on one floor and ended up on a higher floor. With respect to a country's income ladder, the median can remain steady while most people between 20 and 40 have 5 percent gains per year. If the new entrants (young people) have low income and older people have declining incomes, the change in the median will be small.

Obviously, not all individuals follow this smooth path. Yearly variations occur due to random positive or negative events during a specific year. In datasets that follow the same people over time, annual swings are quite common. For example, one-third of households in the top or bottom quintile are not in that quintile in the following year, and, in many cases, the following year's gain or loss is large.

Another indication of people's swings of income is that Rose (2010) reports that data from the Panel Study on Income Dynamics showed that 50 percent of adults had at least 1 year in 15 with incomes of at least $100,000. Using the same dataset, Rank found that 70 percent of adults had at least 1 year in the top income quintile over 40 years. Auten and Gee (2007) also show how one-time snapshots give a distorted picture of how people live over time.

Many economists and sociologists believe that multiyear incomes (sometimes referred to as *permanent income*) are a much more accurate indicator of people's standard of living. Changes in consumption are less volatile than changes in income because people can go into debt when they have a temporary decline in income or they can save more when their incomes are above their permanent level. If continued lower or higher incomes tend to persist, then the sense of permanent income will change. Using the Survey of Consumer Expenditures, Meyer and Sullivan (2017) claim that poverty rates are much lower than official rates based on levels of consumption for low-income individuals. They argue that consumption is a better indicator of permanent income than reported monetary income in a specific year.

Rose (2020) combines 15 years of incomes and finds that the share of adults in his poor and near-poor group (up to 150 percent of poverty) is lower than what exists in each single year of the 15 years. A few good income years can pull up the 15-year average. A similar effect can be seen at the high end of the income ladder, where a number of people have unusually good years that do not reflect their 15-year averages. Since both the bottom and top of the income scale show movement towards the middle, long-term inequality is lower than single-year inequality.

This is validated by computing Gini coefficients for long-term and short-term incomes (Figure 1.2). The first set of bars presents the 1979 Gini with the combined 1968 to 1982 Gini, while the second set of bars shows the 2014 Gini next to the 2001 to 2015 Gini. These figures show a remarkable symmetry: in

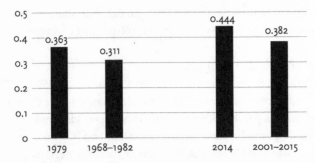

Figure 1.2 Comparing 15-year and Single-year Gini Coefficients.

each pair, the single-year Gini is about 16.5 percent higher than the 15-year average income Gini, and the Ginis in the second group of bars for both the single-year and 15-year Ginis are about 22.5 percent higher than the first group of bars.

Amid all these choices, most agree on which method to use: in 2001 and 2011, the Expert Group on Household Incomes recommended using post-tax, post-transfer, and post-employer benefits and adjusting for family size to report incomes (The Canberra Group 20012011).

RESULTS

The key findings of the original PS 2003 paper were the rising share of income for the top 1 percent and stagnant incomes for those on the bottom and middle rungs of the income ladder. These two findings were linked by the claim that 91 percent of income growth went to the top 10 percent. This "hogging" of growth meant that there were only crumbs for those in the 50th to 90th percentiles. For the bottom 50 percent, there were not any crumbs because the average income of the whole bottom half declined by 21 percent from 1979 to 2014.

In this section, I start by comparing the changes in real median incomes from 1979 to 2014 found in six studies (two by Piketty and coauthors) because median income is usually cited as a standard on how middle-income people are faring. The second part of this section looks at the evolution of the shares of the top one and top ten percent multiple studies.

Before presenting the results, the income coverage of the different studies needs to be addressed. First, the CPS survey only includes 55 percent of national incomes because of its limited coverage and underreporting of capital income. Second, the incomes reported on IRS records for capital gains accounts for 60 percent of national income. Third, CBO adjusts for underreporting of the CPS and includes employer-provided benefits that bring its coverage up to 75 percent of national income. Fourth, studies that include the value of home ownership and other imputations, but do not include the value of government service, cover

83 percent of national income. And fifth, studies that allocate all national income, including government services, reach 100 percent coverage.

Change in Median Incomes

As Table 1.2 shows, the real growth in median income from 1979 to 2014 as reported by major income inequality studies varies from negative 8 percent to positive 51 percent. The pathbreaking PS (2003) study provided intellectual backing for the "stagnating middle-class income" assertion and is the outlier on this list, showing real median decline.[7] The low incomes and the negative growth of the bottom 60 percent of their income ladder is caused by several factors that result in many cases with very low incomes. First, PS limit their definition of income to that recorded on tax forms and exclude many large and growing components of income, such as Social Security income, all other government transfer payments, and employer healthcare contributions. This leads to many retired people appearing to have no or very little income. Second, they include children who file separately from their parents. Instead of being in middle-class household, these children appear as individuals with minimal income. Third, fewer married couples and more adult children filing separately meant that the share of single

Table 1.2 Median income growth (1979–2014), six studies

Study	Change in median	Price deflator	Income concept	Adjust for size	Unit of analysis, 2014 in millions
Piketty and Saez (2003 updated)	−8 percent	CPI-U-RS	Gross income as report on tax forms without government transfers	No	165 M tax filers[a]
CPS	7 percent	CPI-U-RS	Pre-tax, post cash transfers, no employer benefits	No	123 M households
Rose (2016)	30 percent	PCE	Pre-tax, post cash transfers. no employer benefits	Yes	186 M independent adults
Piketty, Saez, and Zucman (2017)	33 percent	National income deflator	All of national income, including value of home ownership and government services	No	All 234 M over 20 years old
Burkhauser et al. (2010)[b]	37 percent	CPI-U-RS	Post-tax, post-transfers with value of health benefits	Yes	117 M households
CBO (2018)	51 percent		Post-tax, post cash, and non-cash transfers and employer benefits	Yes	310 M people

Sources: Piketty, Saez, and Zucman (2014, Appendix Tables II, Distribution), Table 2D13 for PS (2003) and Table 2C13 for Piketty, Saez, and Zucman (2017); CBO (2018), Supplemental Data Spreadsheet 4; Rose (2016); Burkhauser et al. (2010).

[a]Some people who did file tax returns were give imputed incomes and included as a tax filer.
[b]This study compares 2007 with 1979; the median values in 2007 and 2014 are very close to the 2014 median.

filers grew from 44 percent in 1979 to 56 percent in 2014. Because single filers tend to have much lower incomes than married filers, the increase in share of single filers reduces the median income level. This effect would be smaller if they adjusted incomes for family size.

In contrast, the PSZ (2018) study shows a real gain of 33 percent over these years. Several reasons exist for this 41 percentage point difference from the PS (2003) numbers. First, 14 percentage points of the difference are due to the inclusion of more sources of income, especially employer benefits, government transfers to the elderly, and government provision of services (e.g., Medicare, Medicaid, Supplemental Security Income [SSI], and Temporary Assistance for Needy Families [TANF]). Second, another 7 percentage points are due to a different price deflator being used.

Third, the PSZ unit of observation is all Americans 20 and older, with married couples splitting their incomes. Most of the extra 70 million observations are married spouses with modest incomes (incomes of husbands and wives are shared). In the supporting appendix tables, the PSZ study shows that changing the unit of analysis from tax filers to all individuals 20 years and older results in an extra 20 percentage points in income gain.

Finally, it should be noted that these PSZ calculations do not use size-adjusted incomes even though the authors state that this would more accurately reflect standards of living. However, they define their task as allocating all national income to individuals and not measuring changing standards. If PSZ had used size adjustments, real median income growth over these years would have been higher by 6 to 8 percentage points over these same years.

The widely cited CPS median income numbers show only a 7 percent gain from 1979 to 2014. Using the raw data available from the Census, Rose (2016) reported a 30 percent gain over these years. Three reasons exist for the 23 percentage-point difference between Rose and the CPS change in median growth: using a price deflator that shows more growth and less inflation, adjusting for family size, and using independent adults as the unit of analysis rather than households. This last factor is significant because larger families have considerably higher incomes than do single-adult households. With the household weighting used by the Census, married-couple families are counted only as one observation versus being counted as two observations in Rose (2016). Both Rose and CPS do not include employer benefits (Rose, 2007, estimated benefits and found a 33 percent median gain from 1979 to 2005) and other government services that directly serve people. If these were included, then the real median income growth in the Rose study would have been higher by 7–10 percentage points.

Burkhauser, Larrimore, and Simon (2011) expand the base of CPS incomes by imputing the value of employer and government health benefits to individuals. While this is not the broadest definition of income, health benefits are an income stream that grew very quickly. The authors then size incomes for household size and use the National Bureau of Economic Research's (NBER) TaxSim

9.0 to estimate post-tax incomes. In reporting the change in median income from 1979 to 2007, they start by using their simulation of the PS tax filer approach showing a 3.2 percent gain of median income. Step by step, they show that using households rather than tax filers results in a 12.5 percent real median growth. Adjusting for household size adds another 8 percentage points to growth and adding transfers and adjusting for taxes paid lead to a 29.3 percent median growth. And the final adjustment of adding health benefits results in their best estimate of 36.7 percent in real median growth. If this study had used the PCE as its price deflator, real median growth would have been 5 percentage points higher.

Finally, CBO goes beyond just cash income by including employer benefits (including the employer's Federal Insurance Contributions Act [FICA] share), government cash benefits (mostly Social Security payments), and a higher amount of capital income (including capital gains) than the CPS. Incomes are then size adjusted, and the final income series subtracts federal taxes and adds non-cash benefits (mostly Medicare and Medicaid). Because of all the additions, CBO median income was much higher in 2014 than was the CPS median: $77,100 versus $53,000. In terms of trend, the CBO post-tax, size-adjusted incomes grew by 51 percent. This 44 percentage point difference from the CPS median gain is larger than the 23 percentage point gain found in Rose (2014). This is due to three reasons: inclusion of many more income elements, use of post-tax incomes, and a different unit of analysis.

The CBO slightly overstates growth because of two factors related to employer-provided retirement benefits. First, employers' contributions to deferred compensation plans start at $0 dollars per household in 1979 and rise to $2,100 in 2014. However, this gain does not represent more employer contributions but instead the switch from defined benefit plans (which are not included in the CBO approach) to defined contribution plans (which are included in this category). The second overstatement involves the double counting of employer's contributions and the gain of nearly $5,700 of "other market income" (which is mainly retirement income) over these years. Adjusting for these two factors would decrease their real median income change by 8–10 percentage points. Third, the CBO uses capital gains as a proxy for corporate profits not distributed as interest and dividend payments; Auten and Splinter (2018) finds that this increases the income shares of high-income people.

Income Inequality Measures

The release of PS's original paper in 2003 propelled income inequality into a major public issue because the authors reported that that the rich (top 10 percent) monopolized income growth (91 percent). Figure 1.3 shows the share of income growth between 1979 and 2014 that went to the richest 10 percent of the population in four different studies.

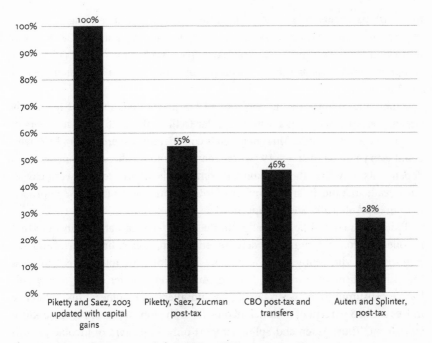

Figure 1.3 Share of income growth from 1979 to 2014 going to top 10 percent.

Using the original PS methodology and including capital gains, the average income of the bottom 90 percent was almost exactly equal in both years, meaning that all income growth went to the top 10 percent. The average income of the bottom 50 percent declined by 21 percent during these years, while the 51st to 90th percentile families made modest gains.

To show how sensitive this finding is to a specific methodology, Armour, Burkhauser, and Larrimore (2013) show that the income growth of the bottom quintile went from declining by 33 percent using PS's methodology from 1979 to 2007 to rising by 31 percent by adjusting for household sizes, including government transfers, accounting for taxes, and including in-kind private and public income.

The next three bars show the post-tax share of the top 10 percent from 1979 to 2014 for three studies. PSZ's 55 percent of growth going the top 10 percent differs greatly from the earlier PS approach. Instead of filers, all adults are represented, all sources of incomes are included, and the studies uses post-tax income while the original study uses only pre-tax income. The CBO, in contrast, did not add as many income sources but did include employer-paid benefits, government cash benefits, and government non-cash benefits.

Auten and Splinter (2018) also allocate all national income but do it in a way that is different from PSZ. They note that many high-income individuals have control of how and when they get paid. When marginal rates were high prior to 1980 (at least 70 percent), many executives and business owners minimized their cash payments in favor of gains in the net worth of their ownership stake. In 1986, marginal rates were reduced greatly (eventually going to 28 percent), thus changing the incentives for how executives and business owners took their compensation. Consequently, Auten and Splinter developed a "consistent market income" for each year.

Auten and Splinter exclude dependent tax filers, adjust incomes for family size, and stratify people in a fashion similar to the CBO, with equal numbers of people in each percentile. This approach is considerably different from PSZ, who count every person over age 19 (where married couples share joint income and dependents only have their personal income). This difference may seem trivial, but it leads to a much larger number of low-income cases in the PSZ approach than in the Auten and Splinter approach.

Finally, Auten and Splinter allocate the 17 percent of national income that is collective consumption (e.g., defense, education, police, fire, courts, and administration) differently from PSZ who apportion this total based on each individual's disposable income. Instead, Auten and Splinter evenly divide collective consumption between per capita and after-tax incomes. This difference moves about 3 percent of national income from the top 10 percent to the bottom 50 percent. Thus, Auten and Splinter report only 28 percent of income growth going to the top 10 percent between 1979 and 2014.

Once again, the PS, 2003 study is an outlier, with 100 percent of the growth going to top 10 percent. Though the other studies' estimates vary, their average estimate of income growth going to the top 10 percent is 45 percent.

Changing Share of Top 1 Percent

PS made the share of income going to the top 1 percent of the income ladder the central figure in their analysis. The four studies in Table 1.3 reveal differing trends in the top 1 percent's rising income share. PS's data include capital gains (but exclude taxes, nontaxable government transfers, and employer benefits) and show that the top 1 percent's income share grew from 10 percent in 1979 to 22 percent in 1983. After 1983, the top 1 percent's share of income rose to 24 percent before declining slightly to 22 percent in 2014. PS find that the top 1 percent increased their share of income by nearly 12 percentage points between 1979 and 2014 (Table 1.2).

Table 1.3 Changes in top one percent's income share

	1979	2014	Percentage point change
Piketty and Saez (2003), updated with capital gains, pre-tax	10.0	22.0	11.9
Piketty, Saez, and Zucman (2018), post-tax	9.1	15.7	6.5
Auten and Splinter (2018), post-tax	7.2	8.5	1.3
CBO (2018), post-tax	7.4	13.3	5.9

For the third time, the PS study is the outlier, with the income share of the top 1 percent more than doubled, growing by almost 12 percentage points. PSZ do not emphasize how different their results are from PS, but their methodology shows only a 6.6 percentage point gain—more than 5 percentage points less than PS's figure.

In contrast, Auten and Splinter's consistent market income series shows a much smaller gain in the top 1 percent's income share. Their 1979 estimate is similar to PSZ's, but their 2014 estimate is nearly 7 percentage points lower than PS's 2014 estimate. Auten and Splinter find a 1.3 percentage point increase in the top 1 percent's income share between 1979 and 2014. Both Auten and Splinter and PSZ allocate all national income, but many of Auten and Splinter's methodological choices lead to less income growth among the top 1 percent and more income growth among middle and lower income people.

CBO's estimate of the post-tax income share of the top 1 percent in 1979 is 7.4 percent, in line with Auten and Splinter's estimates. The CBO estimates that the top 1 percent's income growth of 13.3 percent in 2014 is slightly below the 2014 share of PSZ. One reason that the CBO share of the top 1 percent has grown so much more than the Auten and Splinter 1 percent gain comes from Early's (2018) finding that the CBO does not include many government non-cash assistance activities that primarily benefit people in the bottom half.[8]

Three other studies are worth mentioning but do not have data for 1979 and 2014. Burkhauser, Feng, Jenkins, and Larrimore (2009) use nonpublic CPS data to better estimate the top 1 percent's income. They argue that using households (rather than tax filers) as the observation unit and including government transfer incomes will reduce inequality, especially in post-tax distributions. They report the first and last available data from 1967 to 2006 and find that the top 1 percent's share of income grew by 5 percentage points, one-half of PS's and PSZ's estimates over the same period.

Bricker, Enriques, Krimmel, and Sabelhaus (2016) is authored by researchers at the Federal Reserve Board closely involved in producing and disseminating information from the SCF.[9] Because this triennial survey was first fielded in 1989 (reporting 1988 incomes), it is limited to those years for which the survey is available. Like Auten and Splinter and PSZ, the study attempts to allocate all national income to families and finds a small gain in the top 1 percent's income share, from nearly 16 percent in 1988 to nearly 18 percent in 2012.

Larrimore and colleagues (2017) find a small gain (less than 2 percentage points) in the top 1 percent's income share. This study uses a combination of income tax records, the CPS, and the SCF to estimate capital gains accrual by year for every class of capital ownership, including home ownership by county and by tax-preferred retirement accounts. The combination of data sources allows more options to impute missing incomes. Because the study uses tax records for income and the SCF for capital income estimates, the study's analysis begins in 1989 and ends in 2013.

Excluding PS's findings of a 12 percentage point gain in the top 1 percent's income share, two studies show sizeable gains in the top 1 percent's share of 5.9 and 6.6 percentage points, and four studies show at most a 2 percentage point gain. The average of these six studies shows a gain of the top 1 percent's income share of 3.5 percentage points.

Other Income Inequality Measures

All metrics support the finding that income inequality has increased in the United States at least since 1979. For a long time, researchers mainly reported just the Gini coefficient as the measure of inequality. For example, the CPS reports that the Gini across US households was .404 in 1979 and .480 in 2014, for a gain of 19 percent.

Most studies show that income inequality increased throughout the income ladder. For example, Rose (2016) showed that size-adjusted incomes between 1979 and 2014 increased steadily with each progressive percentile. While the first 5 percentiles had negative income growth, the 1 percent at the 6th percentile was 30 percent, at the 75th percentile was 40 percent, and the 95th percentile was 68 percent. An exception to this finding was the CBO after-tax and transfer income series, where they reported that the income growth of the bottom quintile was 69 percent but 39 percent, 36 percent, 47 percent, and 97 percent, respectively, for the remaining four quintiles (and 228 percent for the top 1 percent). Larrimore et al. (2011) also found that the bottom quintile did well under some methodologies: while PS showed that the bottom quintile's income in 2007 was down by 33 percent, this group's income was up 33 percent when post-tax incomes were adjusted for size and included government transfers.

Finally, an outlier in the inequality literature is the work of Meyer and Sullivan (2017) using the Survey of Consumer Expenditures. They argue that consumption is a better measure of standard of living and of permanent income. An oddity in the consumption expenditure data is that consumption expenditures of the bottom income quintile are about 150 percent greater than reported incomes. This is possible because these people can spend out of savings or go into debt.

Because consumption is so high among low-income households, Meyer has reported that consumption poverty is very low: his last press release said that it was just 3 percent.[10] In terms of inequality, Meyer and Sullivan report a 7 percent rise in the 90/10 ratio of consumer expenditures from 1961 to 2014 and a 29 percent rise in the 90/10 ratio of post-tax and post-transfer incomes over these years.

CONCLUSION

In the physical sciences, when a new experiment reveals new findings, other researchers replicate the experiment to ensure that they find the same conclusion. The social sciences are messier in that researchers cannot control all factors in a way that isolates one issue that can be tested. Furthermore, rarely does a dataset exist that contains all the elements needed to measure complex relationships. As has been shown, various researchers get different answers about the growth of income inequality because they use different units of analysis and different definitions of income and differ in whether to adjust for family size, how to measure capital income, and what price deflator to use.

While it is not the purpose of this chapter to anoint a single study as being the most accurate, a couple of observations can be made. First, the original PS use of IRS microdata opened the way for a new method by which to study income inequality. Yet their methodology shows the median income was lower in 2014 than it was in 1979 and equal to its 1968 level. This is not credible and is not supported by any other data. Furthermore, they report that the top 10 percent got 100 percent of the income growth from 1979 to 2014 and that the share of the top 1 percent grew by 12 percentage points. Neither of these findings is supported by other research.

PS seemed to be aware of these problems, and they combined with Zucman to expand incomes dramatically and to stop using tax filers as their unit of observation. Their findings on the growth of real median incomes from 1979 to 2014 are in line with those of several other studies. But in terms of share of income held by the top 1 percent, both the PS approach and the PSZ approach had similar levels and the largest increases in these shares from 1979 to 2014. In both approaches, the Piketty team has emphasized the limited gains of the bottom half of the population.[11]

Burkhauser et al. (2011) and Rose (2007, 2014, 2016) paint a more positive vision of those in the 35th to 75th percentiles of the income ladder. While stagnating middle-class incomes is a clear story line, a 30–50 percent increase over 37 years is a middling result that is less than good but not terrible. But when this level of increase trails the 80–100 percent increase of the top 20 percent of the population and the 200-plus percent gains of the top 1 percent, the issue of fairness has led many to say that income inequality in the US today is too high.

Rose (2010, 2017) points to several factors behind white working-class dissatisfaction. First, people are nostalgic about how good things were in the 1950s and 1960s. But this is a very myopic view of these years. In 1960, the elderly poverty rate was 35 percent while the overall poverty rate was 22 percent. Houses were smaller, people traveled less for vacations, and those who reached 65 could expect to live 5 fewer years than today.

Second, non-college white men had more opportunities. Rose (2017) shows that, in 1960, non-college white men held 55 percent of the most coveted managerial and professional jobs. By 2014, they held only 15 percent of these jobs even though the share of these coveted jobs in the labor force increased from 17 to 35 percent over these years. The people who "snatched these jobs away" from white non-college men were college-educated white women and college-educated people of color.

Third, this discontent includes a cultural dimension because many people feel that they "losing their country." To some, the notion that minorities may become a majority later in this century is upsetting. To others, the acceptance of gay marriage and transgender bathroom rights is a sign that their values are not shared.

Fourth, Rose (2016) documents the huge growth of the mainly college-educated upper middle class from 13 percent in 1979 to 29 percent in 2014. Instead of the most important income divide being the 1 percent versus the 99 percent, I argue that the divide is driven by the 30 percent (upper middle class and rich) versus the 70 percent. So, members of a "liberal elite" who have access to high-end consumer goods and services, including foreign travel, are setting cultural standards that seem intolerant to many of the views of the bottom 70 percent. Further, the bottom 70 percent worry that their children may not thrive in the economy of the future.

These comments show that the working-class rage that gets so much media attention is based on reasons other than middle-class stagnation. Many polls show that widespread satisfaction with people's own perceptions of their personal living conditions: Pew reports that 32 percent of Americans say that they are "very happy with their life" and another 51 are "pretty happy." Also, a 2018 Federal Reserve Board survey on the well-being of Americans finds 69 percent saying that they are "living comfortably" or are "doing okay." One of the reasons that these numbers do not seem to align with the current incomes of people is due to the tendency of the press to print bad news because it sells or gets more clicks. Another reason is the difference between current income and "permanent income "(the average of many years). As shown, yearly fluctuations result in more people having low incomes in a single year than their income average over multiple years.

Measuring inequality is difficult, but the findings of four studies show that real median incomes have grown from 30 percent to 51 percent since 1979. Many people think that middle-class incomes have stagnated even though their evaluation of their own condition is positive. Instead the press is biased against good news (it is not interesting), and both the left and the right have reasons to proclaim that people are doing badly. This study shows that the best estimates of changes between 1979 and 2014 are that real median income grew by 42 percent, that the share of growth going to the top 10 percent over these years was 45 percent, and that the share of the top 1 percent grew by 3.5 percentage points.

NOTES

1. In December 1978, I released the Social Stratification in the United States poster and factbook highlighting how "unequal" incomes were: it was prominently noted in the explanatory notes that the position of the 1,124 families who declared more than $1 million on their tax returns would be 130 feet above the nearly 4-foot high poster (Rose, 1978).
2. State tax rates on companies vary by their experience of laying off qualified workers; see https://www.taxpolicycenter.org/statistics/state-unemployment-tax-rates.
3. Studies of the "wealth effect" show that people increase their consumption by 3 cents on the dollar of unexpected wealth gains.
4. Burkhauser et al. (2011) show that the size adjustments often change a specific household's place on the income scale: for those in the first quintile of size-adjusted incomes, just a little more than half were in the bottom quintile of non-size-adjusted incomes; for the middle three quintiles, just over a third were in the same quintiles. It was in the top quintile that two-thirds were in the same quintile.
5. The sum of size-adjusted incomes, even for family-of-three equivalents, may not add up to the total income reported by the Bureau of Economic Analysis. For those who want an exact accounting of national income, this is a problem.
6. Cage, R., Greenlees, J., and Jackman, P. (2003). Introducing the Chained Consumer Price Index. Accessed August 19, 2018, at https://www.bls.gov/cpi/additional-resources/chained-cpi-introduction.pdf.
7. The original data used the unadjusted historical CPI through 2002, when PS moved to the CPI-U-RS price deflator. If the unadjusted CPI was used for the 1979–2014 comparison, then the 2014 median income would have been 15 percent lower than the 1979 median.
8. The earlier study only covers 2015 and does not show any changes over time.
9. Smeeding and Thompson (2011) and Wolff and Zacharias (2009) also used the SCF, but for a different time frame.
10. Available at http://www.aei.org/publication/annual-report-on-us-consumption-poverty-2016/
11. Saez (2012) argued that all the income gains from 2009 to 2012 went to the top 1 percent. But Rose (2015) showed that if the starting date was 2007, even using Saez's data, the top 1 percent would have been the biggest losers. Saez went from trough to peak rather than use the more common method of going from peak to peak.

REFERENCES

Abraham, Katherine. 2016. Comment. *Brookings Papers on Economic Activity.* Spring 2016: 313–321.

Armour, Phillip, Richard Burkhauser, and Jeff Larrimore. 2013. "Levels and Trends in US Income and Its Distribution: A Crosswalk from Market Income to a Comprehensive Haig-Simon Income Approach." Cambridge, MA: NBER Working Paper 19110.

Auten, Gerald, and Geoffrey Gee. 2007. *Income Mobility in the United States: Evidence from Income Tax Returns for 1987 and 1996.* Washington, DC: Department of Treasury, Office of Tax Analysis.

Auten, Gerald, and David Splinter. 2018. *Income Inequality in the United States: Using Tax Data to Measure Long-Term Trends.* Washington, DC: Joint Committee on Taxation.

Bricker, Jesse, Alice Enriques, Jacob Krimmel, and John Sabelhaus. 2016. *Measuring Income and Wealth at the Top Using Administrative and Survey Data.* Washington, DC: Brookings Papers on Economic Activity.

Burkhauser, Richard V., Shuaizhang Feng, Stephen P. Jenkins, and Jeff Larrimore. 2009. "Recent Trends in Top Income Shares in the USA: Reconciling Estimates from March CPS and IRS Tax Return Data." Cambridge, MA: NBER Working Paper 15320.

Burkhauser, Richard, Jeff Larrimore, and Kosali Simon. 2011. "A 'Second Opinion' on the Economic Health of the American Middle Class." Cambridge, MA: NBER Working Paper 17164.

Burkhauser, Richard V., Shuaizhang Feng, Stephen P. Jenkins, and Jeff Larrimore. 2011. "Recent Trends in Top Income Shares in the United States: Reconciling Estimates from March CPS and IRS Tax Return Data." *Review of Economics and Statistics,* 94(2): 371–388.

Canberra Group. 2001. *Final Report and Recommendations.* Ottawa: Expert Group on Household Income Statistics, the Canberra Group.

Canberra Group. 2011. *Handbook on Household Income Statistics* (2nd ed.). Geneva: United Nations Economic Commission for Europe.

Congressional Budget Office (CBO). 2018. "The Distribution of Household Income, 2014." In *2015 US Census Bureau, Current Population Reports, P60-252, Income and Poverty in the United States: 2014,* edited by Carmen DeNavas-Walt and Bernadette D. Proctor. Washington, DC: US Government Printing Office.

Early, John F. 2018. "Reassessing the Facts About Inequality, Poverty and Redistribution." Washington, DC: Cato Institute, Policy Analysis No. 839.

Larrimore, Jeff, Richard V. Burkhauser, Gerald Auten, and Philip Armour. 2017. "Recent Trends in US Top Income Shares in Tax Record Data Using More

Comprehensive Measures of Income Including Accrued Capital Gains." Cambridge, MA: NBER Working Paper 23007.

Meyer, Bruce, and James Sullivan. 2017. "Consumption and Income Inequality in the US Since the 1960s." Cambridge, MA: NBER Working Paper 23655.

Mishel, Lawrence, Josh Bivens, Elise Gould, and Heidi Shierholz. 2012. *The State of Working America* (12th ed.). Ithaca, NY: Cornell University Press.

Piketty, Thomas, and Emmanuel Saez. 2003 (data updated to 2014). "Income Inequality in the United States, 1913–1998." *Quarterly Journal of Economics*, 113 (1): 1–39.

Piketty, Thomas, Emmanuel Saez and Gabriel Zucman. 2018. "Distributional National Accounts: Methods and Estimates for the United States." *Quarterly Journal of Economics*, 553–609. Appendix tables available at http://gabriel-zucman.eu/usdina/

Payne, Keith. 2017. *The Broken Ladder: How Inequality Affects the Way in Which We Think, Live, and Die.* New York: Viking Press.

Rose, Stephen J. 1978. *Social Stratification in United States.* Baltimore, MD: Social Graphics Company.

Rose, Stephen J. 2007. *Does Productivity Growth Still Benefit Working Americans? Unraveling the Income Growth Mystery to Determine How Much Median Incomes Trail Productivity Growth.* Washington, DC: The Information Technology & Innovation Foundation.

Rose, Stephen J. 2010. *Rebound: How America Will Emerge Stronger After the Financial Crisis.* New York: St. Martin's Press.

Rose, Stephen J. 2014. *Was JKF Wrong? Does Rising Productivity No Longer Lead to Substantial Middle Class Income Gains.* Washington, DC: The Information Technology & Innovation Foundation.

Rose, Stephen J. 2015. *Social Stratification in United States.* New York: The New Press.

Rose, Stephen J. 2016. *The Growing Size and Incomes of the Upper Middle Class.* Washington, DC: Urban Institute.

Rose, Stephen J. 2017. *White Working Class Men in a Changing American Labor Force.* Washington, DC: Third Way.

Rose, Stephen J. 2020. *Middle Class Income Trajectories, Three 15-Year Periods, 1967 to 2014.* Washington, DC: Brookings Institute.

Saez, Emmanuel. 2012. "Striking it Richer: The Evolution of Top Incomes in the United States." http://www.econ.berkeley.edu/~saez/saez-UStopincomes-2007.pdf

Smeeding, Timothy M., and Jeffrey P. Thompson. 2011. "Recent Trends in Income Inequality: Labor, Wealth and More Complete Measures of Income." In *Who Loses in the Downturn? Economic Crisis, Employment and Income*

Distribution, edited by H. Immervoll, A. Peichl, and K. Tatsiramos. Bingley, UK: Emerald Group

Edward Wolff., and Ajit Zacharias. 2009. "Household Wealth and the Measurement of Economic Well-being in the United States." *Journal of Economic Inequality*, 7: 83–115.

APPENDIX A
RECENT BOOKS ON THE PROBLEMS OF RISING INEQUALITY

Jared Bernstein. 2008. *Crunch: Why Do I Feel So Squeezed (and Other Unsolved Economic Mysteries).*

Tyler Cowen. 2011. *The Great Stagnation: How Americans Ate All the Low-Hanging Fruit of Modern History, Got Sick, and Will (Eventually) Feel Better.*

Thomas Edsall. 2012. *The Age of Austerity: How Inequality Will Remake American Politics.*

Jeff Faux. 2006. *The Global Class War: America's Bipartisan Elite Lost Our Future.*

Robert Frank. 2007. *Falling Behind: How Rising Inequality Harms the Middle Class.*

David Cay Johnson. 2008. *How the Wealthiest Americans Have Enriched Themselves at Government's Expense (and Stuck You with the Bill).*

Robert Kuttner. 2007. *The Squandering of America: How the Failure of Our Politics Undermines Our Prosperity.*

James Lardner and David Smith, editors. 2007. *Inequality Matters: The Growing Economic Divide in America and Its Ruinous Consequences.*

David Madland. 2014. *Hollowed Out: Why the Economy Does Not Work Without a Strong Middle Class.*

Timothy Noah. 2012. *The Great Divergence: America's Growing Inequality Crisis and What We Can Do About It.*

George Packer. 2013. *The Unwinding: An Inner History of the New America.*

Don Peck. *Pinched: How the Great Recession Has Narrowed Our Futures and What We Can Do About It.*

Stephen Pearlstein. 2018. *Can American Capitalism Survive? Why Greed Is Not Good, Opportunity Is Not Equal, and Fairness Will Not Make Us Poor.*

Robert Reich. 2008. *Supercapitalism: The Transformation of Business, Democracy, and Everyday Life.*

Robert Reich. 2013. *Aftershock: The Next Economy and America's Future.*

Robert Reich. 2016. *Saving Capitalism: For the Many, Not the Few.*

Isabelle Sawhill. 2018. *Forgotten Americans: An Economic Agenda for a Divided Nation.*

Joseph Stiglitz. 2013. *The Price of Inequality: How Today's Divided Society Endangers Our Future.*

Joseph Stiglitz. 2015. *Rewriting the Rules of the American Economy: An Agenda for Growth and Shared Prosperity.*

Joseph Stiglitz. 2016. *Unequal Societies and What We Can Do About Them.*

Matt Taibbi. 2014. *Divide: American Injustice in the Age of the Wealth Gap.*

Peter Temin. 2018. *The Vanishing Middle Class: Prejudice and Power in a Dual Economy.*

2

INCOME AND WEALTH INEQUALITY

EVIDENCE AND POLICY IMPLICATIONS

Emmanuel Saez

MEASURING INEQUALITY

Inequality is an important issue because the public cares about it.[1] People have a sense of fairness, and they have views on whether the distribution of economic resources is fair. Given this intrinsic public interest in inequality, our first job as economists is to help enlighten the debate by providing very transparent inequality measures that the broad public can understand. Once we have appropriately measured inequality, we then want to understand the drivers of inequality trends and the effects of public policy on inequality.

Two concepts of economic resources are *income* and *wealth*. Income is a flow typically measured on an annual basis. You get *labor income* from working. You also get income from your wealth, which is *capital income*, or effectively the return on wealth. Wealth is a stock of economic resources that are accumulated either from your own savings or from inheritances you may have received, typically from your parents. Here are the basic aggregate economic facts for the United States. Labor income is about 70–75 percent of total national income. Capital income is the rest: about 25–30 percent. For the bottom 90 percent of income earners, capital income is negligible relative to labor income. Total accumulated wealth measured at market prices is around four times the total annual national income. Given the ratio of 25–30:400, the implicit annual rate of return on wealth in the form of capital income is around 6–7 percent before taxes.

Emmanuel Saez, *Income and Wealth Inequality* In: *United States Income, Wealth, Consumption, and Inequality.* Edited by: Diana Furchtgott-Roth, Oxford University Press (2021). © Oxford University Press. DOI: 10.1093/oso/9780197518199.003.0003.

Wealth inequality is always much higher than income inequality because a lot of people do not have any wealth. The bottom 50 percent of families, ranked by wealth, basically have zero wealth, and hence zero capital income as well.

Advanced economies, or advanced societies, have decided through the will of the community, as represented by the government, to affect the distribution of pre-tax incomes through public policy. Effectively, advanced economies tax between 30 and 50 percent of pre-tax market income. On the low end, the United States and Japan tax about 30 percent of national income. At the high end, European countries with larger welfare states tax about 50 percent of national income. Taxes are used to fund transfers, the welfare state, and a number of public goods. The fact that we have decided to do so much redistribution means that, as societies, we do care about distribution. We find it fair to have the community do substantial amounts of redistribution through its government. Once you take out taxes and you add back transfers, post-tax income inequality is consequently substantially lower than pre-tax income inequality.

A very simple way to measure inequality, and one that the broader public can understand, is to estimate top income shares. What share of total, say, pre-tax, income goes to certain groups, such as the top 10 percent of families, or top 1 percent of families, or the top 0.1 percent of families? Individual income tax statistics are an excellent resource to estimate such top income share series because they cover very long time periods. Advanced economies typically started their progressive income taxes about a century ago (e.g., in 1913, in the United States). These data also capture very well top incomes because governments have typically produced distributional statistics based on individual income tax returns. These statistics provide a very clear picture of the top of the distribution, something you cannot get with survey data. In survey data, there are too few high-income people in samples, and there is measurement error due to substantial nonresponse rates.

Thomas Piketty studied the case of France in Piketty (2001, 2003). Shortly afterward, Piketty and I studied the United States in Piketty and Saez (2003). Since then, more than 25 countries have been studied through a collective effort involving many researchers (see, e.g., Alvaredo et al., 2013). The data are posted online in the World Wealth and Income Database (Alvaredo et al., 2016). It is truly a global project including statistics that cover most of Western Europe and North America and a number of developing countries as well, such as China and India.

The richness of the series produced and the time periods covered vary across countries. Typically, the more advanced economies have data for longer time periods. One caveat is that, in these data, the income concept is *fiscal income*, defined as income reported on individual income tax returns, which is a narrower concept than national income from national accounting. The focus, so far, has been on pre-tax and pre-transfer incomes. This measures inequality as it is generated by the market, before any government taxation and redistribution.

Both pre-tax and post-tax income inequality measures are interesting. You want to study both to assess the redistributive effects of the government.

US PRE-TAX AND POST-TAX INCOME INEQUALITIES

Figure 2.1 shows the time series of the top 10 percent pre-tax income share in the United States for almost a century, from 1917 to 2015.

The figure shows that the United States has gone through large variations in income concentration. Before World War II, the top 10 percent of families were getting a large fraction, around 45 percent of total income. Then there was a precipitous decline that exactly lines up with World War II. After World War II, there were decades during which income concentration was much lower, with the top 10 percent of families getting about one-third of total income. And then, of course, what is striking in this figure—and what has been very much debated—is the extraordinary rise that started in the late 1970s. The top 10 percent income share has grown from 33 percent to more than 50 percent in recent years and has even surpassed the peaks of pre-World War II.

The tax data capture the top very well, and they allow us to disaggregate further within the top 10 percent. A simple way to do that is to decompose the top 10 percent income group into three groups: the top 1 percent, the next 4 percent, and the next 5 percent (bottom half of the top decile). In Figure 2.2, the top 1 percent income share is shown in black, the next 4 percent in light grey, and the next 5 percent in dark grey. The sum of those three series is the top 10 percent income share shown in Figure 2.1.

Figure 2.1 Top 10% Pre-tax Income Share in the United States, 1917–2015.

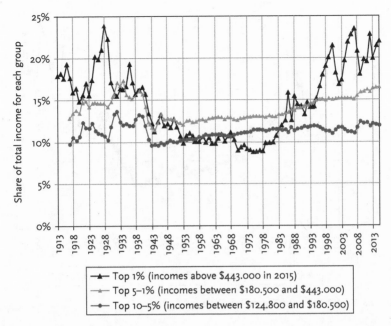

Figure 2.2 Decomposing the U.S. Top 10% Pre-tax Income into Three Groups, 1913–2015.

This decomposition is interesting because the top 10 percent income share gained 17 percentage points since the late 1970s, going from 33 to 50 percentage points: almost all of the 17 percentage point gain, 12–13 percentage points, has gone to the top 1 percent of income earners (families with incomes above $443,000 in 2015), whose share of total pre-tax income rose from 9 percentage points to somewhere between 21 and 22 percentage points in recent years. The next 4 percent, the blue series in the figure, are families making between about $180,500 and $443,000 in 2015, and they have gained, but only 3 or 4 points. And the last income share series for the bottom half of the top 10 percent, families with incomes between $125,000 and $180,000 in 2015, does not experience much gain at all since the 1970s. Even within the top 1 percent, gains are unequal and grow larger as incomes increase.

Figure 2.3 shows the example of the top 0.1 percent, families with more than $2 million in income today. Their share of income has gone up from 3 percent in the late 1970s to 11 percent in 2015, an increase of 8 percentage points. Therefore, a big part of the increasing income concentration comes from this top income group.

Tax data also allow you to look at the composition of income between labor and capital. Figure 2.4 plots the top 0.1 percent income share, stacked by income components: wage and salary earnings, business income, capital income (such as interest, dividends, and rents), and realized capital gains. Even though the level of the very top income shares today is similar, or perhaps even higher, than it was

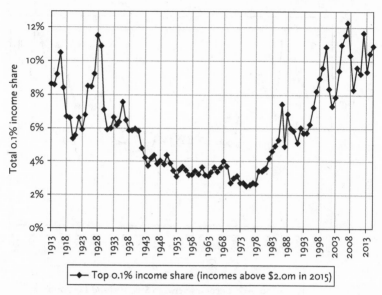

Figure 2.3 Top 0.1% U.S. Pre-Tax Income Share, 1913–2015.

almost a century ago, the composition has changed substantially. A century ago, the very top incomes were mostly capital income. Effectively, people at the top of the income distribution owned large fortunes from which they derived substantial capital incomes in the form of dividends and interest income. Labor income

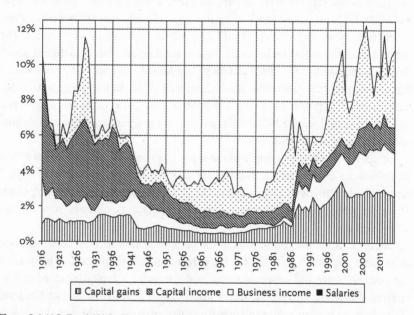

Figure 2.4 U.S. Top 0.1% Pre-Tax Income Share and Composition.

was minimal among top income earners. These top income families were likely the inheritors of the "Robber Barons" of the Gilded Age of the late 19th century. Big fortunes were created and then were passed on to the next generation, and the people at the top could live off these fortunes.

When inequality reemerged beginning in the late 1970s, a significant fraction of this inequality increase, at least up to the year 2000, was a labor income phenomenon. Wages, salaries, and business income—which is, in part, mixed labor and capital—were growing very fast. The best illustration of that is the explosion of Chief Executive Officer (CEO) compensation, which would be captured in the wages and salaries component because the profits from exercised stock options are part of wages and salaries for tax purposes.

Since 2000, capital income at the top has surged. The high labor income earners probably accumulate fortunes and start to derive significant capital income from their fortunes. A good illustration is Bill Gates, who started as an entrepreneur. Initially his income is labor income. He creates a business and then retires from managing Microsoft, but he still gets billions, literally, in dividends every year from the fortune he accumulated, which is capital income.

These data are based on fiscal income; that is, income reported on individual income tax returns. Fiscal income does not include all of total US national income.

INEQUALITY IN DISTRIBUTION OF US NATIONAL INCOME GROWTH

The Piketty-Saez time series we have discussed capture only about two-thirds of national income because a number of income components are not reported on tax returns. On the labor income side, fringe benefits, such as health and pension contributions and employer payroll taxes, are not included in tax data. On the capital income side, the returns on pension funds, corporate retained earnings, corporate taxes, and imputed rents to homeowners are all missing. All of these components are truly economic incomes and go into national income estimated by national accounts, but they are not included here. Another challenge is that the Piketty-Saez data are based on tax units (a *tax unit* is a married couple with dependents if any, or a single adult with dependents if any) instead of adults. Tax units have become smaller over time as the fraction of the population that is married has declined.

Therefore, the Piketty-Saez data are not well designed to understand economic growth at the same time as distribution because the economic growth from the Piketty-Saez data is relatively far apart from the growth in national income that is widely discussed in the public debate. The next step in our research agenda is to impute missing income to line up with national income, in what we are calling *distributional national accounts*. That would allow the analysis of the distribution

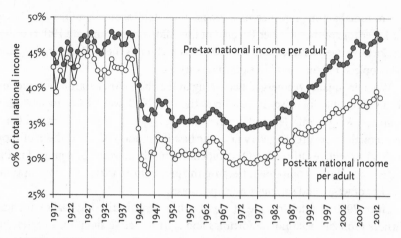

Figure 2.5 Top 10% U.S. National Income Share: Pre-tax versus Post-tax.

of economic growth, both on a pre-tax and a post-tax basis. Thomas Piketty, my colleague Gabriel Zucman, and I (Piketty, Saez, and Zucman, 2016) have some preliminary findings. In Figure 2.5 the share of total national income going to the top 10 percent of adults pre-tax is shown in red. These trends look similar to previous illustrations.

The figure also depicts in white the post-tax national income share for the top 10 percent of families. To compute post-tax income, we start from pre-tax income, deduct all taxes (federal and local), and add back all forms of government spending, including both transfers and public good spending. The comparison of the pre-tax and post-tax series therefore provides a global vision of the redistribution done by the government through taxes and spending.

In Figure 2.5, the post-tax series are very similar to pre-tax series in the early period a century ago when taxes and government spending were small (around 10 percent of all national income). On a post-tax basis, the drop in the top 10 percent income share during World War II is even bigger because taxes increased enormously at that time to fund the war, and taxes on high incomes stayed high afterward. On a post-tax basis, the increase in income concentration since World War II is less than on a pre-tax basis so that post-tax income concentration is not quite as high today as it was a century ago. That is due to the growth of government over time and the overall progressivity of the US tax system.

Growth in average national income is shown in Figure 2.6. In black, we observe the series of real national income per adult for the full population from 1946 to 2013, with a tripling of national income per adult from $20,000 to $60,000 in real terms. Living standards increased by a factor of three since the end of World War II. We can see that the growth rate was 2 percent annually up to 1980, which can be characterized as fast. The growth rate has been slightly lower since 1980, about 1.4 percent.

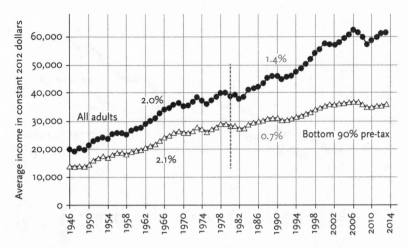

Figure 2.6 Growth in U.S. Real Average National Income: Full Adult Population versus Bottom 90%.

It is interesting to look at pre-tax income growth for the bottom 90 percent, shown in white, also in Figure 2.6. In the first period, from 1946 to 1980, the growth rate is 2.1 percent for the bottom 90 percent, very close to the 2 percent growth rate for the full population. In the second period, however, the pre-tax growth rate for the bottom 90 percent is only 0.7 percent or half of what it is for the full population.

Why study top incomes? Why do we care how the rich are doing? Don't we want to know how living standards evolve? Yes, that is what we want to know, but Figure 2.6 precisely shows why top incomes matter enormously to assess how living standards evolved for the vast majority of American families. The macroeconomic data that are discussed all the time are the black series in Figure 2.6, shown again in Figure 2.7 as national income per adult. Because the share of income going to the top 10 percent has increased so much since 1980, if we just restrict ourselves to the bottom 90 percent, the growth rate we obtain for this group is only about half of the average growth rate. That will be the experience for the vast majority (90 percent) of the population.

This is why developing distributional national accounts was an important missing piece to help enlighten the debate on inequality and growth. The post-tax series depicted in blue in Figure 2.7 subtracts taxes paid by the bottom 90 percent and adds back the transfers they receive. On net, the bottom 90 percent families receive a little bit more from the government than they pay in taxes. We observe in Figure 2.7 that, since 1980, the growth rate of the bottom 90 percent of incomes, on a post-tax basis, has been somewhat better, about 1 percent per year, which closes about a third of the gap in growth rates between the bottom 90 percent and the aggregate.

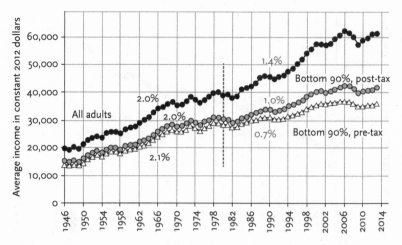

Figure 2.7 Growth in U.S. Real Average National Income: Full Adult Population versus Pre-tax and Post-tax Bottom 90%.

Further down the income distribution, there has been stagnation over the past 45 years, as shown in Figure 2.8 for the bottom 50 percent of adults, pre-tax and post-tax. On a pre-tax basis, there was total stagnation in the real incomes of the bottom 50 percent from the late 1960s to the present, with the bottom 50 percent of adults making about $15,000 a year over that entire period. On a post-tax basis, the bottom 50 percent does slightly better since the late 1960s. Average post-tax income of the bottom 50 percent increases, but this is still a growth rate that is extremely low relative to the full population.

To summarize, distributional national accounts are important because they change the picture of growth. From 1980 to 2013, average national income per

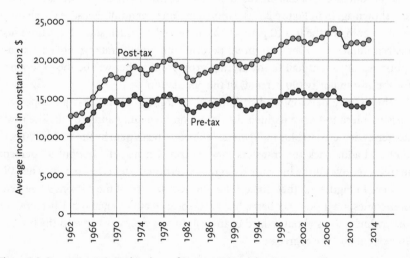

Figure 2.8 Stagnating U.S. Real Income of Bottom 50% Adults: Pre-tax vs. Post-tax.

adult has grown by about 60 percent in real terms economy-wide, but national income per adult for the bottom 90 percent has grown only by 30 percent. National income per adult for the bottom 50 percent has essentially stagnated since 1980.

US WEALTH INEQUALITY

Is income inequality driven solely by labor income, or is wealth and capital concentration also increasing, thus skewing capital income?

In a recent paper (Saez and Zucman, 2016) we capitalized dividends, interest, and other forms of capital income reported on individual tax returns to infer wealth and create distributional statistics for wealth in the United States since 1913.

Figure 2.9 shows that inequality in wealth has also surged in recent decades, but the phenomenon is even more concentrated for wealth than for income because the gains happen for the top 0.1 percent of families (families with wealth greater than $20 million in 2012). Figure 2.9 depicts the share of total wealth going to the top 0.1 percent of families. This time series shows a U-shaped pattern, with a substantial decrease in wealth concentration over the first part of the 20th century, followed by a resurgence in wealth concentration so that today the top 0.1 percent of families have slightly more than 20 percent of household wealth, almost as much as in the peak years of wealth inequality just before the Great Depression.

US wealth is so concentrated today that the share of wealth owned by the bottom 90 percent of families is only slightly above 20 percent and hence about the same as the share for the top 0.1 percent, as seen by comparing Figures 2.9 and 2.10. This means that the wealth of the top 0.1 percent of families is 900

Figure 2.9 Top 0.1% (above $20 million) Wealth Share in the United States, 1913–2012.

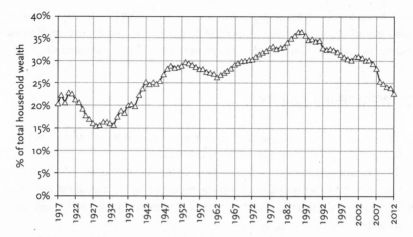

Figure 2.10 Bottom 90% Wealth Share in the United States, 1917–2012.

times bigger, on average, than the average wealth of the bottom 90 percent of families. While this comparison for today is a snapshot, wealth inequality has changed over time, both in amount and composition.

What is striking on the wealth side, clearly seen in Figure 2.10, is that there was democratization of wealth during the first part of the 20th century, when the share of wealth going to the bottom 90 percent doubled, from between 15 percent and 20 percent of total household wealth in the 1920s and 1930s to a peak of above 35 percent in the 1980s. Figure 2.11 shows the composition of the bottom 90 percent wealth and its share since 1917.

Figure 2.11 shows that the democratization of wealth was mostly due to two phenomena. One is that home ownership became much more widespread. The second is the development of funded pensions, which are a form of wealth more

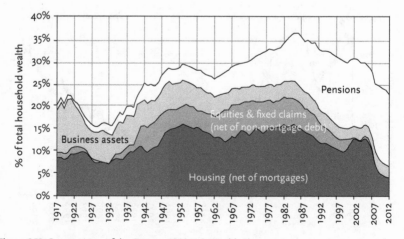

Figure 2.11 Composition of the Bottom 90% U.S. Wealth Share.

equally distributed than other forms of financial wealth. Those gains have been lost over the past 30 years, mostly due to an increase in debt. Pensions have stayed relatively strong, but the indebtedness of the vast majority of American families has increased enormously. On the housing front it is well known that the explosion of mortgage refinancing has eaten into the equity of the bottom 90 percent of families. Other forms of debt, including consumer credit cards and student loans, have also reduced the wealth of the bottom 90 percent of families.

This explosion in debt means effectively that the bottom 90 percent has been saving 0 percent of their income over the past 30 years. The bottom 90 percent of families save zero on average while top wealth holders save a lot, in part because their incomes have increased so much that they can afford to save large shares of their incomes. The result is a huge increase in wealth inequality that, unfortunately, is likely to persist, short of adopting more drastic policies aiming at curbing the wealth at the top and encouraging wealth accumulation at the bottom.

Another way to represent this alarming trend in wealth disparity is shown in Figure 2.12. Figure 2.12 depicts the real wealth per family of the bottom 90 percent of families in white and the top 1 percent of families in black since 1946. Today, the bottom 90 percent of families have about $80,000 in wealth on average and the top 1 percent have about $14 million on average. The figure shows that average wealth for the bottom 90 percent in 2012 was the same as it was in the mid-1980s, at the time when their wealth share peaked. There was an increase in the bottom 90 percent average wealth in the 1990s and early 2000s, but that was really the housing bubble. When the Great Recession hit, destroying the value of housing, the wealth of the 90 percent plummeted. There has not been much of a

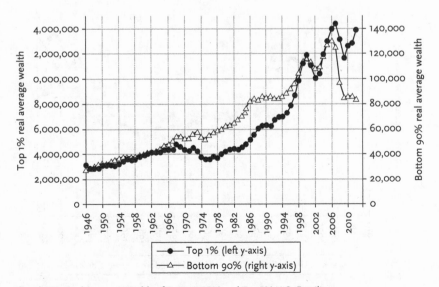

Figure 2.12 Real Average Wealth of Bottom 90% and Top 1% U.S. Families.

comeback, at least up to 2012. In contrast, the top 1 percent wealth holders were less affected by the Great Recession, and their wealth, mostly in the form of corporate stock, bounced back much faster as the stock market recovered quickly.

In sum, US income and wealth concentrations both fell dramatically during the first part of the 20th century and remained low and stable during three decades after World War II, but there has been a sharp increase in inequality since the 1970s. The United States now combines extremely high labor income inequality with very high wealth inequality. What are the drivers of these trends?

INTERNATIONAL COMPARISONS

International evidence is useful to understand the drivers of inequality. Drawing from the World Wealth and Income Database (Alvaredo et al., 2016), Figure 2.13 shows the top 1 percent income share for three English-speaking countries. What is striking is that all three countries follow an overall similar U-shape, with high inequality initially, a big drop during the first part of the 20th century, and then a big increase again since the late 1970s, although the increases for the United Kingdom and Canada have not been quite as large as for the United States.

From Figure 2.13, it might be thought that this evolution is universal and due to deep economic forces such as globalization or technological progress (e.g., the Information Revolution and computers). In reality, that is not so. Figure 2.14 depicts the top 1 percent income share in France, Sweden, and Japan. The first part of the graph looks similar to the English-speaking countries. All three

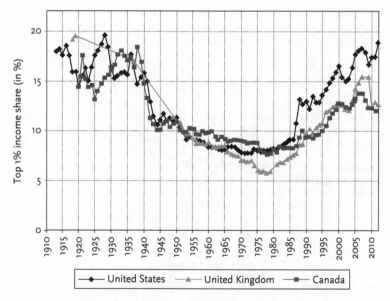

Figure 2.13 Top 1% Income Share: English Speaking Countries (U-shaped).

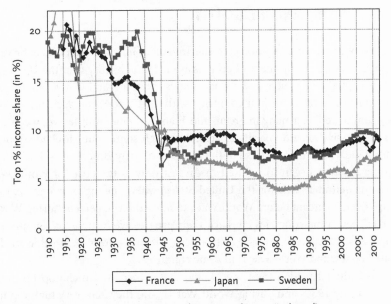

Figure 2.14 Top 1% Income Share: Continental Europe and Japan (L-shaped).

countries had very high levels of income inequality a century ago, as high if not higher than the English-speaking countries from Figure 2.13. Sweden was literally off the charts around World War I, even though today it is known as a country with low inequality. Looking at that data gathered in the World Wealth and Income database, what is striking is that, almost universally, a century ago, after the Industrial Revolution but before government had really started to grow, income inequality was high in practically all advanced economies of the time.

Then inequality declined, and the decline reflects the history of each country. For example, in Japan, the traumatic event is obviously World War II, which had an enormous effect on Japanese inequality while it did not for Sweden, which stayed out of the war. The striking contrast between Figures 2.13 and 2.14 is that France, Sweden, and Japan have not experienced nearly as large an increase in income concentration since the 1970s compared to the United States. Contrasting the two sets of countries (Figures 2.13 and 2.14), this simple finding is important because it tells us that growing income inequality since the 1970s is not just due to globalization or technological progress (e.g., computers) because all six countries depicted in Figures 2.13 and 2.14 have gone through the same process of technological progress, and they are subject to the same forces of globalization, yet the evolution of inequality or income concentration varies. Globalization and technological progress undeniably likely play a big role, but the data show that these phenomena interact with the institutions specific to each country to produce an outcome in inequality that varies significantly across countries.

PUBLIC POLICY AND INEQUALITY

The role of progressive taxation as a determinant of inequality appears to be very important. A quick summary of progressive taxation history over the 20th century is depicted in Figure 2.15, which shows the top marginal tax rate for the individual income tax for four countries, with the US series in black, the United Kingdom in red, Germany in green, and France in blue. A little over a century ago progressive taxation hardly existed. Although some countries had adopted modest individual income taxes in the late 19th or early 20th century, individual income taxation began to be used in earnest only at the onset of World War I. That is definitely true for the United States, where the top marginal tax rate jumps from 7 percent before World War I to more than 60 percent during World War I. Then some countries cut back their progressive income tax. Significant progressive taxation was then reintroduced with the Great Depression in the United States, and World War II in some countries.

The United Kingdom and the United States increased their top tax rates greatly in the 1930s and during World War II, and they kept very high top tax rates for decades after World War II. The US top tax rate was greater than 70 percent from 1936 to the beginning of the Reagan administration in 1980. During the Reagan administration the top tax rate fell from 70 percent to 28 percent, as you can see in the black series in Figure 2.15. During Prime Minister Thatcher's tenure, the UK top tax rate also drops dramatically from greater than 90 percent down to 40 percent, shown in red. The United States and the United Kingdom had the most progressive tax systems in the post–World War II decades, at least

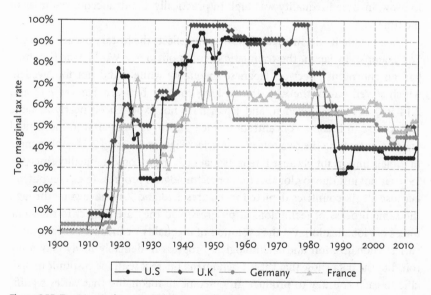

Figure 2.15 Top Marginal Income Tax Rates, 1900–2013.

at the very top of the income scale, and then they moved to being the least progressive. France and Germany did not have nearly as big a change in this period. Germany implemented very progressive income taxation only briefly during the Allied Occupation after World War II, when the United States was effectively in charge of designing the German income tax system.

Why does this matter? Figure 2.16 plots together the top marginal tax rate (in red) in the United States and the pre-tax top 1 percent income share (in black). This is the share of income going to the top 1 percent pre-tax, so that there is no mechanical effect here of the taxes on the incomes because the incomes are pre-tax. Nevertheless, those two time series appear to be mirror images of each other. Namely, pre-tax top income shares were high when top tax rates were low. Conversely, pre-tax income shares were low when top tax rates were high.

Similarly, looking at international evidence, we can make use of the different paths of top tax rates in various countries, especially since the 1960s. In Figure 2.17, we line up countries by how much they cut their top marginal tax rate from the early 1960s to the 2005–2009 period. The United States and the United Kingdom cut marginal tax rates the most, and a number of countries, like Germany, did not change top marginal tax rates much.

To compare the two periods 1960–1964 to 2005–2009, the y-axis in Figure 2.18 shows the change in the top 1 percent income share, again pre-tax. The x-axis shows the change in the top marginal tax rates. This graph shows that the countries roughly line up along a diagonal, meaning that those countries that

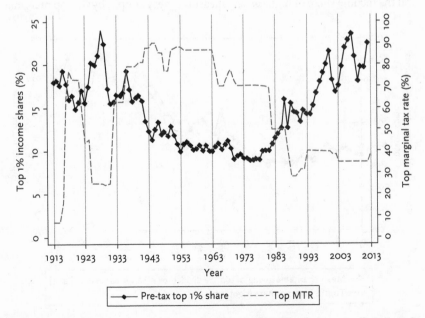

Figure 2.16 Top 1% U.S. Pre-tax Income Share and Top Marginal Tax Rate.

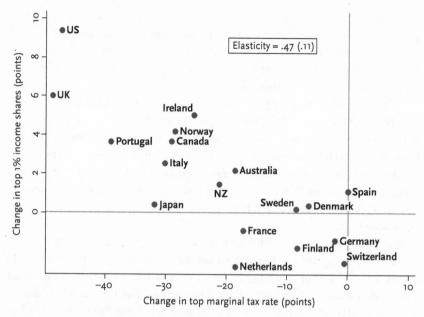

Figure 2.17 Change in Top 1% Pre-tax Income Share and Change in Marginal Tax Rates from 1960–1964 to 2005–2009.

experienced a surge in their top incomes are those that cut the top tax rates the most. Both the US historical evidence and the cross-country evidence since the 1960s suggest that a strong link exists between the level of progressive taxation and the income share of high earners measured, very simply, by the top marginal

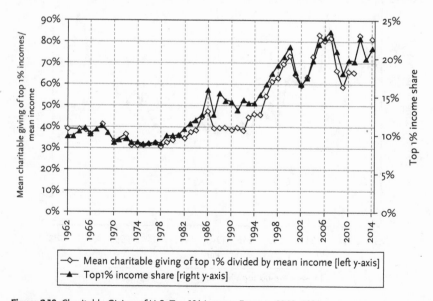

Figure 2.18 Charitable Giving of U.S. Top 1% Income Earners, 1962–2014.

tax rate and the size of the top income share (Piketty, Saez, and Stantcheva, 2014, discuss this evidence in more detail).

Why are pre-tax top incomes negatively affected by top tax rates? In Piketty, Saez, and Stantcheva (2014), we discuss three main possible scenarios that have very different policy implications.

First, all economists learn the standard supply-side scenario whereby top earners work less and earn less when the top tax rate increases. In that scenario, top tax rates should not be too high because they reduce economic activity. Indeed, that is exactly the argument that was used by Reagan and Thatcher when they argued for cutting top tax rates. The argument went as follows: the most talented people are not working that hard because the government is taking too much of their income, so cutting top tax rates will incentivize them to work more. They are going to work harder and make more, and that is going to be good for overall economic growth.

In the second scenario, top earners avoid and evade tax obligations more when top tax rates increase. It is similar to the supply-side scenario, but it has very different policy implications. If people work less when taxes are high, the government cannot do much about it. In contrast, if people avoid taxes more when tax rates are high, the government can do things to fix the tax system. A situation where tax avoidance is easy is typically due to a malfunctioning or poorly designed income tax system. If you are in that second scenario, you want to first eliminate loopholes and improve enforcement, and then, once your tax base has become less elastic, you can increase top tax rates.

The third scenario is what we call the *rent-seeking scenario*, where top earners extract more pay when marginal tax rates are low, but this is at the expense of the rest of the economy. With a high top tax rate, for example, an executive has less incentive to try to increase his or her compensation package because most of the pay raise will be taken away in taxes. To put it simply, high top tax rates put a lid on greed, defined as the ability to extract more pay at the expense of others.

The example of academics will be familiar to some. Faculty pay, at least at the University of California, is rigid. It might reflect, in some vague way, your product, but there is no systematic market force leading it to do this. The way market forces play a role here is that if you get a competitive outside offer you can get a salary increase through a retention case. Your success in gaining a raise affects the limited budget of the University of California and, therefore, taxpayers and students. The higher education sector is not necessarily the place where this phenomenon is most prevalent. In the corporate world, top managers certainly can use their marketability to influence compensation boards. The point is that successful rent-seeking imposes a cost elsewhere. In the rent-seeking scenario, high top tax rates are actually desirable precisely to prevent people at the top of the labor income distribution from extracting too much at the expense of others.

Empirically, Which Scenario Best Reflects Reality?

First, let us rule out the tax avoidance scenario. The reaction to Figure 2.16 is often that it is a nice time series, but perhaps the data do not tell us anything about real income concentration: the data just reflect tax avoidance. When tax rates were very high, the rich were doing everything they could to report taxable incomes as small as possible to the Internal Revenue Service (IRS) to avoid paying those very high tax rates. Then, since tax rates have come down, the rich no longer need to be as careful, so they avoid less. The underlying critique is that real inequality may not have changed much. In the 1960s and 1970s, the rich looked like they were not so rich, but this could be because they were hiding a very large fraction of their incomes.

What evidence can disprove the tax-avoidance scenario? The simplest way is to look at charitable giving of top income earners because charitable giving is tax deductible, which means that the incentives to give are stronger when tax rates are higher. Under the tax avoidance scenario, the rich in the 1960s were actually super-rich, but they were reporting only a fraction of their real incomes. They should have been able to give a lot to charity because, in reality, they were rich and also they would have saved a lot in taxes by deducting charitable giving because tax rates were so high.

However, empirically, charitable giving of top income earners has grown pretty much in tandem with reported top incomes. This is illustrated in Figure 2.19, where there are two scales, the top 1 percent income share (shown in black triangles) and a comparable measure of how much the wealthy give relative to the mean income (shown in white diamonds).

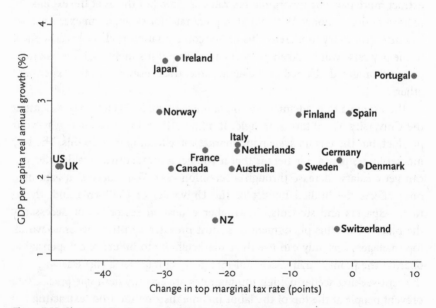

Figure 2.19 Change in Top Tax Rate and GDP per Capita Growth Since 1960.

Over time these two series tightly line up. In the 1960s, the top 1 percent income earners gave on average about 35 percent of the average income economy-wide. Today, they give 80 percent of the average income in the economy. Their ability to give has grown almost parallel to the share of their reported income, which grew from about 10 percent to 22 percent today. This strongly suggests that, in reality, the surge in reported top income shares reflects real income increases because it follows so closely from real behavior, in the form of charitable giving. To put it simply: the rich are richer today (relative to the average income) than in the 1960s and so they are able to give a lot more today (again relative to the average income) than in the 1960s.

The second scenario, tax avoidance, implies that there is a change in the size of tax avoidance with a change in the marginal tax rate. While this may occur, from Figure 2.19 we can conclude that the size of any change in tax avoidance is insufficient to explain the inverse relationship between the change in the highest tax rates and the change in pre-tax income shown in Figure 2.16 for the United States over a century and shown in Figure 2.17 across countries.

Discarding the tax-avoidance scenario, this leaves the two other scenarios: supply-side versus rent-seeking. It is hard to disprove one relative to the other fully convincingly. Probably the world is a mix of both. You can find examples where taxes reduce work incentives and work behavior and other examples where taxes reduce the ability to extract more pay at the expense of others. We want to know quantitatively what is the closest to reality.

What separates the two scenarios the most starkly is the real growth effects of top tax rate cuts. Under the supply-side scenario, growth in the top 1 percent of incomes due to cuts in the top tax rate comes from more economic activity and should therefore register as more economic growth. In contrast, under the rent-seeking scenario, growth of the top 1 percent of incomes due to top tax rate cuts comes at the expense of the bottom 99 percent and hence is not associated with more economic growth. Based on the international macro-evidence, it is hard to find an effect of top tax rate cuts on economic growth.

While it is clear that there is a strong correlation between top tax rates and the share of pre-tax income going to the top 1 percent of income earners (as we have seen in Figures 2.16 and 2.17), it is much harder to see any link between top tax rates and economic growth. For the international comparison, in Figure 2.18, we change the y axis from Figure 2.17 to measure economic growth instead of top income shares. There is no clear correlation between cuts in top tax rates since the 1960s and growth in gross domestic product (GDP) per capita since the 1960s. Certainly, the United States or the United Kingdom did not show growth performance much better than, say, Germany, another advanced economy.

Obviously, growth per capita since 1960 is higher for countries that started poorer in 1960, such as Japan, Ireland, or Portugal. Hence, it is useful to control for the initial level of economic development, as shown in Figure 2.20. When per capita growth is used, growth rates are closer across countries. But even

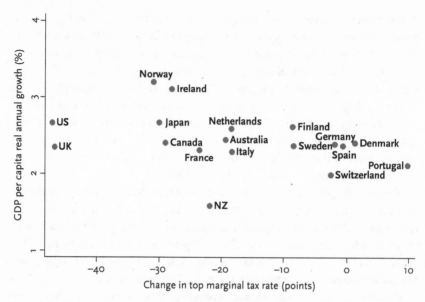

Figure 2.20 Change in Top Tax Rate and GDP per Capita Growth Since 1960 Growth Adjusted for Initial (1960) GDP.

then, there is no obvious correlation in which the United States and the United Kingdom, which cut the top tax rate the most, experience better growth than the European countries that did not adopt those policies. As economists, we know that this lack of correlation is not a compelling test, and it is not sufficient to fully disprove the supply-side scenario. The challenge for economists is to understand whether the surge in top incomes really aligns with a similar increase in actual economic activity. It might be possible that such studies would be doable in specific case studies using, for example, data linking employees and employers.

The rent-seeking scenario asks whether the growth in income share of the top 1 percent comes at the expense of the bottom 99 percent, and I do not know for sure. In Figure 2.21 there is a contrast between the growth of the bottom 99 percent (in white) and the top 1 percent (in black) relative to the top marginal tax rate (in red) for the United States. For this comparison, both the bottom 99 percent and top 1 percent groups start at a base indexed to 100 in 1913, and they end up at about 400 one century later. In the long run, economic growth lifts all boats, and that is indeed what has happened in the United States over the course of a century. Real incomes per adult for the top and for the bottom have multiplied roughly by four in real terms. What is striking is that the timing of growth differs across groups. The period from the New Deal in 1933 to the late 1970s, when top tax rates were extremely high, was a time when the income of the bottom 99 percent grew pretty quickly, while the income of the top 1 percent was growing much more slowly. Conversely, after top tax rates came down in the 1980s, the pattern of growth flips. Namely, this is the time when the incomes of

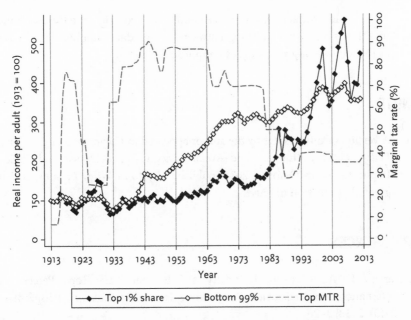

Figure 2.21 U.S. Top 1% and Bottom 99% Income Growth and Marginal Tax Rates.

the top 1 percent are growing extremely quickly, while the incomes of the bottom 99 percent are growing much more slowly.

The pattern of growth for the top 1 percent and bottom 99 percent income for the United States shown in Figure 2.21, and the cross-sectional international comparison of differential cuts in marginal tax rates and economic growth since the 1960s shown in Figures 2.18 and 2.20 are consistent with the rent-seeking scenario. Consistent, but they do not prove the rent-seeking scenario definitively because this is, again, a correlation in terms of growth. The debate has to go on, and hopefully economic research will provide better insights on this key issue for the proper taxation of top incomes in the future.

CONCLUSION

The US and international historical evidence shows that tax policy measured, very simply, by progressivity at the top of the individual income tax system seems to play a big role in shaping income concentration. High top tax rates reduce the pre-tax income gap without, so far, having a clear negative effect on economic growth. The public will favor more progressive taxation only if it is convinced that top income gains are detrimental to economic growth of the 99 percent and that taxation can ameliorate this. In America, people do not have a strong view against inequality per se, as long as inequality is fair. And what does fair mean? As an economist, you would say "fair" means that individual income and wealth reflect the value of what people produce or otherwise contribute to the economic system. This is why distinguishing between the standard supply-side scenario versus the rent-seeking scenario is so important.

NOTE

1. A version of this chapter by the author appeared in *Contemporary Economic Policy*, entitled "Income and Wealth Inequality: Evidence and Policy Implications," in October, 2014, published by John Wiley & Sons, which granted permission to reuse.

REFERENCES

Alvaredo, F., A. Atkinson, T. Piketty, and E. Saez. "The Top1 Percent in International and Historical Perspective." *Journal of Economic Perspectives*, 27(3), 2013, 3–20.

Alvaredo, F., A. Atkinson, T. Piketty, E. Saez, and G. Zucman. "The World Wealth and Income Database." Accessed January 7, 2016. http://www.wid.world.

Piketty, T. Les Hauts Revenus en France au 20e Siècle : Inégalités et Redistribution, 1901–1998. Paris, France: B. Grasset, 2001.

Piketty, T. "Income Inequality in France, 1901–1998." *Journal of Political Economy*, 111(5), 2003, 1004–42.

Piketty, T., and E. Saez. "Income Inequality in the United States, 1913–1998." *Quarterly Journal of Economics*, 118(1), 2003, 1–39.

Piketty, T., E. Saez, and S. Stantcheva. "Optimal Taxation of Top Labor Incomes: A Tale of Three Elasticities." *American Economic Journal: Economic Policy*, 6(1), 2014, 230–71.

Piketty, T., E. Saez, and G. Zucman. "Distributional National Accounts: Methods and Estimates for the United States." NBER Working Paper, 2016.

Saez, E., and G. Zucman. "Wealth Inequality in the United States since 1913: Evidence from Capitalized Income Tax Data." *Quarterly Journal of Economics*, 131(2), 2016, 519–78.

3

IMPROVING ECONOMIC OPPORTUNITY IN THE UNITED STATES

Jared Bernstein

A s of this writing, the US economy is in year 10 of a historically long expansion characterized by low national unemployment. And yet many barriers to economic opportunity and mobility remain in place. These barriers include high levels of income inequality, unequal access to educational opportunities, residential segregation by income, inadequate investments in children and certain areas, and a disparity between the strength and depth of the recovery in rural relative to metro areas.

After presenting evidence in support of these contentions, this chapter offers near-term policy solutions aimed at reducing these barriers, including running tight labor markets, infrastructure investment, direct job creation, healthcare and other work supports, apprenticeships, and more.

Longer term solutions invoke policy interventions targeting inequality, inadequate housing, income and wage stagnation, nutritional and health support, the criminal justice system, and educational access.

Avoiding policies that keep opportunity barriers in place is just as important as the proactive agenda items I recommend. Reducing the provision of public healthcare, regressive tax cuts, and budget cuts to programs that help low- and moderate-income families all reduce opportunity.

Jared Bernstein, *Improving Economic Opportunity in the United States* In: *United States Income, Wealth, Consumption, and Inequality.* Edited by: Diana Furchtgott-Roth, Oxford University Press (2021). © Oxford University Press. DOI: 10.1093/oso/9780197518199.003.0004.

OPPORTUNITY BARRIERS AND THEIR CAUSES

No fixed definition of economic opportunity exists, but most will agree that it corresponds to the realization of personal potential. If a child faces an inadequate school system or a toxic environment, it will be much harder for her to realize her intellectual, and later, her economic potential. If a parent lives in a community with an insufficient quantity of jobs, or jobs that pay wages that are too low to support a family, or jobs for which she lacks the necessary skills, both she and her family face opportunity shortfalls. Such barriers can meaningfully be extended beyond schooling and jobs to housing, nutrition, healthcare, and even infrastructure. For example, consider the fact that due to toxic infrastructure—lead leaching into water pipes—children in parts of our country may suffer brain impairments (though, importantly, such damage need not be permanent). [1] This is a clear example of an opportunity barrier constructed by a public policy failure, one that should be unacceptable in an economy as wealthy and advanced as our own.

Given this framing of the problem, a clear role for policy in the opportunity space is to take down the barriers that get between people and the realization of their economic potential. The extent of the problem can be at least roughly measured through a set of proxies that indicate the existence of opportunity barriers.

Labor Market Barriers Associated with Income, Race, and Education

In a 2017 speech, then Federal Reserve chair Janet Yellen noted that unemployment rates "averaged 13 percent in low- and moderate-income communities from 2011 through 2015, compared with 7.3 percent in higher income communities."[2] Chair Yellen also noted that, in majority minority areas, the jobless rate averaged 14.3 percent between 2011 and 2015. The share of 25- to 54-year-old (so-called prime age) workers in these areas was nearly 9 percentage points lower than in non–majority-minority communities. Racial disparities exist in unemployment rates even controlling for education.[3] Among white people with terminal high school degrees, unemployment was about 5 percent in 2015. For black people, it is twice that. Black people with at least BAs have unemployment rates of 4.1 percent, compared to the 2.4 percent for whites with at least BAs.

Labor Market Barriers Associated with Rural Areas

My own work has documented periods of slack labor markets and their negative impact on the earnings and income growth of low- and moderate-income working families.[4] The Economic Research Service of the United States Department of Agriculture recently analyzed different trends in employment in rural (or nonmetro) labor market indicators versus those from metro areas.[5]

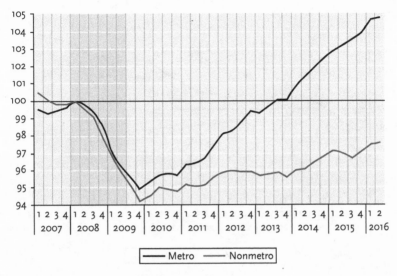

Figure 3.1 Urban job growth outpaced rural, 2009–16.

Figure 3.1 shows employment growth in rural and metro areas, with both indexed to 100 in 2008, first quarter. While employment levels fell about the same amount in percentage terms in both areas over the Great Recession of 2007–2009, metro employment has recovered much more quickly, as the gap at the end of the figure reveals. In the middle of 2016, rural employment was still well below its pre-recession peak.

Labor force participation rates have been particularly slow to recover over this expansion, and while part of that trend is driven by the retirement of baby boomers and thus is not necessarily an indicator of weak labor demand, participation rates have yet to recover for prime-age workers as well. Figure 3.2 shows that the size of the labor force has significantly declined in rural areas, a trend all the more striking when compared to the labor force growth in metro areas during this same time period. Part of the discrepancy is due to differential population growth rates—while population grew over this period in metro areas, it was flat in rural places—but the rural labor force grew even more slowly than the rural population.

Mobility Barriers Associated with Regional Economic Segregation

In recent decades, families with children have lived in increasingly segregated neighborhoods,[6] a trend driven both by rising income inequality and by wealthier parents segregating themselves into areas with higher performing schools, among other factors. Both Chetty et al. and Barbara Sard and Doug Rice find that residential segregation by income exacerbates the

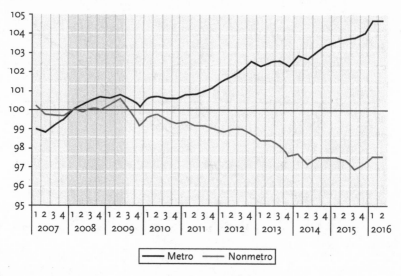

Figure 3.2 Urban labor force growth outpaced rural, 2009–16.

gaps in opportunities between children from low-income and high-income backgrounds.[7] Researcher Ann Owens also connects this development to diminished future opportunities for children: "Rising income inequality provided high-income households more resources, and parents used these resources to purchase housing in particular neighborhoods, with residential decisions structured, in part, by school district boundaries. Overall, results indicate that children face greater and increasing stratification in neighborhood contexts than do all residents, and this has implications for growing inequalities in their future outcomes."

Education Barriers Associated with Income

Yellen noted that close to 100 percent of children of parents with higher incomes and levels of educational attainment pursued higher education, and 60 percent earned a bachelor's degree. But among children of parents with lower incomes and education levels, 72 percent pursued higher education and only 14 percent completed a BA. Figure 3.3, from Chetty et al., shows that the likelihood that a child from a wealthy family will attend an Ivy League or similarly elite school is 50 times that of a child from a low-income family.[8]

Federal Reserve data also show that as inequality has increased, college debt burdens have become much larger for low- relative to high-income families.[9] In 1995, families with education debt in the bottom half of the net worth (a broader definition of income, including assets minus liabilities) distribution had a mean debt-to-income ratio of around 0.26 (for every dollar of their net worth, they owed 26 cents in college debt). For families in the top 5 percent, that ratio was 8 cents on the dollar. By 2013, the debt-to-income ratio had more than doubled to

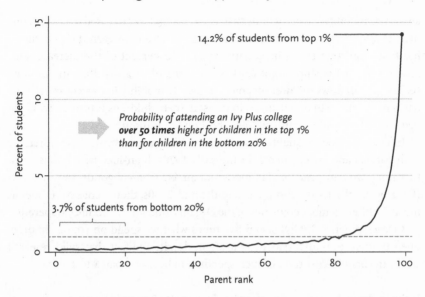

Figure 3.3 Probability of attending "Ivy Plus" college based on parents' income ranking.

0.58 for the bottom half (some of whom are poor but many of whom are middle class) while remaining unchanged for those at the top.

Mobility Barriers Associated with Income, Inequality, and Inadequate Investments in Children

While higher educational attainment is clearly associated with higher earnings, it is also the case that children who grow up in affluent households but do not graduate from college are *2.5 times* as likely to have high incomes in adulthood as children who grow up poor but *do* graduate from college (see Figure 3.4). Recent research by Raj Chetty and others finds correlations between higher inequality

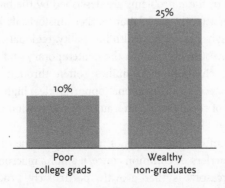

Figure 3.4 Chance of reaching top income fifth higher for non-college graduates from wealthy families than graduates from poor families.

and lower mobility.[10] Chetty finds that as inequality has increased over time, one metric of mobility—the likelihood that adult children out-earn their parents—has fallen and that rising inequality explains 70 percent of the increase. One reason this relationship might exist is that, when less gross domestic product (GDP) growth flows to lower income families, their ability to overcome mobility barriers—to move to opportunity, to invest in their children's future, to avoid the negative externalities of difficult neighborhoods—is diminished.

In fact, growing inequality is associated with less investment in children, by both parents and governments. In the early 1970s, high-income families spent four times what low-income families spent on "enrichment goods" for their kids (tutoring, books, trips, art supplies); in the mid-2000s, they spent seven times as much.[11] Other member countries of the Organisation for Economic Cooperation and Development (OECD) spend five times what we spend on young children, often through pre-kindergarten education, despite the fact that solid research shows the benefit-cost ratio of such spending to be more than 8 to 1.[12]

Employment and Opportunity Barriers Associated with the Criminal Justice System

The National Employment Law Project (NELP) reports that 70 million people in America now have a conviction or arrest history that can show up on a routine background check for employment.[13] NELP also points out that more employers are conducting background checks wherein these records are likely to show up. Research shows extensive employment and earnings disadvantages to those with criminal records, with serious negative spillovers to the families of those who face incarceration.[14] The opportunity/mobility costs of having a criminal record are high: men with criminal records are twice as likely to remain in the bottom fifth of the income scale as are men without records. The fact that these problems disproportionately affect racial minorities is partially a function of institutionalized racism associated with the criminal justice system, so the barrier of discrimination is germane here as well.

The root causes of these problems are described by the barriers themselves. Discrimination, persistently slack labor markets, historically high levels of inequality and even higher levels of wealth inequality, regional economic segregation, inadequate investments in both the contemporary and future well-being of less-advantaged children and families (often through disinvestment in public goods), low access to educational opportunities, high exposure to toxic environments—all of these factors are causes of the erosion of opportunity for many in our society.

I stress the role of our high levels of inequality as one of the most important opportunity barriers. A common concern among macroeconomic analysts today, for good reason, is that growth, particularly productivity growth, has slowed sharply over the past decade (a problem seen across advanced economies). I would characterize this deceleration as one of the most important constraints on growth and, thereby, on aggregate living standards. But the key word is "aggregate." In the presence of high inequality, stronger growth is necessary but not sufficient to take down mobility barriers. If most of the growth flows to the top of the scale, as has occurred in recent decades, then, absent aggressive redistribution, we cannot expect to push back on the many problems just documented.

HOW CAN PUBLIC POLICY ENGENDER MORE OPPORTUNITY?

A useful way to think about policies targeting opportunity is to consider those that can address near-term opportunity barriers and those that address longer term barriers. Near-term policies address opportunity deficits with negative effects on people's economic circumstances today, like the absence of gainful employment opportunities or the effect on living standards when inequality contributes to stagnant paychecks. Long-term interventions, like quality preschools or improved access to higher education, can enhance the future opportunities of children. As I report later, considerable research has found that many safety net programs, like nutritional and healthcare support, both help reduce poverty in the near term *and* improve longer term outcomes for children.

Near-Term Opportunity Enhancers
Running a Tight Labor Market
Extensive evidence shows that lower wage and minority workers are disproportionately helped by tight labor markets. As I showed in a recent analysis for Brookings Institution Hamilton Project, labor market *slack*, or the gap between the quantity of work desired by workers (jobs, hours) and the amount of work available, puts strong downward pressure on real wage growth and incomes.[15] The negative effects of labor market slack tend to fall disproportionately on low-wage workers and low/middle-income households, as illustrated by Figures 3.5 and 3.6.

Figure 3.5 shows how the wage effects of increasing employment and unemployment rates vary by income decile. As expected, increases in employment cause wages to rise and increases in unemployment cause wages to fall, but the effects are much greater for workers in low-wage jobs rather than for highly paid workers. Figure 3.6 simulates the evolution of real median household income for various economic recovery scenarios: one scenario assumes no improvement in employment after 2010, and another assumes that unemployment fell half as fast as it really did between 2010 and 2016. Under the "slower recovery" and "no recovery scenarios," real median incomes either stagnate or fall significantly from their 2010 levels.[16] The strong relationship between tight labor markets and wage

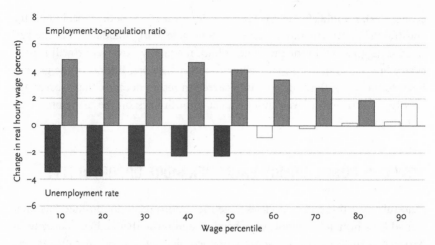

Figure 3.5 Low and middle-wages more responsive to labor market conditions than high wages.

growth, especially for the most marginalized workers, shows that robust pursuit of full employment can play a key role in equalizing access to opportunity.

These findings imply an important role for the Federal Reserve: in balancing its dual mandate of stable prices and full employment, it must be careful not to tap the economic growth brakes (i.e., raise the benchmark interest rate they control) too aggressively. For example, as of this writing, the recovery appears to finally be reaching some places left behind (as shown in some of the preceding illustrations), so, absent clear evidence of inflationary pressures, the Fed should proceed with caution. It also implies a role for fiscal policy to help create more labor demand where it is lacking, as with my next policy suggestion: infrastructure investment.

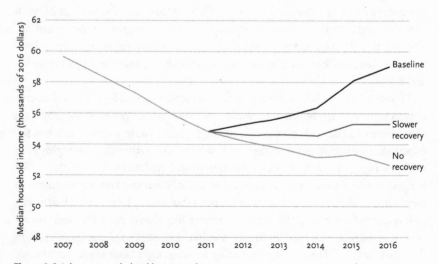

Figure 3.6 Jobs recovery helped boost median income.

Investing in Infrastructure

It is widely agreed that underinvesting in maintaining and improving the nation's public goods is harmful economic policy. I should note that complaints about the conditions of our public capital are bipartisan: both poverty advocates and Chambers of Commerce argue that Congress must work together to address this investment shortfall. Civil engineers have identified[17] the productivity-dampening deterioration of our roads, bridges, public transit, and other transportation infrastructure. The Obama administration's Environmental Protection Agency argued that our water treatment and distribution systems need $384 billion in investments over the next 20 years.[18] More than half of America's public schools need to be repaired, renovated, or modernized[19]; the average age of the main building of a public school today is about 44 years. Roofs, windows, boilers, and ventilation, plumbing, and electrical systems need to be fixed, upgraded, or replaced.[20]

Such investments fit both here and under longer term opportunity enhancers, especially if we consider, as we should, investments in human capital as another dimension of investing in public goods. Improving water systems can yield profound long-term benefits in children's brain development, and upgraded school facilities have been shown to improve teacher retention and academic outcomes.[21]

But in the near term, infrastructure investment can create employment for blue-collar laborers, making it a particularly strategic investment in parts of the country with too little labor demand.[22] Economists have documented that when and where job markets are slack, infrastructure investment has a relatively high "multiplier," meaning a bigger bang for the buck on jobs and economic activity.[23] Economist Josh Bivens points out that, by boosting longer-run productivity growth, well-placed infrastructure investment can allow the Federal Reserve to target lower rates of unemployment, an important complement to my previous point about tight labor market policy.[24]

Direct Job Creation

While Congress often tries to provide help to left-behind places through targeted tax credits, such incentives have a poor track record. One viable conclusion is that these policies are simply too indirect and that if we want to help places with too little labor demand, we must consider direct job creation policies, meaning either jobs created by the government sector or publicly subsidized private employment (as noted later, an alternative is to "move people to jobs," but that is an insufficient response to the problem). Infrastructure ideas, like renovating our stock of public schools by directly creating temporary jobs, fit into this space as well, but Bernstein and Spielberg (2016) elaborate a more ambitious approach.[25]

We stress that subsidized jobs and job creation programs provide income to people who need it and will spend it, thereby helping to boost weak local economies while providing opportunities to workers disconnected from the labor market. We also cite research showing that there can be lasting benefits from helping such workers overcome labor market barriers that are preventing them from gainful employment.

Though our work largely focused on direct jobs to offset recessions, today many policy makers are legitimately concerned about places facing recession-like conditions even while other places are doing much better. We therefore recommend "an employment fund that supports a set of national service jobs on an ongoing basis *and* includes a flexible funding stream that can ramp up in economic downturns. This initiative should enable states to try different approaches to subsidized jobs, encouraging them to experiment to learn more about what works best and for whom."

Healthcare and Other Work Supports
Another important way to help less advantaged persons get into and stay in the labor force—and to tap entrepreneurial opportunities—is to ensure a solid system of work supports, with healthcare as a standout example. Extensive research shows significant, positive labor supply effects from the Earned Income Tax Credit (EITC; a wage subsidy for low-wage workers), and policies that support working parents, especially help with child care, have been shown to raise women's ability to join and stay in the labor force.[26]

Opportunities related to entrepreneurship are particularly germane to this part of the agenda, as research finds that employer-provided health coverage is a constraint on business formation by potential entrepreneurs.[27] These studies find that people who can secure health coverage through non-employment sources have higher levels of self-employment and "entrepreneurship probabilities" than those who lack such access. Such work is consistent with other research by Nick Buffie showing the release of insurance-driven "job lock" as the Affordable Care Act (ACA) has ramped up.[28] These findings underscore a commonsense connection between access to affordable coverage outside of employment, the ACA, and entrepreneurial opportunities.

Helping Small Manufacturers Join Global Supply Chains
Instead of pursuing trade protectionism, a policy that most economists view as hurtful to growth and aggregate social welfare, a better alternative is to implement policies that will help our manufacturers compete more effectively in the global economy. In an analysis I did with Congressman Ro Khanna, we argued that policy should target smaller manufacturers from areas with displaced workers, helping such firms modernize and find their way into the global supply chain.[29] We identify three policies consistent with this goal: expanding the Commerce Department's Manufacturing Extension Partnership (MEP), pushing back on currency interventions, and investing in new, high-demand industries.

The MEP's mission is to "enhance the productivity and technological performance of US manufacturing." It does not provide direct financing, but it does provide guidance by helping small manufacturing firms adopt new technologies, integrate into global supply chains, strengthen regional partnerships, and connect with national labs. According to a 2014 report from the nonpartisan Congressional Research Service, the 30,000 companies served by the MEP "reported $2.5 billion in new sales, $4.2 billion in retained sales, $1.1 billion in cost savings, $2.7 billion in new client investment, the creation of 17,833 jobs and the retention of 46,069 jobs."[30]

The program costs $130 million annually, or 0.003 percent of federal government spending. In the interest of helping small manufacturers and boosting US net exports, its funding should at least be doubled. It is notable, and disheartening in this regard, that recent budget proposals by the Trump administration attempt to zero out the MEP, a counterproductive cut if our goal is to create more opportunity and jobs in this space.

In some of my own recent writings, I suggest two other measures to level the trade playing field and push back on currency manipulation: *currency reciprocity* (the ability to purchase the currency of manipulators to neutralize their intervention) and *countervailing duties* on exports from countries that use currency depreciation to subsidize exports.[31]

Invest in Renewable Energy

Pollin et al. find that a combination of market incentives (carbon caps and taxes) alongside public and private investment in renewable energy would improve both environmental and employment outcomes.[32] In terms of public investment, they call for retrofitting publicly owned buildings, initiating green infrastructure projects (e.g., building out a "smart" grid), implementing procurement policy such as supplying the US military with renewable energy, and expanding federal research and development into renewable energy development, storage, and distribution. They estimate that their investment agenda (private and public) would generate 2.7 million jobs.

Khanna and I agree and highlight a role for public investment in battery/ energy storage technology. We also note the utility of public–private innovation centers that build connections between university labs and factory floors.[33] Such multilevel workforce investments that involve everyone from research programs and scientists to engineers and manufacturers have the potential to revitalize communities that have lost manufacturers and experienced years of disinvestment.

Apprenticeship Programs

Economist Robert Lerman makes a strong case that apprenticeship programs, or *work-based learning*, can be highly effective in connecting young workers with limited prospects to good jobs. Public policy can help (and is doing so in some states and other advanced economies) through grants and credits to employers who start up apprenticeship programs, as well as by spreading the word to the broader employment community. Lerman writes that "expanding apprenticeship offers a long-term, evidence-based strategy that increases productivity by increasing skills at very modest cost to the government. Apprenticeships combine serious work-based learning and classroom instruction usually lasting two to four years, aimed at mastering occupational and employability skills, and leading to a recognized credential."[34]

Work-based, "learning-by-earning" programs can address high youth unemployment while preparing young people for "middle-skill" careers in potentially high-demand sectors such as healthcare, advanced manufacturing, construction, and information services. Moreover, these programs can enhance opportunity by setting out career pathways for upward mobility, as well as including postsecondary education as part of their package.

Moving Opportunity

Inequality and mobility expert Raj Chetty and various teams of researchers have identified a set of neighborhood correlates associated with lower and high levels of opportunity and mobility for children. They find that when families with young children "move to opportunity," those children do better as adults relative to children who stay in disadvantaged places. While Chetty et al.'s correlations are rigorously derived, it is important to realize that they represent correlation, not causation, so we cannot assume that neighborhood factors themselves drive mobility. For example, they find that communities with a large share of mother-only families experience relatively low mobility. But two-parent families in those neighborhoods experience the same lower mobility rates, suggesting that single parenthood is likely a correlate more than a cause. Also, policy-makers cannot, of course, simply advocate leaving disadvantaged neighborhoods as a sole strategy for families there. We must apply policies like those noted earlier to help the families that stay behind. Helping people move to opportunity is certainly one valid strategy, but moving opportunity to people where they are is another.

Longer Term Investments in Opportunity

As discussed earlier, the long-term rise of income inequality has negative effects on long-term opportunity and mobility through at least three channels.[35]

First, it makes neighborhoods of concentrated poverty and wealth more common and neighborhoods with more income diversity less common. Children in neighborhoods of concentrated poverty are exposed to more environmental hazards, lower quality public goods, and less privileged social networks than are children in higher income neighborhoods.

Second, income/wealth inequality makes access to quality educational experiences less equal, with strong immobility consequences. Higher income parents can invest in more enrichment opportunities for their children, and children from wealthier families can attend more adequately funded schools. Students from privileged backgrounds can afford to attend elite universities while students from less privileged backgrounds often can't, and, when they can, their debt-to-income ratios can rise to levels that generate a new set of constraints.

Third, inequality directly undermines opportunity by subjecting some people to persistent disadvantages and stressors that others don't face. For example, poverty researchers note that experiences associated with persistent and deep poverty, such as overcrowded or unsafe housing, inadequate nutrition and medical care, and exposure to environmental toxins, can lead to "toxic stress" and delayed physical and social development, with obvious negative implications for future opportunity.

Addressing these long-term barriers requires policy interventions targeting inequality, inadequate housing, income and wage stagnation, nutritional and health support, educational access, and environmental degradation.

Importantly, extensive research on longitudinal data (data that track people or places over time) finds that many of our safety net programs work as long-term mobility enhancers.[36] That is, quasi-experimental designs that follow children over time and compare those who received an intervention to those who didn't (or those who got larger "doses" of the intervention to others who got smaller doses) find that these programs do not simply boost consumption in the present. They work like investments, with lasting effects. Consider:

- Duncan et al. find that a $3,000 annual increase in income to poor children before age 6 is associated with 135 extra hours of work a year for adults between the ages of 25 and 37, with an increase in annual earnings of 17 percent.
- Manoli and Turner find that adding $1,000 of the EITC during a student's senior year of high school boosts college enrollment by 0.4 to 0.7 percentage points.
- Cohodes et al. find that Medicaid eligibility expansions between 1980 and 1990 "had an impact equivalent to cutting today's high school dropout rate by 9.7 to 14 percent and raising the college completion rate by 5.5 to 7.2 percent."
- Hoynes et al. find that access to the Supplemental Nutrition Assistance Program (SNAP, or food stamps) in the 1960s and early 1970s decreased kids' adulthood obesity by 16 percent and their incidence of heart disease by 5 percent while increasing their high school completion rate by 18 percent.
- Former President Obama's Council of Economic Advisers finds that every $1 spent on early childhood education results in roughly $8.60 of "benefits to society . . . about half of which comes from increased earnings for children when they grow up."

- Chetty et al. find that children in families that received a Section 8 voucher when they were younger than 13 under the "Moving to Opportunity" program saw a 15 percent earnings boost in adulthood, while kids in families that got the voucher that had to be used in a low-poverty neighborhood saw a 31 percent earnings increase.

These findings suggest that public policy can boost longer term opportunities by tapping the elasticities implicit in this research. One measure to consider is significantly increasing the value of the EITC for childless adults, an idea with considerably bipartisan political support.[37] Such workers under 25 are ineligible for the wage subsidy and, if they earn poverty-level wages, are exposed to payroll and income taxes that can push them into or deeper into poverty. Older low-income childless workers are eligible for only a very small credit (e.g., a full-time minimum wage worker is eligible for a credit of under $50). Proposals to significantly increase the value of the credit would lift hundreds of thousands of workers out of poverty and bring millions closer to the poverty threshold.

Increasing the EITC is sometimes promoted as a substitute to higher minimum wages. But longtime antipoverty advocate Robert Greenstein points out that proposals to raise the minimum wage and the EITC should not be viewed as substitutes; their designs have several complementary attributes, and it will take both to raise living standards and boost opportunities.[38]

The Center on Budget and Policy Priorities (CBPP) has argued for strengthening the Child Tax Credit (CTC), which currently excludes the first $3,000 of a worker's earnings from consideration, for very poor families with young children.[39] That can be accomplished by either "making the *current* CTC fully refundable for families with a young child or by creating a fully refundable *supplement* to the CTC just for families with young children (an option that is more expansive because it boosts the tax credit for all families with young children that receive the CTC, not just those at lower income levels)."

With respect to the findings of Chetty et al., as well as those of Ann Owens (on residential segregation by income), the CBPP also views renewing and boosting the funding of Housing Choice Vouchers (HCV) as an opportunity-enhancing policy intervention.[40] Housing expert Barbara Sard notes that HCV has a strong track record in reducing homelessness, foster care placements, and frequent disruptive moves, and it has been associated with lower rates of "alcohol dependence, psychological distress, and domestic violence victimization among the adults with whom the children live." She finds that HCV "has an important, positive impact on minority families' access to opportunities," one that is particularly pronounced for minority families. But Sard also notes that relatively few families are able to use vouchers to find housing in low-poverty areas with access to better educational opportunities, and she suggests improvements that would enable more such moves, including increased incentives for state and local agencies to seek higher opportunity locations, setting subsidy caps and jurisdictional rules that facilitate moving to opportunity, and direct assistance and encouragement both to landlords in low-poverty areas and to families who would benefit from moving to such areas.[41]

A full treatment of criminal justice reform is beyond the scope of this essay, but many changes could begin to reduce the harm caused by mass incarceration. For example, Mitchell and Leachman recommend state-level policies that can reduce the negative effects of incarceration rates: reducing penalties for low-level felonies, many of which fall disproportionately on minorities; reexamining sentencing laws; reducing sentences; and more.[42] Congress could accelerate such progress with legislation allowing federal judges to impose sentences below the mandatory minimums when warranted. Emsellem and Ziedenberg have also written about the need for expanding "fair chance" hiring practices such as "ban-the-box" (which allows those with records to not reveal them in initial interview stages), and they find positive results in many places that are trying these interventions. They also underscore the importance of making background checks more reliable and accurate and recommend "clean slate" or expungement laws for minor, nonviolent felonies.[43]

Finally, the long-term benefits of Medicaid access underscore the importance of tapping the ACA's Medicaid expansion in the 14 states that have yet to do so.[44] The expansion led to significantly improved coverage of low-income families in states that took it up, and Medicaid is particularly important to residents of rural areas, which, as shown earlier, have faced less employment growth in recent years.[45] In this regard, efforts by conservatives to significantly cut the Medicaid program as part of their American Health Care Act (AHCA) go in exactly the opposite direction of creating more opportunity for less advantaged families. I now turn to that and other policies that should be strongly resisted in the interest of promoting opportunity.

POLICIES THAT WOULD DIMINISH OPPORTUNITY

Policy-makers have, in recent years, promoted programs in at least three areas that threaten to significantly reduce opportunities: healthcare, budgets, and taxes.

Healthcare

I have already underscored the opportunity-enhancing characteristics of publicly provided healthcare, including how it unlocks entrepreneurial opportunities and improves the long-term health and educational attainment of children who receive it. Subsidized coverage, a key component of the ACA, also provides income relief for families whose budgets are already tight even before paying for health coverage.

In contrast, various political factions have consistently tried to both roll back the ACA's subsidies to lower income and older persons and cut funding to support the Medicaid expansion part of the program. For example, in evaluating one proposal—the AHCA—the Congressional Budget Office (CBO) found that the bill would have completely unwound the coverage gains of the ACA, adding 24 million to the ranks of the uninsured.[46] Based on the research cited earlier, such ideas clearly run counter to an opportunity agenda. Instead, as noted earlier, policy-makers should build on the successes of the ACA and improve its flaws. That would mean expanding Medicaid to the 19 states that have yet to adopt it, introducing a public option (e.g., Medicare or Medicaid) into the insurance exchanges, and strengthening the risk pool by raising enrollment and marketplace subsidies to lower out-of-pocket costs.[47]

Taxes

As noted throughout this chapter and as the work of Chetty and others have underscored, high levels of inequality are associated with immobility, wage and income stagnation, residential segregation, and diminished opportunity in both the near term and—especially regarding poor children facing educational and environmental barriers—the long term. Yet regressive tax cuts "pile on" and exacerbate market-driven inequalities that are already too high from an opportunity perspective. They also reduce the revenues needed to implement many of the opportunity-inducing policy ideas touted throughout this chapter.

The large tax package passed at the end of 2017 is exhibit A in exacerbating this destructive chain of higher inequality, less mobility, and less resources to offset immobility. According to the CBO, the deficit-financed legislation increases the debt by $1.9 trillion over 10 years as it delivers "windfall gains to wealthy households and profitable corporations, further widening the gap between those at the top of the income ladder and the rest of the nation."[48] According to the Tax Policy Center, the cuts to the richest 1 percent of households increase their after-tax income by 2.9 percent, more than twice the increase to the middle fifth and more than seven times the increase to the bottom fifth.[49]

My own research finds strong evidence that the tax cuts are doing serious damage to the revenue flow necessary to support opportunity-enhancing policy measures.[50] According to the CBO, from the summer of 2017, before the tax cuts were enacted, the Treasury was expected to collect 17.7 percent of GDP in revenue in 2018. The actual share came in well below that, at just 16.4 percent. Note that the CBO's estimate of the 2018 spending share was almost right on target, at 20.5 percent of GDP (the actual share was 20.3 percent). Note also that the 20.3 percent spending share in 2018 was precisely equal to the 50-year average. What's unusual is the low revenue number.

In other words, these plans thwart opportunity in two ways: by exacerbating after-tax inequality, a problem clearly associated with immobility and diminished opportunity, and by reducing revenues needed to support the many ideas elaborated earlier, ideas which would lower barriers to opportunity.

Budget Policy

One recent, underappreciated trend in federal budget policy seems designed to buttress rather than reduce opportunity barriers: the decline in support for non-defense discretionary (NDD) programs. Many programs in this budget category are associated with reducing the opportunity barriers discussed throughout this essay, including housing assistance programs, job training programs, Head Start, aid for poor school districts, Pell grants, the MEP discussed earlier (a program within the Commerce Department that helps small manufacturers access global supply chains), and block grants that support community and economic development.[51] CBPP analysis shows that NDD funding is already heading for its lowest levels on record as a share of GDP.[52] Recent budget proposals by the current administration have followed a similar "architecture": large tax cuts that worsen after-tax inequality and spending cuts that fall mostly on low- and moderate-income households.[53]

Instead, I have argued that supporting an opportunity agenda in a fiscally responsible manner while protecting key income and health security programs like Medicare, Medicaid, Social Security, and SNAP (food assistance) will require additional, not less, revenue.[54] That is, revenue neutrality is too low a bar for our tax debate. In the interest of maintaining and supporting the opportunity enhancers discussed earlier, we must raise revenues, not try to break even (or, worse, use questionable scoring practices to claim neutrality). In this regard, recent proposals to raise revenues through a much increased top marginal tax rate[55] or a tax on the ultrawealthy[56] are wholly consistent with a fiscally responsible opportunity agenda.

CONCLUSION

This chapter documents extensive barriers to opportunity and mobility stemming from income inequality, discrimination, residential economic segregation, low access to educational opportunities, inadequate job opportunities, and more. I then elaborate a set of short- and long-term policies to reduce these barriers. Finally, I argue that there are policies under discussion in the areas of health, taxes, and budgets that push in precisely the wrong direction, threatening to reinforce these barriers.

In discussing some of the long-term benefits to children who were in families that received certain antipoverty benefits, I highlighted several rigorous analyses showing how these programs have improved the life chances of these recipients. This information is important both as a guide to opportunity-enhancing policy and as a reminder that, too often, those who oppose these programs wrongly claim that "nothing works."

In fact, continuing evidence shows that healthcare policy, child-centered educational policies, antipoverty policies, and workforce policies (recall the earlier discussion around apprenticeships) are having their intended effects.[57] If we are serious about providing Americans with the opportunities they deserve to realize their potential, then the policies and programs discussed herein must be nurtured, strengthened, and improved.

NOTES

1. Ellen Ruppel Shell, "The Brains of Flint's Children, Imperiled by Lead, Could Still Escape Damage," *Scientific American*, July 1, 2016, https://www.scientificamerican.com/article/the-brains-of-flint-s-children-imperiled-by-lead-could-still-escape-damage/.

2. Janet Yellen, "Addressing Workforce Development Challenges in Low-Income Communities," remarks at the 2017 Annual Conference of the National Community Reinvestment Coalition, Washington, DC, March 28, 2017. https://www.federalreserve.gov/newsevents/speech/files/yellen20170328a.pdf.

3. Jared Bernstein, "What Racial Injustice Looks Like in America's Economy," *The Washington Post*, July 11, 2016, https://www.washingtonpost.com/posteverything/wp/2016/07/11/racial-economic-injustice-jobs-incomes-and-wealth/?utm_term=.0a52e8e36f9c.

4. Jared Bernstein, "Wage Outcomes and Macroeconomic Conditions: What's the Connection?" Jared Bernstein Blog, August 16, 2016, http://jaredbernsteinblog.com/wp-content/uploads/2016/08/wg_macro_8_25.pdf.

5. US Department of Agriculture Economic Research Service, "Rural Employment and Unemployment," updated September 23, 2019, https://www.ers.usda.gov/topics/rural-economy-population/employment-education/rural-employment-and-unemployment/.

6. Ann Owens, "Inequality in Children's Contexts: Income Segregation in Households with and without Children," American Sociological Review 81, no. 3 (2016): 549–574, http://journals.sagepub.com/doi/abs/10.1177/0003122416642430.

7. Douglas Rice, "Groundbreaking Studies: Good Neighborhoods Help Low-Income Children Succeed," Center on Budget and Policy Priorities, May 4, 2015, http://www.cbpp.org/blog/groundbreaking-studies-good-neighborhoods-help-low-income-children-succeed.

8. Raj Chetty et al., "Mobility Report Cards: The Role of Colleges in Intergenerational Mobility," The Equality of Opportunity Project, January 2017, http://www.equality-of-opportunity.org/papers/coll_mrc_paper.pdf.

9. Jared Bernstein and Ben Spielberg, "Inequality Matters," *The Atlantic*, June 5, 2015, https://www.theatlantic.com/business/archive/2015/06/what-matters-inequality-or-opportuniy/393272/.

10. Raj Chetty et al., "The Fading American Dream: Trends in Absolute Income Mobility Since 1940," NBER Working Paper 22910, December 2016, http://www.equality-of-opportunity.org/papers/abs_mobility_paper.pdf.

11. Jared Bernstein, "The Biggest Public Policy Mistake We're Continuing to Make, Year After Year," *The Washington Post*, February 1, 2016, https://www.washingtonpost.com/posteverything/wp/2016/02/01/the-biggest-public-policy-mistake-were-continuing-to-make-year-after-year/?utm_term=.119fe0b31153.

12. Executive Office of the President of the United States, "The Economics of Early Childhood Investments," January 2015, https://obamawhitehouse.archives.gov/sites/default/files/docs/early_childhood_report_update_final_non-embargo.pdf.

13. National Employment Law Project and Center for Community Change, "The 'Wild West' of Employment Background Checks," August 2014, https://www.nelp.org/wp-content/uploads/2015/03/Wild-West-Employment-Background-Checks-Reform-Agenda.pdf.

14. Jared Bernstein, Ben Spielberg, and Scott Winship, "Policy Options for Improving Economic Opportunity and Mobility," Peter G. Peterson Foundation, June 2015, http://www.pgpf.org/sites/default/files/grant_cbpp_manhattaninst_economic_mobility.pdf.

15. Jared Bernstein, "The Importance of Strong Labor Demand," The Hamilton Project, February 27, 2018. http://www.hamiltonproject.org/papers/the_importance_of_strong_labor_demand.

16. The results in Figure 3.6 are derived from a model run on data from 1968 to 2016. It regresses the percentage change in nominal median household income on lagged inflation (CPI-U-RS), the percentage change in wages, employment, and the unemployment rate gap. The R-squared from the regression is 0.8.

17. American Society for Civil Engineers, "2017 ASCE Infrastructure Report Card," updated February 2019, https://www.infrastructurereportcard.org/wp-content/uploads/2019/02/Full-2017-Report-Card-FINAL.pdf.

18. Jared Bernstein, "Make American Infrastructure Great Again!" *The Washington Post*, June 14, 2016, https://www.washingtonpost.com/posteverything/wp/2016/06/14/talking-infrastructure-with-liz-mcnichol/?utm_term=.acbfb71e6fd1.

19. Jared Bernstein, "Fixing Our School Facilities: An Essential Combination of Education and Infrastructure Policy," *The Washington Post*, March 30, 2016, https://www.washingtonpost.com/posteverything/wp/2016/03/30/fixing-our-school-facilities-an-essential-combination-of-education-and-infrastructure-policy/?utm_term=.86f4a390877f.

20. Mary Filardo, Jared Bernstein, and Ross Eisenbrey, "Creating Jobs Through FAST!, a Proposed New Infrastructure Program to Repair America's Public Schools," 21st Century School Fund and Economic Policy Institute, August 11, 2011, http://www.21csf.org/best-home/docuploads/pub/237_FixAmericasSchoolsFinal.pdf.

21. "The Importance of School Facilities in Improving Student Outcomes," Penn State Center for Evaluation and Education Policy Analysis, June 7, 2015, https://sites.psu.edu/ceepa/2015/06/07/the-importance-of-school-facilities-in-improving-student-outcomes/.

22. Heather Boushey, "Now is the Time to Fix Our Broken Infrastructure," Center for American Progress, September 22, 2011, https://www.americanprogress.org/issues/economy/news/2011/09/22/10231/now-is-the-time-to-fix-our-broken-infrastructure/; US Department of Transportation Federal Highway Administration, "Employment Impactsof Highway Infrastructure Investment," April 4, 2017, https://www.fhwa.dot.gov/policy/otps/pubs/effects/; Joseph Kane and Robert Puentes, "Beyond Shovel-Ready: The Extent and Impact of US Infrastructure Jobs," Brookings Institution, May 9, 2014, https://www.brookings.edu/interactives/beyond-shovel-ready-the-extent-and-impact-of-u-s-infrastructure-jobs/.

23. US Council of Economic Advisors, "Economic Report of the President," February 2016, https://obamawhitehouse.archives.gov/sites/default/files/docs/ERP_2016_Book_Complete%20JA.pdf.

24. Josh Bivens, "The Short- and Long-Term Impact of Infrastructure Investments on Employment and Economic Activity in the US Economy," Economic Policy Institute, July 1, 2014, http://www.epi.org/publication/impact-of-infrastructure-investments/.

25. Jared Bernstein and Ben Spielberg, "Preparing for the Next Recession: Lessons from the American Recovery and Reinvestment Act," Center on Budget and Policy Priorities, March 21, 2016, http://www.cbpp.org/research/economy/preparing-for-the-next-recession-lessons-from-the-american-recovery-and.

26. Chuck Marr et al., "EITC and Child Tax Credit Promote Work, Reduce Poverty, and Support Children's Development, Research Finds," Center on Budget and Policy Priorities, October 1, 2015, http://www.cbpp.org/research/federal-tax/eitc-and-child-tax-credit-promote-work-reduce-poverty-and-support-childrens?fa=view&id=3793; Francine Blau and Lawrence Kahn, "Female Labor Supply: Why is the US Falling Behind?" NBER Working Paper No. 18702, January 2013, http://www.nber.org/papers/w18702.

27. Robert Fairlie, Kanika Kapur, and Susan Gates, "Is Employer-Based Health Insurance a Barrier to Entrepreneurship?" RAND Working Paper Series No. WR-637-EMKF, November 2008, https://papers.ssrn.com/sol3/papers.cfm?abstract_id=1305280; Allison Wellington, "Health Insurance Coverage and Entrepreneurship," *Contemporary Economic Policy* 19, no. 4 (2001): 465–478, http://onlinelibrary.wiley.com/doi/10.1093/cep/19.4.465/full.

28. Nick Buffie, "Obamacare and Part-Time Work, Part 1: Voluntary Part-Time Employment," Center for Economic and Policy Research, December 6, 2016, http://cepr.net/blogs/cepr-blog/obamacare-and-part-time-work-part-1-voluntary-part-time-employment.

29. Jared Bernstein and Ro Khanna, "How to Help Small Manufacturers (And How Not to)," *The Washington Post,* February 23, 2017, https://www.washingtonpost.com/posteverything/wp/2017/02/23/how-to-help-small-manufacturers-and-how-not-to/?utm_term=.50148c5f7430#comments.

30. John Sargent Jr., "The Manufacturing Extension Partnership Program," Congressional Research Service, December 14, 2015, http://nationalaglawcenter.org/wp-content/uploads/assets/crs/R44308.pdf.

31. Jared Bernstein, "Ditching T.P.P. Won't Solve the Trade Deficit," *The New York Times,* January 24, 2017, https://www.nytimes.com/2017/01/24/opinion/ditching-tpp-wont-solve-the-trade-deficit.html?_r=2.

32. Robert Pollin et al., "Green Growth: A US Program for Controlling Climate Change and Expanding Job Opportunities," Center for American Progress and Political Economic Research Institute, September 2014, https://cdn.americanprogress.org/wp-content/uploads/2014/09/PERI.pdf.

33. Manufacturing USA: National Network for Manufacturing Innovation. "Manufacturing USA Programs." https://www.manufacturing.gov/programs/manufacturing-usa.

34. Robert Lerman, "Bipartisan Support Emerges for Expanding Apprenticeships," Urban Institute, February 27, 2015, http://www.urban.org/urban-wire/bipartisan-support-emerges-expanding-apprenticeships; Robert Lerman, "Evidence-Based Policy Calls for Expanding Apprenticeships," Urban Institute, August 7, 2013, http://www.urban.org/urban-wire/evidence-based-policy-calls-expanding-apprenticeships.

35. Bernstein, Spielberg, and Winship, "Policy Options for Improving Economic Opportunity and Mobility."

36. Ibid.; Jason Furman and Krista Ruffini, "Six Examples of the Long-Term Benefits of Anti-Poverty Programs," US Council of Economic Advisors, May 11, 2015. https://obamawhitehouse.archives.gov/blog/2015/05/11/six-examples-long-term-benefits-anti-poverty-programs.

37. Chuck Marr et al., "Strengthening the EITC for Childless Workers Would Promote Work and Reduce Poverty," Center on Budget and Policy Priorities, April 11, 2016, http://www.cbpp.org/research/federal-tax/strengthening-the-eitc-for-childless-workers-would-promote-work-and-reduce.

38. Robert Greenstein, "Strengthen Minimum Wage — and EITC," Center on Budget and Policy Priorities, May 27, 2015, http://www.cbpp.org/blog/strengthen-minimum-wage-and-eitc.

39. Chuck Marr, Chloe Cho, and Arloc Sherman, "A Top Priority to Address Poverty: Strengthening the Child Tax Credit for Very Poor Young Children," Center on Budget and Policy Priorities, August 10, 2016, http://www.cbpp.

org/research/federal-tax/a-top-priority-to-address-poverty-strengthening-the-child-tax-credit-for-very.

40. Douglas Rice, "55,000 Housing Vouchers at Risk under 2017 Funding Bills," Center on Budget and Policy Priorities, March 28, 2017, http://www.cbpp.org/blog/55000-housing-vouchers-at-risk-under-2017-funding-bills.

41. Barbara Sard, "The Future of Housing in America: A Better Way to Increase Efficiencies for Housing Vouchers and Create Upward Economic Mobility," Center on Budget and Policy Priorities, September 21, 2016, http://www.cbpp.org/housing/the-future-of-housing-in-america-a-better-way-to-increase-efficiencies-for-housing-vouchers.

42. Michael Mitchell and Michael Leachman, "Changing Priorities: State Criminal Justice Reforms and Investments in Education," Center on Budget and Policy Priorities, October 28, 2014, http://www.cbpp.org/research/changing-priorities-state-criminal-justice-reforms-and-investments-in-education.

43. Maurice Emsellem and Jason Ziedenberg, "Strategies for Full Employment Through Reform of the Criminal Justice System," Center on Budget and Policy Priorities, March 30, 2015, http://www.cbpp.org/research/full-employment/strategies-for-full-employment-through-reform-of-the-criminal-justice.

44. As of this writing, Medicaid expansion was passed and implemented in 34 states. In 3 states, Medicaid expansion had been passed but not yet implemented. 14 states had not adopted Medicaid expansion. Kaiser Family Foundation. "Status of State Medicaid Expansion Decisions: Interactive Map." Updated September 20, 2019. https://www.kff.org/medicaid/issue-brief/status-of-state-medicaid-expansion-decisions-interactive-map/.

45. "Rural America Will Benefit from Medicaid Expansion," Center on Budget and Policy Priorities, June 7, 2013, http://www.cbpp.org/sites/default/files/atoms/files/Fact-Sheet-Rural-America.pdf.

46. "American Health Care Act," Congressional Budget Office, March 13, 2017, https://www.cbo.gov/publication/52486.

47. Barack Obama, "United States Health Care Reform: Progress to Date and Next Steps," The Journal of the American Medical Association, August 2, 2016, pp. 525–532, http://jamanetwork.com/journals/jama/fullarticle/2533698; Sarah Lueck, "Insurers Must Recalibrate Premiums and Costs," The New York Times, August 24, 2016, http://www.nytimes.com/roomfordebate/2016/08/24/is-obamacare-sustainable/insurers-must-recalibrate-premiums-and-costs.

48. Chuck Marr, Brendan Duke, and Chye-Ching Huang, "New Tax Law Is Fundamentally Flawed and Will Require Basic Restructuring," Center on Budget and Policy Priorities, updated August 14, 2018, https://www.cbpp.org/research/federal-tax/new-tax-law-is-fundamentally-flawed-and-will-require-basic-restructuring.

49. Ibid.

50. Jared Bernstein, "Let's Be Honest: We Also Have a Revenue Problem," Written testimony at House Financial Services Committee Hearing, December 11,

2018, https://financialservices.house.gov/uploadedfiles/12.19.2018_jared_bernsteinl_testimony.pdf.

51. Isaac Shapiro et al., "Trump Budget Would Cut Block Grants Dramatically, Underscoring Danger of Block-Granting Social Programs," Center on Budget and Policy Priorities, March 28, 2017, http://www.cbpp.org/research/federal-budget/trump-budget-would-cut-block-grants-dramatically-underscoring-danger-of.

52. "Non-Defense Discretionary Programs," Center on Budget and Policy Priorities, updated August 12, 2019, http://www.cbpp.org/research/policy-basics-non-defense-discretionary-programs.

53. Richard Kogan and Isaac Shapiro, "House GOP Budget Gets 62 Percent of Budget Cuts from Low- and Moderate-Income Programs," Center on Budget and Policy Priorities, March 28, 2016, http://www.cbpp.org/research/federal-budget/house-gop-budget-gets-62-percent-of-budget-cuts-from-low-and-moderate-income.

54. Jared Bernstein, "The Nonreality of the Current Tax Debate," *The Washington Post*, March 30, 2017, https://www.washingtonpost.com/posteverything/wp/2017/03/30/the-nonreality-of-the-current-tax-debate/?utm_term=.77282f0d7de9.

55. Matthew Choi, "Ocasio-Cortez Floats 70 Percent Tax on the Super Wealthy to Fund Green New Deal," *Politico*, January 4, 2019, https://www.politico.com/story/2019/01/04/ocasio-cortez-70-percent-tax-1080874

56. US Senator of Massachusetts, Elizabeth Warren, "Senator Warren Unveils Proposal to Tax Wealth of Ultra-Rich Americans," January 14, 2019, https://www.warren.senate.gov/newsroom/press-releases/senator-warren-unveils-proposal-to-tax-wealth-of-ultra-rich-americans.

57. Sean Reardon, Jane Waldfogel, and Daphna Bassok, "The Good News About Educational Inequality," *The New York Times*, August 26, 2016, https://www.nytimes.com/2016/08/28/opinion/sunday/the-good-news-about-educational-inequality.html?_r=0; Danilo Trisi, "Safety Net's Anti-Poverty Effectiveness Has Grown Nearly Ten-Fold Since 1967," Center on Budget and Policy Priorities, January 4, 2016, http://www.cbpp.org/blog/safety-nets-anti-poverty-effectiveness-has-grown-nearly-ten-fold-since-1967; Arloc Sherman and Danilo Trisi, "Safety Net More Effective Against Poverty Than Previously Thought," Center on Budget and Policy Priorities, May 6, 2015, http://www.cbpp.org/research/poverty-and-inequality/safety-net-more-effective-against-poverty-than-previously-thought.

REFERENCES

American Society for Civil Engineers. February 2019. "2017 ASCE Infrastructure Report Card." https://www.infrastructurereportcard.org/wp-content/uploads/2019/02/Full-2017-Report-Card-FINAL.pdf

Bernstein, Jared. February 1, 2016. "The Biggest Public Policy Mistake We're Continuing to Make. Year After Year." *The Washington Post*. https://www.

washingtonpost.com/posteverything/wp/2016/02/01/the-biggest-public-policy-mistake-were-continuing-to-make-year-after-year/?utm_term=.119fe0b31153

Bernstein, Jared. March 30, 2016. "Fixing Our School Facilities: An Essential Combination of Education and Infrastructure Policy." *The Washington Post.* https://www.washingtonpost.com/posteverything/wp/2016/03/30/fixing-our-school-facilities-an-essential-combination-of-education-and-infrastructure-policy/?utm_term=.86f4a390877f

Bernstein, Jared. June 14, 2016. "Make American Infrastructure Great Again!" *The Washington Post.* https://www.washingtonpost.com/posteverything/wp/2016/06/14/talking-infrastructure-with-liz-mcnichol/?utm_term=.acbfb71e6fd1

Bernstein, Jared. July 11, 2016. "What Racial Injustice Looks Like in America's Economy." *The Washington Post.* https://www.washingtonpost.com/posteverything/wp/2016/07/11/racial-economic-injustice-jobs-incomes-and-wealth/?utm_term=.0a52e8e36f9c

Bernstein, Jared. August 16, 2016. "Wage Outcomes and Macroeconomic Conditions: What's the Connection?" On The Economy: Jared Bernstein Blog. http://jaredbernsteinblog.com/wp-content/uploads/2016/08/wg_macro_8_25.pdf

Bernstein, Jared. January 24, 2017. "Ditching T.P.P. Won't Solve the Trade Deficit." *The New York Times.* https://www.nytimes.com/2017/01/24/opinion/ditching-tpp-wont-solve-the-trade-deficit.html?_r=2

Bernstein, Jared. March 30, 2017. "The Nonreality of the Current Tax Debate." *The Washington Post.* https://www.washingtonpost.com/posteverything/wp/2017/03/30/the-nonreality-of-the-current-tax-debate/?utm_term=.77282f0d7de9

Bernstein, Jared. February 27, 2018. "The Importance of Strong Labor Demand." The Hamilton Project. http://www.hamiltonproject.org/papers/the_importance_of_strong_labor_demand

Bernstein, Jared. December 11, 2018. "Let's Be Honest: We Also Have a Revenue Problem." Written testimony at House Financial Services Committee Hearing, Washington DC. https://financialservices.house.gov/uploadedfiles/12.19.2018_jared_bernsteinl_testimony.pdf

Bernstein, Jared, and Ro Khanna. February 23, 2017. "How to Help Small Manufacturers (And How Not To)." *The Washington Post.* https://www.washingtonpost.com/posteverything/wp/2017/02/23/how-to-help-small-manufacturers-and-how-not-to/?utm_term=.50148c5f7430comments

Bernstein, Jared, and Ben Spielberg. June 5, 2015. "Inequality Matters." *The Atlantic.* https://www.theatlantic.com/business/archive/2015/06/what-matters-inequality-or-opportuniy/393272/

Bernstein, Jared, and Ben Spielberg. March 2, 2016. "Preparing for the Next Recession: Lessons from the American Recovery and Reinvestment Act." Center on Budget and Policy Priorities. http://www.cbpp.org/research/economy/preparing-for-the-next-recession-lessons-from-the-american-recovery-and

Bernstein, Jared, Ben Spielberg, and Scott Winship. June 2015. "Policy Options for Improving Economic Opportunity and Mobility." Peter G. Peterson Foundation. http://www.pgpf.org/sites/default/files/grant_cbpp_manhattaninst_economic_mobility.pdf

Bivens, Josh. July 1, 2014. "The Short- and Long-Term Impact of Infrastructure Investments on Employment and Economic Activity in the US Economy." Economic Policy Institute. http://www.epi.org/publication/impact-of-infrastructure-investments/

Blau, Francine, and Lawrence Kahn. January 2013. "Female Labor Supply: Why is the US Falling Behind?" NBER Working Paper 18702. http://www.nber.org/papers/w18702

Boushey, Heather. September 22, 2011. "Now Is the Time to Fix Our Broken Infrastructure." Center for American Progress. https://www.americanprogress.org/issues/economy/news/2011/09/22/10231/now-is-the-time-to-fix-our-broken-infrastructure/

Buffie, Nick. December 6, 2016. "Obamacare and Part-Time Work. Part 1: Voluntary Part-Time Employment." Center for Economic and Policy Research. http://cepr.net/blogs/cepr-blog/obamacare-and-part-time-work-part-1-voluntary-part-time-employment

Center on Budget and Policy Priorities. June 7, 2013. "Rural America Will Benefit from Medicaid Expansion." http://www.cbpp.org/sites/default/files/atoms/files/Fact-Sheet-Rural-America.pdf

Chetty, Raj, John N. Friedman, Emmanuel Saez, Nicholas Turmer, and Danny Yagan. January 2017. "Mobility Report Cards: The Role of Colleges in Intergenerational Mobility." The Equality of Opportunity Project. http://www.equality-of-opportunity.org/papers/coll_mrc_paper.pdf

Chetty, Raj, David Grusky, Maximilian Hell, Nathaniel Hendren, Robert Manduca, and Jimmy Narang. December 2016. "The Fading American Dream: Trends in Absolute Income Mobility Since 1940." NBER Working Paper 22910. http://www.equality-of-opportunity.org/papers/abs_mobility_paper.pdf

Choi, Matthew. January 4, 2019. "Ocasio-Cortez Floats 70 Percent Tax on the Super Wealthy to Fund Green New Deal." Politico. https://www.politico.com/story/2019/01/04/ocasio-cortez-70-percent-tax-1080874

Congressional Budget Office. March 13, 2017. "American Health Care Act." https://www.cbo.gov/publication/52486

Emsellem, Maurice, and Jason Ziedenberg. March 30, 2015. "Strategies for Full Employment Through Reform of the Criminal Justice System." Center on Budget and Policy Priorities. http://www.cbpp.org/research/full-employment/strategies-for-full-employment-through-reform-of-the-criminal-justice

Executive Office of the President of the United States. January 2015. "The Economics of Early Childhood Investments." https://obamawhitehouse.archives.gov/sites/default/files/docs/early_childhood_report_update_final_non-embargo.pdf

Farlie, Robert, Kanika Kapur, and Susan Gates. November 2008. "Is Employer-Based Health Insurance a Barrier to Entrepreneurship?" RAND Working Paper Series No. WR-637-EMKF. https://papers.ssrn.com/sol3/papers.cfm?abstract_id=1305280

Filardo, Mary, Jared Bernstein, and Ross Eisenbrey. August 11, 2011. "Creating Jobs Through FAST! A Proposed New Infrastructure Program to Repair America's Public Schools." 21st Century School Fund and Economic Policy Institute. http://www.21csf.org/best-home/docuploads/pub/237_FixAmericas SchoolsFinal.pdf

Furman, Jason, and Krista Ruffini. May 11, 2015. "Six Examples of the Long-Term Benefits of Anti-Poverty Programs." US Council of Economic Advisors. https://obamawhitehouse.archives.gov/blog/2015/05/11/six-examples-long-term-benefits-anti-poverty-programs

Greenstein, Robert. May 27, 2015. "Strengthen Minimum Wage—and EITC." Center on Budget and Policy Priorities. http://www.cbpp.org/blog/strengthen-minimum-wage-and-eitc

Kaiser Family Foundation. September 20, 2019. "Status of State Medicaid Expansion Decisions: Interactive Map." https://www.kff.org/medicaid/issue-brief/status-of-state-medicaid-expansion-decisions-interactive-map/

Kane, Joseph, and Robert Puentes. May 9, 2014. "Beyond Shovel-Ready: The Extent and Impact of US Infrastructure Jobs." Brookings Institution. https://www.brookings.edu/interactives/beyond-shovel-ready-the-extent-and-impact-of-u-s-infrastructure-jobs/

Kogan, Richard, and Isaac Shapiro. March 28, 2016. "House GOP Budget Gets 62 Percent of Budget Cuts from Low- and Moderate-Income Programs." Center on Budget and Policy Priorities. http://www.cbpp.org/research/federal-budget/house-gop-budget-gets-62-percent-of-budget-cuts-from-low-and-moderate-income

Lerman, Robert. February 27, 2015. "Bipartisan Support Emerges for Expanding Apprenticeships." Urban Institute. http://www.urban.org/urban-wire/bipartisan-support-emerges-expanding-apprenticeships

Lerman, Robert. August 7, 2013. "Evidence-Based Policy Calls for Expanding Apprenticeships." Urban Institute. http://www.urban.org/urban-wire/evidence-based-policy-calls-expanding-apprenticeships

Lueck, Sarah. August 24, 2016. "Insurers Must Recalibrate Premiums and Costs." The New York Times. http://www.nytimes.com/roomfordebate/2016/08/24/is-obamacare-sustainable/insurers-must-recalibrate-premiums-and-costs

Manufacturing USA: National Network for Manufacturing Innovation. "Manufacturing USA Programs." https://www.manufacturing.gov/programs/manufacturing-usa

Marr, Chuck, Chye-Ching Huang, Cecile Murray, and Arloc Sherman. April 11, 2016. "Strengthening the EITC for Childless Workers Would Promote Work and Reduce Poverty." Center on Budget and Policy Priorities.

http://www.cbpp.org/research/federal-tax/strengthening-the-eitc-for-childless-workers-would-promote-work-and-reduce

Marr, Chuck, Chye-Ching Huang, Arloc Sherman, and Brandon DeBot. October 1, 2015. "EITC and Child Tax Credit Promote Work, Reduce Poverty, and Support Children's Development, Research Finds." Center on Budget and Policy Priorities. http://www.cbpp.org/research/federal-tax/eitc-and-child-tax-credit-promote-work-reduce-poverty-and-support-childrens?fa=view&id=3793

Marr, Chuck, Chloe Cho, and Arloc Sherman. August 10, 2016. "A Top Priority to Address Poverty: Strengthening the Child Tax Credit for Very Poor Young Children." Center on Budget and Policy Priorities. http://www.cbpp.org/research/federal-tax/a-top-priority-to-address-poverty-strengthening-the-child-tax-credit-for-very

Marr, Chuck, Brendan Duke, and Chye-Ching Huang. August 14, 2018. "New Tax Law Is Fundamentally Flawed and Will Require Basic Restructuring," Center on Budget and Policy Priorities, updated, https://www.cbpp.org/research/federal-tax/new-tax-law-is-fundamentally-flawed-and-will-require-basic-restructuring

Mitchell, Michael, and Michael Leachman. October 28, 2014. "Changing Priorities: State Criminal Justice Reforms and Investments in Education." Center on Budget and Policy Priorities. http://www.cbpp.org/research/changing-priorities-state-criminal-justice-reforms-and-investments-in-education

National Employment Law Project and Center for Community Change. August 2014. "The 'Wild West' of Employment Background Checks." https://www.nelp.org/wp-content/uploads/2015/03/Wild-West-Employment-Background-Checks-Reform-Agenda.pdf

"Non-Defense Discretionary Programs." August 12, 2019. Center on Budget and Policy Priorities. http://www.cbpp.org/research/policy-basics-non-defense-discretionary-programs

Obama, Barack. 2016. "United States Health Care Reform: Progress to Date and Next Steps." *The Journal of the American Medical Association*, 525–532. http://jamanetwork.com/journals/jama/fullarticle/2533698

Owens, Ann. 2016. "Inequality in Children's Contexts: Income Segregation in Households with and without Children." *American Sociological Review*, 81 (3): 549–574. http://journals.sagepub.com/doi/abs/10.1177/0003122416642430

Penn State Center for Evaluation and Education Policy Analysis. June 7, 2015. "The Importance of School Facilities in Improving Student Outcomes." https://sites.psu.edu/ceepa/2015/06/07/the-importance-of-school-facilities-in-improving-student-outcomes/

Pollin, Robert, Heidi Garrett-Paltier, James Heintz, and Bracket Hendricks. September 2014. "Green Growth: A US Program for Controlling Climate Change and Expanding Job Opportunities." Center for American Progress and Political Economic Research Institute. https://cdn.americanprogress.org/wp-content/uploads/2014/09/PERI.pdf

Reardon, Sean, Jane Waldfogel, and Daphna Bassok. August 26, 2016. "The Good News About Educational Inequality." *The New York Times*. https://www.nytimes.com/2016/08/28/opinion/sunday/the-good-news-about-educational-inequality.html?_r=0

Rice, Douglas. May 4, 2015. "Groundbreaking Studies: Good Neighborhoods Help Low-Income Children Succeed." Center on Budget and Policy Priorities. http://www.cbpp.org/blog/groundbreaking-studies-good-neighborhoods-help-low-income-children-succeed

Rice, Douglas. March 28, 2017. "55,000 Housing Vouchers at Risk under 2017 Funding Bills." Center on Budget and Policy Priorities. http://www.cbpp.org/blog/55000-housing-vouchers-at-risk-under-2017-funding-bills

Ruppel Shell, Ellen. July 1, 2016. "The Brains of Flint's Children, Imperiled by Lead, Could Still Escape Damage." *Scientific American*. https://www.scientificamerican.com/article/the-brains-of-flint-s-children-imperiled-by-lead-could-still-escape-damage/

Sard, Barbara. September 21, 2016. "The Future of Housing in America: A Better Way to Increase Efficiencies for Housing Vouchers and Create Upward Economic Mobility." Center on Budget and Policy Priorities. http://www.cbpp.org/housing/the-future-of-housing-in-america-a-better-way-to-increase-efficiencies-for-housing-vouchers

Sargent Jr., John. December 14, 2015. "The Manufacturing Extension Partnership Program." Congressional Research Service. http://nationalaglawcenter.org/wp-content/uploads/assets/crs/R44308.pdf

Shapiro, Isaac, David Reich, Chloe Choe, and Richard Kogan. March 28, 2017. "Trump Budget Would Cut Block Grants Dramatically. Underscoring Danger of Block-Granting Social Programs." Center on Budget and Policy Priorities. http://www.cbpp.org/research/federal-budget/trump-budget-would-cut-block-grants-dramatically-underscoring-danger-of

Sherman, Arloc, and Danilo Trisi. May 6, 2015. "Safety Net More Effective Against Poverty Than Previously Thought." Center on Budget and Policy Priorities. http://www.cbpp.org/research/poverty-and-inequality/safety-net-more-effective-against-poverty-than-previously-thought

Trisi, Danilo. January 4, 2016. "Safety Net's Anti-Poverty Effectiveness Has Grown Nearly Ten-Fold Since 1967." Center on Budget and Policy Priorities. http://www.cbpp.org/blog/safety-nets-anti-poverty-effectiveness-has-grown-nearly-ten-fold-since-1967

US Council of Economic Advisors. February 2016. "Economic Report of the President." https://obamawhitehouse.archives.gov/sites/default/files/docs/ERP_2016_Book_Complete%20JA.pdf

US Department of Agriculture Economic Research Service. September 23, 2019. "Rural Employment and Unemployment." https://www.ers.

usda.gov/topics/rural-economy-population/employment-education/rural-employment-and-unemployment/

US Department of Transportation Federal Highway Administration. April 4, 2017. "Employment Impacts of Highway Infrastructure Investment." https://www.fhwa.dot.gov/policy/otps/pubs/effects/

Warren, Elizabeth, US Senator of Massachusetts. January 14, 2019. "Senator Warren Unveils Proposal to Tax Wealth of Ultra-Rich Americans." https://www.warren.senate.gov/newsroom/press-releases/senator-warren-unveils-proposal-to-tax-wealth-of-ultra-rich-americans

Wellington, Allison. 2001. "Health Insurance Coverage and Entrepreneurship." *Contemporary Economic Policy,* 19(4): 465–478. http://onlinelibrary.wiley.com/doi/10.1093/cep/19.4.465/full

Yellen, Janet. March 28, 2017. "Addressing Workforce Development Challenges in Low-Income Communities." Remarks at the 2017 Annual Conference of the National Community Reinvestment Coalition, Washington, DC. https://www.federalreserve.gov/newsevents/speech/files/yellen20170328a.pdf

4

INCOME GROWTH AND ITS DISTRIBUTION FROM EISENHOWER TO OBAMA

THE GROWING IMPORTANCE OF IN-KIND TRANSFERS (1959–2016)

James Elwell, Kevin Corinth, and Richard V. Burkhauser

INTRODUCTION

Using public-use Annual Social and Economic Supplement to the Current Population Survey (ASEC-CPS) data stretching over three business cycles (1979–1989, 1989–2000, and 2000–2007), Burkhauser, Larrimore, and Simon (2012b) were the first to show systematically the sensitivity of measures of income and its distribution to the types of income included in the data, the sharing unit over which the data were collected, and the unit of analysis considered by the researcher.[1,2] In this chapter, we extend the analysis of Burkhauser et al. (2012b) back to 1959 (capturing the business cycles of the 1960s and 1970s) and forward over the current business cycle to 2016.[3]

Because the Census Bureau did not begin to estimate the market value of in-kind government transfers in general, and Medicare, Medicaid, and employer-sponsored health insurance (ESI) in particular, until 1979, doing so is the first contribution of this chapter.[4] We first use public-use ASEC-CPS data (income years 1967–2016) to create common yearly source-of-income categories, including estimates of the market value of in-kind transfers, back to 1967. We create analogous series using the decennial Census for the years 1960, 1970, 1980, and 1990 (income years 1959, 1969, 1979, and 1989) and reassuringly show

James Elwell, Kevin Corinth, and Richard V. Burkhauser, *Income Growth and Its Distribution from Eisenhower to Obama* In: *United States Income, Wealth, Consumption, and Inequality.* Edited by: Diana Furchtgott-Roth, Oxford University Press (2021). © Oxford University Press. DOI: 10.1093/oso/9780197518199.003.0005.

that they yield similar values to those found using ASEC-CPS data for 1969, 1979, and 1989. We then couple our decennial Census-based 1959 values to our ASEC-CPS values from 1967–2016 to create common yearly source-of-income categories, including estimates of the market value of in-kind transfers, back to decennial Census income year 1959.

Using this newly created dataset, we then show that choice of income sources, sharing unit, and the unit of analysis substantially change our measures of how the American middle class fared both absolutely and relative to the rest of the income distribution over a period stretching from near the end of the Eisenhower administration in 1959 to the end of the Obama administration in 2016.[5]

Using either of our most restrictive income definitions—labor earnings or market income—and a tax unit as both our sharing unit and our unit of analysis (choices researchers using tax record-based data are forced to make; e.g., Piketty and Saez, 2003), the resources available to the middle class (measured as the median American tax unit or the mean value of the middle quintile of American tax units) peaked in 1969 and trended downward thereafter. While these yearly values fell and rose within all subsequent business cycles, with the exception of the business cycle of 1989–2000, these values were lower at the end than at the beginning of each cycle.

In contrast, as we broaden our income definition to the disposable size-adjusted household income (including both cash and some in-kind transfers) of persons—the measure of income most commonly used in the survey data–based literature—middle class Americans have made peak-to-peak gains over all completed business cycles since 1959, including the 2000–2007 business cycle. In 2016, this disposable income measure finally returned to its peak year 2007, pre-Great Recession high at the start of the current, ongoing business cycle. However, this is a lower bound measure of the importance of government tax and transfer policies for the growth in the median American's disposable income. When we include the market values of Medicare, Medicaid, and ESI in our upper bound measure of the median American's disposable income, we find even greater growth.

Disaggregating the US population into quintiles, we show similar differences in the pattern of income growth between 1959 and 2016 based on the choice of income sources, sharing unit, and unit of analysis. Focusing only on the market income of tax units, the rich got richer, the poor got poorer, and the income of the middle class stagnated.[6]

However, these results change dramatically once we use more comprehensive measures of income that are more consistent with Haig-Simon principles.[7] When we adjust for government taxes, include cash and in-kind transfers, but exclude the value of Medicare, Medicaid, and ESI benefits—thus creating a lower bound measure of disposable income—we find that all five quintiles have experienced gains of more than 100 percent since 1959, with the highest gains among the top and bottom quintiles. When we include the market values of Medicare,

Medicaid, and ESI (the former two of which are programs that only began in 1966) in our upper bound measures of disposable income, the bottom quintile of the income distribution registers the greatest gains since 1959 and there are much smaller differences in gains across the other quintiles.

We find similar results when we focus on the single most common scalar measure of income inequality, the Gini coefficient. For all business cycle peak years and for 2016, using either of our most restrictive income definitions—labor earnings or market income—and a tax unit as both our sharing unit and our unit of analysis, Gini values are highest (most unequal) but decline as we increasingly take into account government taxes and transfers. We conclude that measures of median income and income inequality that exclude the market value of in-kind transfers will substantially understate the success of government policies in off-setting the stagnation in median market income and the rise in market income inequality since 1969.

ALTERNATIVE MEASURES OF THE ECONOMIC WELL-BEING OF THE MIDDLE CLASS

Economic growth in gross domestic product, measured in either aggregate or per capita terms, indicates a nation's progress in producing goods and services. How this progress translates into resources for the middle class, however, depends on how these gains in output are distributed across the population. Household survey data are the usual source for monitoring income and its distribution—at the household, family, and individual levels. Each year the Census Bureau uses household survey data to derive its official statistics on income and poverty.[8] Household survey data are also the basis for cross-national comparative studies and are the source for most other distributional analyses, such as those done by the Organisation for Economic Cooperation and Development (OECD, 2008, 2011, 2015). The definitions that underlie the way that household surveys ask income questions provide best-practice measures of personal living standards. The "income-sharing" unit that researchers choose when using these data is virtually always the household (all persons living in the dwelling), and the "income definition" is disposable (post-tax, post-transfer) income, adjusted for differences in household size and composition using an equivalence scale.[9]

The "unit of analysis" is the individual (regardless of age). Hence, median income is based on the equivalized income assigned to each person in the population. Gottschalk and Smeeding (1997), d'Ercole and Förster (2012), and the Canberra Group (2011) make the case for this standard methodology.[10]

A long-standing challenge to survey-based estimates is that they do not provide a complete picture of the income distribution and its trends because survey estimates fail to fully capture the highest incomes. In contrast, the tax-based data used in the top income shares literature do a much better job of capturing the highest incomes. (For the seminal article on US top incomes, see Piketty and Saez, 2003; for a review of this literature, see Atkinson, Piketty, and Saez, 2011.)

This tax data benefit is gained at the cost of being constrained to use the definitions of income and income-sharing unit mandated by each country's tax administration (definitions that differ from the survey-based ones) and being restricted to summary inequality measures that do not incorporate differences across the full income range (i.e., top income shares). However, we are primarily focusing on the middle class and are using a median rather than a mean income measure to track changes in middle-class income. Therefore, undercoverage of income at the very top of the distribution is unlikely to affect the results on median income that we report. In addition, survey data allow us to consider various definitions of income and sharing units and to consider different units of analysis. This is not possible when using tax record–based data.

Likewise, those using tax record–based data in the standard labor economics literature are forced to focus on the median wage earnings of workers or tax units. As a result, they do not account for the many workers who live in households that share labor earnings as well as other resources. This can lead to a misrepresentation of the distribution of income available to all Americans. The set of seven measures of median income from the survey- and tax-based literatures we discuss in the next section are all derived, as noted earlier, from data contained in the unrestricted, public-use ASEC-CPS and decennial Census. These are the most common cross-sectional, survey-based sources of data for those interested in measuring the incomes and income distributions of Americans. The ASEC-CPS contains a detailed questionnaire on the sources of income for household members and is commonly used to evaluate levels and trends of income and income inequality (see, e.g., Danziger and Gottschalk, 1995; Daly and Valletta, 2006; Blank, 2011; Burkhauser et al., 2011).

Drawing on previous work, we use the public-use ASEC-CPS to construct estimates of household income, building on income series from Burkhauser et al. (2012b) and Armour et al. (2014) and supplemented with cell-means from Larrimore et al. (2008) to address top-coding of high sources of income in households. With these data we extend the ASEC-CPS household income series created in Larrimore, Burkhauser, and Armour (2015) back to 1959—the last business cycle peak year before major increases in government cash and in-kind transfers related to both the maturing of Social Security (Old-Age, Survivor, and Disability Insurance) and the launch of New Frontier and Great Society programs in the 1960s—and forward to include the current business cycle through 2016.

To do so, we must address two important breaks in the ASEC-CPS data during this period. The first is the well-known break in the data that occurs between income years 1992 and 1993, caused by a redesign of the survey questions covering income sources. We follow Larrimore et al. (2015) and adjust for this break by assuming that the entire decrease in median income between 1992 and 1993 is caused by the improvement of ASEC-CPS data collection efforts, and therefore we adjust median income in 1992 and in all preceding years by the same percentage, resulting in no change in measured median incomes between 1992 and 1993 (see Atkinson et al., 2011; Burkhauser et al., 2012a; and Armour et al., 2014, for examples of this correction method).

The second break occurs for income year 2013, when the ASEC-CPS used past years' methods for one part of the survey population and a new method for the other part, to test the effect of the new method on outcomes. We use the median value based on these new methods for 2013 and adjust median income in all preceding years by the ratio of median values in 2013 based on the new and the old methods, similar to our adjustment for the break between 1992 and 1993.

The modern ASEC-CPS series begins in 1968 (income year 1967). We use these data to estimate the labor earning and market income of tax units back to 1967, utilizing methods that are consistent with those in the tax record–based inequality literature. However, we then contrast our findings with alternative definitions of income using methods that are consistent with those in the household survey–based literature.[11] Because many major Great Society programs began before 1967, including Medicare and Medicaid, this is not an ideal year to begin a study of the importance of government taxes and transfers on household income. Furthermore, to separate trends in income growth from variations introduced by business cycles, previous studies have compared peak years in the business cycle. Since 1967 is not a peak year in the business cycle, the earliest year in a series beginning in 1967 that we can consistently compare with subsequent peak years is 1969.

For these reasons, we create a second set of income series using the decennial Census of 1960. This corresponds to income year 1959, which is a peak year in the business cycle. Thus, we can make comparisons between peak years 1959 and 1969 and thereby capture the importance of in-kind transfers, including the insurance value of Medicare and Medicaid during the 1960s. To establish that the Census-based data points in 1959 can reasonably be combined with those of our ASEC-CPS income series, we repeat the process for the 1970, 1980, and 1990 decennial Censuses that can be directly compared to data for the same years in the CPS and find that the ASEC-CPS and Census values are similar.

Next, we briefly describe the seven measures we will use to document median income trends. In all cases we compare trends in real median income using the Consumer Price Index Research Series (CPI-U-RS).[12] We more fully discuss the details of our sources of income imputations in these series in an online appendix.[13]

Labor Earnings of Tax Units

The first measure is the *labor earnings of the median tax unit*. This income measure only looks at one source of market income, labor earnings (i.e., wages and salaries, self-employment income, and farm income) and uses the tax unit as both its sharing unit and its unit of analysis.[14] Such a measure is in the style of the tax record–based literature because labor earnings are a component of market income and the sharing unit is the tax unit. Tax units are not explicitly defined in the ASEC-CPS or the decennial Census, and so we assign tax units using the same assumptions from Piketty and Saez (2003).

Important in its own right, we also use this measure of median income as an additional check on the comparability of our decennial Census and ASEC-CPS series. We do this because these datasets ask similar questions with respect to the labor earnings of tax units. This is not the case with respect to the market income of tax units, necessitating some imputation (see the online appendix for details).

Market Income of Tax Units

The second is the *market income of the median tax unit*. A major new international literature based on data from administrative tax records of rich countries traces the share of income held by the very top part of the income distribution of these countries back to the early part of the 20th century. However, for the United States, this literature's measure of income is limited to taxable market income (wages, interest, dividends, etc.) of tax units. (See Atkinson et al. (2011) for a review of this international literature and Piketty and Saez (2003) for the first effort to measure top US income shares in this way.)

We follow Piketty and Saez (2003) and define market income to include gross income from wages and salaries, farm income, self-employment and business income, retirement income from pensions, dividends, interest, rent, and alimony. These sources of income are summed across individuals in a tax unit within each ASEC-CPS household, without adjusting for number of persons in a tax unit. Our unit of analysis, therefore, is the tax unit. While some of these separate sources of income are combined in earlier ASEC-CPS years, each is included in some questions back to 1967. Some of these sources of income are not specifically included as decennial Census questions. In particular, in earlier years, retirement and pension income, dividends, interest, rent, and alimony are grouped as "other" income, a category that also includes some non-market sources of income such as Social Security. Some of these sources are covered separately in later years while other sources continue to be grouped as "other" income. As a result, imputation of these sources varies, both across decennial Census and ASEC-CPS surveys and over time within the decennial Census. See the online appendix for details.

Although the level of median income of this measure is likely to be greater than one that looks at labor earnings alone, its trend will depend on the relative growth of other sources of market income.

Household Size-Adjusted Labor Earnings of Persons

The third is the *household size-adjusted labor earnings of the median person*. Consistent with the survey-based literature, this measure of median income expands the sharing unit from the tax unit to the household and makes the unit of analysis the person. We adjust this measure's household income using the square root of the number of people in the household and assume equal sharing across household members. This size adjustment is common in US and international research studies of median income trends and inequality (e.g., see Ruggles, 1990; Gottschalk and Smeeding, 1997; Atkinson and Brandolini, 2001; d'Ercole and Förster, 2012).

Burkhauser et al. (2012b) first showed that because the number of tax units within households has grown over time, while the number of people in those households has fallen, these demographic characteristics will tend to increase this measure of median income over time relative to a tax unit–based measure of labor earnings.

Household Size-Adjusted Market Income of Persons

The fourth is the *household size-adjusted market income of the median person*. In the same manner as discussed earlier, this measure of median income expands the sharing unit from the tax unit to the household and makes the unit of analysis the person. For the same reasons as discussed previously, this measure of median income will increase over time relative to a tax unit–based measure of market income.

Household Size-Adjusted Pre-Tax Post-Transfer Income of Persons

The fifth is the *household size-adjusted pre-tax post-transfer income of the median person*. While the Census Bureau reports the *pre-tax, post-transfer income of households* in the first figure of its annual report (Semega, Fontenot, and Kollar 2017), the Census Bureau uses this household size-adjusted median income measure in its more sophisticated discussions of income trends. To calculate this income measure, it adds government cash transfers to the income measure used in the previous series. These programs include Aid to Families with Dependent Children and its successor, Temporary Assistance for Needy Families, as well as social insurance programs such as Social Security and Workers' Compensation. This measure excludes, however, transfers directly tied to the tax system, such as the Earned Income Tax Credit (EITC). It also excludes any in-kind government transfers, such as food and housing assistance and the market value of Medicare or Medicaid insurance.

Because this measure adds government cash transfers but does not subtract government taxes, its level of median income will be greater than one that looks at market income alone, but its trend will depend on the relative growth of other sources of government cash transfers to market income.

As with market income, the income categories covering these income sources are less granular in earlier ASEC-CPS surveys. However, when aggregated, the various categories are still covered by some questions in the ASEC-CPS back to 1967. This is also the case with respect to the decennial Census. Therefore, unlike our measure of market income, it is not necessary for us to impute any decennial Census income sources to align them with the ASEC-CPS for this measure of income. The reason is that while the different income categories are grouped by survey questions, the groups all align with the income sources included as pre-tax post-transfer income. For example, retirement, investment, and public assistance income are all grouped under a single question in the 1960 decennial Census. This mixes market sources of income with government transfers, but all three sources of income are included in a pre-tax post-transfer measure of income. As a result, this is our most comparable income series over all our years since it requires no income source or tax unit imputations.

Household Size-Adjusted Post-Tax Post-Transfer Plus In-Kind Transfer Income of Persons

The sixth measure is the *household size-adjusted post-tax, post-transfer income (including some in-kind transfers) of the median person*. This lower bound disposable income measure more fully captures the importance of government tax and transfer policies for the resources of the median person. It uses the National Bureau of Economic Research's (NBER) TaxSim 9.3 (Feenberg and Coutts, 1993) to estimate federal and state taxes and liabilities, including Social Security and Medicare payroll taxes. In addition, it captures the market value of some in-kind transfers. The Census Bureau reports or imputes the value of the Supplemental Nutrition Assistance Program (SNAP, or food stamps), housing subsidies, and school lunches on an annual basis beginning in 1979. We use these values in our estimates. All are now generally recognized as important resources that are primarily available to low-income households, and the Census Bureau now includes them as resources in its Supplemental Poverty Measure (Garner and Short 2012). Larrimore et al. (2015) use this measure in their analysis. Because it both adds government in-kind transfers and tax credits (e.g., the EITC) but subtracts taxes, the level of median income of this measure could be higher or lower than the Census Bureau's median (pre-tax, post-cash transfer) income values as well as median market income alone. Its trends will depend on the relative growth of net government transfers to market income.

We discuss the details of how we extend these tax and in-kind series back to 1967 in the online appendix. Our decennial Census series does not provide a measure of in-kind transfers in 1959 or in any other Census year. This is not a problem for the years in which we have ASEC-CPS values of these transfers. But, in our analysis, we effectively assume that there were no federal in-kind transfer programs in 1959 with the exception of housing subsidies and ESI, which we impute.[15]

Household Size-Adjusted Post-Tax Post-Transfer Plus In-Kind Transfer Income (Including Medicare, Medicaid, and ESI) of Persons

The seventh measure is the *household size-adjusted post-tax, post-transfer income plus in-kind transfers (including the market values of Medicare, Medicaid and ESI) of the median person*. Burkhauser et al. (2012b) were the first to use the market value of health insurance in a disposable income measure in order to show the growing importance of access to health insurance for explaining differences between survey- and tax record–based analyses of income and its distribution. The Congressional Budget Office (CBO), in 2012, was the first government agency to include the market values of both government- and employer-sponsored health insurance (ESI) in their measure of income (CBO, 2013). Larrimore et al. (2015) use this same fuller measure of income in an appendix table for the period 1979–2012.[16] Lyons (2015)—as well as Burkhauser, Larrimore, and Lyons (2017)—show its importance for estimating the income of working age people with disabilities.

Here we use it to measure after-tax income (including the market values of Medicare, Medicaid, ESI, and other in-kind transfers) and its distribution across American households back to 1959—just before the major expansions of government tax and transfer programs associated with the New Frontier and Great Society programs of the 1960s.[17] Due to the rapid growth in government-provided health insurance and ESI, this upper bound value of the disposable income of the median American will be greater than all other measures in levels and trends, particularly in the bottom half of the income distribution where receipt of government-provided insurance sources is concentrated.

In constructing this measure, we note that in-kind benefits in the form of health insurance, like all other in-kind benefits, have value to individuals—otherwise government actors would have a strong incentive to replace Medicare and Medicaid benefits with cash transfer programs or lower taxes, and employers would have an incentive to replace ESI with higher wages. Measures that exclude Medicare, Medicaid, and ESI as resources undervalue their worth by effectively placing a zero value on this form of health insurance. This exclusion understates not only the level of household resources but also their trend, as the costs of Medicare, Medicaid, and ESI have substantially increased in real terms and as a share of all government transfers to households.

Following the approach of Armour et al. (2014), Burkhauser et al. (2012b), and the CBO (2012, 2013), we include the market value of Medicare, Medicaid, and ESI in this measure of income back to 1979 based on the Census Bureau's imputed value of health insurance, although we use the full market value rather than just its fungible value.

For government-subsidized health insurance (Medicare and Medicaid), the Census Bureau determines, by state and risk class back to 1979, the average government cost of providing Medicare and Medicaid to those persons reporting that they have this insurance. The two risk classes for Medicare are aged and disabled. The four risk classes for Medicaid are aged, blind and disabled, nondisabled children (younger than 21), and nondisabled adults (21–64).[18] Thus, the imputed average cost of government-provided health insurance varies by state and by the government insurance pool through which beneficiaries access it.

In determining the values of Medicare and Medicaid for individuals who qualify for both programs (dual eligible), we follow the Census Bureau's approach and estimate the value of their health insurance as the combined cost of insurance from each program. This assumes that the total value of the insurance that dual-eligible individuals receive is not only greater to them than the value for those insured under only one of these programs, but is greater by the average cost of the other program. This may overstate this value to the degree that there is overlap in coverage. However, it might understate it to the degree that dual-eligible individuals have higher than average medical expenses relative to those who are only covered by one program. Therefore, this value still may be less than the cost dual-eligible individuals would incur if they purchased equivalent insurance in the market.[19]

Prior to 1979, the ASEC-CPS contains no information on the value of health insurance benefits and no direct information on coverage of health insurance from any source. Thus, to calculate income under this definition we must impute both receipt and market value of insurance for Medicare, Medicaid, and ESI. See the online appendix for details on this procedure. The Census Bureau ceased reporting the market values of Medicare and Medicaid coverage after the 2014 survey. Therefore, these sources are calculated for the income years 2014–2016 based on methodology published by the Census Bureau.

TRENDS IN MEDIAN INCOME, 1959–2016

The earliest starting point for ASEC-CPS-based income measures that include both in-kind transfers and taxes is 1979, since this is the first year that the Census Bureau provides measures of in-kind transfers. As can be seen in Figure 4.1, using our estimates of in-kind transfers and taxes allows us to extend all seven of our income series back to 1967 using ASEC-CPS data and to 1959 using decennial Census data. It reports trends for these seven measures of real median income, normalized to 100 percent in 1979.[20]

The trends found during 1979–2007 are well known in the literature and replicate those found by Burkhauser et al. (2012b), Armour et al. (2014), and

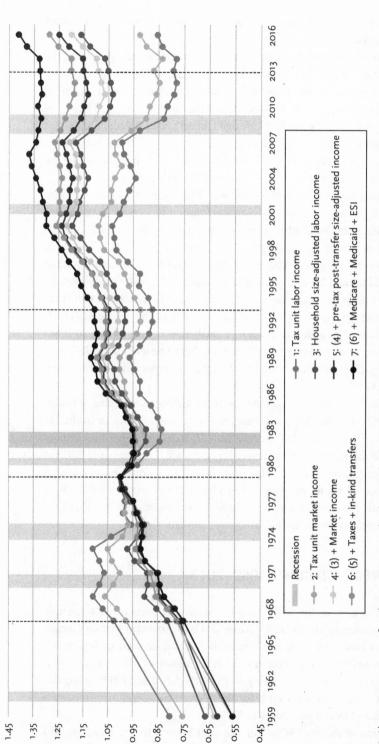

Figure 4.1 Alternative measures of median income normalized to 1979 levels (1959–2016). Median income trends normalized to one in 1979 with National Bureau of Economic Research (NBER) recession dates in gray. In keeping with previous work (Armour et al., 2014; Burkhauser et al., 2012b; Larrimore et al., 2015), "Series 1: Tax Unit Labor Income" measures the size-unadjusted labor income of tax units. Series 2 adds market income. In series 3–7, we adjust for persons in the household using the square-root of household size. Vertical dashed lines signify breaks in the data due to start of our use of Annual Social and Economic Supplement to the Current Population Survey (ASEC-CPS) data with our new imputations in 1967, start of standard ASEC-CPS data in 1979, and assumption that all changes in income between 1992 and 1993 and between 2013 and 2014 were due to the change in CPS survey methods with prior years adjusted accordingly.

Authors' calculations using the ASEC-CPS, National Health Expenditures Accounts (NHEA), White House Budget Historical Tables, Statistical Abstracts of the US, Census Bureau population estimates, US Department of Agriculture Supplemental Nutrition Assistance Program (SNAP) Data Tables and Child Nutrition Tables, US Bureau of Labor Statistics Consumer Price Index for Medical Care in US City Average, Center for Medicare and Medicaid Services Medicare Enrollment Data, Medicaid and CHIP Payment and Access Commission (MACPAC) Medicaid Enrollment Data, Kramer (1988), Collinson et al. (2016), Hoynes et al. (2016). Taxes calculated using National Bureau of Economic Research (NBER) TaxSim

Larrimore et al. (2015) and extends them to 2016 for all measures. We denote NBER-defined business cycles by shading recession years. Note that, although the total population we include in each of our seven trend lines is the same, the median person in that population will not be the same person because the income sources and sharing unit we use to capture income differ.[21]

There are a number of similarities in the trends of five of our seven measures of income. The median values of the five income measures that use the household as their sharing unit and the person as their unit of analysis are greater at the ending peaks of the 1980s and the 1990s business cycles than at their starting peaks. During both cycles, median income falls from its pre-recession high to a trough (with the year varying by measure). However, in both cycles, we find that strong post-recession growth increases median income well above its initial pre-recession business cycle high.

This is not the case for growth in the *labor earnings of the median tax unit*. The median value of this measure is noticeably lower at the end of the 1980s business cycle than at the beginning. Although it recovers somewhat from its 1984 trough, it remains below its 1979 high in 1989. During the 1990s cycle, post-recession growth is strong enough to lift it above its pre-recession high, but it only manages to return to just above its 1979 pre-recession high in 2000, well below the other five household size-adjusted measures of income in 2000. Those focusing on the growth in the labor earnings of the median tax units will greatly understate the actual increase in labor earnings available to the median American during this period because that median American lives in a household that may contain more than one tax unit. The same is true for using growth in the labor earnings of the median worker to make inferences about the labor earnings available to the median American.

As can also be seen in Figure 4.1, growth in *the market income of the median tax unit* is higher than the growth in the labor income of the median tax unit in all years. Nevertheless, it is still substantially below the median income of the five measures that use the household as their sharing unit and the person as their unit of analysis.

These five measures all take into consideration that workers live in households, not in tax units or by themselves, and that these household members share their individual labor earnings. Some also include other sources of market income as well as the net returns of government taxes and transfers. All show substantially higher growth in the resources available to the median American over these first two post-1979 business cycles than do either the labor earnings or market income of the median tax unit.

The inconsistency of tax unit measures vis-à-vis the other five measures continues during the 2000–2007 business cycle. Both tax unit measures dramatically fall from 2000 to 2004. Although they then increase, both are substantially below their 2000 value by the end of the business cycle in 2007. Both measures then fall precipitously during the Great Recession and do not begin increasing until 2013. Since then, both have slowly recovered, but by 2016 they were still well below their value at the start the current business cycle and even further below their 2000 business cycle peaks.

However, both these measures fail to recognize the social insurance value of living in a household—which is the pooling of income over all household members. Thus, sharp reductions in the income (labor earnings or other forms of market income) from one tax unit in a household are softened by the continued income from its other tax units. At the same time, the number of people living in each household falls during this period, so fewer people are sharing household resources. These are important distinctions.

Although our preferred measure of median labor earnings, *the household size-adjusted labor earnings of the median person*, also falls at the start of the 2000 business cycle, during the recovery years it increases and almost reaches its 2000 level by 2007. This measure then falls precipitously during the Great Recession and does not begin increasing until 2012. It then increases and is closer to its 2007 peak level by 2016 than is the flawed labor earnings of the median tax unit measure. More important, the pooling of labor earnings in households reduces the depth of the drop in median income in the years between the business cycle's pre-recession and post-recession peaks.

The *household size-adjusted market income of the median person* follows a very similar path within business cycles. Growth by the end of the 2000–2007 cycle was not enough to raise median market income above its level in 2000. However, because nonwage market income has grown faster at the median during the current cycle, this measure of median income almost reaches its 2007 pre–Great Recession peak by 2016 and experiences a less severe drop in the years between 2000 and 2016.

The *household size-adjusted pre-tax, post-transfer income of the median person*, as used by the Census Bureau—which adds cash transfers to market income—closely follows the market income trends. Growth by the end of the 2000–2007 business cycle was not quite enough to raise it to its level in 2000, but government transfers offset market income declines during the cycle, so its interim-year declines were smaller. Because government transfers have grown faster than market income during the current cycle, this measure of median income finally exceeded its pre–Great Recession high by 2016, greatly offsetting market income declines in the interim years. What is less clear is the degree to which this observed growth in net government transfers for the median American had negative effects on their employment and hence on measures of labor and market income in the previous series.[22]

The measure *household size-adjusted post-tax, post-transfer income (including some in-kind transfers) of the median person*—which is recommended by the OECD and is used by most European Union members—is also our preferred lower bound measure of median total income because it more fully takes into consideration both government taxes and transfers. Doing so shows how effective government tax and transfer policy has been in increasing the median income of Americans and in offsetting the decline in their market income during both the 2000–2007 business cycle and the present cycle. Although the growth of median income during the first two cycles is much greater than during the last two, this fuller measure of income shows growth over all four business cycles since 1979. More important, it shows that government tax and transfer policies since 2000 have largely offset the interim-year declines in median market income during this period.

The measure *household size-adjusted post-tax, post-transfer income plus in-kind transfers (including the insurance value of Medicare, Medicaid, and ESI) of the median person*, our upper bound measure of disposable income, is somewhat controversial because it adds the market value of health insurance provided by the government (i.e., Medicare and Medicaid) as well as by employers (ESI) to the previous measure. Because of the rapid growth in the value of health insurance provided by the government and employers since the mid-1980s, this measure's median income trends are considerably greater than all the other median income trends shown in Figure 4.1 through 2006. Median values then fall somewhat until 2009 and are flat through 2014, but they exceed the previous high in 2015 and 2016.[23]

But how does our understanding of these trends from 1979 to 2016 change once we are able trace our seven measure of median income back to 1959?

The labor earnings of the median tax unit rose substantially between the peak years of the 1959–1969 business cycle. However, 1969 would prove to be the second highest yearly value for this measure of income. Its business-cycle–peak year 1973 only barely exceeded its 1969 peak, and it then dropped substantially over the late 1970s and 1980s business cycles. While it did rise over the 1990s business cycle, returning to its 1979 level in 2000, it then fell over the 2000–2007 business cycle and remained far below its 2007 peak in 2016, nine years later.

The market income of the median tax unit also rose substantially between the peak years of the 1959–1969 business cycle. However, this peak was not surpassed until the final growth years of the 1990s business cycle before falling substantially over the 2000–2007 business cycle, and it remained far below its 2007 peak in 2016. Hence, the secular decline in both the labor earnings and market income of the median tax unit found in studies beginning in 1979, and therefore first observed over the two peak years of the 1980s business cycle, was in fact an extension of a secular decline in both these measures beginning in 1969.

However, once we look at labor earnings and market income within a household sharing unit and focus on the household size-adjusted income of the median person, our findings are more consistent with those based on our other three measures of income using a household sharing unit and the person as the unit of analysis. All five measures increase over the 1959–1969 business cycle. But unlike the two measures using the tax unit as sharing unit and unit of analysis, all five measures increase over the two business cycles of the 1970s as well.

However, in contrast to subsequent business cycles, differences in trends over these three business cycles are much smaller across these five measures, especially compared to the trend since 1999, as discussed earlier.

Figure 4.1 shows that a measure of income that focuses solely on either the labor earnings or market income of tax units as a measure of the resources available to the median American from 1959 to 2016 will dramatically understate the importance of labor earnings and market income to the median American's household size-adjusted income. Rather than trending downward since their 1969 peak when measured at the tax unit level, labor earnings and market income sources increased over every business cycle from 1959 through 2000. Since then, they declined slightly over the 2000–2007 business cycle, fell precipitously during the Great Recession and its aftermath, and still had not reached their 2007 levels by 2016. But this is a far more optimistic story than the one told by those who focus on the labor earnings or market income of tax units since 1959.

Figure 4.1 also shows that the growth in the redistribution of market income via government tax and transfer policies dating back to the Great Society has not only mitigated the cyclical decline in the median American's household size-adjusted market income during recessions but has, more importantly, mitigated the secular stagnation of median labor and market income since 2000.

TRENDS IN THE DISTRIBUTION OF INCOME

The importance of taxes and transfers over this entire period can be seen in more detail in Table 4.1. Row 1 (Panel A) reports cumulative median income growth, controlling for inflation (CPI-U-RS), for the entire period of our data from 1959 through 2016 for each of our income definitions based on values underlying Figure 4.1.

In the remaining rows, it shows how cumulative income growth has varied over the entire income distribution. It does so by estimating cumulative mean income growth for each quintile and the top 5 percent for each of our income definitions. (As discussed in note 6 data limitations in the public-use version of the ASEC-CPS prevent us from capturing the top 1 percent.) However, since 2016 is not a peak year in a business cycle, and thus the interpretation for income growth ending in that non-peak year also contains cyclical effects (the cyclical effects of the Great Recession and its aftermath between 2007 and 2016), we will primarily focus on trends in income growth between business cycle peak years 1959 through 2007. Those values are reported in Table 4.1 (Panel B). As discussed earlier in the text and in note 21, the quintile composition is not constant across measures: that is, persons may switch quintiles for different measures of income.

Table 4.1 Income growth for 1959–2016 and 1959–2007 using alternative measures of income by quintiles

| | Labor income of tax units (1) | Market income of tax units (2) | Household size-adjusted labor income of persons (3) | Household size-adjusted market income of persons (4) | Household size-adjusted post-transfer | | |
					Pre-tax income of persons (5)	Post-tax income + in-kind income of persons (6)	Post-tax income + in-kind income + Medicare + Medicaid + ESI of persons (7)
Panel A:							
Median	6.4%	23.0%	75.1%	91.3%	103.1%	130.4%	153.7%
Q1	−52.7%	−75.5%	−61.3%	18.0%	109.0%	183.8%	262.0%
Q2	−4.7%	20.7%	35.5%	63.3%	88.5%	119.7%	157.6%
Q3	8.6%	24.3%	75.7%	91.9%	103.8%	130.4%	154.5%
Q4	41.6%	54.0%	103.4%	116.2%	120.4%	145.1%	162.2%
Q5	110.6%	121.2%	149.8%	160.4%	157.2%	164.7%	175.7%
Top 5%	146.7%	155.0%	190.6%	193.4%	184.9%	179.3%	186.8%
Panel B:							
Median	24.0%	36.2%	78.2%	92.4%	100.8%	126.4%	141.2%
Q1	−75.7%	−20.4%	−30.9%	34.9%	108.9%	188.1%	246.8%
Q2	21.0%	47.9%	45.7%	68.2%	85.3%	116.5%	144.9%
Q3	28.5%	37.1%	78.0%	93.4%	101.0%	126.7%	141.9%
Q4	56.4%	63.7%	99.5%	113.5%	115.4%	140.0%	149.1%
Q5	108.5%	119.2%	135.5%	148.0%	144.0%	154.0%	155.7%
Top 5%	134.5%	142.2%	168.6%	173.9%	164.9%	165.4%	163.5%

Note: Panel A: 1959–2016, Panel B: 1959–2007.

Source: Authors' calculations using the Annual Social and Economic Supplement to the Current Population Survey (ASEC-CPS), National Health Expenditures Accounts (NHEA), White House Budget Historical Tables, Statistical Abstracts of the US, Census Bureau population estimates, US Department of Agriculture Supplemental Nutrition Assistance Program (SNAP) Data Tables and Child Nutrition Tables, Bureau of Labor Statistics Consumer Price Index for Medical Care in US City Average, Centers for Medicare and Medicaid (CMI) Medicare Enrollment Data, Medicaid and CHIP Payment and Access Commission (MACPAC) Medicaid Enrollment Data, Kramer (1988), Collinson et al. (2016), Hoynes et al. (2016). Taxes calculated using the National Bureau of Economic Research's TaxSim.

As was the case in Figure 4.1, the first two columns in Table 4.1 present the growth in labor earnings and market income of tax units. The remaining five columns use the household as the sharing unit and the person as the unit of analysis.

Growth in the first two columns in Table 4.1 (Panel A) is consistent with growth estimates by Piketty and Saez (2003), Atkinson et al. (2011), and others who focus on tax units without adjusting for the number of persons in those tax units. When focusing solely on either labor earnings or market income of tax units in Panel A, the rich get richer, the poor get poorer, and median income has been mostly stagnant since 1959. Mean market income among the top 5 percent of tax units increased by 155.0 percent (1.66 percent annual rate) between 1959 and 2016 while declining by 75.5 percent (2.43 percent annual decrease) for those in the bottom quintile and increasing by only 24.3 percent (0.38 percent annual increase) for those in the middle quintile. Note that this mean value of the middle quintile is close to the 23.0 percent growth (0.36 percent annual growth) in the median value from the entire distribution of market incomes in the second-column of Panel A that we also use in showing trends in middle-class income in Figure 4.1.

Part of the slow growth in both the labor earnings of tax units and the market income of tax units captured at the median and more generally for the mean value of each of the bottom four quintiles of those measures of income is the result of comparing 1959 with 2016. The former is a peak year while the latter is the most recent year of our data, but one in which this part of the income distribution (using these two measures of income) is still recovering from the Great Recession. In contrast, the top income quintile (and the top 5 percent) had fully recovered from the Great Recession by 2016 and the mean value of these two measures of income exceeded their mean values in 2007.

Hence, growth rates for all but the top quintile are higher when peak year 1959 is compared with peak year 2007, as can be seen in Panel B. But even when we control for this difference in the timing of recovery with the current business cycle and focus on 1959–2007, the differences in growth in these two measures of income are still dramatic across the distribution. The lowest quintile has negative growth in market income, while the growth in the middle quintile is quite small over this 48-year period. The poorest got poorer, the growth of the middle three quintiles of the income distribution is dramatically lower than the top quintile and the rich, captured here as the top 5 percent.

But as Table 4.1 also shows, when we broaden our measure of income across the remaining columns in Panels A and B to those used in the standard survey-based income and income inequality literatures, the growth in median income and in the mean value of the bottom four quintiles dramatically increases relative to the top quintile.

Growth in median market income between 1959–2007 increases from 36.2 percent (column 2) in Panel B (the stagnation of the middle class) to 92.4 percent (column 4) when we expand our sharing unit to the household from the tax unit, make the unit of analysis the person rather than the tax unit, and adjust our sharing unit's income to account for the number of people in the household. All the other columns of Panel B show the result of adding additional sources of income. Median income growth increases to 100.8 percent when other cash income, including government transfers, are added to market income (column 5). Median income growth increases to 126.4 percent in our lower bound measure of disposable income (column 6) when we subtract taxes and add income from in-kind transfers (but not the values of Medicare, Medicaid, and ESI). Finally, median income growth increases to 141.2 percent in our upper bound measure of disposable income when we add the market values of Medicare, Medicaid, and ESI (column 7).

For the bottom quintile, income growth reverses from a decrease of −20.4 percent to an increase of 34.9 percent when we more properly capture market income using our preferred household sized-adjusted income of persons measure. It jumps to 108.9 percent when looking at pre-tax post-transfer income—an increase greater than that found in the second and third quintiles. When taxes and in-kind transfers (but not Medicare, Medicaid, or ESI) are included, income growth in the bottom quintile increases to 188.1 percent—an increase greater than that found in all other quintiles and the top 5 percent. The growth rate rises to 246.8 percent when we add the market values of Medicare, Medicaid, and ESI, far greater than the increases found in all the other quintiles as well as in the top 5 percent. While this last comparison is controversial since it assigns the full market values of Medicare and Medicaid as well as ESI to income, even when we effectively assign a value of zero to this major in-kind transfer in our lower bound measure of median disposable income in column 6, growth in the bottom quintile from 1959 to 2007 was greater than for all other quintiles.

Furthermore, when using this lower bound disposable income measure, we can see the importance of government taxes and transfers in redistributing market income gains across the income distribution. While growth in the mean value of the income of the top 5 percent (165.4 percent) was higher than growth in the mean value of four of the five quintiles, mean income in all five more than doubled over this period. Notably, the bottom quintile had the largest increase in average income, albeit off a much lower base level. Unlike our measures of labor earnings and market income of tax units, the median income and the mean income in all five quintiles as well as the top 5 percent are greater in 2016 than they were in 2007. Hence, even using the lower bound measure of disposable income, not only did the rich get considerably richer between 1959 and 2016, but so did the rest of the population.

Gini Coefficient Trends

The single most common scalar measure of income inequality is the Gini coefficient. Using our seven measures of income in Table 4.2, we report Gini values for peak years of all business cycles over the period 1959–2007 as well as for the most recent year of our data, 2016. For all business cycle peak years and for 2016, Gini values are highest (most unequal) when we use our most restrictive income definitions—labor earnings or market income—and a tax unit as both our sharing unit and our unit of analysis; Gini values fall as we increasingly take into account government taxes and transfers.

This is reassuring since one of the goals of government tax and transfer policy is to shift market income from Americans living in higher income households to Americans living in lower income households, and this occurred in all years. But what our new dataset now shows is how Gini value trends have changed across each of these income measures since 1959. Focusing solely on the market income of tax units or the household size-adjusted market income of persons, Gini values increase over the period from 1959 to 1979: 0.488 to 0.495 and 0.411 to 0.419, respectively. However, the reverse is the case when government in-cash transfers are taken into account. Gini values decline from 0.392 to 0.366. Gini values decline even more when using our preferred lower and upper bound measures of disposable income, which fell from 0.362 to 0.304 and 0.350 to 0.288, respectively. Since 1979, income inequality has increased over all business cycle peak-to-peak years regardless of how we measure income. However, it is also the case that, over the entire period from 1959 to 2007, income inequality has risen less the fuller the measure of income chosen. As discussed previously, the current business cycle began in 2007 and is not yet complete since median income continued to grow from its business cycle trough up through 2016, our last year of data. Over the period 2007 through 2016, income inequality has also grown but it is still the case that this growth is slowest in our fuller measures of income.

Our results with respect to the distribution of income in these last three sections are largely consistent with the findings of Moffitt (2015) and Fox et al. (2015). Moffitt (2015) focuses on government spending on both in-cash and in-kind welfare programs. He found significant growth in the early 1970s, slow growth in the late 1970s to the mid-1980s, and higher growth from the late 1980s onward. Fox et al. (2015) compare US poverty rates back to 1967 using income concepts from the Supplemental Poverty Measure (SPM) (which uses a measure of income similar to our lower bound disposable income measure of income), and comparing this measure to the Official Poverty Measure that excludes in-kind transfers. Our findings show that these are roughly the periods during which in-kind transfers including Medicare, Medicaid, and ESI (which neither Moffitt [2015] nor Fox et al. [2015] include in their analyses) largely mitigated income inequality in market income.

Table 4.2 Gini coefficients for business cycle peaks (1959–2007) and 2016

	Labor income of tax units (1)	Market income of tax units (2)	Household size-adjusted labor income of persons (3)	Household size-adjusted market income of persons (4)	Pre-tax income of persons (5)	Pre-tax income + in-kind income of persons (6)	Pre-tax income + in-kind income + Medicare + Medicaid + ESI of persons (7)
							Household size-adjusted post-transfer
1959	0.507	0.488	0.423	0.411	0.392	0.362	0.350
1969	0.496	0.479	0.409	0.401	0.363	0.319	0.308
1973	0.519	0.498	0.430	0.419	0.366	0.320	0.306
1979	0.532	0.495	0.443	0.419	0.366	0.304	0.288
1989	0.566	0.523	0.479	0.451	0.401	0.346	0.326
2000	0.595	0.558	0.505	0.480	0.436	0.369	0.342
2007	0.603	0.568	0.509	0.485	0.439	0.376	0.342
2016	0.635	0.594	0.532	0.502	0.448	0.384	0.341

Note: Gini values are for all business cycle peaks and the final year of the Obama administration.

Source: Authors' calculations using the March Annual Social and Economic Supplement to the Current Population Survey (ASEC-CPS), National Health Expenditures Accounts (NHEA), White House Budget Historical Tables, Statistical Abstracts of the United States, Census Bureau population estimates, US Department of Agriculture Supplemental Nutrition Assistance Program (SNAP) Data Tables and Child Nutrition Tables, Bureau of Labor Statistics Consumer Price Index for Medical Care in US City Average, Centers for Medicare and Medicaid (CMI) Medicare Enrollment Data, Medicaid and CHIP Payment and Access Commission (MACPAC) Medicaid Enrollment Data, Kramer (1988), Collinson et al. (2016), Hoynes et al. (2016). Taxes calculated using NBER TaxSim.

MEAN (PER CAPITA GDP) AND MEDIAN INCOME GROWTH SINCE 1959

A new literature attempts to capture the long-term relationship between aggregate measures of growth using National Accounts data (e.g., per capita gross domestic product [GDP/N]) and the real income of the median person (median real GDP). This literature argues that median real GDP is a more appropriate measure of the resources available to the average person than is a measure of mean income like GDP/N that can rise even when most of the income growth accrues to the top end of the distribution. While median real GDP may be conceptually appropriate, operationally it is not possible to directly capture median real GDP using National Accounts data alone. To solve this problem, researchers have turned to either survey or administrative tax record data or some combination of the two to capture trends in median income. But it is critical that the sources of income used in the National Accounts match those used in the survey or administrative tax record data or "like is not compared to like" (see Nolan, Roser, and Thewissen, 2018, for a review of this literature).[24] Piketty, Saez, and Zucman (2018) create the first comprehensive "distributional national accounts" by starting with tax return microdata, adding in income sources covered in survey data such as in-kind transfers, and distributing items in the national accounts that are not included in microdata across tax units. By including these sources of income, they attempt to create estimates that are consistent with macroeconomic growth, and they find a dramatic rise in income inequality consistent with their prior work using the market income of tax units.

Gordon (2016: table 18.4) uses such a measure of median income derived from survey data in his estimates of median real GDP from 1975 to 2012. This measure is based on CBO estimates using ASEC-CPS data statistically matched to income from tax record data. But while the CBO has been including the market value of Medicare and Medicaid in its measures of income since 2012, these values are not included in previous years. More problematic, for earlier years, Gordon estimates median real GDP using top income data from the World Top Income Database (Alvaredo et al., n. d.). However, these data contain information on the taxable market income of the median tax unit as it comes from the series developed by Piketty and Saez (2003).

In Figure 4.2 we use our new survey-based data set to show the problem of comparing trends in real GDP/N to trends in real market income of the median tax unit. We first compare growth in GDP/N from 1959 to 2016 taken from the Bureau of Economic Analysis to growth in the real market income of the median tax unit based on the same ASEC-CPS and decennial Census data that underlie the values reported for this income measure in Figure 4.1.[25]

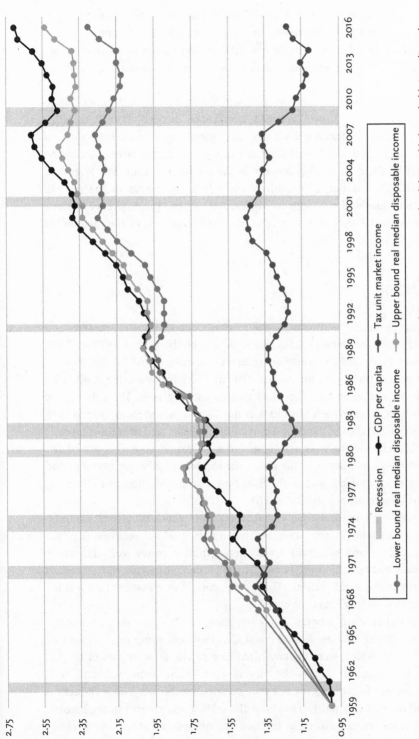

Figure 4.2 Trends in real gross domestic product (GDP) per capita, real taxable market income of the median tax unit, and real disposable household size-adjusted income (lower and upper bound) of the median person normalized to 1959. Income series reported here are the same as in Figure 4.1 except with values normalized to income year 1959.

Market income of the median tax unit and the upper and lower bound household size-adjusted disposable income of the median person are from authors' calculations using Annual Social and Economic Supplement to the Current Population Survey (ASEC-CPS) and the 1960 decennial Census.

Income per capita from the Bureau of Economic Analysis NIPA table 7.1. All series adjusted using Consumer Price Index Research Series (CPI-U-RS).

We normalize these two trends to 1.00 in 1959 to show differences in growth. Between 1959 and 1969, the market income of the median tax unit increased at approximately the same rate as real GDP/N. But, since then, GDP/N has increased substantially while the market income of the median tax unit has trended downward.

This picture changes when we compare it to our lower and upper bound measures of the median American's disposable income—household size-adjusted disposable income excluding and including the market values of Medicare, Medicaid, and ESI of persons—in Figure 4.1, measures more in line with GDP/N than the market income of the median tax unit. While growth in real GDP/N has outpaced both of these fuller measures of the median American's household size-adjusted disposable income, the difference is much less than when GDP/N is compared to the market income of the median tax unit, especially since 1973.

CONCLUSION

Using Census Bureau estimates of the market value of in-kind transfers and Current Population Survey (ASEC-CPS) data over the period 1979 to 2007, Burkhauser et al. (2012b) construct measures of income and its distribution. Here we extend their work forward to 2016 and back to 1967 using ASEC-CPS data, and we couple it with decennial Census data for 1959. With this newly linked dataset, we provide a fresh look at the 20-year period from 1959 to 1979 and show that the choice of income sources, sharing unit, and the unit of analysis substantially change our understanding of how the American middle class fared both absolutely and relative to the rest of the income distribution over a period stretching from near the end of the Eisenhower administration in 1959 to the end of the Obama administration in 2016.

Focusing solely on the market income of tax units, which is the most common measure of income in the tax-based income inequality literature (e.g. see Atkinson, Piketty, and Saez, 2011, for a review of this literature), we find that over the business cycle of 1959–1969 cumulative real market income of the median tax unit rose substantially and the Gini coefficient of this measure of income fell as a growing economy "lifted all boats."

This result is more pronounced when using our broader measures of income. The launch of New Frontier and Great Society programs during this business cycle, which were heavily tilted toward the bottom part of the income distribution, as well as the maturing of Social Security, led to even larger increases for the bottom of the income distribution and a reduction of overall income inequality. However, since 1969, the growth in the median market income of tax units has trended flat or downward. Researchers focusing on this narrow measure of economic well-being since 1969 will find that the rich got richer, the poor got poorer, and the income of the middle class stagnated.

Consistent with accepted standards in the survey-based literature this dismal picture dramatically changes when we broaden our measure of income to include government taxes and transfers, expand our sharing unit to include all members of the household, make the person our unit of analysis, and adjust household income to account for the number of persons in the household. After doing so, we show that, between 1969 and 1979, rather than declining, income increased for the median American and Gini coefficients continued to fall.

Thus by extending our survey-based dataset back to the business cycle peak year 1959 and using it as the starting point for our study of median income and income inequality we are able to demonstrate that the stagnation of the market income of the median tax unit effectively began in 1969, as did the increase in Gini coefficients for that measure of income.

However, we also show that government tax and transfer policies have transformed a 23.0 percent cumulative increase (0.36 percent annual rate) in the market income of the median tax unit between 1959 and 2016 into a lower bound 130.4 percent or an upper bound 153.7 percent increase (1.47 and 1.65 percent annual rate, respectively) when we more fully account for taxes and transfers and use the proper sharing unit and unit of analysis. Doing so, we show that, while over this period the rich got substantially richer, so did poor and middle-class Americans.

Measures of median income and income inequality that exclude the market value of in-kind transfers will substantially understate the success of government policies in offsetting the stagnation in median market income and the rise in market income inequality since 1969.

NOTES

1. The views in this chapter reflect those of the authors and should not be attributed to the Joint Committee on Taxation, the Council of Economic Advisers, or their staffs. Elwell's work on this research was funded by the Lynde and Harry Bradley Foundation while he was a graduate student at Cornell University.

2. We define a business cycle peak year as the peak in our median market income of tax unit series since it is capturing market income. These years usually correspond to the last full year of macroeconomic growth as defined by the NBER and identified in our figures but are the second to last full year of macroeconomic growth before the recessions of early 1990s and 2000s. This measure is similar to that used by Armour, Burkhauser, and Larrimore (2014) and Daly and Valletta (2006). In all cases, our findings are not sensitive to using the last full year before a recession.

3. We use the Consumer Price Index Research Series (CPI-U-RS) (Stewart and Reed, 1999) for all estimates related to ASEC-CPS data. We do so because this is the standard deflator used in the income inequality literature.

4. We produce the market value of Medicare/Medicaid for 1967–1978. These values are consistent with those produced by the Census Bureau thereafter. We created a similar market value of employer-provided health insurance series for 1959 and from 1967–1978. See the online appendix for additional details on all these health insurance series.

5. "Middle class" is a term of art that potentially has many definitions. Here we focus only on two: the median of the total US population and the mean of its middle quintile. Other measures are possible. Our main results based on our coupled ASEC-CPS and Census data are not sensitive to using the mean value of the middle quintile.

6. We use the top 5 percent throughout this chapter rather than the top 1 percent used in the tax record–based income inequality literature due to undercoverage of top incomes in the public use ASEC-CPS data, a problem it shares with all other survey-based datasets. See Burkhauser et al. (2012a), which uses the restricted access ASEC-CPS, for more details.

7. The "gold standard" Haig-Simon income definition measures yearly income of an individual as equal to their consumption plus their net change in wealth. This standard is used by both the Canberra Group (2011) and the OECD (d'Ercole and Forster, 2012) in their conceptualization of income. Poor data on consumption generally constrains researchers from operationalizing this definition. A more comprehensive measure of income that includes taxes and in-kind transfers comes closer to meeting this standard, however, than does the market value of tax units measure based on tax record data alone. See Larrimore, Burkhauser, Auten, and Armour (2019).

8. See Semega, Fontenot, and Kollar (2017) for income year 2016, the last year of data used in this chapter.

9. Size-adjusted household income accounts for economies of scale in household consumption by dividing household income by the square root of household size. This income measure is commonly used in US and cross-national studies of inequality (see, e.g., Gottschalk and Smeeding, 1997; Atkinson and Brandolini, 2001; Burkhauser et al., 2011), as well as by the OECD in its official measures of income inequality and poverty (d'Ercole and Förster, 2012). It also closely matches the adjustments for household size implied by the Census Bureau's poverty thresholds (Ruggles, 1990). This measure assumes that income is shared equally among all household members, so each member receives the same amount for personal consumption.

10. The International Expert Group on Household Economic Statistics (Canberra Group) was convened as an initiative of the Australian Bureau of Statistics under the auspices of the United Nations Statistical Commission. Its report was largely adopted as the standard for measuring household income by the International Conference of Labour Statisticians. In 2011, the United Nations Economic Commission for Europe provided an updated reference outlining its latest standards and recommendations.

11. We extend our ASEC-CPS series back to 1967 rather than to 1965 or earlier even though ASEC-CPS data does exist for these years. We do so because sample sizes are smaller and because income questions in these years are considerably less detailed. This makes it more difficult to establish income categories consistent with those beginning in 1967.

12. We do so since the CPI-U-RS is the standard deflator used in the survey-based income inequality literature. However, we test the sensitivity of our results using the Personal Consumption Expenditures (PCE) price index that is a chain-type (or Tornqvist) price index, so it does not systematically over-state inflation, as do the CPI-U and its variations, which are Laspeyres indices. Again, we use this price index rather than the Chained-CPI-U, which only begins in 2000, because it has been available since 1947. See Appendix Figure 4.1A at the end of this chapter, which shows that, though this deflator slightly increases real growth in median income, our main findings are not sensitive to this deflator choice.

13. Online appendix can be found at https://www.nber.org/papers/w26439.

14. There are a substantial number of individuals who report large negative farm income values, especially in earlier years when a larger share of workers were self-employed farmers. These individuals to some degree cause the mean values to be low in the lowest quintile and our estimates of growth in mean income in this quintile to be volatile. But this is not the case for the rest of the distribution. When we restrict farm incomes to be non-negative, we generate nearly identical results outside of the lowest quintile. However, the results for the bottom quintile remain fairly volatile. This is largely due to a much larger number of non-working tax units in this quintile that results in a low base level of income, such that even small or moderate income variation produce large percentage changes.

15. This is only approximately correct. While the Food Stamp Act of 1964 launched the food stamps program, there was a pilot program from 1961–1964. Housing benefits began with the Housing Act of 1937, but benefits were small prior to the Department of Housing and Urban Development Act of 1965. For instance, total outlays were $80 million in 1959, rose to $327 million in 1966, and to more than $1 billion by 1970 in 2016 dollars (see Office of Management and Budget [OMB], 2016). Likewise, the school lunch program began in 1946 and was expanded and modified several times in the 1960s. The National School Lunch Program (NSLP) is somewhat larger, with expenditures of $236 million in 1960 and $591 million in 1970 (United States Department of Agriculture [USDA], 2013). The relatively small size of the benefits in these programs suggests attempting to estimate their exact value in 1959 would only minimally affect our estimates. A predecessor program to Medicare/Medicaid (Kerr-Mills) began in 1961, but there were otherwise no Medicare or Medicaid benefits in 1959. By 1967, the first year for which

we have ASEC-CPS estimates, the programs' combined expenditures were more than $20 billion in 2016 dollars.

16. A small academic literature has begun to include the market value of health insurance in its measures of income. See Burtless and Svaton, 2010; Burkhauser, Larrimore, and Simon, 2013; Burtless and Milusheva, 2013; CBO, 2013; Sommers and Oellerich, 2013; Armour, Burkhauser, and Larrimore, 2014; and Kaestner and Lubotsky, 2016). But because this literature has been dependent on Census Bureau measures of the market value of health insurance, its analyses only go back to 1979.

17. Fox et al. (2015) estimate US poverty rates back to 1967 using income concepts from the Supplemental Poverty Measure (SPM). Hence, they also subtract taxes from gross income and include the market value of some in-kind transfers as resources and in their threshold measures. However, the SPM ignores the market value of government-provided health insurance and ESI in its measures of household resources and thresholds. Although the SPM provides a consistent relationship between the resources counted as income and included in its poverty thresholds, it fails to capture Medicare, Medicaid, and ESI's growing importance. Instead of treating the market value of health insurance as a resource, it subtracts medical out-of-pocket expenses from total household resources.

18. The Medicare and Medicaid risk classes reflect the channel through which benefits were accessed. The Medicare risk class "aged" applies to all persons on Medicare aged 65 or older. The Medicare risk class "disabled" applies to all persons accessing Medicare benefits through the SSDI program. The Medicaid risk class "children" applies to children accessing Medicaid benefits through either traditional Medicaid or a state's Children's Health Insurance Program (CHIP). The Medicaid risk class "adults" applies to all adults under the age of 65 accessing Medicaid benefits. The Medicaid risk class "aged" applies to all persons accessing Medicaid aged 65 or older. Last, the Medicaid risk class "disabled" applies to all persons accessing Medicaid benefits due to their qualification for SSI benefits (see Burkhauser et al., 2017, for a more complete discussion of this issue).

19. Given the Affordable Care Act of 2010, this may no longer be the case, since insurance companies, beginning January 1, 2014, are no longer permitted to adjust their premiums based on preexisting conditions. However, for the years in this study prior to 2014, insurers could deny insurance to those with preexisting conditions and/or charge such individuals higher premiums (see Burkhauser et al., 2017, for a more complete discussion of this issue).

20. When we use the PCE index rather than the CPI-U-RS index to adjust our series for inflation (see Appendix Figure 4.1A), the qualitative conclusions are identical.

21. The median individual for each measure will also change year-to-year. For instance, substantial shifts in the composition of the population, such as through the immigration of low-skill workers or the aging of the population into

retirement, may increase the share of the population living in households with low labor earnings, thus reducing the household size-adjusted labor earnings of the median person even when, over the same period, the median earnings of employed individuals is rising. Alternatively, the increase in the share of persons living in two- or three-labor earner households may reduce the share of the population living in households with low labor earnings, thus increasing the household size-adjusted labor earnings of the median person, even when over the same period the earnings of employed individuals is falling.

22. Mulligan (2012) finds that the expanded safety net programs over the Great Recession substantially increased the marginal tax on work. He concludes that this caused at least half the drop in hours worked between 2007 and 2009. Moffitt (2015) presents a counterpoint to Mulligan's analysis, arguing that Mulligan overestimates the marginal tax rates faced by workers moving from the social safety net to employment and that the actual rates imply much smaller reductions in labor supply as a result. Similarly, Moffitt's review of the literature on the labor supply effects of individual programs suggests much weaker labor supply responses to these changes, although Moffitt acknowledges that these effects are generally estimated outside recession periods.

23. The Census Bureau discontinued its series on the market value of Medicare and Medicaid in 2014 (income year 2013). In addition, Burkhauser et al. (2017) argue that the Affordable Care Act's rules regarding community ratings of health insurance, which came into effect in 2014, by law reduced the cost of private market health insurance to persons with above-average expected healthcare costs. This, in turn, reduced the market value of Medicare and Medicaid to their beneficiaries because they are now eligible for this less expensive community-rated private market health insurance.

24. Atkinson et al. (2015) use data from EU-SILC country surveys from 2004 to 2011 to demonstrate the problems of replicating National Accounts measures of mean income with survey data. To the degree that the survey data capture mean income based on National Accounts concepts of income, it allows researchers to compare such a measure with a median income measure, which can be captured in survey data.

25. Between 1959 and 1969, real GDP per capita increased from $22,321 to $30,566 (36.9 percent) while the real median market income of tax units rose from $30,628 to $39,806 (40.9 percent) in 2018 dollars. But, since then, the increase in real mean GDP has substantially outpaced the growth in median market income of tax units. Both series were adjusted using the CPI-U-RS. When we instead use the PCE index to adjust both series (see Appendix Figure 4.2A), the qualitative conclusions are identical, but measured GDP per capita grows slightly faster because the PCE measures inflation to be lower than the CPI-U-RS, particularly after 1980. The same is the case for our measurements of tax unit or household income when comparing the two different indices.

REFERENCES

Alvaredo, Facundo, Anthony B. Atkinson, Thomas Piketty, Emmanuel Saez, and Gabriel Zucman. n.d. *WID—The World Wealth and Income Database, May 25, 2016.* http://www.wid.world/

Armour, Philip, Richard V. Burkhauser, and Jeff Larrimore. 2014. "Levels and Trends in US Income and Its Distribution: A Crosswalk from Market Income Towards a Comprehensive Haig-Simons Income Approach." *Southern Economic Journal,* 81(2): 271–293.

Atkinson, Anthony B., and Andrea Brandolini. 2001. "Promises and Pitfalls in the Use of Secondary Data Sets: Income Inequality in OECD Countries as a Case Study." *Journal of Economic Literature,* 39(3): 771–779.

Atkinson, Anthony B., Anne-Catherine Guio, and Eric Marlier. March 2015. *Monitoring the Evolution of Income Poverty and Real Incomes over Time.* London: Centre for Analysis of Social Exclusion Report No. 188.

Atkinson, Anthony B., Thomas Piketty, and Emmanuel Saez. 2011. "Top Incomes in the Long Run of History." *Journal of Economic Literature,* 49(1): 3–71.

Blank, Rebecca. 2011. *Changing Inequality.* Berkeley: University of California Press.

Bureau of Economic Analysis (BEA). 2016, May 25. NIPA table 7.1. http://www.bea.gov/iTable/index_nipa.cfm

Burkhauser, Richard V., Shuaizhang Feng, Stephen P. Jenkins, and Jeff Larrimore. 2011. "Trends in United States Income Inequality Using the Internal March Current Population Survey: The Importance of Controlling for Censoring." *Journal of Economic Inequality,* 9(3): 393–415.

Burkhauser, Richard V., Shuaizhang Feng, Stephen P. Jenkins, and Jeff Larrimore. 2012a. "Recent Trends in Top Income Shares in the USA: Reconciling Estimates from March CPS and IRS Tax Return Data." *The Review of Economics and Statistics,* 94(2): 371–388.

Burkhauser, Richard V., Jeff Larrimore, and Sean Lyons. 2017. "Measuring Health Insurance Benefits: The Case of People with Disabilities." *Contemporary Economic Policy,* 35(3): 439–456.

Burkhauser, Richard V., Jeff Larrimore, and Kosali I. Simon. 2013. "Measuring the Impact of Valuing Health Insurance on Levels and Trends in Inequality and how the Affordable Care Act of 2010 Could Affect Them." *Contemporary Economic Policy,* 31(4): 779–794.

Burkhauser, Richard V., Jeff Larrimore, and Kosali I. Simon. 2012b. "A 'Second Opinion' on the Economic Health of the American Middle Class." *National Tax Journal,* 65(1): 7–32.

Burtless, Gary, and Sveta Milusheva. 2013. "Effects of Employer-Sponsored Health Insurance Costs on Social Security Taxable Wages." *Social Security Bulletin,* 73(1): 83–108.

Burtless, Gary, and Pavel Svaton. 2010. "Health Care, Health Insurance, and the Distribution of American Incomes." *Forum for Health Economics & Policy*, 13(1). doi:10.2202/1558-9544.1194

Canberra Group. 2011. *Handbook on Household Income Statistics* (2nd ed.). Geneva: United Nations Economic Commission for Europe.

Congressional Budget Office (CBO). 2012. *The Distribution of Household Income and Federal Taxes, 2008 and 2009*. Washington, DC: US Government Printing Office.

Congressional Budget Office (CBO). 2013. *The Distribution of Household Income and Federal Taxes, 2010*. Supplemental data. http://www.cbo.gov/publication/44604.

Center for Medicare and Medicaid Services (CMS). 2005. "Key Milestones in Medicare and Medicaid History, Selected Years: 1965–2003." *Health Care Financing Review*, 27(2): 1–3.

Collinson, Robert, Ingrid Gould Ellen, and Jens Ludwig. 2016. "Low-Income Housing Policy." In Robert A. Moffitt (ed.), *Economics of Means Tested Transfer Programs in the United States*, Vol. 2 (pp. 59–126), edited by R. A. Moffitt. Chicago, IL: University of Chicago Press for the NBER.

Daly, Mary C., and Robert G. Valletta. 2006. "Inequality and Poverty in United States: The Effects of Rising Dispersion of Men's Earnings and Changing Family Behaviour." *Economica*, 73(289): 75–98.

Danziger, Sheldon and Peter Gottschalk. 1995. *America Unequal*. Cambridge MA: Harvard University Press and New York: Russell Sage Foundation.

d'Ercole, Marco M., and Michael M. Förster. 2012. "The OECD Approach to Measuring Income Distribution and Poverty: Strengths, Limits and Statistical Issues." In *European Measures of Income and Poverty: Lessons for the US*, edited by D. J. Besharov and K. A. Couch (pp. 27–58). New York: Oxford University Press.

Feenberg, Daniel, and Elisabeth Coutts. 1993. "An Introduction to the TAXSIM Model." *Journal of Policy Analysis and Management*, 12(1): 189–194.

Fox, Liana, Irwin Garfinkel, Neeraj Kaushal, Jane Waldfogel, and Christopher Wimer. 2015. "Waging War on Poverty: Historical Trends in Poverty using the Supplemental Poverty Measure." *Journal of Policy Analysis and Management*, 34(3): 567–592.

Garner, Thesia, and Kathleen Short. 2012. *The Supplemental Poverty Measure: A Joint Project between the Census Bureau and the Bureau of Labor Statistics*. Price and Index Number Research Papers, Bureau of Labor Statistics. https://www.bls.gov/pir/sphome.htm

Gordon, Robert. 2016. *The Rise and Fall of American Growth: The US Standard of Living since the Civil War*. Princeton NJ: Princeton University Press.

Gottschalk, Peter, and Timothy Smeeding. 1997. "Cross-National Comparisons of Earnings and Income Inequality." *Journal of Economic Literature*, 35(2): 633–687.

Hoynes, Hilary, Diane W. Schanzenbach, and Douglas Almond. 2016. "Long-Run Impacts of Childhood Access to the Safety Net." *American Economic Review*, 106(4): 903–934.

Kaestner, Robert, and Darren H. Lubotsky. 2016. "Health Insurance and Income Inequality." *Journal of Economic Perspectives*, 30(2): 53–78.

Kramer, Fredrica D. 1988. *From Quality Control to Quality Improvement in AFDC and Medicaid*. Washington, DC: National Academy Press.

Larrimore, Jeff, Richard V. Burkhauser, and Philip Armour. 2015. "Accounting for Income Changes over the Great Recession: The Importance of Taxes and Transfers." *National Tax Journal*, 68(2): 281–318.

Larrimore, Jeff, Richard V. Burkhauser, Gerald Auten, and Phillip Armour. 2019. *Recent Trends in US Top Income Shares in Tax Record Data Using More Comprehensive Measures of Income, Including Accrued Capital Gains*. NBER Working Paper 23007 revised. Cambridge, MA: National Bureau of Economic Research.

Larrimore, Jeff, Richard V. Burkhauser, Shuaizhang Feng, and Laura Zayatz. 2008. "Consistent Cell Means for Topcoded Incomes in the Public Use March CPS (1976–2007)." *Journal of Economic and Social Measurement*, 33: 89–128.

Lyons, Sean. 2015. *Health Reform, Physician Market Power, and Income Disparity*, Ph.D. diss. Ithaca, NY: Cornell University.

Moffitt, Robert A. 2015. "The Deserving Poor, the Family, and the US Welfare System." *Demography*, 52(3): 729–749.

Mulligan, Casey. 2012. *The Redistribution Recession: How Labor Market Distortions Contracted the Economy*. New York: Oxford University Press.

Nolan, Brian, Max Roser, and Stefan Thewissen. 2018. "GDP per Capita versus Median Household Income: What Gives Rise to Divergence over Time." *Review of Income and Wealth*. https://doi.org/10.1111/roiw.12362

Office of Management and Budget (OMB). 2016. Table 12.3—Total Outlays for Grants to State and Local Governments, by Function, Agency, and Program: 1940–2017. https://www.whitehouse.gov/omb/budget/Historicals.

Piketty, Thomas, and Saez, Emmanuel. 2003. "Income Inequality in the United States, 1913–1998." *The Quarterly Journal of Economics*, 118(1): 1–39.

Piketty, Thomas, Emmanuel Saez, and Gabriel Zucman. 2018. "Distributional National Accounts: Methods and Estimates for the United States." *Quarterly Journal of Economics*, 133(2): 553–609.

Organisation for Economic Cooperation and Development (OECD). 2008. *Growing Unequal? Income Distribution and Poverty in OECD Countries*. Paris: OECD Publishing.

Organisation for Economic Cooperation and Development (OECD). 2011. *Divided We Stand: Why Inequality Keeps Rising/* Paris: OECD Publishing.

Organisation for Economic Cooperation and Development (OECD). 2015. *In It Together: Why Less Inequality Benefits All*. Paris: OECD Publishing.

Ruggles, Patricia. 1990. *Drawing the Line: Alternative Poverty Measures and their Implication for Public Policy*. Washington, DC: Urban Institute Press.

Ruggles, Steven, Sarah Flood, Ronald Goeken, Josiah Grover, Erin Meyer, Jose Pacas, and Matthew Sobek. 2019. IPUMS USA: Version 9.0 [1960, 1970, 1980, 1990]. Minneapolis, MN: IPUMS. https://doi.org/10.18128/D010. V9.0

Semega, Jessica L., Kayla R. Fontenot, and Melissa A. Kollar. 2017. *Income and Poverty in the United States: 2016*. Washington, DC: US Census Bureau, Washington.

Sommers, Benjamin D., and Donald Oellerich. 2013. "The Poverty-Reducing Effect of Medicaid." *Journal of Health Economics*, 32(5): 816–832.

Stewart, Kenneth J., and Stephen B. Reed. 1999. "Consumer Price Index Research Series Using Current Methods, 1978–98." *Monthly Labor Review*, 122(6): 29–38.

United States Census Bureau. 1973. Statistical Abstracts of the United States, 1967–1978. https://www.census.gov/prod/www/statistical abstract.html

United States Census Bureau. 2000. Historical National Population Estimates, 1900–1999. http://www.census.gov/popest/data/national/totals/pre-1980/tables/popclockest.txt

United States Department of Agriculture (USDA). 2013. National School Lunch Program Fact Sheet. http://www.fns.usda.gov/sites/default/files/NSLPFactSheet.pdf

United States Department of Agriculture (USDA). 2014. National Level Annual Summary Tables: FY 1969–2014. http://www.fns.usda.gov/pd/child-nutrition-tables

APPENDIX

Appendix Figure 4.1A recreates Figure 4.1 using the Personal Consumption Expenditure (PCE) index instead of the CPI-U-RS to adjust for inflation. While overall growth is slightly higher since 1959 (because the PCE measures inflation as being slightly lower than the CPI), the qualitative results are essentially unchanged. Appendix Figure 4.2A repeats this exercise for Figure 4.2. Appendix Table 4.1A compares the CPS-based and decennial Census-based medians and means of each income series for years in which both data sources are available.

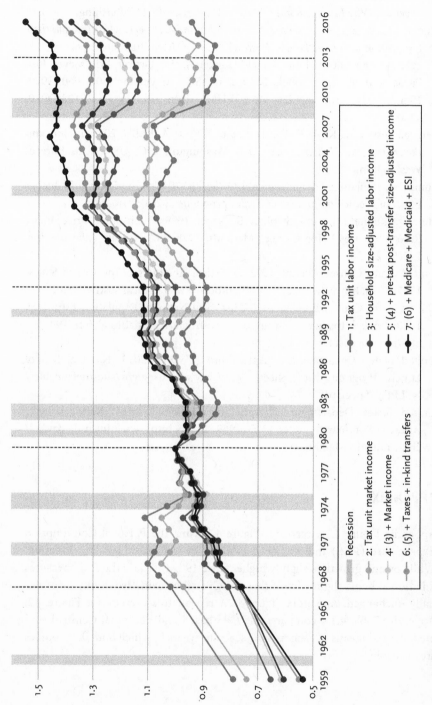

Appendix Figure 4.1A Alternative measures of median income normalized to 1979 levels (1959–2016). Data from Figure 4.1 combined with annual Personal Consumption Expenditure (PCE) series from the Bureau of Economic Analysis.

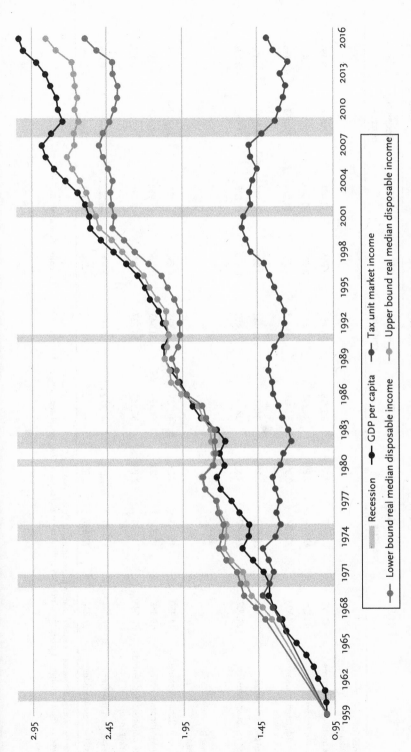

Appendix Figure 4.2A Trends in Real gross domestic product (GDP) per capita, real taxable market income of the median tax unit, and real disposable household size-adjusted income of the median persons normalized to 1959. Same series as in Figure 4.1 with values normalized to income year 1959. Median market tax unit income and the upper and lower bound median disposable income from authors' calculations using March Current Population Survey and the 1960 decennial Census. Income per capita from the Bureau of Economic Analysis NIPA table 7.1. All series adjusted using Personal Consumption Expenditure (PCE).

Appendix Table 4.1A Comparisons of Current Population Survey (CPS)-based and decennial census-based medians and means (1969, 1979, and 1989)

	1969			1979			1989		
	CPS	Decennial census	%	CPS	Decennial census	%	CPS	Decennial census	%
Panel A: Medians									
Tax units labor income	40,723	41,595	-2.1%	36,719	38,483	-4.6%	35,401	35,294	0.3%
Market income	43,157	42,809	0.8%	40,675	41,624	-2.3%	40,815	43,137	-5.4%
Size-adjusted households market income	27,893	27,634	0.9%	32,411	31,113	4.2%	34,824	35,053	-0.7%
Pre-tax post-transfer	29,125	28,903	0.8%	34,431	34,088	1.0%	37,560	37,411	0.4%
Post-tax post-transfer	24,707	24,342	1.5%	28,720	28,450	0.9%	31,603	31,652	-0.2%
Panel B: Means									
Tax units labor income	44,950	46,443	-3.2%	44,732	46,895	-4.6%	47,475	48,128	-1.4%
Market income	49,378	49,304	0.2%	51,398	51,643	-0.5%	55,953	57,842	-3.3%
Size-adjusted households market income	32,643	31,986	2.1%	37,543	35,727	5.1%	42,694	42,885	-0.4%
Pre-tax post-transfer	34,594	33,927	2.0%	40,472	39,658	2.1%	46,227	45,898	0.7%
Post-tax post-transfer	27,878	27,667	0.8%	31,566	32,050	-1.5%	36,391	37,412	-2.7%

Note: Percentage differences are the deviation of the decennial Census from the CPS.

Source: Authors' calculations using the March CPS and the decennial Census. Taxes calculated using the National Bureau of Economic Research's TaxSim.

5

TOP INCOME SHARES AND THE DIFFICULTIES OF USING TAX DATA

Gerald Auten and David Splinter

The conventional view of the US income distribution paints a dark picture: inequality increased dramatically in recent decades, top incomes grew substantially while lower and middle incomes have stagnated, the tax system has become less progressive, and most economic growth has been "captured" by the top of the distribution. Our analysis suggests, however, that this conventional view may be overstated. After addressing limitations of the data and assumptions used to support this view, a different picture emerges: income inequality has increased only modestly in recent decades, incomes of the bottom 50 percent have not stagnated, the overall tax system has become more progressive, and economic growth has been more widely shared.

Researchers need to account for a number of challenges in measuring the distribution of income, especially when trying to compare distributions over long time periods. While tax data are superior to survey data in many ways, especially for measuring the top of the distribution, researchers need to be mindful of their limitations. Tax returns are designed to report income and collect taxes according to the current Internal Revenue Code, which often deviates from economists' view of what constitutes economic income. Tax reforms, especially the Tax Reform Act of 1986, have changed both how income is defined in tax data and who is required to file tax returns. In addition, as much as 40 percent of national income is missing from tax returns. Accounting for this missing income is necessarily sensitive to the decisions of researchers about how to allocate it.

Gerald Auten and David Splinter, *Top Income Shares and the Difficulties of Using Tax Data* In: *United States Income, Wealth, Consumption, and Inequality.* Edited by: Diana Furchtgott-Roth, Oxford University Press (2021).
© Oxford University Press. DOI: 10.1093/oso/9780197518199.003.0006.

Social and economic conditions have also changed dramatically since the 1960s, in ways that can affect income distribution estimates in both tax and survey data. Among these changes are differential declines in marriage rates, increases in post-secondary education, and substantial increases in government transfer programs (including Social Security). Failing to adequately account for changes in social and economic conditions as well as issues associated with tax data can result in misleading estimates of inequality levels and trends.

The conventional view of dramatically increasing income inequality largely reflects the influential Piketty and Saez (2003) paper and the more recent paper by Piketty, Saez, and Zucman (PSZ, 2018).[1] The original paper used tax return data and suffered from a number of well-recognized problems: using a narrow measure of income that omitted Social Security and other transfers, failing to account for the effects of tax reforms, and basing income groups on tax units, which creates an upward bias in their estimated top income shares over time because of differential decreases in marriage rates. PSZ addressed a number of these issues by targeting total national income and basing income groups on the number of adults rather than tax units. National income is a broad measure that includes compensation of employees, proprietorship income, net interest, rental income, and corporate profits. The new paper, however, created additional issues, primarily due to certain assumptions about how to allocate the increasing share of income not reported on tax returns.

The estimates presented in this chapter reflect our analysis as of mid-2019, which fully accounts for national income and improves upon PSZ by paying more careful attention to the allocation of income missing from individual tax returns. We start with income reported on individual tax returns, as did Piketty and Saez. However, we then account for the effects of tax reforms as well as important technical details of how income is reported in tax data. We account for social changes such as declining marriage rates and the increase in single-parent households. We provide a step-by-step comparison between our estimates and those of PSZ, and we discuss how different assumptions for allocating missing income affect estimates of top income shares.

Our estimates suggest a modest increase in the top 1 percent share of national income of 3 percentage points (pp) between 1962 and 2014. The period since 1979, however, differs from the earlier period. Our estimates suggest that the top 1 percent share of pre-tax income declined by about 2 pp from 1962 to 1979 and increased by just under 5 pp from 1979 to 2014.

The expansion of transfers and increased progressivity of the overall tax system largely offset the increases in pre-tax income inequality. We find that the top 1 percent share of after-tax/transfer income increased by less than 1 percentage point over the full period. In spite of the drop in top statutory income tax rates from 91 percent in 1960 to 39.6 percent in 2015, total effective tax rates on the top of the distribution exhibit no long-term trend due to tax reforms that broadened the tax base. However, the overall tax system became more progressive as a result of tax reductions and refundable credits targeted at lower and middle-income taxpayers.

The first section of this chapter summarizes our estimates of the top 1 percent and bottom 50 percent shares of pre-tax national income and the effects of transfers and taxes. The second section discusses how our estimates of the distribution of national income are constructed, presenting step-by-step effects on top 1 percent shares when moving from income reported on tax returns to national income, and it examines why our estimates differ from PSZ. The following two sections discuss changes over time in high-income tax avoidance and estimates of the distribution of economic growth.

DISTRIBUTION OF NATIONAL INCOME

The Top 1 Percent

As shown in Figure 5.1, our estimate is that the top 1 percent share of pre-tax national income has increased about 3 pp since the early 1960s, from 11 to 14 percent. This increase is more modest than that observed when only considering income reported on tax returns (i.e., *fiscal income*). The addition of income missing from fiscal income increases top shares in the 1960s, largely from adding corporate retained earnings, and it reduces top shares in recent decades, largely from adding non-taxable employee compensation. This explains why the increase in top shares is more modest when using a broader measure of pre-tax

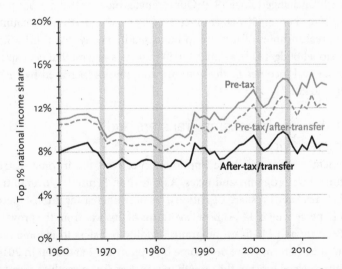

Figure 5.1 Top 1 percent national income shares. Shaded years show initial years of National Bureau of Economic Research (NBER) recessions.
National Bureau of Economic Research (NBER), Auten and Splinter (2019a), and authors' calculations.

income that includes income sources missing from tax returns. Figure 5.1 also illustrates how top 1 percent shares tend to increase during expansionary periods and decrease during recessionary periods.

Including the effects of taxes and transfers, top 1 percent shares increased less than 1 pp between 1962 and 2014. For the more recent period between 1979 and 2014, top 1 percent pre-tax (pre-transfer) shares increased 5 pp, but after-tax/transfer shares increased by only 1 pp.

Pre-Tax Incomes of the Bottom 50 Percent and Upper-Middle Class

Changes in income shares outside the top 1 percent are also important to consider. PSZ argue that their estimated increase in the top 1 percent share is almost exactly matched by a decrease in bottom 50 percent share and that real incomes of the bottom have increased little in recent decades. What do our estimates show?

As illustrated in Figure 5.2A, the bottom 50 percent pre-tax share of national income increased slightly from 21 to 22 percent from 1962 to 1979, but then declined to 16.4 percent by 2014. As discussed in the following section, transfers and taxes offset almost all of this pre-tax decline in the bottom 50 percent share. Figure 5.2B shows that the income shares of those in the 50th to 90th percentiles, who might be considered the upper-middle class, were relatively constant over the past five decades and are much less affected by transfers and taxes.

While income shares are a common focus, it is at least as important to consider changes in levels of real incomes. One of the arguments of PSZ and the conventional wisdom is that real pre-tax incomes of the bottom 50 percent have been nearly unchanged since 1979. Our estimates indicate that average per capita incomes of the bottom 50 percent increased by nearly one-third. Accounting for transfers, real incomes of this group increased by nearly two-thirds. Similarly, Congressional Budget Office (CBO, 2018) estimates suggest that per capita after-tax/transfer real incomes of the bottom two quintiles increased by 62 percent from 1979 to 2014.

Redistribution: Increasing Transfers and Tax Progressivity

Government policies can have important effects on the income distribution through transfer programs and taxes. As shown in Figure 5.3, overall transfers more than tripled as a share of national income, increasing from 5 percent in 1962 to 17 percent by 2014. Almost two-thirds of this was from the growth in the Social Security and Medicare programs. Adding transfers to income increases the bottom 50 percent share of income by 3 pp in 1962 and 8 pp in 2014 since this group received most of the growth in transfers. The growth of transfers also resulted in larger decreases in top 1 percent income shares over time: 0.5 pp in 1962 and 1.9 pp in 2014.

(A)

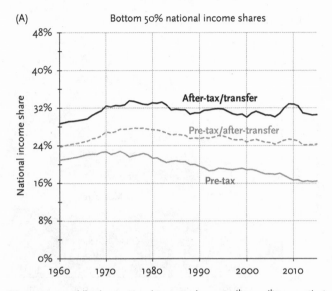

Bottom 50% national income shares

(B)   Upper-middle class national income shares (50th to 90th percentiles)

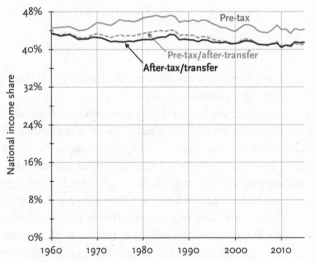

Figure 5.2 A. Bottom 50 percent national income shares. B. Upper-middle class national income shares (50th to 90th percentiles).
Auten and Splinter (2019a).

Our analysis also indicates that the overall tax system has become more progressive since the 1960s. This is primarily a result of top tax burdens showing no clear trend while lower and middle-income tax burdens declined due to tax cuts and the expansion of refundable credits. The combined effects of transfers and taxes almost completely offset the changes in pre-tax shares of both the top 1 percent and the bottom 50 percent of the population.

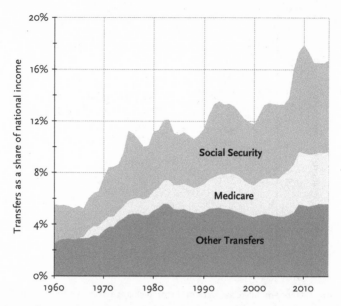

Figure 5.3 Transfers as a share of national income. Other transfers includes the refundable portion of tax credits.
Bureau of Economic Analysis and authors' calculations.

Figure 5.4A shows how total tax burdens (i.e., average effective tax rates from all taxes) of the top 1 percent evolved over the past five decades. Total top 1 percent tax burdens fluctuated around 39 percent but were lower in the 1970s (37 percent) and highest in the late 1990s and 2013–2015 (44 percent).[2] The federal individual income tax accounts for the largest share of taxes paid by the top 1 percent and has been the most volatile. Individual income taxes increase during economic expansions, such as 1991–2000 and 2003–2007, as high-income taxpayers move into higher tax brackets, and they decrease during recessions, such as 2001 and 2008–2009. They were also affected by the top tax rate increase in 1993 (from 31 to 39.6 percent), the reduction in 2003 to 35 percent, and the restoration of the 39.6 percent rate in 2013 along with the imposition of two new taxes and other provisions targeting high-income taxpayers.[3]

Individual income taxes paid by the top 1 percent have increased despite top federal individual tax rates falling from 91 percent to 39.6 percent. In 1962, only about 1 in 1,000 of the top 1 percent paid the top tax rate, as it only applied to extremely high incomes. But, in 2014, the majority paid the top rate. Another factor is base broadening targeted at high-income taxpayers, especially in the Tax Reform Act of 1986 (TRA86), as discussed later. In addition, the shift from C corporations to pass-through businesses after TRA86 resulted in the large decline in the importance of the corporate income tax seen in Figure 5.4A. Income previously taxed under the corporate income tax is now reported and taxed under the individual income tax. While the effect of payroll taxes is relatively

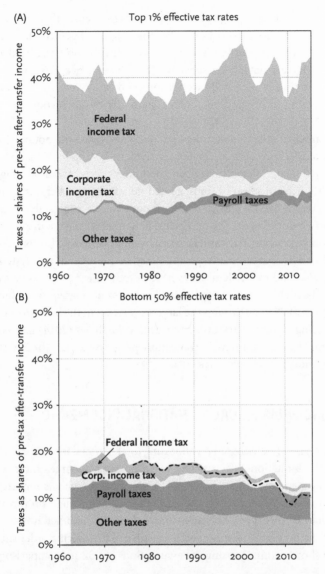

Figure 5.4 A. Top 1 percent effective tax rates. B. Bottom 50 percent effective tax rates. Income is pre-tax/after-transfer income, which is the broadest income definition. The refundable portion of tax credits is included in government transfers rather than taxes, but the effects are shown by the dashed line.
Auten and Splinter (2019a) and authors' calculations.

small for high-income taxpayers, these taxes have become more important since the uncapping of the Medicare tax in 1994.

In contrast, Figure 5.4B shows that total tax burdens of the bottom 50 percent have declined over time, especially after 1979. Since 1962, tax burdens of the bottom 50 percent decreased from 17 to 13 percent. If the refundable portion of tax credits is counted as part of the tax system—rather than as transfers, as in the national accounts—tax burdens of the bottom 50 percent decreased from 17 to 10 percent (the dashed line in Figure 5.4B). Income tax burdens of the bottom 50 percent have been substantially reduced since 1962 by various tax cuts and expansions of earned income and child tax credits. Accounting for the refundable portion of tax credits more than fully offsets income tax liabilities since 2002.

The combined effects of transfers and taxes increased the bottom 50 percent after-tax/transfer income share by 8 pp in 1962 and 14 pp in 2014. Note that the 2008 to 2010 bump in after-tax/transfer bottom 50 percent shares in Figure 5.2A resulted from the increase in transfers and tax credits enacted during the Great Recession as an economic stimulus. Overall, our estimates suggest that transfers and taxes offset almost all of the pre-tax decline in bottom 50 percent income shares.

The combination of flat top tax burdens and decreasing bottom 50 percent tax burdens has increased the progressivity of the overall tax system. Other estimates also find that federal taxes have become more progressive over time. CBO estimates show that average federal tax rates decreased for all but the top quintile from 1979 to 2013, with the largest decreases in the bottom of the distribution.[4] Using several distributional measures, Mathews (2014) also concluded that federal income taxes have become more progressive since the late 1960s and have been most progressive since 2000.

CHANGING FROM FISCAL TO NATIONAL INCOME

Distributional estimates based on allocating total national income can overcome some of the limitations of estimates based on fiscal income. Table 5.1 shows our step-by-step adjustments to change from fiscal income as reported on tax returns to national income and the effect of each adjustment on top 1 percent income shares.[5] This approach stacks changes one after another, however, so that estimated effects on top shares may be sensitive to the specific order shown. The table also shows estimates using the assumptions of PSZ for comparison.[6]

Step-by-Step Effects on Top 1 Percent Income Shares

The first steps are to ensure that our sample is consistent with the baseline population of the US resident population age 20 and older, to define our unit of analysis for determining income groups, and to account for the non-filer population as well as individuals represented on tax returns.[7] To make our sample consistent with the baseline Census population, we drop non-resident filers and other filers under age 20. We also drop dependent filers age 20 and older, primarily full-time students aged 20–23 who have not provided more than half of their own support and are being claimed as a dependent on another tax return. The income of young and dependent filers is allocated to returns claiming dependent

Table 5.1 Top 1% national income shares

	Auten-Splinter		Piketty, Saez, and Zucman		1962–2014 increase		
	1962	2014	1962	2014	AS	PSZ	PSZ–AS diff.
Panel A: Summary of changes							
Fiscal income with cap. gains	9.8	21.8	9.8	21.8	12.0	12.0	—
Pre-tax changes (Panel B)	1.3	−7.7	2.8	−1.6	−9.0	−4.4	—
Pre-tax national income	11.1	14.1	12.6	20.2	3.0	7.6	4.6
Transfers and Taxes (Panel C)	−2.8	−5.6	−2.5	−4.5	−2.8	−2.0	—
After-tax/transfer income	8.3	8.5	10.1	15.7	0.2	5.6	5.4
Panel B: Fiscal income to pre-tax national income							
Unit of observation & sample	−0.6	−2.2	−0.7	−1.6	−1.6	−0.9	0.6
+ employer-sponsored insurance	−0.1	−1.3	−0.1	−1.3	−1.2	−1.2	*
+ corporate income taxes	1.1	0.1	1.4	0.5	−1.0	−0.8	0.2
+ payroll & other taxes	−0.2	−1.2	*	−0.4	−1.1	−0.5	0.6
+ private retirement income	−0.2	−0.2	−0.2	1.1	0.1	1.3	1.2
+ income corrections	0.4	0.1	0.6	0.6	−0.3	*	0.4
+ underreported income	0.1	−0.6	0.5	1.4	−0.7	0.9	1.6
+ imputed rent	−0.1	−0.3	0.2	−0.2	−0.1	−0.4	−0.3
− realized capital gains	−1.2	−2.6	−0.9	−2.2	−1.5	−1.3	0.1
+ corporate retained earnings	2.1	0.6	2.0	0.6	−1.5	−1.4	0.1
Panel C: Pre-tax to after-tax/transfer income							
+ transfers	−0.5	−1.9	−0.2	−1.8	−1.4	−1.6	−0.1
− taxes	−1.9	−2.5	−2.3	−3.0	−0.6	−0.7	*
+ government surplus	0.4	−0.4	*	0.2	−0.8	0.2	1.0
+ government consumption	−0.8	−0.7	—	—	*	—	*

Note: * denotes change between −0.05 and 0.05. In Panel B, the PSZ addition of social insurance and deduction of associated taxes is not shown.
Source: Auten and Splinter (2019a), Piketty, Saez, and Zucman (2018), and authors' calculations.

exemptions. Following an approach similar to that of the CBO, we define income groups based on the total number of individuals, which accounts for all individuals on a tax return. This means that each percentile has the same number of individuals instead of the same number of tax units. For purposes of ranking tax units, income is size-adjusted by dividing by the square root of income, a standard equivalence scale in distribution studies.[8]

Our approach accounts for both differential changes in marriage rates by income groups and the increasing fraction of single-parent households. Marriage rates have declined significantly in the lower and middle-income population, but have remained high in the top 1 percent. The lower marriage rate increases the total number of returns filed—unmarried individuals file separate returns whereas married couples usually file one joint return—and therefore increases the number of returns in the top 1 percent. The returns added to the top 1 percent will have higher than average incomes, thereby mechanically increasing top income shares in recent decades. Basing income groups on the numbers of individuals rather than tax units controls for both changes in household structure. Relative to baseline tax return data and tax units, these adjustments reduce top 1 percent income shares by 0.6 pp in 1962 and 2.2 pp in 2014. The 2014 effect is similar to the 2.4 pp decrease estimated by Bricker et al. when income groups are based on families rather than tax units.[9]

The baseline income for this analysis is fiscal income including capital gains. Our analysis makes three basic types of adjustments to distribute national income: adjustments that account for major tax reforms, technical adjustments to account for certain features of how income is reported on tax returns, and additions to account for income not included in tax data.

The largest effect on top 1 percent income shares is from adding sources of national income not on tax returns, such as employer-sponsored insurance and the employer portion of payroll taxes. The growth in employer-sponsored insurance contributions results in larger reductions in top 1 percent shares in more recent years: a negligible decrease in 1962 and a 1.3 pp decrease in 2014. The portion of payroll taxes paid by employers is included in pre-tax income because they help fund programs benefitting workers and because economists generally assume the incidence falls on workers. The effect of payroll taxes has grown over time and, by 2014, including these and other taxes decreased top 1 percent income shares by 1.2 pp.

An important aspect of allocating total national income is accounting for all the components of corporate pre-tax income: retained earnings, dividends, and corporate taxes paid. We replace realized capital gains, which are included on individual tax returns but excluded from national income, with corporate retained earnings, which are excluded from individual tax returns but included in national income. Realized capital gains can be considered less appropriate for measuring current-year incomes because they tend to be lumpy and generally reflect gains accrued over many years. Replacing realized capital gains with retained earnings increases the top 1 percent share in 1962 but decreases it by 2 pp in 2014, largely because of the increased share of stock held by retirement accounts.

The inclusion of retained earnings and corporate taxes is an important factor in accounting for the base-broadening effects of the TRA86. Before TRA86, business activity was concentrated in C corporations, which had substantial retained earnings and were subject to the corporate income tax. TRA86, however, greatly changed tax incentives so that it was often more advantageous to organize businesses as pass-through businesses (S corporations, partnerships, and sole proprietorships) whose income is reported directly on individual tax returns and is not subject to the corporate income tax. Failing to include business income on a consistent basis would tend to overstate top income shares after TRA86 compared to before its enactment. The effects can be seen in Table 5.1. In 1962, the combined effect of including corporate retained earnings and corporate taxes increased the top 1 percent share by about 3.2 pp. By 2014, the increase was only 0.7 pp. An additional factor in this change is that the share of corporate ownership in retirement accounts grew from about 5 to 50 percent over this period. Assets in these accounts are more equally distributed than direct corporate ownership.

Other adjustments necessary to conform to national income have smaller effects on top income shares, although they may be important for ranking individual tax units and for other parts of the distribution. These adjustments include technical income corrections and accounting for sources of income missing from tax returns: income accruing in retirement accounts, underreported income, and imputed rent. Corrections for technical features of income reporting on tax returns make our income definition more consistent over time. For example, we add back deductions for net operating loss carryovers, which reflect losses incurred in prior year, and subtract gambling losses included in itemized deductions up to the amount of gambling income, which better reflects net income from this source.

We allocate income accruing inside retirement accounts (i.e., inside buildup) based on wages for defined benefit accounts and asset ownership for defined contribution accounts. Underreported income is defined here as the difference between national income totals and amounts reported in tax data for wages and pass-through businesses. As discussed later, we allocate these underreported amounts based on detailed Internal Revenue Service (IRS) audit studies that are representative of the entire filing population. Finally, we add imputed rent, the non-taxable value of living in owner-occupied housing net of expenses.

After-tax/transfer national income accounts for the effect of transfers and taxes, as well as government surpluses or deficits and government consumption. Starting with our measure of pre-tax national income, we first add transfers. As discussed earlier, the increasing size of transfers results in larger reductions in top 1 percent income shares over time: 0.5 and 1.9 pp in 1962 and 2014, respectively. Subtracting taxes reduces top 1 percent income shares by 1.9 and 2.5 pp in 1962 and 2014, respectively. This increasing effect is due to the growing progressivity of individual income taxes that resulted from tax credit expansions and other changes that primarily benefitted lower and middle income households.[10] This is partially offset by decreasing progressive effects from corporate taxes.

We allocate government surpluses or deficits by federal taxes. Historical experience suggests that federal surpluses have been followed by tax cuts (e.g., 1964 and 2001) and large federal deficits have preceded tax increases (e.g., 1982, 1984, and 1991). The surplus in 1962 therefore slightly increases top income shares and the deficit in 2014 decreases them. Finally, we add government consumption, which includes non-transfer spending consisting primarily of education and national defense expenditures. These expenditures are allocated half per capita and half by income. While recognizing uncertainties involved in allocating government expenditures, our approach acknowledges both that the benefits of government services may increase with income as well as the public goods aspect of government consumption.[11]

Comparison with Piketty, Saez, and Zucman

Our estimates differ considerably from those in PSZ, especially for the most recent periods. This section examines the reasons for these differences and shows their effects on top 1 percent shares in Table 5.1. The largest differences from PSZ include our differing assumptions for allocating retirement income and our more careful treatment of business losses. In recent years, the largest difference is in allocating underreported income, part of which is from our accounting for business losses.

Before considering specific differences, it is important to note that PSZ have made several important improvements over their earlier paper. These include using a broader definition of income that accounts for total national income and basing income groups on adults (i.e., primary and secondary taxpayers). The definition of national income does not include transfer payments, but PSZ finessed this issue by including Social Security and unemployment compensation benefits and netting out the associated payroll taxes. In addition, many of our estimated effects of including income not in tax data are very similar to PSZ's findings. For example, we use similar approaches to allocate corporate retained earnings and estimate that including employer-sponsored insurance benefits reduce the top 1 percent share by similar amounts.

The first difference to consider is units of observation and sample selection. PSZ changed from tax units to the number of adults to set income groups and evenly split incomes of married couples by dividing them in half. While it accounts for the decline in marriage rates, the PSZ approach does not account for the increase in single-parent households or decreasing household size and also implies no economies of scale in households. The PSZ approach reduces the top 1 percent share by 0.7 pp in 1962 and by 1.6 pp in 2014. Our approach bases income groups on all individuals and ranks by size-adjusted income. While we both exclude filers under age 20, our analysis also excludes dependent filers age 20 and older and non-resident filers who are not in the baseline population. While our results are very similar in 1962, by 2014 the approach used by PSZ decreases the top 1 percent share by 0.6 pp less than ours.

Different treatments of retirement account income result in large differences in estimated top income shares. Our 2014 private retirement income is about half from taxable amounts reported on tax returns and half from non-taxable income accruing in retirement accounts. The top 1 percent receives about 2 percent of taxable retirement income and almost 10 percent of retirement account income associated with retirement wealth. This allocation is comparable to Federal Reserve economist estimates that the top 1 percent by wealth owns about 8 percent of retirement wealth.[12] For 2014, PSZ's online data suggest that they overstate top income shares by allocating about 16 percent of private retirement income to the top 1 percent, a much higher share than suggested by either taxable retirement benefits or retirement wealth estimates. This results from PSZ using non-taxable retirement income as well as taxable retirement income amounts reported on tax returns when allocating this income. Nearly all of these non-taxable amounts reflect rollovers of assets that should not be treated as retirement income for this purpose.

Another important difference is the treatment of business losses. Our analysis accounts for business losses in three ways not done in PSZ: the effects of TRA86 in limiting the deduction of losses on passive investments, the fact that net operating loss carryovers do not reflect current-year income, and that a significant share of underreported business income is from tax returns with losses. Although not shown separately in Table 5.1, we estimate that imposing post-TRA86 loss limits in earlier years to make business income consistent over time increases the top 1 percent share in 1985 by 0.5 pp. Removing net operating losses in 2015 reduces the top 1 percent by 0.5 pp. Relative to tax return income, these two adjustments result in a 1 pp smaller increase in the top 1 percent share. As discussed in more detail in the next section, we also account for business losses in allocating underreported business income, which explains part of our difference with PSZ's top 1 percent shares.

Important steps to getting to total national income are allocating corporate retained earnings and corporate taxes. Our approach to allocating corporate retained earnings is very similar to that of PSZ. As a result, our estimated effects on top income shares are almost identical. The allocation of corporate taxes, however, is an issue which continues to challenge economists. As compared to our allocation of one-quarter to wages—as done by the CBO[13]—and three-quarters by corporate capital ownership, PSZ allocate it by all capital ownership. The larger PSZ allocation to the top 1 percent in recent years results from the increasing share of capital held by pass-through businesses. Smith et al., however, concluded that most pass-through income from S corporations reflects human capital rather than the conventional understanding of capital likely to be affected by corporate taxes.[14]

After-tax/transfer income incorporates the effects of adding transfers and subtracting taxes. PSZ estimates suggest that the top 1 percent share of after-tax/transfer income increased by 5.6 pp from 1962 to 2014 compared to only 0.2 pp in our estimates. Most of this difference, however, is a result of the 4.6 pp difference in pre-tax income increases.

The PSZ estimates of the effects of adding transfers on the top 1 percent share is virtually identical to ours. While PSZ estimates of the effects of taxes on top

1 percent shares are larger than ours by 0.5 pp or less, the differences over time are almost the same.

When estimating effective tax rates, as opposed to the effect of taxes on income shares, our results differ significantly from those of PSZ. Our estimates show that tax rates are significantly higher for high-income groups than for low-income groups. This suggests the overall tax system is progressive and is similar to the pattern for federal taxes found by the CBO and the Tax Policy Center. In comparison, the PSZ tax rates are much flatter over the income distribution. By shifting underreported income away from the bottom of the distribution and to the top of the distribution (relative to our audit-based approach), PSZ's calculations increase average effective tax rates for low-income taxpayers and decrease tax rates for high-income taxpayers. In addition, the PSZ income definition excludes transfers other than Social Security and unemployment compensation and subtracts the payroll taxes for these programs. This reduces income for low-income taxpayers, thereby further increasing estimated tax rates for this group relative to broader measures of income typically used to estimate effective tax rates.

The PSZ approach for allocating government surpluses or deficits results in a 1.0 pp increase in top 1 percent shares since 1962, relative to our approach. While we allocate surpluses and deficits by federal taxes, PSZ allocate them half by all taxes paid and half by transfers received in the current year. Their approach implies that deficit financing effectively offsets a portion of transfers actually received. While large deficits may eventually result in some cutbacks in transfer programs, this assumption is inappropriate from a current-year perspective. Although it has little effect on the trend, the PSZ allocation of government consumption by after-tax income increases top 1 percent after-tax/transfer shares by three-quarters of a percentage point in both 1962 and 2014 compared to our approach. This is because their allocation essentially implies that government consumption has no additional redistributive effect relative to after-tax/transfer income. As discussed earlier, we allocate it half per capita to account for the public goods aspect of this spending.

ISSUES IN MEASURING INCOME: ALTERNATIVE DEFINITIONS, TAX REFORMS, UNDERREPORTED INCOME, AND TAX AVOIDANCE

While the earlier part of this chapter presented our methodology and results and discussed the reasons that our results differ from those of PSZ, some income measurement issues deserve additional attention. This section examines alternative definitions of income, changes in the tax base reported on individual returns due to tax reforms, the underreporting of income due to tax evasion, and how high-income tax avoidance has evolved over time.

National Income, Personal Income, and Other Income Measures

Many different income measures are used to estimate the distribution of income. This section briefly discusses the major components of national income and other commonly used income measures.[15] National income is the sum of compensation of employees, proprietorship income, net interest, rental income, and corporate profits, which equals gross domestic product (GDP) plus foreign-source income less capital depreciation. Thus the conceptual basis for national income is earnings from both labor and capital. Transfers are not considered in determining total national income.

Personal income is defined as all income of persons. A large share of personal income sources are the same as for national income, and total personal income is about equal to total national income. Personal income, however, excludes social insurance taxes and includes cash and non-cash transfers: Social Security benefits, unemployment insurance, veterans' benefits, Medicare, Medicaid, and other similar benefits. Instead of including all economic income of corporations, personal income includes only dividends received by individuals. Fixler, Gindelsky, and Johnson, in several papers, have estimated the distribution of personal income.[16]

Another long-standing approach used by public finance economists has been to obtain broader measures of economic income than that reported on tax returns by including additional sources received or accrued in a given year although not targeting national income. Examples include studies by Pechman and Okner in the 1960s and 1970s, transfer-inclusive cash income used by Treasury's Office of Tax Analysis, and expanded income used by the staff of the Joint Committee on Taxation.

Other studies have used narrower definitions of income that can produce misleading distributional estimates because of the omission of important sources of income. Census money income omits capital gains (or any related measure such as corporate retained earnings on stock holdings) and non-cash transfers. In addition, survey-based estimates suffer from measurement error, especially in the bottom and top tails of the distribution.[17] While tax data can attenuate this measurement error, fiscal income as defined in Piketty and Saez only includes non-transfer income reported on tax returns, missing up to 40 percent of national income.

Since a large fraction of national income is not reported on individual tax returns (or related information returns), it must necessarily be imputed when using tax data. While a number of missing income sources can be reasonably allocated using data available in surveys, the distribution of some income components is inherently ambiguous. Estimates of the income distribution will therefore always be subject to some uncertainties. For this reason, in other work, we present sensitivity analysis.[18] For example, accounting for income from unreported offshore wealth increases top 1 percent income shares by only about 0.3 pp in 2014. Combining the effects of several alternative allocation assumptions that increase or decrease the top 1 percent income share results in changes of about 1 pp. This analysis suggests a relatively narrow range around our main estimates.

Tax Reforms Affecting Fiscal Income of High-Income Taxpayers

The income tax system in the 1960s was characterized by high statutory tax rates but relatively modest effective tax rates for the top of the distribution. Hellerstein concluded that this was because the tax base was "full of leaks, loopholes, exemptions and preferences."[19] The combination of high tax rates and loopholes provided both the incentive and opportunity for tax avoidance. This situation was described as "dipping deeply into great incomes with a sieve."[20] While some loophole-closing provisions were enacted starting in 1969, the Economic Recovery Tax Act of 1981 created new opportunities for tax shelters. Some of these new sheltering opportunities were limited in 1982 and 1984, but major reform was not accomplished until TRA86.[21]

TRA86 was based on the principle of lowering tax rates and broadening the tax base to achieve revenue and distributional neutrality. Individual income tax rates were reduced and simplified to two basic rates: 15 and 28 percent. To achieve distributional neutrality and target tax shelters, the base broadening was targeted at the top of the distribution. The 60 percent exclusion for long-term capital gains was repealed, increasing the top capital gains rate from 20 to 28 percent. Real estate tax shelters were addressed by lengthening depreciation periods and making the tax rate on capital gains the same as that on ordinary income. Deductions for rental losses were capped and phased out for high-income taxpayers, and the use of passive losses on investments to offset positive income was limited. These changes resulted in higher reported incomes on the individual tax returns of wealthy taxpayers.[22]

TRA86 also created strong incentives to change the form of business organization. Before TRA86, the top individual tax rate was greater than the top corporate tax rate (50 vs. 46 percent), causing shifting into C corporations.[23] After TRA86, the top individual tax rate was less than the top corporate tax rate (28 vs. 34 percent), causing shifting into pass-through businesses (S corporations, partnerships, and sole proprietorships). This shifting of entity form further increased reported top incomes because pass-through income is reported directly on individual tax returns but C corporation retained earnings are not. This shift from C corporations to pass-through businesses caused an exaggerated jump in top fiscal income shares in the late 1980s. Measures based on national income address this issue by including corporate retained earnings, which were more important prior to TRA86.

Underreported Income

US national income includes estimates of underreported income that are based on periodic detailed audit studies by the IRS. These audit studies are based on stratified random samples of tax returns representative of the potential for underreporting. They are much more comprehensive than normal operational audits, making full use of information returns and generally requiring taxpayers to provide adequate proof of income and deductions. Based on the extent of information reporting, the IRS increases the amounts found to account for income not found. Early studies were called the Taxpayer Compliance Measurement Program (TCMP). Starting in 2001, these were replaced by the National Research Program (NRP).

Table 5.2 shows the distribution of underreported business income in the 1988 TCMP. Since research on the income distribution is based on reported incomes (i.e., underreporting-inclusive incomes are not observed in annual tax data), the table shows the distribution by adjusted gross income (AGI) as originally reported on income tax returns. One notable result is that the percentage change in income from adding underreported income is highest at the bottom of the distribution and declines among returns with higher reported incomes. For taxpayers with a negative AGI, usually the result of current-year business losses and/or large net operating losses carried over from prior years, the TCMP found enough income to make the overall corrected income of this group positive. In some cases, adding underreported income moves taxpayers from the bottom of the distribution to the top 1 percent. For the bottom two quintiles by reported income, business income is increased by more than 400 percent. For the top 1 percent by reported income, business income is increased by only 10 percent. Recent

Table 5.2 Underreporting rates of pass-through business income by reported adjusted gross income (AGI), 1988

Reported AGI group	Reported on return ($billion)	Income gap ($billion)	Corrected income ($billion)	Percentage change in income	Share of income change	Share of positive business income (PSZ)
Less than $0	−10	20	10	∞	13%	1%
0–40 (excl. < $0)	9	42	51	441%	27%	6%
40–80	34	50	84	145%	32%	19%
80–95	32	24	55	75%	16%	16%
95–99	40	11	51	26%	7%	20%
Top 1%	77	8	85	10%	5%	38%
Total	183	153	336	84%	100%	100%

Note: Pass-through business income includes net income of sole proprietorships, partnerships, and S corporations.
Source: Tabulations by the authors of the 1988 Taxpayer Compliance Measurement Program File.

research suggests that these patterns persist through recent periods and confirm the importance of accounting for overstated business losses when allocating underreported income.[24]

Auten and Splinter (2019a) national income estimates are based on the results of these TCMP and NRP data.[25] In contrast, PSZ allocate underreported business income in proportion to positive amounts of reported business income. Their approach implies that all those who do report large amounts of income have hidden even more and nearly doubles the highly concentrated pass-through income of the top 1 percent in many years. Moreover, the PSZ approach disregards underreporting on returns with business losses. In 1988, for example, our audit-based approach allocates about one-sixth of underreported business income to returns with negative AGI, compared to almost none being allocated to these returns with the PSZ approach.

In recent decades, these differences in allocating underreported income explain one-third of the larger PSZ top 1 percent pre-tax shares. In 2014, about $500 billion of the income of the top 1 percent came from the profits of pass-through businesses.[26] This represented about 50 percent of total positive pass-through income, and therefore PSZ allocated about half of underreported pass-through income to the top 1 percent, or about $350 billion. In comparison, the 2001 NRP audit study shows that only 5 percent of the underreported income of filers was received by the top 1 percent by *reported* income.[27] Based on the NRP data and accounting for non-filer underreporting, we allocate about $35 billion to these returns. Re-ranking from adding underreporting income means our final top 1 percent has a bit more underreported income than the initial allocation suggests.[28] This difference of more than $300 billion results in PSZ increasing top 1 percent income shares by about 2 pp more than our audit-based approach.

The PSZ estimates are the basis for US incomes in the World Inequality Database,[29] which is intended to allow international comparisons of income distributions. Because of concerns about some of the assumptions behind the US data, especially regarding the allocation of retirement and underreported income, we hope that improvements can be made to this important new database.

Changes in Tax Avoidance

Given the tax rules in effect in the 1960s, the introduction of information reporting on additional types of income, and the effects of TRA86 in closing tax shelters and inducing the shift of businesses from corporate to pass-through form, it is no surprise that changes in tax avoidance help explain the increase in top fiscal income shares. Saez, however, dismisses the importance of the tax-avoidance channel based on two arguments: (1) a perceived inverse relationship between top statutory tax rates and top income shares and (2) high-income charitable contributions.[30] Evidence suggests that both arguments are flawed.

While top federal individual tax rates and pre-tax top income shares since 1960 could appear to have a negative correlation, this is fully driven by changes in TRA86: a large drop in the top tax rate, base-broadening, and entity-shifting. Using our top 1 percent pre-tax national income shares, for 1960–2015, the correlation with top tax rates is −0.58, consistent with the negative correlation narrative. But for the sub-periods 1960–1986 and 1988–2015, the correlations are +0.61 and +0.23. Removing the effects of TRA86 reverses the sign of the correlation, suggesting no consistent relationship between top rates and income shares.

There are additional issues with such correlation analysis. The fraction of taxpayers subject to the top rate has changed dramatically. For example, in 1962, only 0.001 percent of tax units were subject to the top tax rate, while in 1988, it was more than 20 percent and in 2014, it was 0.6 percent.

With respect to charitable giving, Saez argues that because deductions for charitable contributions of the top 1 percent increased from 35 percent to 80 percent of average economy-wide income since the 1960s, this shows that "their ability to give has grown almost parallel to the share of their reported income" and thus their income share must have increased as well.[31] Leaving aside the question of whether this is a sensible comparison, it is important to note that these numbers are partly explained by changes in tax laws. In the 1960s, deductions for charitable contributions were limited to 30 percent of AGI for donations to certain 501(c) charitable organizations and 20 percent for other donations, including to donations to private foundations. Starting with the 1969 Act, these limits were increased to 50 and 30 percent (20 percent in some cases), respectively, allowing much larger deductions of charitable contributions. Furthermore, AGI in the 1960s included only 50 percent of capital gains, making the limits on maximum charitable deductions even stricter than implied by the percentage limits alone. Since post-TRA86 law income includes all capital gains, this further relaxed the contribution deduction limits.

DISTRIBUTION OF ECONOMIC GROWTH

Comparisons of cross-sectional inequality over time have been used to calculate the "fraction of total growth (or loss) captured by top 1%."[32] Using this method, updated estimates by Piketty and Saez suggest that the top 1 percent received about three-quarters of the increase in fiscal income between 1979 and 2014. But the question of who has benefited from economic growth can only be answered by using data that tracks individuals over time, such as the panels used in income mobility studies.

The basic issue is that the same people are not at the top all the time. Instead, there is substantial turnover. For example, Auten, Gee, and Turner examined persistence in the top 1 percent before and after 2005. They found that 48 percent had not been in the top 1 percent the prior year, and 39 percent dropped out of the top 1 percent by the next year. Only 16 percent were continuously in the top 1 percent for the five previous years and 24 percent for the five following years. From a longer-term perspective, they found that the combined Greatest Generation and Silent Generation occupied 79 percent of the top 1 percent in 1987. But, by 2010, their share fell to 22 percent, and they had been replaced by the Baby Boomers, who occupied a 59 percent share.[33] The turnover rate is also high on the 400 taxpayers with the highest incomes. Over the period from 1992 to 2008, the IRS found that more than 3,600 taxpayers appeared in this group.[34] More than two-thirds of primary filers appeared only once, and fewer than 10 appeared in all 17 years.

Another perspective in the mobility literature comes from examining the income changes of taxpayers initially in top- or bottom-income groups. While the cross-sectional approach implies high income growth for top income groups and little growth for bottom income groups, mobility studies tracking the same individuals over time show that most of those in the top 1 percent in the base year experience income decreases while those starting at the bottom have the largest increases. Between 1996 and 2005, Auten and Gee estimated that, for those starting in the top 1 percent, almost 70 percent had income *decreases*, while 80 percent of those initially in the bottom quintile had income *increases*. Those in the top 1 percent (excluding the top 0.1 percent) had average real income declines of 37 percent, while those in the top 0.01 percent had declines of 67 percent.[35] Similarly, Splinter followed the same primary taxpayers in 1980 and 2014 and found that real incomes decreased for those starting in the top income quintile, but more than doubled for the bottom two quintiles, which earned about three-fourths of fiscal income growth.[36]

Van Kerm found similar results for other countries including Greece, Ireland, Italy, and Portugal.[37] For Britain, Jenkins and Van Kerm concluded that "from a longitudinal perspective, the pattern of individual income growth is progressive: the lower the rank in the base-year distribution, the greater the expected income growth. Expected income growth, absolute or proportionate, is positive for the majority of individuals, but negative for individuals in the richest fifth in the base year."[38]

Mobility studies illustrate that most of those at the top in a particular year earn little, if any, of the economic growth in following years, and those in the lowest income groups experience the largest increase in following years. While some of this reflects transitory income and life cycle effects, the mobility literature highlights the importance of keeping in mind that it is not the same people at the bottom and the top over time.

CONCLUSION

Using tax data to estimate income inequality over long time periods is difficult because of social changes, tax policy changes, and the nearly 40 percent of national income missing from tax returns. Our analysis accounts for important social and tax policy changes, adjusts for important technical issues in using income reported on individual tax returns, and includes estimates of missing income. We show step-by-step how our adjustments affect top income shares, and we compare our approach to those of Piketty and Saez and PSZ.

It is important to note that our analysis is not intended to make any normative judgments about the distribution of income, transfers, or taxes. Instead, our research is intended to improve upon prior estimates by addressing the challenges posed by changes in social and economic conditions and changes in how and where income is reported in tax data. Because an increasing share of national income is not reported in tax data, all such estimates necessarily involve a degree of uncertainty. In addition, there are many areas where information is currently lacking, but we may learn more in the future.

Other studies have found results similar to those we report in this chapter. Using the Survey of Consumer Finance, Bricker et al. estimate that, between 1988 and 2012, the top 1 percent pre-tax income share increased 3 pp. Using internal Census data to deal with top-coding, Burkhauser et al. estimate that, between 1967 and 2004, it increased only 2 pp. Combining survey and tax data, Fixler, Gindelsky, and Johnson estimate a 2012 top 1 percent share of personal income of 13 percent, similar to our pre-tax/after-transfer share.[39]

Our estimates are that pre-tax top 1 percent national income shares increased only 3 pp (from 11 to 14 percent) since the early 1960s, with a decline of about 2 pp from 1962 to 1979 and an increase of about 5 pp from 1979 to 2015. After accounting for taxes and transfers, our estimates suggest that the top 1 percent share was almost unchanged between 1962 and 2014. Redistribution from transfers and taxes almost fully mitigated the increase in pre-tax top income shares. This resulted from the growth of transfers from 5 to 17 percent of national income and more overall progressivity in the tax system, primarily due to increases in refundable credits and other tax reductions targeted at lower and middle-income taxpayers. Another important finding is that real incomes of the bottom 50 percent have increased rather than stagnated. Finally, we find that claims that most of economic growth has gone to the top of the distribution are misleading. Panel data show that those starting with low incomes have the largest percentage increases while incomes fall for those at the top. Moreover, it is not the same people at the top over time.

DISCLAIMER

Auten: Views and opinions expressed are those of the author and do not necessarily represent official positions or policies of the US Department of the Treasury. Splinter: This paper embodies work undertaken for the staff of the

Joint Committee on Taxation, but as members of both parties and both houses of Congress comprise the Joint Committee on Taxation, this work should not be construed to represent the position of any member of the Committee.

ACKNOWLEDGMENTS

For helpful comments and discussions, we thank Thomas Barthold, Edith Brashares, Julie-Anne Cronin, Wojciech Kopczuk, Jeff Larrimore, Janet McCubbin, James Poterba, John Sabelhaus, Emmanuel Saez, Joel Slemrod, Eugene Steuerle, Erick Zwick, and participants of the NBER Summer Institute, CBO Distributional Tax Analysis Conference, Georgetown Tax Law and Public Finance workshop, and annual conferences of the National Tax Association and American Economic Association. We also thank Janet Auten for editorial assistance.

NOTES

1. Thomas Piketty and Emmanuel Saez, "Income Inequality in the United States, 1913–1998," *Quarterly Journal of Economics*, 118(1) (February 2003): 1–39. Thomas Piketty, Emmanuel Saez, and Gabriel Zucman, "Distributional National Accounts: Methods and Estimates for the United States," *Quarterly Journal of Economics*, 131(2) (May 2018): 519–557. Their new book was released shortly before this article went to press and too late to be included. Emmanuel Saez and Gabriel Zucman, *The Triumph of Injustice: How the Rich Dodge Taxes and How to Make them Pay*. New York: W.W. Norton, 2019. One change from PSZ was to allocate corporate income taxes by corporate ownership, which increased top income shares and tax burdens in the 1960s.

2. The estimates in this paper are from the July 2019 version of Auten and Splinter (2019a) estimates and do not account for the Tax Cuts and Jobs Act enacted December 22, 2017. The effects of this act will not be known for several years due to lags in filing and processing of IRS data and short-run behavioral responses. Gerald Auten and David Splinter, "Income Inequality in the United States: Using Tax Data to Measure Long-Term Trends." Working paper. July 2019, http://davidsplinter.com/AutenSplinter-Tax_Data_and_Inequality.pdf (hereafter, Auten and Splinter, 2019a).

3. In 2013, changes to high-income taxpayers included the higher top statutory rate, the phaseout of itemized deductions, two new surtaxes (the Additional Medicare Tax and the Net Investment Income Tax), as well as other tax increases on capital income. Auten, Splinter, and Nelson (2016, p. 952) estimated that "top individual marginal tax rates increased by about 7 percentage points on earned income. The top effective individual marginal rate

on capital gains and qualified dividends increased from 15 percent to over 25 percent." Gerald Auten, David Splinter, and Susan Nelson, "Reactions of High-Income Taxpayers to Major Tax Legislation," *National Tax Journal,* 69(4) (December 2016): 935–964.

4. Kevin Perese, "CBO's New Framework for Analyzing the Effects of Means-Tested Transfers and Federal Taxes on the Distribution of Household Income." Congressional Budget Office. Working paper 2017-09. December 2017, https://www.cbo.gov/publication/53345.

5. This section only provides a brief description of our methodology. For more details, see the online appendix to Auten and Splinter (2019a), http://davidsplinter.com/AutenSplinter-Tax_Data_and_Inequality_onlineapp.pdf.

6. Auten and Splinter (2019b) provide a similar step-by-step comparison to CBO estimates, another frequently cited source of US income inequality estimates using tax data. Gerald Auten and David Splinter, "Top 1% Income Shares: Comparing Estimates Using Tax Data," *AEA Papers and Proceedings,* 109(May 2019b): 307–311.

7. The age 20 standard was used in PSZ as well as the Piketty and Saez (2003). This has the advantage of making it easier to estimate the non-filer population, although it excludes independent households under age 20 and does not account for later entry into the labor force due to rising college attendance in recent decades. As discussed in the text, we address these issues by our treatment of taxpayers under age 20 and dependent filers age 20 and older.

8. Julie-Anne Cronin, Portia DeFilippes, and Emily Y. Lin, "Effects of Adjusting Distribution Tables for Family Size," *National Tax Journal,* 65(4) (December 2012): 739–758.

9. Jesse Bricker, Alice Henriques, Jacob Krimmel, and John Sabelhaus, "Estimating Top Income and Wealth Shares: Sensitivity to Data and Methods," *American Economic Review,* 106(5) (May 2016b): 641–645.

10. David Splinter, "Who Pays No Tax? The Declining Fraction paying Income Taxes and Increasing Tax Progressivity," *Contemporary Economic Policy,* 37(3) (October 2019b): 413–426.

11. Our approach is halfway between the two extremes considered by Congressional Budget Office. 2013, "The Distribution of Federal Spending and Taxes in 2006." Congressional Budget Office, https://www.cbo.gov/publication/44698.

12. Sebastian Devlin-Foltz, Alice M. Henriques, and John Sabelhaus, "Is the US Retirement System Contributing to Rising Wealth Inequality?" Russell Sage Foundation. *Journal of the Social Sciences,* 2(6) (October 2016): 59–85.

13. Estimates by Liu and Altshuler (2013) and Suárez Serrato and Zidar (2016) suggest that wages bear an even larger share of the corporate tax. Li Liu and Rosanne Altshuler, "Measuring the Burden of the Corporate Income Tax Under Imperfect Competition," *National Tax Journal,* 66(1) (March 2013): 215–237; Juan Carlos Suárez Serrato, and Owen Zidar, "Who Benefits

from State Corporate Tax Cuts? A Local Labor Markets Approach with Heterogeneous Firms," *American Economic Review,* 106(9) (September 2016): 2582–2624.

14. Matthew Smith, Danny Yagan, Owen M. Zidar, and Eric Zwick, "Capitalists in the Twenty-First Century," *Quarterly Journal of Economics,* 134(4) (November 2019): 1675–1745.

15. See Steven Rose, "The Ins and Outs of Measuring Income Inequality in the United States," Chapter 1 in this volume, for additional discussion of alternative definitions of income and income data.

16. Dennis Fixler, Marina Gindelsky, and David Johnson, "Improving the Measure of the Distribution of Personal Income," *AEA Papers and Proceedings,* 109(May 2019): 302–306.

17. Christopher R. Bollinger, Barry T. Hirsch, Charles M. Hokayem, and James P. Ziliak, "Trouble in the Tails? What We Know about Earnings Nonresponse 30 Years after Lillard, Smith, and Welch," *Journal of Political Economy,* 127(5) (July 2019): 2143–2185.

18. Auten and Splinter, 2019a.

19. Jerome Hellerstein, *Taxes, Loopholes and Morals.* New York: McGraw-Hill, 1963.

20. First used by Simons (1938) to describe the tax system in the 1930s, this phrase was later used to describe the situation in the 1960s. Henry C. Simons, *Personal Income Taxation: The Definition of Income as a Problem of Fiscal Policy.* Chicago, IL: University of Chicago, 1938, 219.

21. For further insights into the base-broadening movement leading up to TRA86 and previous expansions of tax shelters, see Pechman (1987) and Bakija and Steuerle (1991). Joseph Pechman, "Tax Reform: Theory and Practice," *Journal of Economic Perspectives,* 1 (1) (Summer 1987): 11–28. Jon Bakija and Eugene Steuerle, "Individual Income Taxation Since 1948," *National Tax Journal,* 44(4) (December 1991): 451–475.

22. While the focus in this section is on longer term effects of TRA86, there were also important short-term shifting responses that had temporary effects on top income shares. The unlocking of capital gains in 1986 to realize gains ahead of the rate increase roughly doubled reported gains. In addition, ordinary income was deferred from 1987 to 1988, to be taxed at much lower rates. Both of these resulted in temporary spikes in top 1 percent income shares. See Auten, Splinter, and Nelson (2016).

23. Roger Gordon and Joel Slemrod, "Are 'Real' Responses to Taxes Simply Income Shifting Between Corporate and Personal Tax Bases?" In *Does Atlas Shrug? The Economic Consequences of Taxing the Rich,* edited by J. Slemrod (pp. 240–288). New York: Russell Sage Foundation and Harvard University Press, 2000.

24. Gerald Auten and Patrick Langetieg, "The Distribution of Underreported Income: What We Can Learn from the NRP," presentation at the National

Tax Association Spring Symposium and forthcoming in the *National Tax Journal*.

25. This paper's estimates use the 1988 audit distribution to allocate underreported income in years prior to 1992 and the 2001 audit distribution for later years. Since the focus of these audit studies is the overall amount of missing tax revenue, there are few published studies providing information on the distribution of underreported income. One exception using the 2001 NRP study data is Andrew Johns and Joel Slemrod, "The Distribution of Income Tax Noncompliance," *National Tax Journal* 63(3) (September 2010): 397–418.

26. This number is based on Piketty and Saez (2003) online data as currently updated.

27. Johns and Slemrod, "The Distribution of Income Tax Noncompliance," table 3.

28. Johns and Slemrod (2010) shows that the top 1 percent shares of reported income and true income after adding underreported income are essentially the same, but that the top 1 percent by reported income receives a less than proportional amount. This apparent contradiction is reconciled by the effects of re-ranking by true income.

29. Information can be found at https://wid.world/country/usa/

30. Emmanuel Saez, "Income and Wealth Inequality: Evidence and Policy Implications," Chapter 2 in this volume.

31. Ibid.

32. Emmanuel Saez, "Striking It Richer." Working paper. 2013.

33. Gerald Auten, Geoffrey Gee, and Nicholas Turner, "New Perspective on Income Mobility and Inequality," *National Tax Journal*, 66(4) (December 2013): 893–912.

34. Internal Revenue Service, Statistics of Income Division, "The 400 Individual Income Tax Returns Reporting the Highest Adjusted Gross Incomes Each Year, 1992-2006." Washington DC: US Internal Revenue Service. 2008, table 4, https://www.irs.gov/pub/irs-soi/08intop400.pdf.

35. Gerald Auten and Geoffrey Gee, "Income Mobility in the United States: New Evidence from Income Tax Data," *National Tax Journal*, 62(2) (June 2009): 301–328.

36. David Splinter, "Progressive Growth: Comparing Cross-Sectional and Panel Approaches." Working paper. 2019a, http://www.davidsplinter.com/Splinter-ProgressiveGrowth.pdf.

37. Philippe Van Kerm, "Income Mobility Profiles," *Economic Letters*, 102(2) (February 2009): 93–95.

38. Stephen P. Jenkins and Philippe Van Kerm, "Assessing Individual Income Growth," *Economica*, 83(332) (October 2016): 690–691.

39. Jesse Bricker, Alice Henriques, Jacob Krimmel, and John Sabelhaus, "Measuring Income and Wealth at the Top Using Administrative and Survey

Data," *Brookings Papers on Economic Activity* (Spring 2016a): 261–312; Richard V. Burkhauser, Shuaizhang Feng, Stephen Jenkins, and Jeff Larrimore, "Recent Trends in Top Income Shares in the United States: Reconciling Estimates from March CPS and IRS Tax Return Data," *Review of Economics and Statistics*, 44(2) (May 2012): 371–388; and Fixler, Gindelsky, and Johnson, "Improving the Measure of the Distribution of Personal Income."

REFERENCES

Auten, Gerald, and Geoffrey Gee. June 2009. "Income Mobility in the United States: New Evidence from Income Tax Data." *National Tax Journal*, 62(2): 301–328.

Auten, Gerald and Patrick Langetieg. 2020. "The Distribution of Underreported Income: What We Can Learn from the NRP," presentation at the National Tax Association Spring Symposium and forthcoming in the *National Tax Journal*.

Auten, Gerald, Geoffrey Gee, and Nicholas Turner. December 2013. "New Perspective on Income Mobility and Inequality." *National Tax Journal*, 66(4): 893–912.

Auten, Gerald, and David Splinter. 2019a. "Income Inequality in the United States: Using Tax Data to Measure Long-Term Trends." Working paper. http:// davidsplinter.com/AutenSplinter-Tax_Data_and_Inequality.pdf

Auten, Gerald, and David Splinter. May 2019b. "Top 1% Income Shares: Comparing Estimates Using Tax Data." *AEA Papers and Proceedings*, 109: 307–311.

Auten, Gerald, David Splinter, and Susan Nelson. December 2016. "Reactions of High-Income Taxpayers to Major Tax Legislation." *National Tax Journal*, 69(4): 935–964.

Bakija, Jon, and Eugene Steuerle. December 1991. "Individual Income Taxation Since 1948." *National Tax Journal*, 44(4): 451–475.

Bollinger, Christopher R., Barry T. Hirsch, Charles M. Hokayem, and James P. Ziliak. July 2019. "Trouble in the Tails? What We Know about Earnings Nonresponse 30 Years after Lillard, Smith, and Welch." *Journal of Political Economy*, 127(5): 2143–2185.

Bricker, Jesse, Alice Henriques, Jacob Krimmel, and John Sabelhaus. 2016a. "Measuring Income and Wealth at the Top Using Administrative and Survey Data." *Brookings Papers on Economic Activity*, Spring: 261–312.

Bricker, Jesse, Alice Henriques, Jacob Krimmel, and John Sabelhaus. 2016b. "Estimating Top Income and Wealth Shares: Sensitivity to Data and Methods." *American Economic Review*, 106(May): 641–645.

Burkhauser, Richard V., Shuaizhang Feng, Stephen Jenkins, and Jeff Larrimore. May 2012. "Recent Trends in Top Income Shares in the United States: Reconciling Estimates from March CPS and IRS Tax Return Data." *Review of Economics and Statistics*, 44(2): 371–388.

Congressional Budget Office. 2013. *The Distribution of Federal Spending and Taxes in 2006*. Washington, DC: Congressional Budget Office.

Congressional Budget Office. 2018. *The Distribution of Household Income, 2015*. Washington, DC: Congressional Budget Office.

Cronin, Julie-Anne, Portia DeFilippes, and Emily Y. Lin. December 2012. "Effects of Adjusting Distribution Tables for Family Size." *National Tax Journal*, 65(4): 739–758.

Devlin-Foltz, Sebastian, Alice M. Henriques, and John Sabelhaus. October 2016. "Is the US Retirement System Contributing to Rising Wealth Inequality?" *Russell Sage Foundation Journal of the Social Sciences*, 2(6): 59–85.

Fixler, Dennis, Marina Gindelsky, and David Johnson. 2019. "Improving the Measure of the Distribution of Personal Income." *AEA Papers and Proceedings*, 109(May): 302–306.

Gordon, Roger, and Joel Slemrod. 2000. "Are 'Real' Responses to Taxes Simply Income Shifting Between Corporate and Personal Tax Bases?" In *Does Atlas Shrug? The Economic Consequences of Taxing the Rich*, edited by J. Slemrod (pp. 240–288). New York: Russell Sage Foundation and Harvard University Press.

Hellerstein, Jerome. 1963. *Taxes, Loopholes and Morals*. New York: McGraw-Hill.

Jenkins, Stephen P., and Philippe Van Kerm. 2016, October. "Assessing Individual Income Growth." *Economica*, 83(332): 679–703.

Internal Revenue Service, Statistics of Income Division. 2008. *The 400 Individual Income Tax Returns Reporting the Highest Adjusted Gross Incomes Each Year, 1992–2006*. Washington DC: US Internal Revenue Service.

Johns, Andrew, and Joel Slemrod. September 2010. "The Distribution of Income Tax Noncompliance." *National Tax Journal*, 63(3): 397–418.

Liu, Li, and Rosanne Altshuler. March 2013. "Measuring the Burden of the Corporate Income Tax Under Imperfect Competition." *National Tax Journal*, 66(1): 215–237.

Mathews, Timothy. 2014. "Historical Trends in the Degree of Federal Income Tax Progressivity in the United States." *Social Science Journal*, 1(March): 90–99.

Pechman, Joseph. 1987. "Tax Reform: Theory and Practice." *Journal of Economic Perspectives*, 1(1): 11–28.

Perese, Kevin. December 2017. "CBO's New Framework for Analyzing the Effects of Means-Tested Transfers and Federal Taxes on the Distribution of Household Income." Working paper 2017-09. Washington, DC: Congressional Budget Office.

Piketty, Thomas, and Emmanuel Saez. February 2003. "Income Inequality in the United States, 1913–1998." *Quarterly Journal of Economics*, 118(1): 1–39.

Piketty, Thomas, Emmanuel Saez, and Gabriel Zucman. May 2018. "Distributional National Accounts: Methods and Estimates for the United States." *Quarterly Journal of Economics*, 131(2): 519–557.

Saez, Emmanuel. 2013. "Striking It Richer." Working paper.

Saez, Emmanuel, and Gabriel Zucman. 2019. *The Triumph of Injustice: How the Rich Dodge Taxes and How to Make Them Pay*. New York: W.W. Norton.

Simons, Henry C. 1938. *Personal Income Taxation: The Definition of Income as a Problem of Fiscal Policy*. Chicago, IL: University of Chicago.

Smith, Matthew, Danny Yagan, Owen M. Zidar, and Eric Zwick. November 2019. "Capitalists in the Twenty-First Century." *Quarterly Journal of Economics*, 134(4): 1675–1745.

Splinter, David. 2019a. "Progressive Growth: Comparing Cross-Sectional and Panel Approaches." Working paper. http://www.davidsplinter.com/Splinter-ProgressiveGrowth.pdf

Splinter, David. October 2019b. "Who Pays No Tax? The Declining Fraction paying Income Taxes and Increasing Tax Progressivity." *Contemporary Economic Policy*, 37(3): 413–426.

Suárez Serrato, Juan Carlos, and Owen Zidar. September 2016. "Who Benefits from State Corporate Tax Cuts? A Local Labor Markets Approach with Heterogeneous Firms." *American Economic Review*, 106(9): 2582–2624.

Van Kerm, Philippe. February 2009. "Income Mobility Profiles." *Economic Letters*, 102(2): 93–95.

6

THE EFFECTS OF THE MOVEMENT OF WOMEN INTO THE WORKFORCE ON INCOME TRENDS

Diana Furchtgott-Roth and Beila Leboeuf

INTRODUCTION

Studies have documented rising income inequality in the United States over the past four decades. This chapter presents evidence suggesting that the movement of women into the workforce, combined with changing trends in marriage, divorce, and life expectancy, may have been factors leading to higher inequality. The movement of women into the workforce, facilitated by changing social norms, higher educational attainment among women, and advancements in contraceptives, resulted not only in a social revolution but also in a major economic shift. As women started working in greater numbers and pursuing more schooling, two-earner households and single-female led households became more common, which may have led to a polarization of income at the top and at the bottom of the income distribution. At the top, high-earning women married high-earning men to create dual-income households with a high joint income. At the bottom, high divorce rates, higher life expectancy (particularly for women), and a greater prevalence of single motherhood may have led to more single-female led households with low incomes.

The purpose of this chapter is to illustrate that while women's professional progress has raised America's gross domestic product (GDP) and income

Diana Furchtgott-Roth and Beila Leboeuf, *The Effects of the Movement of Women into the Workforce on Income Trends* In: *United States Income, Wealth, Consumption, and Inequality.* Edited by: Diana Furchtgott-Roth, Oxford University Press (2021). © Oxford University Press. DOI: 10.1093/oso/9780197518199.003.0007.

levels, it may have at the same time contributed to increased inequality. This should be kept in mind when considering policies geared toward reducing inequality.

This chapter explains trends from 1980 to 2019. The remainder of this chapter is organized as follows: the next section presents data on women's labor force participation and education from 1980 to the present, documenting the advancements made by women, and mothers in particular, over the past four decades. The following section highlights several limitations in how inequality is measured. The next section presents evidence suggesting that the movement of women into the workforce, along with changes in marriage, divorce, and life expectancy, may have led to greater income inequality. We then review some of the empirical evidence on the effects of the movement of women into the workforce and related factors on inequality and finish with our conclusions.

THE MOVEMENT OF WOMEN INTO THE WORKFORCE

Labor Force Participation

Women's labor force participation rates, which measure the share of employed and unemployed women in the working age population, rose substantially in the second half of the 20th century. In 1980, 51 percent of working-aged women were employed or looking for work.[1] By 1999, 60 percent of women were participating in the labor force, an increase of about 18 percent in just under two decades.[2] Moreover, women were entering fields that had previously been solely the purview of men, such as medicine, dentistry, law, and business. This exodus of women from the home to the office had substantial effects not only on income and its distribution, but also on society and culture.

The first years of the 21st century saw the labor force participation of women decline slightly from the 1999 peak, to just over 57 percent in 2019.[3] However, the changes in women's educational and work outcomes that took place over the second half of the 20th century remained.

Table 6.1 shows female labor force participation rates broken down by age groups over time. While labor force participation has risen on average for women in all age categories, the largest increases are for women in the middle of the age distribution and older. In 1980, women in the 16–24 and 25–54 age groups had the strongest labor force participation rates. By 2019, prime-age working women between the ages of 25 and 54 were the most likely to be in the labor force, with a 76 percent labor force participation rate.[4] In comparison, only 55 percent of younger women, aged 16–24, were in the labor force, a decrease of 7 percentage points since 1980.[5] A major reason for declining labor force participation among younger women is increased enrollment in postsecondary education.

Furthermore, from 1980 until the present, the number of women working later in life has grown substantially. Table 6.1 shows that, since 1980, the share

Table 6.1 Labor force participation rates for women by age group, 1980–2019

Age	1980 (%)	2000 (%)	2019 (%)
16+	52	60	57
16–24	62	63	55
25–54	64	77	76
55+	23	26	35

Source: Bureau of Labor Statistics, Labor Force Participation Rate: 16 years and over, Women {LNS11300002} (2019), https://data.bls.gov/pdq/SurveyOutputServlet, Bureau of Labor Statistics, Labor Force Participation Rate: 25–54 years, Women [LNS11300062] (2019), https://beta.bls.gov/dataViewer/view/timeseries/LNS11300062; Bureau of Labor Statistics, Labor Force Participation Rate: 16–24 years, Women [LNS11324886] (2019), https://data.bls.gov/timeseries/LNS11324886; Bureau of Labor Statistics, Labor Force Participation Rate: 55 years and over, Women [LNU01324232] (2019), https://data.bls.gov/timeseries/LNU01324232

of women over the age of 55 who are in the labor force has grown from 23 to 35 percent.[6] Also, women over 65 years of age have more than doubled their participation rate over the past four decades, from 8 percent in 1980 to more than 16 percent in 2019.[7]

Moreover, gains in labor force participation for women have occurred in more skilled occupations, consistent with a rising demand for social and analytical skills (as opposed to physical skills) since the 1980s.[8] In 2017, women represented more than half of workers in management, professional, and related occupations, surpassing their representation in the overall workforce.[9] Figure 6.1 shows the shares of men and women in these occupations in 2017. While women represented 47 percent of the workforce in 2017, they composed 52 percent of all management, professional, and related occupations, driven largely by strong female representation in community and social services (e.g., social workers, education directors, teachers, paralegals, and designers); life, physical, and social sciences (e.g., biology, physical, and medical scientists, and psychologists); and business and financial operations occupations (e.g., human resource workers, accountants, credit counselors, marketing specialists, and fundraisers).

Working Mothers

One of the primary drivers of increasing female labor force participation over the past four decades is increased participation of mothers. In the past, most women stayed at home to take care of their children, especially young children. With cultural and technological changes, since 1980, more women with children of all ages have been leaving the home to work. The labor force participation rate for women with children under 18 grew from 57 percent in 1980 to 71 percent in 2017.[10] The largest increase has been seen for women with children under 6 years old, suggesting that women are taking less time off from work after having a child. According to the US Census, 73 percent of women who worked during pregnancy were back to

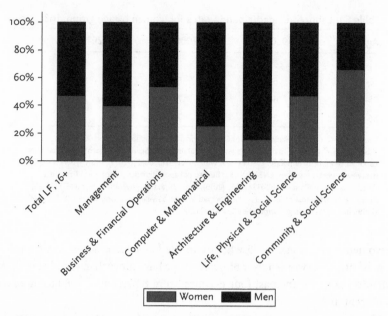

Figure 6.1 Gender distribution in management, professional, and related occupations in 2017.
Bureau of Labor Statistics, Table 11, "Women in the labor force: a databook," (2018), https://
www.bls.gov/opub/reports/womens-databook/2018/pdf/home.pdf
Note: BLS reports the categorization of all employed people by detailed occupation and gender.
Broadly defined categories include (1) management, professional, and related occupations,
(2) service occupations, (3) sales and office occupations, (4) natural resources, construction,
and maintenance occupations, and (5) production, transportation, and materials moving
occupations. In 2017, women represent 52 percent of the first category. A more detailed
breakdown of this category is shown in Figure 1 above.

work within 6 months of giving birth during the 2000s and 60 percent were
back to work within 3 months, compared to 60 percent and 46 percent, respectively, at the beginning of the 1980s.[11]

In 1980, fewer than half of women with children under 6 were in the labor
force, but by 2017, 65 percent of these women were in the labor force.[12] When
children are old enough to go to school, more women tend to rejoin the workforce. As a result, women with children between the ages of 6 and 17 have even
higher participation rates. In 2017, 76 percent of women with children between
the ages of 6 and 17 were in the labor force, up 12 percentage points since 1980.[13]

The movement of mothers into the labor force has increased the participation rates of women in general. However, women participate in the labor force in
different patterns than men. Table 6.2 compares the distribution of women and
men working part-time and full-time. Since 1980, working women have slightly
increased their participation in full-time employment; full-time employment for
working women increased from 73 percent of the labor force in 1980 to 76 percent
in 2017.[14] The opposite is true for working men; while 90 percent of working men
were employed full time in 1980, this proportion declined slightly to 88 percent in

Table 6.2 Share of women and men working part- and full-time in 2017

| | Women | | Men | | Percentage point difference in part-time work |
Year	Full (%)	Part (%)	Full (%)	Part (%)	
1980	73.2	26.8	90.4	9.6	17
1985	73.4	26.6	89.9	10.1	17
1990	74.8	25.2	89.9	10.1	15
1995	72.6	27.4	89.0	11.0	16
2000	75.4	24.6	89.9	10.1	15
2005	74.8	25.2	89.3	10.7	15
2006	75.3	24.7	89.4	10.6	14
2007	75.3	24.7	89.5	10.5	14
2008	75.4	24.6	88.9	11.1	14
2009	73.5	26.5	86.8	13.2	13
2010	73.4	26.6	86.6	13.4	13
2011	73.5	26.5	86.6	13.4	13
2012	73.7	26.3	86.7	13.3	13
2013	74.0	26.0	86.9	13.1	13
2014	74.2	25.8	87.3	12.7	13
2015	74.8	25.2	87.6	12.4	13
2016	75.1	24.9	87.6	12.4	13
2017	75.6	24.4	87.9	12.1	12

Source: Bureau of Labor Statistics, Table 21, "Women in the labor force: a databook," (2018) https://www.bls.gov/opub/reports/womens-databook/2018/pdf/home.pdf

2017.[15] In addition, despite the movement of women into the labor force, 24 percent of women still hold part-time positions, compared to 12 percent of men. This, combined with the slight increase in part-time work for men, results in a shrinking but still notable gender gap of 12 percentage points in part-time work. This gap is likely due to differences in preferences for part-time work as women bear children and still spend more time than men do in caregiving and household activities.[16]

Overall, the increase in participation rates of women, their movement into higher paying jobs, and the higher rates of labor force participation rates among mothers have had profound effects on the distribution of income, as discussed later in this chapter.

Educational Attainment

Growing educational attainment for women has also played a role in women's higher labor force participation rates and in increasing earnings over time. While greater educational attainment may have contributed to the decrease in labor

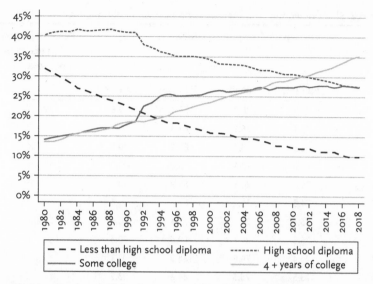

Figure 6.2 Educational attainment of women aged 25 and older, 1980–2018.
US Census Bureau, "Table A-1. Years of School Completed by People 25 Years and Over, by Age and Sex: Selected Years 1940-2018," (2019), https://www2.census.gov/programs-surveys/demo/tables/educational-attainment/time-series/cps-historical-time-series/taba-1.xlsx

force participation rates for young women aged 16–24, higher education also raised overall participation rates. When it became culturally more acceptable for women to work, they began investing in human capital, which led to higher-paying jobs and stronger labor force attachment.

Since 1980, women have gained higher levels of education, including bachelor's, master's, and doctor's degrees, and raised their earnings potential. Figure 6.2 illustrates the rise of higher education for women, showing the highest degree completed by women aged 25 and older from 1980 to 2018. Since 1980, the proportion of women whose highest level of schooling consists of some postsecondary education (some college, a college degree, or more) has steadily risen, while the proportion of women reporting a high school degree or less as the highest level of schooling completed has declined. In 1980, only 68 percent of women had a high school diploma or more. By 2018, more than 90 percent of women did, and the share of women receiving some college education or more had more than doubled from 28 percent in 1980 to more than 62 percent.[17]

Moreover, the upswing of higher education for women since 1980 has surpassed merely associate and bachelor's degrees and has expanded to graduate degrees, including master's and doctor's. Figure 6.3 shows how the shares of postsecondary degrees earned by women have risen over time. In less than 40 years, women nearly doubled their share of doctoral degrees with an increase of 84 percent during the period. Although less sizable, the percentage of associate, bachelor's, and master's degrees conferred to women increased by 11 percent, 15 percent, and 20 percent, respectively.[18] The increase in postsecondary

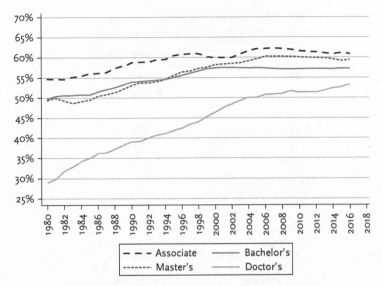

Figure 6.3 Share of degrees earned by women, 1980–1981 to 2016–2017.
US Department of Education, National Center for Education Statistics, Digest of Education Statistics 2018 Table 318.10, "*Degrees Conferred by Postsecondary Institutions, by level of degree and sex of student: selected years 1869-70 through 2028-2029,*" (2018), https://nces.ed.gov/programs/digest/d18/tables/dt18_318.10.asp?current=yes

education for women has been so substantial that, by 2016, the latest data available from the Department of Education, women earned nearly 60 percent of all postsecondary degrees.[19]

Women have moved into the professional world in record numbers. Traditionally, occupations in fields such as medicine, dentistry, and law were held by men. In 1980, women received less than a quarter of medical and dentistry degrees and received less than one-third of all law degrees. Since then, more women have moved into these occupations and have increased their share of these professional degrees by more than 15 percentage points for all three degrees.[20] As shown in Table 6.3, the share of dentistry degrees conferred to women increased

Table 6.3 Share of Professional degrees conferred to women, 1980–2016

	1980 (%)	2016 (%)	% Increase 1980–2016
Medical	24.7	47.4	91.9
Dentistry	14.4	47.9	232.6
Law	32.4	49.6	53.1

Source: US Department of Education, National Center for Education Statistics, Digest of Education Statistics 2018 Table 324.40, "*Number of postsecondary institutions conferring degrees in dentistry, medicine, and law, and number of such degrees conferred, by sex of student: Selected years, 1949–50 through 2016–17,*" (2018) https://nces.ed.gov/programs/digest/d18/tables/dt18_324.40.asp?current=yes

Table 6.4 Contribution of wives' earnings
to family income, selected years: 1980–2018

Year	Median percentage (%)
1980	27.0
1985	28.0
1990	31.0
1995	32.0
2000	32.8
2005	34.9
2010	37.1
2015	36.0
2018	36.9

Source: Women's Bureau, US Department of Labor, *"Mothers and Families: Selected Labor Force Characteristics, Married women's earnings as a percent of total family income,"* (2018) https://www.dol.gov/wb/stats/mother_families-text.htm#earn-married; Bureau of Labor Statistics, "1971 to 2013 Annual Social and Economic Supplements to the Current Population Survey (CPS)," (2014), https://www.dol.gov/wb/stats/mother_families.htm

the most at 233 percent from a level of 14 percent in 1980 to 48 percent in 2016. Women made significant advancements in these professional fields, and by 2016, women earned almost half of all degrees in all three fields.

By obtaining higher levels of education, women have increased their earnings potential, which is one reason that wives' contribution to family income is up 10 percentage points since 1980, from 27 percent to 37 percent.[21] Table 6.4 demonstrates the increase in wives' contribution to family earnings over time.

Furthermore, women's earnings as a percentage of men's have increased by 18 percentage points from 1980 to 2018.[22] Figure 6.4 shows the rise over time in women's earnings as a share of men's earnings. The increase has slowed in the past decade but has made substantial progress since 1980. In addition, more married women are beginning to earn more than their husbands. In 2018, more than 29 percent of married women had a higher income.[23]

ARE MEASURES OF INCOME INEQUALITY RELIABLE?

Economists often divide all households into income quintiles (fifths) and measure the differences in their incomes. This allows them to quantify income inequality and its growth over time. However, these measures of inequality are sensitive to methodological assumptions and choices, such as how to allocate income, what constitutes income, and how to account for inflation. As Steven Rose discusses

Figure 6.4 Female-to-male weekly earnings ratio, 1980–2018.
Women's Bureau, US Department of Labor, "Gender Earnings ratios by weekly earnings
and annual earnings (time series)," (2018), https://www.dol.gov/wb/stats/earnings-text.
htm#earn-gender-week-annual

in Chapter 1 of this volume, depending on how these questions and others are
addressed, researchers can come to very different conclusions. At one extreme,
researchers such as Emmanuel Saez, Thomas Piketty, and Gabriel Zucman have
measured large increases in inequality over time. Making different methodological choices, other researchers such as Gerald Auten and David Splinter have
measured much lower growth in inequality.

Examining the income distribution of households is not sufficient to understand either the extent of inequality in the United States or its drivers. Differences
between the highest earners and lowest earners do not always necessarily reflect
undesirable inequality. The lowest income group contains at least three significant groups of individuals. Some have low incomes because they are not working
or they may be searching for work. A second group comprises elderly individuals
who may have small amounts of retirement income but more substantial assets,
such as stocks and a home. These individuals may not be in the labor force and
therefore may not earn an income. A third group consists of students or recent
graduates who may not be earning much but whose education gives them a
strong shot at a prosperous future. While the first group may be in need of government help, the second and third groups may not.

Furthermore, quantifying inequality can be a dubious process for a number of
reasons. For example, quintiles differ in the number of people per household and
the number of earners per household, making comparisons difficult. Table 6.5

Table 6.5 Characteristics of income quintiles in 2018

	All consumer units	Lowest 20 %	Second 20 %	Third 20 %	Fourth 20 %	Highest 20 %
People	2.5	1.7	2.1	2.5	2.9	3.2
Earners	1.3	0.5	0.8	1.3	1.8	2.1
Housing tenure (%):						
Homeowner	63	41	56	61	72	87
With mortgage	37	12	20	34	52	67
Without mortgage	26	29	36	27	20	20
Renter	37	59	44	39	28	13

Source: Bureau of Labor Statistics, "Table 1101. Quintiles of income before taxes: Annual expenditure means, shares, standard errors, and coefficients of variation, Consumer Expenditure Survey, 2018," (2018) https://www.bls.gov/cex/2016/combined/quintile.pdf

shows that in 2018, households in the lowest fifth had an average of 1.7 people, with 0.5 earners. The highest fifth, however, had 3.2 persons per household, with 2.1 earners.[24] Thus, comparing households at the top to households at the bottom makes an inappropriate comparison between households with more individuals and households with fewer individuals and will result in measures of inequality that are biased upward.

In fact, as illustrated in Table 6.5, characteristics of households along the income distribution reveal trends associated with age. For example, while home ownership predictably increases with income quintile, a higher share of low-income Americans own their homes free of mortgage debt than do upper-income Americans; in 2018, 29 percent of households in the lowest income group and 36 percent in the next to lowest group owned their homes without a mortgage, compared to 20 percent of households in the two highest quintiles.[25]

Another factor that can appear to affect inequality is changes in the tax code. The Tax Reform Act of 1986 lowered the top individual tax rate to 28 percent and the corporate rate to 35 percent. Prior to the 1986 tax reform, the top individual rate was 50 percent, and the top corporate rate was 46 percent, so small businesses paid tax at a lower rate if they incorporated and filed taxes as corporations.

With the implementation of the Tax Reform Act of 1986, the top individual tax rate of 28 percent meant that small businesses were often better off filing under the individual tax code. Revenues shifted from the corporate to the individual tax sector. In the late 1980s and 1990s, that made it appear as though people had suddenly become better off and income inequality had worsened.

Income inequality measures may not accurately represent differences in economic well-being because the cost of living varies substantially in different parts of the country. College graduates on average earn more than those without a degree, and they tend to move to locations with higher costs of housing, food, and services, such as New York City, Boston, Washington, DC, and San Francisco. This leads to a high proportion of individuals with high incomes in more expensive locations where high incomes buy less. Thus, measures of inequality that don't take into account purchasing power do not paint a complete picture of economic hardship.

Moreover, low-income individuals spend a higher proportion of their income on nondurables such as food and clothing, while high-income individuals spend more on services. The price of food and clothing has been rising more slowly than the price of services. For example, high childcare costs may be a necessary expense that allows high earners to go to work in the first place, but that may take up a significant portion of a high income, particularly in expensive cities. Thus, high-income individuals in expensive locations may face high necessary expenses that low-income individuals in less expensive locations do not. This is not accounted for in inequality measures.

Last, income inequality measures may paint a picture that appears worse than the reality because these measures don't reflect the process of income mobility. In reality, those who constitute the bottom of the income distribution don't stay there indefinitely. Individuals move around quintiles as they age and their careers progress. High school or college graduates will start out in the bottom quintile and then move into a higher quintile when they start working. On the other hand, top earners may appear at the top of the income distribution one year only to move down the ranks the next year.

A variety of factors contribute to income inequality between upper and lower quintiles. While some of the difference between the highest and lowest earners may be due to underlying social issues, at least a few other factors may mitigate some concerns about increasing inequality over time.

EFFECTS ON INCOME DISTRIBUTION

Income Growth Driven by Second Earners

Another possible factor contributing to income inequality is the movement of women into the workforce, which may have affected both the level and distribution of household income over time. In other words, as women added a second household income, this may have shifted two-income households higher up in the income distribution. Table 6.6 shows the increasing proportion of joint returns with two earners over time from an analysis of individual tax returns by the Internal Revenue Service.[26] In 1969, 46 percent of joint tax returns had wage and salary income from two earners. By 2009, 73 percent of joint tax returns had income from two earners.

Table 6.6 Share of joint returns with two earners, selected years, 1969–2009

Tax Year	Percentage of joint returns with two earners (%)
1969	46.0
1979	52.6
1989	58.2
1999	60.0
2009	73.0

Sources: Internal Revenue Service, "Wage Income and Elective Retirement Contributions," Statistics of Income Bulletin Summer 2013, (2013), https://www.irs.gov/pub/irs-soi/13sumbul.pdf; Ellen Yau, Kurt Gurka, and Peter Sailer, "Comparing Salaries and Wages of Women Shown on Forms W-2 to Those of Men," 1969–1999, US Internal Revenue, Statistics of Income Branch, http://www.irs.gov/pub/irs-soi/99inw2wm.pdf

Households with second earners experienced the most income growth. Figure 6.5 graphs median income in constant 2018 (Consumer Price Index [CPI] adjusted) dollars for households by number of earners, from 1987 to 2018. While median income seems to have increased rather sluggishly for all

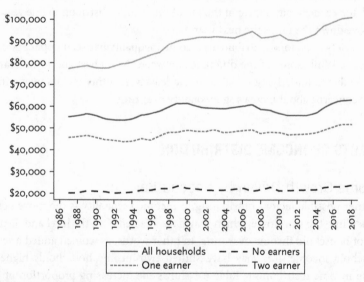

Figure 6.5 Median income by number of earners in household, 1990–2018.
US Census Bureau, "Historical Income Tables, H-12. Number of Earners in Household-All Races by Median and Mean Income: 1980 to 2018," (2018), https://www2.census.gov/programs-surveys/cps/tables/time-series/historical-income-households/h12ar.xls
Note: Median income is measured in constant 2018 dollars, adjusted using the CPI. Data for years 1980 to 1986 are omitted due to missing data.

Table 6.7 Distribution of households within income quintiles by earner type in 2018

	All quintiles (%)	Lowest fifth (%)	Second fifth (%)	Middle fifth (%)	Fourth fifth (%)	Highest fifth (%)	Top 5% (%)
No earners	23.9	63.0	29.3	15.1	7.9	4.2	2.5
One earner	36.1	32.8	51.8	44.7	31.0	20.4	22.0
Two earners	31.9	4.0	17.2	34.6	48.9	54.7	54.3
Three or four earners	8.1	0.3	1.6	5.6	12.3	20.7	21.1
Total	100.0	100.0	100.0	100.0	100.0	100.0	100.0

Source: US Census Bureau, Annual Social and Economic Supplement, 2018 (Table HINC-05. Percent Distribution of Households, by Selected Characteristics within Income Quintile and Top 5 Percent in 2018), https://www.census.gov/data/tables/time-series/demo/income-poverty/cps-hinc/hinc-05.html

households, this average trend masks quite different trends for households with different numbers of earners. In 2018, households with a single earner earned a median income of $51,971, a 14 percent increase from a median income of $45,767 in 1987.[27] Meanwhile, households with two earners saw substantial gains: in 2018, median income for these households was $101,091, up 31 percent from $77,355 in 1986.[28] This increase has been driven largely by the size of the contribution of the second earner, reflecting increasing women's wages as young women have invested in their education in preparation for a full-time career.

Examining the distribution of households within quintiles by number of earners further illustrates that top quintiles have the highest shares of two-earner households, while lower quintiles have higher shares of no-earner or one-earner households. Table 6.7 shows the percent distribution of each household type within each income quintile as well as within the top 5 percent of income, in 2018. Of the households in the highest income quintile, 55 percent have two earners, and another 21 percent have three or four earners. On the other hand, only 4 percent of households in the lowest quintiles have two earners, while 63 percent have no earners and 33 percent have just a single earner. Clearly, there is a strong correlation between the number of earners in a household and where that household falls in the income distribution.[29]

While many would agree that the entry of women into the labor force and the growth in women's wages are together a positive development for women and society overall, these changes may have also contributed to a measured increase in inequality, as income growth has concentrated at the top of the income distribution where a higher proportion of households have two earners and thus have reaped the benefits of women's advancement in the labor force. The trends in Figure 6.5 suggest that if there were more one-earner households, the distribution of income would be far more even.

Changing Self-Selection into Marriage

Changing self-selection into marriage may have further exacerbated measured inequality. Historically, the returns to marriage were largely based on *production complementarities*.[30] In other words, one individual would specialize in market work (usually the man) while the second individual would specialize in home production (usually the woman). Together, the married couple would be more efficient and productive than they would each be individually. However, with technological advancements that reduced the time needed to perform household work, this model has become increasingly outdated. The traditional benefits of marriage for most individuals have declined, leading to declining marriage rates for most categories of individuals.

On the other hand, the returns to marriage may have been replaced with a shift toward *consumption complementarities*.[31] In other words, as individuals have more leisure time and income, marriage may provide increased benefits of enjoying these things together. Thus, those with more income may have more to gain from the modern marriage. Examining the data on marriage trends provides supporting evidence for this hypothesis.[32] While marriage rates declined from 1980 to 2018 for almost all categories of individuals by age, gender, education, and race, the percentage of white, college-educated women aged 40 and older who are married has increased slightly.[33]

Thus, women with higher earnings potential may also be more likely to be married. Together with the reasonable assumption that there is some degree of assortative mating and that there is a positive correlation between a woman's earnings and that of her spouse, this can lead to greater income inequality as more high-income individuals join together to create dual-earner high-income households.

Examining the distribution of households within income quintiles by family characteristics suggests that married women may indeed be driving income growth in higher income quintiles. Table 6.8 shows the distribution of households within income quintiles and the top 5 percent by household characteristics. In the top quintile, 77 percent of households are married couples. In the top 5 percent of income earners, 81 percent are married couples. Meanwhile, most households in the lowest quintile are nonfamily households. More than a third of families in the lowest quintile are nonfamily households headed by a female householder living alone.[34]

Shifting the perspective to examine the percentage of individuals in each quintile by family characteristic similarly points to the same findings. Table 6.9 shows that unmarried men and women living alone are most likely to be in the lowest income quintiles. In 2018, 47 percent of women living alone were in the bottom quintile, and more than 73 percent of women living alone were in the bottom two quintiles. Fewer than 4 percent of women living alone were in the top quintile. The trends are similar for men. In 2018, 62 percent of men living

Table 6.8 Distribution of family and nonfamily households within income quintiles in 2018

	All Quintiles (%)	Lowest fifth (%)	Second fifth (%)	Middle fifth (%)	Fourth fifth (%)	Highest fifth (%)	Top 5% (%)
Family households	**64.9**	**37.1**	**56.4**	**66.6**	**78.4**	**86.1**	**87.1**
Married-couple families	48.2	16.7	35.2	47.8	63.9	77.4	80.7
Male householder, no spouse present	5.0	3.9	5.8	6.5	5.3	3.7	3.5
Female householder, no spouse present	11.7	16.5	15.4	12.3	9.2	5.1	2.9
Nonfamily households	**35.1**	**62.9**	**43.6**	**33.4**	**21.6**	**13.9**	**12.9**
Male householder living alone	12.9	22.7	16.9	13.0	7.5	4.1	4.2
Male householder not living alone	3.9	2.0	3.4	5.0	4.9	4.4	4.1
Female householder living alone	15.5	36.4	20.6	12.1	5.8	2.7	2.5
Female householder not living alone	2.8	1.8	2.7	3.3	3.4	2.7	2.2
Total (%)	**100**	**100**	**100**	**100**	**100**	**100**	**100**

Source: US Census Bureau, Annual Social and Economic Supplement, 2018 (Table HINC-05. Percent Distribution of Households, by Selected Characteristics within Income Quintile and Top 5 Percent in 2018), https://www.census.gov/data/tables/time-series/demo/income-poverty/cps-hinc/hinc-05.html

Table 6.9 Income quintiles by family characteristic in 2018

	Lowest fifth (%)	Second fifth (%)	Middle fifth (%)	Fourth fifth (%)	Highest fifth (%)	Total (%)
Family households	**11.4**	**17.4**	**20.5**	**24.2**	**26.5**	**100**
Married-couple families	6.9	14.6	19.8	26.5	32.1	100
Male householder, no spouse present	15.3	23.2	26.0	21.0	14.5	100
Female householder, no spouse present	28.2	26.4	21.1	15.8	8.6	100
Nonfamily households	**35.9**	**24.8**	**19.0**	**12.3**	**7.9**	**100**
Male householder living alone	35.4	26.3	20.3	11.6	6.4	100
Male householder not living alone	10.3	17.3	25.3	24.9	22.2	100
Female householder living alone	46.9	26.5	15.6	7.5	3.5	100
Female householder not living alone	12.9	19.3	23.7	24.7	19.3	100

Source: US Census Bureau, Annual Social and Economic Supplement, 2018 (Table HINC-05. Percent Distribution of Households, by Selected Characteristics within Income Quintile and Top 5 Percent in 2018), https://www.census.gov/data/tables/time-series/demo/income-poverty/cps-hinc/hinc-05.html

alone were in the bottom two quintiles, and fewer than 7 percent were in the top quintile. In contrast, married couples are more likely to be in the top quintiles. In 2018, 32 percent of married couples were in the top quintile, and 59 percent were in the top two quintiles. Only 7 percent of married-couple families were in the lowest quintile in 2018.[35]

Shrinking Household Size

As second earners in married households drive income growth at the top of the income distribution, the simultaneous shrinkage in household size at the bottom of the income distribution has added to measured inequality. Figure 6.6 shows the percentage distribution of households by size from 1960 to 2019. While the percentage of households with three or more individuals has declined over time, the proportion of households with one or two individuals has increased. The proportion of one-person households has seen the greatest increase over the past six decades. In 1960, 13 percent of households had just one person, but by 2019, more than 28 percent of households had one person, a 117 percent increase.[36] As shown in Tables 6.8 and 6.9, one-person households tend to appear at the low end of the income distribution. Thus, the shift over time toward one-person households may have widened the income distribution and increased measured inequality.

The shrinkage in household size over time can be explained by several factors. The increased longevity of today's seniors, with women outliving men on average,

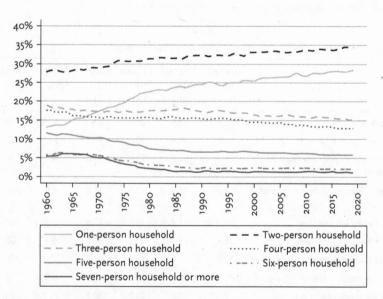

Figure 6.6 Percentage distribution of households by size, 1960–2019.
US Census Bureau, "Historical Household Tables, Table HH-4. Households by Size: 1960 to Present," (2019), https://www.census.gov/data/tables/time-series/demo/families/households.html

has contributed to a rising number of single-senior households. In 1900, 6 percent of Americans older than age 65 lived alone. By 2014, this number had risen to 26 percent. Of those elderly individuals living alone, 69 percent are women (possibly reflecting women's higher life expectancy).[37] These households may have low income, but they are not necessarily poor since at least some of these households have assets such as retirement accounts and real estate. One-third of these households report that they are financially comfortable.[38]

In addition, shifting trends in marriage and divorce have contributed to the rise in one-person households. Accompanying their movement into the workforce, women are postponing marriage, so the number of single never-married women has risen over time. Before the 1970s, the median age at first marriage for women was younger than 21 years of age. Since 1970, the median age at first marriage for women has steadily risen, to age 28 in 2019.[39] This trend reflects the increasing number of women attending college and pursuing career opportunities upon graduation. Figure 6.7 shows the evolution of women's marital status over time from 1950 to 2019. In 1970, 22 percent of adult women were single (never married) and just over 3 percent were divorced. By 2019, the percentage of single women grew to 30 percent and the percentage of divorced women nearly quadrupled to 11 percent.[40]

As shown in Tables 6.8 and 6.9, unmarried men and women living alone are heavily represented in the lowest two income quintiles. Table 6.8 shows that 59 percent of households in the lowest quintile are male or female householders

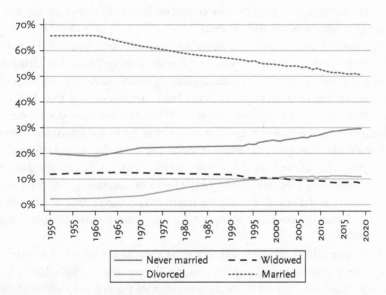

Figure 6.7 Marital status of women, 1950–2019.
US Census Bureau, "Historical Marital Status Tables, Table MS-1. Marital Status of the Population 15 Years Old and Over, by Sex," (2019), https://www2.census.gov/programs-surveys/demo/tables/families/time-series/marital/ms1.xls

living alone. Furthermore, Table 6.9 shows that, of male householders living alone, more than a third are in the lowest income quintile. Examining the population of female householders living alone, almost half are in the lowest quintile.

Thus, the postponement of marriage and the high incidence of divorce have led to an increase in the relative population of single female-headed households, a substantial percentage of which are also susceptible to poverty. Many female-headed households have children present from earlier marriages or from relationships outside of marriage, which makes these households especially vulnerable to economic hardship.

EMPIRICAL EVIDENCE FROM OTHER STUDIES

Turning to empirical research, some evidence suggests over the past 40 years, shifts in women's employment, earnings, and resulting effects on family structure and marriage may have contributed to higher household inequality. A number of studies have sought to quantify the effects of shifting trends in female and male employment, earnings, and household structure on between-household income inequality. These studies generally decompose the rise in inequality over a certain time period and then determine the extent to which the increase can be explained by a variety of factors. These studies are not causal in the sense that they do not exploit a source of random variation in women's workforce participation (or other related measures) to determine effects on household income inequality. However, they provide information on the possible mechanisms driving rising inequality over the past 40 years.

The empirical literature has explored four possible contributors to household inequality trends: increases in male and female earnings inequality, changes in male and female employment rates, increasing incidence of assortative mating (correlation between earnings of household members), and the decline of households headed by married couples.[41] While the literature does not reach a consensus on the effects of these factors across the board (considering many countries and time periods) some findings are generally agreed upon. First, rising inequality in the United States during the 1980s can be explained in large part by increasing inequality among male heads of households.[42] Second, other factors such as the rise of assortative mating[43] and the decline of households headed by married couples[44] also played a significant role in rising inequality in the 1980s.[45]

Larrimore (2014) conducts a thorough analysis of the effects of a variety of factors on income inequality growth over different time periods. Uses March Current Population Survey (CPS) data to estimate the extent to which changes in earnings, employment, and marriage can explain trends in household inequality in the United States since 1979. He shows that the factors explaining rising inequality vary dramatically by time period. He examines household earnings during the 1980s business cycle (1979–1989), the 1990s business cycle (1989–2000), and the 2000s business cycle (2000–2007). He calculates the average annual percentage change in the Gini coefficient for each of the three time periods and decompose the changes to 13 attributable factor components.

He finds that while inequality in male-householder earnings explained most of the rise in household inequality in the 1980s and 1990s, male-householder earnings inequality declined in the 2000s and had the effect of reducing inequality since 2000.

Although assortative mating accounted for rising household inequality in the 1980s and 1990s, by the 2000s, changes in the correlation between spouses' earnings reduced inequality. The authors explain these findings as the result of changes in the types of labor market entries and exits by women over the years. In other words, in the 1980s, the largest increase in labor force participation was for wives of high-earning men. For women married to non-working men, employment increased by much less. Thus, during the 1980s, income inequality increased as high-earning households earned even more income as wives entered the workforce. However, in the 1990s and 2000s, increasing labor force participation came from women with non-working husbands, which led to a decline in no-earner households and reduced inequality. These findings indicate that the effect of women's labor force participation on inequality may be either positive of negative depending on the characteristics of women joining the workforce.

Another study conducted by Esping-Andersen (2007) finds that women's employment raised inequality in the 1990s in several countries (including the United States). Although their results are not consistent with results from many other studies, the authors argue that even if women's earnings rise relative to male earnings over time, the profile of female labor supply (i.e., growth in participation and earnings for those with higher education and earnings potential) is likely to result in rising inequality. They predict that if countries have very high labor force participation rates for women across all households at the top and at the bottom of the income distribution, it would be plausible that inequality would be reduced. The authors examine the effects of assortative mating on inequality and find that, as expected, assortative mating leads to higher inequality.

A more recent study by Grotti and Scherer (2016) uses data from the Luxembourg Income Study (LIS) and a new empirical strategy to measure the effects of female employment and household structure on household income inequality in Denmark, Germany, Italy, the United Kingdom, and the United States. They find that, while women's employment increased more for women living with high-earning men, between the mid-1980s and mid-1990s, these changes contributed very little to rising inequality. The authors also conclude that changes in earnings similarity between household partners has no substantial effect on inequality for any of the countries and time periods.

Additional evidence from Daly and Valletta (2006) suggests that changes in family structure substantially increased inequality between 1969 and 1989. In particular, they find that the increasing incidence of low-income households (such as those led by single women with children) accounted for more than half of the increased dispersion between the median household income and both the right and left tails of the household income distribution.

Thus, the empirical literature suggests that the time period studied as well as the method used to determine the drivers of inequality growth over time can lead to different conclusions. However, it appears that while rising female labor force participation may or may not have not have had a direct effect of raising inequality, higher female employment may have had indirect effects on rising inequality. As women joined the workforce in greater numbers, pursued more education, and gained more independence and control over their lives, household structure and marriage patterns underwent significant change, and the evidence suggests that, at least for some time periods over the past 40 years, these changes may have contributed to rising household income inequality.

CONCLUSION

The movement of women into the workforce, combined with societal shifts in education, life expectancy, marriage, and divorce, has had far-reaching consequences for the level and distribution of income over the past four decades. On the one hand, as women graduated from school in greater numbers, joined the workforce, and entered into professional careers, more households shifted to dual-earner couples with higher incomes. On the other hand, the rise in divorce rates combined with women delaying marriage and higher life expectancy led to more single households with lower incomes. These two forces may have exacerbated measured inequality in the economy.

To properly address inequities in society, it is important to have a clear picture of actual economic well-being faced by individuals along the income distribution, well-being that is not always accurately captured by inequality numbers. This chapter shows that inequality measures can reflect more than economic challenges. Women's advancement in the labor force and positive societal shifts have resulted in income patterns that may have led to an increase in measured inequality but that also reflect great social and economic progress.

Attributing all inequality to an underlying social problem would lead to bad policy and a failure to recognize the progress that American society and women have achieved thus far.

NOTES

1. Bureau of Labor Statistics, Labor Force Participation Rate: Women [LNS11300002] (2019).
2. Ibid.
3. Ibid.
4. Bureau of Labor Statistics, Labor Force Participation Rate: 25–54 years, Women [LNS11300062] (2019), https://beta.bls.gov/dataViewer/view/timeseries/LNS11300062.
5. Bureau of Labor Statistics, Labor Force Participation Rate: 16–24 years, Women [LNS11324886] (2019), https://data.bls.gov/timeseries/LNS11324886.
6. Bureau of Labor Statistics, Labor Force Participation Rate: 55 Years and over, Women [LNU01324232] (2019), https://data.bls.gov/timeseries/LNU01324232.
7. Bureau of Labor Statistics, Labor Force Participation Rate: 65 Years and over, Women [LNU01300354] (2019), https://beta.bls.gov/dataViewer/view/timeseries/LNU01300354.
8. Pew Research Center, October, 2016, "The State of American Jobs: How the Shifting Economic Landscape Is Reshaping Works and Society and Affecting the Way People Think About the Skills and Training They Need To Get Ahead,"https://www.pewsocialtrends.org/2016/10/06/1-changes-in-the-american-workplace/.
9. Bureau of Labor Statistics, table 11, "Women in the Labor Force: A Databook" (2018), https://www.bls.gov/opub/reports/womens-databook/2018/pdf/home.pdf.
10. Ibid., table 7, https://www.bls.gov/opub/reports/womens-databook/2018/home.htm
11. US Census Bureau, "Maternity Leave and Employment Patterns of First-Time Mothers: 1961–2008" (2011), https://www.census.gov/prod/2011pubs/p70-128.pdf.
12. Bureau of Labor Statistics, table 7, "Women in the Labor Force: A Databook" (2018), https://www.bls.gov/opub/reports/womens-databook/2018/pdf/home.pdf.
13. Ibid.
14. Bureau of Labor Statistics, table 21, "Women in the Labor Force: A Databook" (2018), https://www.bls.gov/opub/reports/womens-databook/2018/pdf/home.pdf.
15. Ibid.
16. Aguiar and Hurst (2007).
17. US Census Bureau, "Table A-1. Years of School Completed by People 25 Years and Over, by Age and Sex: Selected Years 1940–2018" (2019), https://

www2.census.gov/programs-surveys/demo/tables/educational-attainment/time-series/cps-historical-time-series/taba-1.xlsx.

18. US Department of Education, National Center for Education Statistics, Digest of Education Statistics 2018, table 321.20, "Associate's Degrees Conferred by Postsecondary Institutions, by Race/Ethnicity and Sex of Student: Selected Years 1976–1977 Through 2016–2017," (2018); US Department of Education, National Center for Education Statistics, Digest of Education Statistics 2018 table 322.20, "Bachelor's Degrees Conferred by Postsecondary Institutions, by Race/Ethnicity and Sex of Student: Selected Years 1976–1977 Through 2016–2017" (2018); US Department of Education, National Center for Education Statistics, Digest of Education Statistics 2018 table 323.20, "Master's Degrees Conferred by Postsecondary Institutions, by Race/Ethnicity and Sex of Student: Selected Years 1976-1977 Through 2016–2017" (2018).

19. US Department of Education, National Center for Education Statistics, Digest of Education Statistics 2018 table 318.10, "Degrees Conferred by Postsecondary Institutions, by Level of Degree and Sex of Student: Selected Years 1869–70 Through 2028–2029" (2018).

20. US Department of Education, National Center for Education Statistics, Digest of Education Statistics 2018, table 324.40, "Number of Postsecondary Institutions Conferring Degrees in Dentistry, Medicine, and Law, and Number of Such Degrees Conferred, by Sex of Student: Selected Years, 1949–50 Through 2016–17" (2018), https://nces.ed.gov/programs/digest/d18/tables/dt18_324.40.asp?current=yes.

21. Women's Bureau, US Department of Labor, "Mothers and Families: Selected Labor Force Characteristics, Married Women's Earnings as a Percent of Total Family Income" (2018); Bureau of Labor Statistics, "1971 to 2013 Annual Social and Economic Supplements to the Current Population Survey (CPS)" (2014), https://www.dol.gov/wb/stats/mother_families.htm.

22. Women's Bureau, US Department of Labor, "Gender Earnings Ratios by Weekly Earnings and Annual Earnings (Time Series)" (2018), https://www.dol.gov/wb/stats/earnings-text.htm#earn-gender-week-annual.

23. US Census Bureau, "Table F-22. Married-Couple Families with Wives' Earnings Greater than Husbands' Earnings" (2018), https://www2.census.gov/programs-surveys/cps/tables/time-series/historical-income-families/f22.xls.

24. Bureau of Labor Statistics, "Table 1101. Quintiles of Income Before Taxes: Annual Expenditure Means, Shares, Standard Errors, and Coefficients of Variation, Consumer Expenditure Survey, 2018" (2018), https://www.bls.gov/cex/2016/combined/quintile.pdf.

25. Ibid.

26. Internal Revenue Service, "Wage Income and Elective Retirement Contributions," Statistics of Income Bulletin Summer 2013" (2013). https://www.irs.gov/pub/irs-soi/13sumbul.pdf; Ellen Yau, Kurt Gurka, and Peter Sailer, "Comparing Salaries and Wages of Women Shown on Forms W-2 to Those of Men," 1969–1999, US Internal Revenue, Statistics of Income Branch, http://www.irs.gov/pub/irs-soi/99inw2wm.pdf.

27. US Census Bureau, "Historical Income Tables, H-12. Number of Earners in Household-All Races by Median and Mean Income: 1980 to 2018" (2018) https://www2.census.gov/programs-surveys/cps/tables/time-series/historical-income-households/h12ar.xls.

28. Ibid.

29. US Census Bureau, "Annual Social and Economic Supplement, 2018 (Table HINC-05. Percent Distribution of Households, by Selected Characteristics Within Income Quintile and Top 5 Percent in 2018)," https://www.census.gov/data/tables/time-series/demo/income-poverty/cps-hinc/hinc-05.html.

30. Becker (1991).

31. Isen and Stevenson (2010).

32. Ibid.

33. Authors' findings using Current Population Survey data on individuals aged 16 and older for the years 1980–2018.

34. US Census Bureau, "Annual Social and Economic Supplement, 2018 (Table HINC-05. Percent Distribution of Households, by Selected Characteristics within Income Quintile and Top 5 Percent in 2018)," https://www.census.gov/data/tables/time-series/demo/income-poverty/cps-hinc/hinc-05.html.

35. Ibid.

36. US Census Bureau, "Historical Household Tables, Table HH-4. Households by Size: 1960 to Present" (2019), https://www.census.gov/data/tables/time-series/demo/families/households.html.

37. American Psychological Association, "By the Numbers: Older Adults Living Alone" (2016), https://www.apa.org/monitor/2016/05/numbers.

38. Ibid.

39. US Census Bureau, "Figure MS-2 Median Age at First Marriage: 1890 to Present" (2019), https://www.census.gov/content/dam/Census/library/visualizations/time-series/demo/families-and-households/ms-2.pdf.

40. US Census Bureau, "Historical Marital Status Tables, Table MS-1. Marital Status of the Population 15 Years Old and Over, by Sex" (2019), https://www2.census.gov/programs-surveys/demo/tables/families/time-series/marital/ms1.xls.

41. Larrimore (2014).

42. Larrimore (2014), Karoly and Burtless (1995), Daly and Valletta (2006).

43. Karoly and Burtless (1995).

44. Bishop et al. (1997), Daly and Valletta (2006).

45. This overview of past literature draws heavily from the discussion included in the work of Larrimore (2014).

REFERENCES

Aguiar, Mark, and Erik Hurst. 2007. "Measuring Trends in Leisure: The Allocation of Time over Five Decades." *The Quarterly Journal of Economics*, 122(3): 969–1006.

Becker, Gary S. 1991. *A Treatise on the Family, Enlarged Edition.* Cambridge, MA: Harvard University Press.

Bishop, John A., John P. Formby, and W. J. Smith. 1997. "Demographic Change and Income Inequality in the United States, 1976–1989." *Southern Economic Journal*, 64(1): 34–44.

Daly, Mary C., and Robert G. Valletta. 2006. "Inequality and Poverty in the United States: The Effects of Rising Dispersion of Men's Earnings and Changing Family Behavior." *Economica*, 73(289): 75–98.

Esping-Andersen, Gosta. 2007. "Sociological Explanations of Changing Income Distributions." *American Behavioral Scientist*, 50(5): 639–658.

Grotti, Raffaele, and Stefani Scherer. 2016. "Does Gender Equality Increase Economic Inequality? Evidence from Five Countries." *Research in Social Stratification and Mobility*, 45: 13–26.

Isen, Adam, and Betsey Stevenson. 2010. "Women's Education and Family Behavior: Trends in Marriage, Divorce, and Fertility." NBER Working Paper 15725.

Karoly, Lynn A., and Gary Burtless. 1995. "Demographic Change, Rising Earnings Inequality, and the Distribution of Personal Well Being, 1959–1989." *Demography*, 32(3): 379–405.

Larrimore, Jeff. 2014. "Accounting for United States Household Income Inequality Trends: The Changing Importance of Household Structure and Male and Female Labor Earnings Inequality." *Review of Income and Wealth*, 60(4): 683–701.

7

EXPLAINING RACE AND GENDER WAGE GAPS

June O'Neill and Dave O'Neill

INTRODUCTION

Although earnings differentials between African Americans and non-Hispanic whites and between men and women have narrowed over the years, they have by no means disappeared. But how much of the current minority–white wage gap and the current gender wage gap is due to labor market discrimination? Or can these wage gaps be explained by other factors, such as differences in work-related skills? These are crucial questions in the analysis of income trends. Our discussion includes not only wage gaps between African Americans and whites and between men and women but additionally wage gaps experienced by ethnic and racial minorities. We focus our discussion on conditions since 2000. Because of the difficulty inherent in directly measuring the prevalence of discriminatory behavior by employers, analysts have turned to empirical studies that seek to measure the extent to which racial and gender wage differences can be attributed to differences in employee productivity. The component of racial and gender wage differences that cannot be attributed to the measured productivity factors may provide a rough indication of the effect of labor market discrimination on the earnings of minorities and women. This is an approximate measure because our ability to explain how much of earnings differences are due to discrimination depends on our ability to measure productivity accurately. Measures of human capital such as years of schooling completed are readily obtained from standard sources such as census data. But differences in

June O'Neill and Dave O'Neill, *Explaining Race and Gender Wage Gaps* In: *United States Income, Wealth, Consumption, and Inequality.* Edited by: Diana Furchtgott-Roth, Oxford University Press (2021). © Oxford University Press.
DOI: 10.1093/oso/9780197518199.003.0008.

years of schooling, although usually correlated with earnings differences, are an imperfect measure even of cognitive skills, in part because schools vary considerably in quality and in part because even within a school quality category, student achievement varies because of differences in parental endowments and personal traits.

Measures of cognitive development, such as those revealed in test score data, are not widely available. When available, they are useful but imperfect measures of individual productivity. Other aspects of individual productivity, such as leadership ability and reliability, are also difficult to obtain. The typical survey has no way to measure those characteristics objectively, although they likely influence success in the labor market. Among groups with a significant proportion of immigrants, ability to speak English is an important aspect of productivity and can now be roughly measured with census data. Other aspects of acculturation are more difficult to assess.

Gender differences in productivity present the greatest challenge to measurement. Labor market outcomes differ between women and men in large part because of differences in lifetime career paths, a consequence of differences in gender roles within the family.[1] Consequently, an analysis of the gender gap requires detailed data on lifetime work experience. In addition, women's continuing family responsibilities influence their preferences for work situations that allow for more flexibility and less intensity. Men and women may therefore make different tradeoffs between pay and job amenities.

We use two data sources for our estimates. One is the American Community Survey (ACS), a large sample survey collected by the US Census Bureau. The ACS data provide large samples which are ideal to estimate earnings differentials between whites and minorities, separately by sex, and for those from small population groups, such as non-Hispanic blacks and American Indians, as well as subgroups of Hispanics and Asians by country of origin.

One drawback of the ACS, a drawback shared by the decennial census and the Current Population Survey (CPS), is that it provides only limited measures of productivity-related factors. For example, it does not have information on lifetime work experience, an important omission for understanding the gender gap in earnings. A strong point of the National Longitudinal Survey of Youth 1979 (NLSY79) cohort, our second major data source, is that it provides information on key productivity-related characteristics such as lifetime work experience and test scores that allow for measurement of cognitive achievement. The NLSY79 does not, however, provide large enough samples for analysis of small minority groups, though it has oversampled Hispanics and African Americans. In this chapter we use statistical analysis to determine how much of the currently observed wage gaps between minority and white workers and between female and male workers might be attributed to productivity factors.

WAGE DIFFERENCES BETWEEN MINORITIES AND WHITES

In this section we start with our findings based on the 2005 and 2009 ACS to analyze the wage gaps between white non-Hispanics and 16 racial and ethnic groups. Separate racial and ethnic analyses are provided for men and women. We then turn to the NLSY79 data to analyze the sources of wage differences between African Americans and whites, as well as between Hispanics and whites in 2000, when the cohort was 35–43 years of age, and in 2008, when the cohort had reached the ages of 43–51. Men and women are once again analyzed separately.

Racial and Ethnic Wage Differentials: Results from the ACS

The various ethnic and racial minorities differ considerably both in their earnings and with respect to their skills. Since men and women have different career paths on average, we will consider these differentials separately, first for men and then for women.

Wage Differentials Among Men

Examining the population of men aged 25–54 who are working full-time (i.e., 35 hours or more per week), wage differentials by race are evident. As a group, Asian men's average hourly wage rates were about the same or slightly above the hourly wages of white men between 1989 and 1999 and have risen well above the white male rate since 1999, reaching a 12 percent advantage in 2010. The Hispanic to white wage ratio declined fairly steadily from 75 percent in 1975 to about 65 percent in 2000, where it has remained. The black to white hourly wage ratio declined from 79 percent in 1979 to 73 percent in 1989 and has stayed at about that level through 2010.[2]

To what extent are these earnings differences explained by differences in skills that can be measured in US Census Bureau surveys? The explanatory analysis is enriched by using a more detailed breakdown of the non-white groups. The Census Bureau divides Asians into subgroups of Chinese, Japanese, Asian Indian, Korean, Vietnamese, Filipino, and Other Asian. It also divides Hispanics into subgroups of Mexican, Puerto Rican, Cuban, Dominican, Other Central American, South American, and Other Hispanic.

We use the 2005 and 2009 ACS and a multiple regression analysis to calculate wage differentials (expressed as ratios of hourly earnings) between each group and the reference group of white men.[3] Results are displayed in Table 7.1. We show results for two models, each of which takes into account an increasing number of explanatory variables. The variables included in each model are indicated at the bottom portion of the table, which displays an "X" for the particular variable included. Model I shows the effect of adjusting for age, geographic region, metropolitan/central city location, schooling, part-time work, and type of

Table 7.1 Minority/white wage ratios for men aged 25–54, before and after controlling for skill-related characteristics

	Unadjusted (No control)		Model I		Model II	
	2005	2009	2005	2009	2005	2009
Race/Ethnicity Indicators						
American Indian	77	78	87	86	87	87
Black non-Hispanic	74	74	83	81	83	82
Chinese	113	114	89	90	98	99[NS]
Japanese	120	124	95	97[NS]	101[NS]	104[NS]
Asian Indian	128	141	99[NS]	106	105	113
Korean	108	108	86	86	96	94
Vietnamese	88	88	88	88	98[NS]	97[NS]
Filipino	93	96	84	86	89	90
Other Asian	82	89	80	86	86	91
Mexican	62	65	82	84	92	92
Puerto Rican	81	82	91	91	95	94
Cuban	89	85	91	88	100[NS]	96[NS]
Dominican	69	67	79	78	89	86
Other Central American	60	61	79	81	91	92
South American	79	83	79	84	90	93
Other Hispanic	79	86	89	90	94	93
Control Variables						
Age			X		X	
Region, MSA, Central City			X		X	
Schooling			X		X	
Work part-time			X		X	
Type of employer			X		X	
Yrs. since migration to US					X	
English-speaking ability					X	

Note: The ratios shown were estimated from OLS regressions of an individual's log hourly wage rate on a set of explanatory variables including an indicator variable (or variables) specifying race/ethnicity, with white non-Hispanic as the omitted reference category. The anti-log of the partial regression coefficients of these indicator variables yields the wage ratios. The other variables controlled are indicated above for each model. The sample is restricted to wage and salary workers who worked 20 hours or more a week and 26 weeks or more a year. Hourly wages are obtained by dividing annual earnings by the product of weeks and hours worked during the year. "NS" indicates not significant at 1% level.
Source: Public Use Microdata, American Community Survey (ACS), 2005 and 2009.

employer (government, nonprofit, private); model II additionally adjusts for the number of years in the United States and proficiency in English.

Table 7.1 presents the hourly wage in each racial or ethnic group as a percent of the hourly wage of white men. Results using the 2005 ACS are shown in the first column and results using the 2009 ACS are shown alongside in the second column. The initial wage ratios, unadjusted for any skill factors, stayed the same or increased a bit between 2005 and 2009. We report the ratios for 2009, noting any significant change.

Wage ratios vary considerably among groups. Most Asian groups of men earn more than white men. Wages of Asian Indian and Japanese men are the highest of any group: 41 percent and 24 percent respectively higher than wages of white, non-Hispanic men in 2009. Chinese and Korean men earned 14 percent to 8 percent higher wages than white men. However, the group "Other Asian" (including Thai, Hmong, Pakistani, and Cambodian groups) earn only about 89 percent as much as white men.

All Hispanic groups earn less than white non-Hispanic men and Asian men. Mexicans, Dominicans, and other Central Americans have the lowest earnings of any group shown: about one-third below those of white men. Cubans, Puerto Ricans, and those from South America have the highest earnings among Hispanics, but still earn about 15–18 percent less than white men. African American and American Indian men earn 22–26 percent less than white men.

Model I shows the effect of adjusting for age, geographic division, metropolitan/central city location, schooling, part-time work, and type of employer (government, nonprofit, private). Asians tend to live in high-wage areas and have much more education than most other groups. More than half of Asian men hold a bachelor's or advanced degree. Once differences in geographic location and education are taken into account, the earnings advantage of Asian men over white men is largely eliminated.

Hispanic groups, on the other hand, have relatively low levels of schooling: almost half of Hispanic men have not completed high school, and only 9 percent are college graduates. Consequently their earnings converge significantly with those of white (non-Hispanic) men when education variables are added to the model. The differential between Mexican and white men is cut in half, although the change for other Hispanic groups with stronger education backgrounds is less dramatic. Wages of African American and American Indian men relative to those of white men also rise when differences in years of schooling are accounted for.

A relatively large proportion of Asians and Hispanics are immigrants. In model II we add variables indicating the number of years since migrating to the United States and self-reported English language proficiency. This adjustment raises the wage ratios for Hispanics and Asians. At this final step, wages of the Asian groups are mostly either slightly above or below those of white men. Wages of Asian Indians, still the highest earning group, are 13 percent above those of whites. Wage gaps for Hispanic men are sharply reduced. In 2009, the wages of all Hispanic groups except for Dominicans are more than 90 percent as high as those of white men. Cuban men essentially reach parity with white men.

Groups with a significant proportion of immigrants present particular difficulties for analysis because of cultural differences among them that may influence the speed of assimilation. Such differences are only partly captured by measures of years of schooling and self-reported measures of English-speaking ability. Different cohorts of migrants from the same country can differ because of changing selection factors. Second-generation and higher order–generation immigrants are likely to be more assimilated. In the next part of this section, we present additional analyses of Hispanic and black men using the better measures of skills available in the NLSY79 data.

Wage Differentials Among Women

The hourly wage ratios of ethnic/racial groups to whites are relatively higher for women than is the case for men. Asian women have earned more than white women in every year between 1989 and 2010, and their wage advantage rose sharply after 2002.[4]

To understand better the effect of differences in skills on these wage ratios we replicate the analysis conducted for men, looking at a similar array of groups within the broad categories. Results are given in Table 7.2. Although patterns of wage differentials among different groups of women are similar to those of men, the size of gaps between white women and black and Hispanic women is, for the most part, strikingly smaller than the corresponding gap among men. In the ACS for 2009, the unadjusted black to white ratio among men is 74 percent, and among women it is 86 percent (Table 7.2). The differential between white and Hispanic women is also much smaller than the corresponding male gap for all subgroups of Hispanic women. The adjustments in model I (which include schooling and geographic location) raise ratios for groups with less education than white women (e.g., African American and Mexican women) and lower ratios for groups with superior education (e.g., Japanese and Asian Indian women). After adjusting for all variables in model II, which adds to model I immigration and English-speaking skills, gaps among non-Asian women are further reduced and wage ratios are mostly on the order of 95 percent for all groups except American Indians (88 percent), Dominicans and African Americans (93 percent), and Cuban women (who are at parity with white women).

The Asian–white differentials are quite similar for women and men. Asian women, like Asian men, typically earn more than white counterparts because of higher education levels. After adjusting for schooling, migration, and language variables, Asian women still appear to earn more than white women (up to 10 percent more for both Chinese and Asian Indian women).

In general, given limited availability of detailed productivity measures in the ACS, it remains difficult to say with certainty how much, if any, of the current earnings differentials could be due to labor market discrimination. In fact, including all variables, among men, most Asian groups earn about as much or more than white men, and, among women, the Asian groups mostly earn more than white women.

Table 7.2 Minority/white wage ratios for women aged 25–54, before and after controlling for skill-related characteristics

	Unadjusted (No control)		Model I		Model II	
	2005	2009	2005	2009	2005	2009
Race/Ethnicity Indicators						
American Indian						
Black non-Hispanic						
Chinese	121	124	97	100[NS]	107	110
Japanese	121	123	96	96	100[NS]	99[NS]
Asian Indian	122	131	98[NS]	103	105	110
Korean	107	109	92	94	102[NS]	103[NS]
Vietnamese	89	88	94	95	105	107
Filipino	115	117	97	99[NS]	102	104
Other Asian	88	89	90	90	96	96
Mexican	72	73	89	90	96	96
Puerto Rican	92	91	97	96	100[NS]	98[NS]
Cuban	98	94	97	94	104	101[NS]
Dominican	71	74	79	83	89	93
Other Central American	68	69	84	87	94	96
South American	85	87	83	86	94	95
Other Hispanic	84	90	94	94	97	96
Control Variables						
Age			X		X	
Region, MSA, Central City			X		X	
Schooling			X		X	
Work part-time			X		X	
Type of employer			X		X	
Yrs. since migration to US					X	
English-speaking ability					X	

Note: The ratios shown were estimated from OLS regressions of an individual's log hourly wage rate on a set of explanatory variables including an indicator variable (or variables) specifying race/ethnicity, with white non-Hispanic as the omitted reference category. The anti-log of the partial regression coefficients of these indicator variables yields the wage ratios. The other variables controlled are indicated above for each model. The sample is restricted to wage and salary workers who worked 20 hours or more a week and 26 weeks or more a year. Hourly wages are obtained by dividing annual earnings by the product of weeks and hours worked during the year. "NS" indicates not significant at 1% level.
Source: Public Use Microdata, American Community Survey (ACS), 2005 and 2009.

Once we adjust for all the variables considered, most Hispanic men earn 90 percent as much as white (non-Hispanic) men (Cubans are at parity, and the gaps for Mexicans and Puerto Ricans are extremely small). Among women, the adjusted Mexican to white wage ratio rises to 96 percent, and the Cuban and Puerto Rican ratios reach parity. The adjusted black to white wage ratio is 93 percent.

In this broad overview we find that, after we control for readily measured variables such as age, region, residence in a city, part-time work, years of schooling, class of employer (government, nonprofit, and private), migration history, and self-reported English-speaking ability, remaining differentials between whites and minorities are small or eliminated. The largest between-group wage differential that remains after adjusting for these characteristics is that between African American and white men: a ratio of 83 percent. Among women the African American–white differential is smaller: 93 percent. The wage gap between white women and minority women is generally smaller than the parallel wage gaps for men. In fact, white women earn less than Asian women as well as less than Cuban women once we account for differences in migration and English-speaking ability.

Black–White and Hispanic–White Wage Differentials: Results from the NLSY79

We now turn to the much richer NLSY79 data for a more nuanced analysis of the black–white and Hispanic–white wage gaps among male and female workers. The NLSY79 cohort was first interviewed in 1979 (at ages 14–22) and was initially reinterviewed each year (more recently every other year). Detailed information was obtained on lifetime work experience, education, and many other individual characteristics and behaviors of relevance to labor market outcomes. One unique variable of considerable value is the individual's score on the Armed Forces Qualification Test (AFQT), which was administered to survey participants in 1980. The test reflects differences in cognitive skills that are influenced by the quality and quantity of schooling and human capital acquired at home.

We report on results from both the 2000 survey taken when the cohort was 35–43 years of age and the 2008 survey taken when the cohort had reached ages 43–51. Our sample of wage and salary workers was 5,399 in 2000 and 4,673 in 2008. Attrition as well as some movement in and out of the labor force led to the change in sample size between 2000 and 2008. African Americans and Hispanics were oversampled by the survey, allowing for adequate samples for analyses of these groups. Because the initial cohort was fixed, recent immigrants are not present in the dataset.

Wage Differentials Among Men

To estimate effects of differences in characteristics on wage differentials between black and white men and Hispanic and white men, we use a methodology similar to that employed in the preceding analysis of data from the ACS. White men are again restricted to white non-Hispanic men, although for convenience we continue to refer to them simply as "white." We again use multiple regression analysis to examine the effects of different explanatory variables on individuals' hourly wages.[5] We include characteristics that are likely to affect productivity and therefore wages.

Key characteristics and their mean values for white, African American, and Hispanic men are displayed in Table 7.3 for 2000 and 2008. Due to attrition, the sample for men declined by 15 percent for white men, 18 percent for black men, and 24 percent for Hispanic men. However, most characteristics showed little change, the main exceptions being years of work experience (which is expected to increase over an 8-year period) and the wage rate, which also increased after adjusting for inflation.[6] In our analysis we use detailed breakdowns of schooling completed. Hispanic men have the lowest levels of schooling. In 2008, almost 7 percent completed fewer than 10 years of schooling; another 18 percent completed 10 or 11 years and may have attended the twelfth grade but never graduated high school; another 36 percent completed high school with a diploma or a GED but never attended college. About 27 percent of Hispanic men attended college but only 12 percent of those who attended college ever graduated with a bachelor's or higher degree.

African American men have completed more schooling than Hispanic men, particularly at the high school level. About 21 percent never completed high school, but another 40 percent ended their schooling with a high school diploma or a GED. About the same percentage of African American men as Hispanic men attended college, but a somewhat larger percentage attained a bachelor's or advanced degree.

White men have considerably more education than either African Americans or Hispanics. Only 11 percent were high school dropouts. More than half of white men attended college and close to 60 percent of those who attended obtained a bachelor's or advanced degree.

Education obtained by the three groups is likely to differ in quality because of differences in family income and other aspects of family background. Years of schooling can be a poor proxy for cognitive skills when the quality of schools attended and family background differ among groups. One variable unique to the NLSY79 and of considerable value to the measurement of cognitive skills is the individual's score on the AFQT, administered to nearly all survey participants in 1980 when they were 15–23 years of age. The AFQT is a component of a larger test of vocational aptitude developed by the military many decades ago

Table 7.3 Selected characteristics of men by race

	2000 (Ages 35–43)			2008 (Ages 43–51)		
	White	Black	Hispanic	White	Black	Hispanic
Hourly Rate of Pay[a]	22.1	15.8	18.1	24.1	16.9	19.5
Region (%)						
Northeast	17.3	14.0	15.2	26.8	20.0	15.9
North Central	34.9	17.1	7.1	30.5	16.3	6.8
South	31.4	61.5	31.0	26.9	56.6	31.6
West	16.4	7.4	46.6	15.8	7.0	45.7
Education (Highest Level Attained, %)						
<10 yrs	4.3	4.1	9.3	2.9	2.6	6.8
10–12 yrs (no diploma or GED)	8.3	14.9	19.8	7.8	18.4	17.9
HS grad (diploma)	32.8	35.8	27.4	31.8	34.9	28.3
HS grad (GED)	4.1	7.9	6.2	4.1	5.4	7.8
Some college	21.6	23.9	26.4	22.8	25.4	26.8
BA or equiv. degree	20.7	10.9	7.9	21.5	10.1	9.6
MA or equiv. degree	5.9	2.1	1.9	7.0	3.2	2.3
PhD or prof. degree	2.3	0.4	1.2	2.2	0.3	0.5
AFQT percentile score	55.4	24.1	33.6	57.1	24.2	33.3
Work Experience						
Avg. years worked in civilian jobs since age 18[b]	17.8	15.9	17.3	24.9	22.7	24.4
Avg. yrs. worked in the military since 1978[b]	0.5	0.8	0.4	0.7	1.1	0.7
Sample size	1,416	759	519	1,199	625	396

[a]Hourly rate of pay in 2008 dollars (geometric mean).
[b]Years are full year equivalents based on total weeks worked divided by 52.
Note: Characteristics above are for wage and salary workers included in the regression analysis.
Source: National Longitudinal Survey of Youth (NLSY79).

to determine eligibility for service and for job placement within the service. The test is a measure of verbal and mathematical skills and has been validated over the years as an effective and unbiased predictor of job performance.[7] Of course, in common with any test of skill or achievement, the aptitude it measures is influenced by the quantity and quality of schooling and by the home environment from early childhood, as well as by intrinsic abilities.[8] Mean test scores on the AFQT are shown in Table 7.3, and they differ considerably by race. On average, in 2008, the white men in the sample were reported to have scored at the

57th percentile, African Americans at the 24th percentile, and Hispanics at the 33rd percentile.

We also take account of differences in work experience and include measures of total weeks worked in civilian employment since age 18 (divided by 52 to convert to full-year equivalents) and total weeks served in the military since 1978 (also divided by 52). Close to 17 percent of African American men served in the military, compared to 8.5 percent for Hispanic men and 9.6 percent for white men. Partly for this reason, black men accumulated fewer years of civilian employment than did white or Hispanic men. Also, the average combined total lifetime employment of African American men is lower than that of the other two groups. Thus the average years of work by black men was 16.7 in 2000, 1.6 years lower than the average years worked by white men. Hispanic men worked only 0.6 year less than white non-Hispanic men. All three groups added a little more than 7 years to their work experience by 2008, and differentials among groups remained about the same.

The male black–white wage ratio in the NLSY79 sample was 71 percent and the male Hispanic–white ratio was 82 percent in 2000. In 2008, both ratios were about a percentage point lower. In Table 7.4 we show how these ratios change when we control for different groups of characteristics. We group variables into three stages, each of which builds on the prior level, to observe effects of adding particular factors on wage ratios. Stage 1 controls for differences in age, geographic location, and schooling; stage 2 additionally controls for AFQT score; and stage 3 additionally controls for civilian and military work experience.

Table 7.4 Explaining the black–white and Hispanic–white wage gaps among men

	Black–white wage ratio		Hispanic–white wage ratio	
	2000 (ages 35–43)	2008 (ages 43–51)	2000 (ages 35–43)	2008 (ages 43–51)
Unadjusted hourly wage ratio (%)	71.2**	70.1**	82.0**	80.9**
Hourly wage ratio controlling for:				
1) Schooling	83.0**	82.0**	91.5**	91.4**
2) Variables in 1) and AFQT	94.0**	95.8	97.9	100.6
3) Variables in 2) and work experience	102.1	99.9	97.4	100.0

Note: The log wage ratios are exponentiated log wage differentials, which are the partial regression coefficients of dummy (0,1) variables for black (Hispanic) from a series of OLS regressions containing the explanatory variables noted. The reference group is white non-Hispanic. All regressions starting with stage 1 also control for age, MSA, central city, and region. The analysis is restricted to wage and salary workers. The statistical significance of the black and Hispanic coefficients is indicated as follows (two-tailed test): **significant at the 5% level or less. All other ratios are not statistically significant.
Source: National Longitudinal Survey of Youth (NLSY79).

We find that, for 2008, the unadjusted hourly wage rate of black men is about 70 percent of the unadjusted white male wage rate, leaving a differential or gap of 30 percent (Table 7.4). When we control for differences in age, geographic location, and schooling, the black–white ratio rises to 82 percent both because of differences in schooling and because a larger proportion of African American than of white men live in the South, where wages are lower (stage 1).

After adding a variable measuring AFQT score (stage 2) the black–white wage ratio jumps to 96 percent, leaving a gap of only 4 percent (100 minus the ratio) and is no longer statistically significant. The effect of AFQT scores on the wage ratio is large because the differential in scores is large: African American men scored at the 24th percentile and white men at the 57th, and the effect of a percentile point increase in AFQT score on wages is large for both African Americans and whites. Our findings with respect to the explanatory power of the AFQT variable are similar to those of Neal and Johnson (1996) and O'Neill (1990), who analyzed the same NLSY79 cohort when the survey participants were still in their twenties.[9] The black–white hourly wage ratio rises above 100 percent and the gap is eliminated when we control for differences in civilian and military work experience (model 3).

Table 7.5 shows the effect on the black–white wage ratio of the same series of regression adjustments for two subsets of men: those who completed no more than high school and those who are college graduates or have advanced degrees. The initial, unadjusted wage ratios are somewhat higher within education group but the effects of moving from stage 1 to stage 3 are similar to what we observed for the total group. The effect of AFQT is similarly large. For college graduates the wage gap is eliminated in 2008 with the addition of AFQT in stage 2 (in 2000, the wage ratio rises to 95, not 100 percent, but is not statistically significant). With all of the variables added in stage 3, the black–white wage gap is no longer of statistical or practical significance for either education group in both 2000 and 2008.

The differential between Hispanic and white men (Table 7.4) is smaller than the black–white gap before adding any explanatory variables (less than 20 percent overall and less than 10 percent for the subgroups of those who had at most a high school diploma and those who had completed college or had higher degrees (Table 7.5). The addition of detailed schooling plus age and the geographic variables (stage 1) reduces the overall differential by half and marginally reduces the gaps for the high school and college groups since the grouping by education has already accounted for much of the education difference. The gap for Hispanic men is no longer statistically or practically significant for the total group as well as for the two education subgroups once AFQT scores are added (stage 2). The addition of the work experience variable has no significant effect on the outcome.

Table 7.5 Explaining the male black–white and Hispanic–white wage gaps at different education levels

	High school graduate or less				College graduate or more			
	Black–white wage ratio		Hispanic–white wage ratio		Black–white wage ratio		Hispanic–white wage ratio	
	2000 (Ages 35–43)	2008 (Ages 43–51)	2000 (Ages 35–43)	2008 (Ages 43–51)	2000 (Ages 35–43)	2008 (Ages 43–51)	2000 (Ages 35–43)	2008 (Ages 43–51)
Unadjusted hourly wage ratio (%)	78.3**	77.9**	91.8**	91.6**	77.0**	80.5**	94.3	94.1
Hourly wage ratio controlling for:								
1) Schooling	82.7**	82.7**	93.4**	92.9**	82.4**	84.8**	96.1	95.9
2) Variables in 1) and AFQT	92.8**	94.7	100.3	101.5	95.1	100.9	101.9	104.3
3) Variables in 2) and work experience	97.3	99.0	99.1	100.2	96.6	102.7	103.8	105.0

Note: The log wage ratios are exponentiated log wage differentials, which are the partial regression coefficients of dummy (0, 1) variables for black (Hispanic) from a series of OLS regressions containing the explanatory variables noted. The reference group is white non-Hispanic. All regressions starting with stage 1 also control for age, MSA, central city, and region. The analysis is restricted to wage and salary workers. The statistical significance of the black and Hispanic coefficients is indicated as follows (two-tailed test): **significant at the 5% level or less. All other ratios are not statistically significant.
Source: National Longitudinal Survey of Youth (NLSY79).

Our analysis of the NLSY79 data indicates that differences in schooling, scores on the AFQT, and lifetime work experience explain virtually all of the difference in hourly pay between African American men and white men. The difference in schooling and AFQT alone accounts for the pay difference between Hispanic men and white men. In our analysis of data from the ACS, we found significant residual wage gaps mainly because the data provide no standardized measure of actual attainment of cognitive skills or of accumulated work experience. Years of schooling completed are a weak proxy for learned skills when standards for promotion and the attainment of diplomas and degrees vary widely. The AFQT provides a standardized measure of attainment, which reflects cognitive skills acquired in school and at home.

Without including the AFQT or work experience variables, the ACS and the NLSY79 both indicate about the same adjusted black–white wage gap. In fact, comparing the results of models that include only age, geographic location, and schooling, we find that the black–white wage ratio using the ACS 2009 is 81 percent (model I of Table 7.1), about the same as the ratio observed in the NLSY79 data (stage 1 of Table 7.4).[10] It is the addition of the AFQT variable (and also the work experience variables) that sets the NLSY79 results apart from the standard results using data like the ACS.

In sum, we find that differences in years of schooling and, more importantly, AFQT scores alone explain most of the black–white wage gap among men and all of the Hispanic–white wage gap. When years of work experience are included in the regression, the black–white gap is eliminated. The question remains, however, whether these results are reliable or instead reflect bias in the explanatory variables or other problems that typically confound statistical analysis of wage differentials.

First, do the explanatory variables themselves reflect employer discrimination? Differences in years of schooling and the AFQT are not likely to have been influenced by current employer discrimination, although societal discrimination had a crucial influence in the past on the educational attainment of African Americans. Because AFQT scores are likely influenced by early schooling and parental background, they, too, could have been affected by the lingering effects of early segregationist policies. However, those effects should not be confused with current employer discrimination.

Another question is whether it is appropriate to include work experience in an analysis of the wage gap that aims to determine the role of employer discrimination. It would be inappropriate if employer discrimination were an important reason for the lower employment of African American men. However, factors other than employer discrimination appear to be more important determinants of black–white employment differences. The relative decline in the employment of young African American men (particularly high school dropouts) that started in the 1970s and continued in the 1980s has been related to the broader decline in demand for low-skilled workers as well as to increased crime and incarcerations (Bound and Freeman, 1992).

Using data from the NLSY79, we also find that African American men are much more likely than white men to have been incarcerated. In the 2000 survey, close to 13 percent of African American men had been interviewed in jail in at least one of the survey years (compared to 6 percent of Hispanics and 3 percent of whites). Incarceration directly reduces years of work experience and, if it lasts long enough, may lead to depreciation of work-related skills. It also makes it more difficult to obtain future employment. In an analysis of the determinants of lifetime work experience we found that jail experience had a strong and significant negative effect on work experience.

The argument is sometimes also made that employer discrimination takes the form of rewarding minorities less than whites for higher levels of work-related skills, which would appear as lower coefficients in our regression analysis. Lower returns to additional years of work experience and education (and, less plausibly, to higher scores on the AFQT) for minorities than for whites could be evidence of employer discrimination that might discourage investment in work-related skills.

To address these issues we have estimated separate regressions for African Americans, whites, and Hispanics, and we report here on our findings of results for the major explanatory variables in 2000. With respect to AFQT scores, we find that the wage gain associated with a 10 percentile point increase in the AFQT score is larger for African American and Hispanic men than it is for white men, suggesting that employers recognize and reward skill among minority men at least to the same extent as they do among white men (i.e., holding constant the variables indicated in model I, a 10 percentile point increase in the AFQT score increases the wage rates of African American and Hispanic men by about 6 percent and white men by about 5 percent).

When work experience is added to the model, the return to AFQT is slightly smaller for all groups, presumably because AFQT scores are correlated with work experience. However, the same pattern by race is maintained and the coefficients remain robust and significant. The even stronger relation between the AFQT score and wage rates among African Americans and Hispanics than for whites is good evidence that the AFQT provides an unbiased measure of skills.[11] The question of bias in the AFQT, however, has been analyzed more directly by the US. Department of Defense, which uses it extensively as a tool for assigning military personnel to occupational training and tasks. Such tests have concluded that the AFQT predicts African American performance as well as it does white performance.[12]

Most men have at least a high school diploma or a GED (87 percent among whites, 81 percent among African Americans, but dropping to 71 percent among Hispanics). The differences in attainment are more pronounced at the postsecondary level, where white men are much more likely to graduate from college than African American or Hispanic men. Holding AFQT constant, increases in schooling through high school do not have a significant effect on earnings for any group. However, the increases in wages associated with college graduation and with attainment of higher degrees are large and roughly similar for all groups. White and Hispanic men have a higher return to college graduation than do black men, while black men have higher returns at the master's, doctoral, and professional degree levels.

With regard to returns to work experience, holding constant education and AFQT, wage gains associated with an additional year of civilian experience are somewhat lower for African Americans than for the other groups: about 4 percent for black men, 4.7 percent for white men, and 4.9 percent for Hispanic men. The return to a year of military service is lower than the return to a year of civilian work experience for all three groups.[13] The small black–white difference in work experience coefficients may be due to discontinuities in African American male employment that we have not accounted for in this analysis.[14]

When we take into account minority–white differences in characteristics and the difference in the wage premiums associated with these differences, we find that the single largest factor contributing to the wage gaps is the differential in the AFQT. The AFQT differential alone explains 45 percent of the black–white wage gap and half of the Hispanic–white gap. AFQT and education together account for two-thirds of the black–white gap and 89 percent of the Hispanic–white gap. Differences in geographic location and work experience fully explain the remaining gaps.[15]

We conclude from this analysis that labor market discrimination is not a likely cause of either the black–white or Hispanic–white wage gap among men. Nonetheless, these wage gaps are troubling, particularly the persistent black–white gap. Our analysis suggests that the source of the problem lies in the fact that black men on average accumulate less in the way of cognitive skills before they enter the labor market and less continuous work experience after entry. The public policy issue that we face is what should be done to help eliminate the productivity gaps.

Some observers advocate eliminating the effects of the skill gap rather than acknowledging its existence and devoting the energy and other resources needed to closing it. That is essentially the approach of affirmative action. Other analysts and commentators, concerned about the problems of young African American men, have focused on the causes of the skill gap. Jencks and Phillips (1998a) comment that "if racial equality is America's goal, reducing the black–white skill gap would probably do more to promote this goal than any other strategy that could command broad political support." Researchers have increasingly turned their attention to the sources of the skill gap and to the study of ways to change the provision of schooling, as well as the environmental conditions and parental attitudes that have negative impacts on the development of skills from early childhood. For example, see Jencks and Phillips (1998b), Fryer and Levitt (2004), and Heckman (2008).

Wage Differentials Among Women

The initial unadjusted minority–white wage gaps are considerably smaller among women than those we observed for men. In 2008 the black–white wage ratio for men in the NLSY79 is 70 percent, while the ratio for women is 87 percent. The Hispanic–white wage ratio for men is 81 percent and for women 92 percent. We analyze the sources of the black–white and Hispanic–white wage differences among women using the same methodology that we applied to our analysis of wage gaps among men. We conduct wage regressions for all women (and separately for women with high school education and women who are college graduates) and use the coefficients of variables indicating African American race and Hispanic origin to estimate wage differentials between the two minority groups and the reference group of white women.

The salient characteristics of black, white, and Hispanic women are displayed in Table 7.6. In addition to the variables used in our analysis of racial and ethnic differences among men, we include two variables that are particularly relevant to women. One indicates whether the person ever had a spell out of the labor force due to family responsibilities, and the other is a measure of the proportion of total weeks worked part-time since age 22.

Table 7.6 Selected characteristics of women by race

	2000 (ages 35–43)			2008 (ages 43–51)		
	White	Black	Hispanic	White	Black	Hispanic
Hourly rate of pay[a]	16.5	13.7	15.1	17.3	15.0	15.9
Region (%)						
Northeast	17.2	13.5	13.8	25.8	16.5	13.4
North Central	32.6	18.8	8.1	30.7	18.6	7.5
South	33.3	61.2	33.9	29.5	58.9	36.5
West	16.9	6.6	44.1	14.1	6.0	42.6
Education (Highest Level Attained, %)						
<10 yrs	1.8	2.8	7.5	0.9	2.1	7.3
10–12 yrs (no diploma or GED)	8.2	11.1	14.6	8.0	10.9	12.5
HS grad (diploma)	32.6	29.2	24.0	29.7	24.6	23.0
HS grad (GED)	3.6	5.3	5.7	3.3	4.2	5.0
Some college	26.0	36.6	34.2	26.5	40.2	36.2
BA or equiv. degree	19.7	12.2	8.5	20.7	13.4	9.1
MA or equiv. degree	7.4	2.5	4.7	10.1	4.1	5.9
PhD or prof. degree	0.8	0.4	0.8	0.9	0.5	0.9
AFQT percentile score	53.0	24.5	30.1	54.1	25.8	30.6
Work Experience						
Avg. years worked in civilian jobs since age 18[b]	16.5	14.5	15.0	22.9	21.3	21.3
Avg. yrs. worked in the military since 1978[b]	0.0	0.1	0.1	0.1	0.1	0.0
Proportion of total weeks worked PT since age 22 (%)	16.9	9.7	12.0	16.7	9.8	11.6
% ever out of labor force due to family responsibilities	49.6	57.8	64.4	55.5	58.9	66.7
Sample size	1,358	855	492	1,236	778	439

[a]Hourly rate of pay in 2008 dollars (geometric mean).
[b]Years are full year equivalents based on total weeks worked divided by 52.
Source: National Longitudinal Survey of Youth (NLSY79).

In 2008, black women were almost as likely as white women to have completed at least high school (87 percent for black women vs. 91 percent for white women; only 80 percent of Hispanic women completed high school). Similar to the comparison among men, education differences are more pronounced at the college level. About 32 percent of white women completed college or got an advanced degree, compared to 18 percent of black women and 16 percent of Hispanic women. All three groups of women slightly increased their educational attainment between 2000 and 2008. AFQT scores differ considerably by race and Hispanic origin among women, much as they did among men. The average percentile score on the AFQT was 54 percent for white women compared to 26 percent for black women and 31 percent for Hispanic women.

In terms of work experience, white women accumulated more years of work experience in civilian jobs since age 18 than African American or Hispanic women, but white women were much more likely to have worked part-time. (About 17 percent of the total time worked by white women was part-time, compared to 10 percent for black women and 12 percent for Hispanic women.) Black women accumulated more years in the military than white or Hispanic women.

The results of our regression analysis are shown in Table 7.7. The results for women, as for men, are given sequentially in three stages, each of which adds new groups of independent variables. The initial unadjusted black–white earnings ratio was 87 percent in 2008, somewhat higher than in 2000. The earnings ratio rises to 94 percent after controlling for schooling and the

Table 7.7 Explaining the black–white and Hispanic–white wage gaps among women

	Black–white wage ratio		Hispanic–white wage ratio	
	2000 (ages 35–43)	2008 (ages 43–51)	2000 (ages 35–43)	2008 (ages 43–51)
Unadjusted hourly wage ratio (%)	82.8**	87.1**	91.2**	91.9**
Hourly wage ratio controlling for:				
1) Schooling	90.8**	94.3**	97.0	98.3
2) Variables in 1) and AFQT	104.1*	106.6**	107.3**	107.5**
3) Variables in 2) and work experience	105.4**	105.7**	106.5**	105.8**

Note: The log wage ratios are exponentiated log wage differentials, which are the partial regression coefficients of dummy (0, 1) variables for black (Hispanic) from a series of OLS regressions containing the explanatory variables noted. The reference group is white non-Hispanic. All regressions starting with stage 1 also control for age, MSA, central city, and region. The analysis is restricted to wage and salary workers. The statistical significance of the black and Hispanic coefficients is indicated as follows (two-tailed test): **significant at the 5% level or less, *significant at the 10% level.
Source: National Longitudinal Survey of Youth (NLSY79).

geographic and age variables. The addition of the AFQT variable eliminates any disparity. In fact it raises the black–white ratio for women to 106.6 percent. Lifetime work experience has no additional effect. (It lowers the ratio slightly to 105.7 percent.)

In 2008, the unadjusted Hispanic–white hourly wage ratio among women was 92 percent (a gap of 8 percent). When we control for differences in schooling and geographic location, the Hispanic–white ratio rises to 98 percent, leaving a gap of 2 percent (not statistically significant). Controlling for differences in AFQT scores, the Hispanic–white wage ratio rises above 100 percent (to 107.5 percent without the work experience variables and slightly lower when the work experience variables are added).

Table 7.8 presents results of the same set of black–white and Hispanic–white regressions conducted for women who attended or graduated from high school and women who attained a college degree or advanced degree. At the college level, Hispanic women earned 16 percent more than white non-Hispanic women in 2008 before adjusting for any explanatory factors. This result is not significantly altered by the addition of other factors. Black women earn almost as much as white women before adjusting for other factors, and that ratio rises above 100

Table 7.8 Explaining the female black–white and Hispanic–white wage gaps at different education levels

	High school graduate or less				College graduate or more			
	Black–white wage ratio		Hispanic–white wage ratio		Black–white wage ratio		Hispanic–white wage ratio	
	2000 (ages 35–43)	2008 (ages 43–51)	2000 (ages 35–43)	2008 (ages 43–51)	2000 (ages 35–43)	2008 (ages 43–51)	2000 (ages 35–43)	2008 (ages 43–51)
Unadjusted hourly wage ratio (%)	85.6**	87.2**	94.4**	92.6**	85.3**	96.7	105.9	116.1**
Hourly wage ratio controlling for:								
1) Schooling	91.7**	93.7*	96.0	97.6	89.0**	97.7	101.3	107.8
2) Variables in 1) and AFQT	105.7**	105.0	106.5	105.7	96.6	105.9	107.3	114.5*
3) Variables in 2) and work experience	108.7**	105.1	104.9	103.0	95.0	103.0	110.0	117.8**

Note: The log wage ratios are exponentiated log wage differentials, which are the partial regression coefficients of dummy (0, 1) variables for black (Hispanic) from a series of OLS regressions containing the explanatory variables noted. The reference group is white non-Hispanic. All regressions starting with stage 1 also control for age, MSA, central city, and region. The analysis is restricted to wage and salary workers. The statistical significance of the black and Hispanic coefficients is indicated as follows (two-tailed test): **significant at the 5% level or less, *significant at the 10% level.
Source: National Longitudinal Survey of Youth (NLSY79).

once we control for AFQT scores. Among the high school subgroup, the wage ratios for both black and Hispanic women exceed 100 once we adjust for AFQT.

Examining the results of separate regressions for black, white, and Hispanic women allows us to examine regression coefficients to determine how the pecuniary returns to key variables vary by race and Hispanic ethnicity. We find, as we did in the same comparison among men, that the increase in the wage rate associated with an increase in AFQT is not only large and significant for all groups but is much larger for black and Hispanic women than for white women. A 10 percentile point increase in the AFQT score raises the wage rate by about 8 percent for African American women, 7 percent for Hispanic women, and 4 percent for white women when schooling, age, and geographic location are held constant. The return to additional years of work experience is about the same for all three groups (marginally higher for black and Hispanic women). Black women have worked more years in the military than the other groups, and their return to military service is also higher. Part-time work has a negative effect on hourly pay. Black women are less likely to have worked part-time than the other groups, and their wage penalty for part-time work is larger than it is for the other groups. White women were much more likely to have worked part-time, but their penalty for doing so is not as large as it is for black women.

When we take into account minority–white differences in characteristics and the difference in the wage premiums associated with these differences, we find, as we did for men, that the single largest factor contributing to the wage gaps is the differential in the AFQT score. In fact, the AFQT differential alone explains 94 percent of the female black–white wage gap and more than explains the female Hispanic–white gap.[16]

In sum, our analysis of female wage differentials by race and Hispanic ethnicity provides no support for the view that the differences observed—which are smaller than those observed among men—are due to employment discrimination.

THE GENDER WAGE GAP

Although the gender gap in pay has narrowed considerably since the late 1970s, women's hourly pay was only 79 percent of men's in 2000 among the NLSY79 cohort (who had reached ages 35–43 by that year). Yet women and men in the NLSY79 have approximately the same amount of schooling and scores on the AFQT test. Gender differences in productivity, however, arise for reasons other than differences in cognitive skills. The most important source of the gender wage gap is the difference in human capital acquired through labor market experience and in job choice, both of which reflect differences in the relative importance of home and market activities in the lives of women and men.

The division of labor in the family is less delineated than it once was. A majority of married women with children now work. Nonetheless, women still assume greater responsibility for child rearing than men do, and that responsibility influences the extent and continuity of market work as well as choice of occupation and preferences for working conditions that facilitate the combination of work in the market and housework.[17] These gender differences in preferences translate into wage differences, partly because they lead to differences in human capital acquired on the job and partly because flexible schedules at work, a less stressful work environment, and other working conditions compatible with meeting the demands of home responsibilities are likely to come at the price of lower wages.

The Tradeoff Between Work in the Market and Housework

The labor force participation of women has greatly increased over the years. Yet even today labor force data show the strong effect of the presence of children, particularly young children, on women's work participation. Among parents of children under the age of 6 years, 58 percent of women were employed in 2009 compared to 88 percent of men. Among parents of children whose youngest child was aged 6–17, 72 percent of women were employed compared to 86 percent of men. Thus many women are out of the labor force during a time of life when labor market skills would otherwise be acquired.[18]

Even if they are in the labor force, women with children differ from working men with respect to hours spent at work. In 2009, 29 percent of women with children under the age of 6 worked part-time compared to 6 percent of men with similarly aged children. The percentage of women working part-time is reduced to 24 percent when their children reach ages 6–17, while the percentage of men working part-time falls just slightly to 5 percent. Gender differences in hours are also present among full-time workers, in that women are less likely than men to work long hours in a week: in 2010, 25 percent of male full-time workers but only 14 percent of female full-time workers worked 41 hours or more a week.[19]

Are women steered into part-time jobs by prejudiced employers harboring negative views of women? Polls on job preferences indicate that free choice, not employer choice, is the reason for the gender difference in part-time work. Results of a poll conducted by the Pew Research Center (2007) show that, in answer to the question "What would be the ideal situation for you-working full-time, working part-time, or not working at all outside the home?" 50 percent of all mothers of children under age 18 responded that part-time would be ideal, 20 percent said full-time, and 29 percent said not working at all. In contrast, 72 percent of fathers preferred full-time work, 12 percent part-time work, and 16 percent no work (Table 7.9). Even among mothers who were employed full-time, 49 percent said that their ideal would be part-time work, while 80 percent of mothers working part-time said that part-time was their ideal and only 5 percent indicated a preference for full-time work. These results are not an anomaly. Over the years, periodic polls on job preferences have found similar results.[20]

Table 7.9 What working situation would be ideal for you? Results from a 2007 Pew Research Center Survey

	Ideal situation would be			
	Not working (%)	Part-time work (%)	Full-time work (%)	N
Have children under 18				
Fathers	16	12	72	343
Mothers	29	50	70	414
Mothers with children under 18				
Employed full-time	21	49	29	187
Employed part-time	15	80	5	75
Not employed	48	33	16	153

Source: From "Fewer Mothers Prefer Full-time Work" in *A Social and Demographic Trend Report*, Pew Research Center, p. 3, July 12, 2007.

Data collected by the Department of Labor's American Time Use Survey (ATUS) provide further insight into the tradeoffs that women and men make in apportioning their time between market work, housework, and other activities. The ATUS collects information from individuals who keep detailed diaries, recording how they spend their time during a 24-hour period. Table 7.10 displays our tabulations from the combined 2003–2004 ATUS for employed men and women aged 20–44 who reported their time use on a weekday.[21]

The table shows the allocation of hours among five categories of primary activity: sleeping, housework, childcare, market work, and socializing, sports, and all other activities. The time allocations are given separately according to the age of the youngest child (<1, 1–5, 6–12, and 13–17) as well as for those who have no children under age 18 present in the household. Primary activities are mutually exclusive, so with allowance for rounding error, the time spent in the four activities plus sleeping adds up to 24 hours.

We report data for those who are currently employed, kept a diary on a weekday, and were employed on the diary day. Time spent on childcare is measured in two ways: hours during the day spent on primary childcare when it is the main activity and total hours spent with children present in either a primary capacity or a secondary capacity while engaged in other activities. (Total hours were not collected for children after they reached age 13.)

Several distinct patterns of time use stand out. No matter how measured, working mothers devote significantly more time to childcare than do fathers. Hours spent on childcare by both mothers and fathers decline as children age. Working mothers of infants spent 3.1 hours on primary childcare, and those hours declined to 2.3 when the youngest child was aged 1–5 and to 1.5 once

Table 7.10 Average hours spent per day in child care, work, and other activities by age of youngest child, for employed women and men ages 20–44

Age of youngest child:	Currently employed and work on diary day				
	<1	1–5	6–12	13–17	No child
Women					
Household work	2.4	1.6	1.9	1.8	1.4
Primary child care	3.1	2.3	1.5	0.5	0.1
Market work	7.2	7.6	7.7	8.4	8.2
Socializing, sports, eating, and other	3.8	4.7	5.4	5.8	6.3
Sleeping	7.5	7.9	7.5	7.4	8.1
Total hours with children in respondent's care	8.7	6.9	6.2	NC	NA
Men					
Household work	1.0	0.9	1.0	0.9	1.0
Primary child care	1.1	1.1	0.8	0.3	0.0
Market work	9.9	9.5	9.5	9.8	8.9
Socializing, sports, eating, and other	4.4	5.0	5.2	5.3	6.4
Sleeping	7.5	7.5	7.6	7.7	7.6
Total hours with children in respondent's care[a]	3.7	4.1	3.7	NC	NA

[a]Total waking hours in a day spent with children in a primary or a secondary capacity.
Note: Sample includes employed women and men aged 20–44 reporting time use on a weekday. 2003–2004 annual averages are reported. Means are weighted. NC: Data not collected for children over 12 years of age. NA: Not applicable.
Source: Pooled 2003 and 2004 data from the American Time Use Survey (ATUS).

the child reached school age (6–12), falling to only 0.5 hour when the youngest child was a teenager. Over the same span, fathers of infants devoted 1.1 hours to primary childcare, falling to 0.8 hours by the time the youngest child reached 6–12 years.

Mothers also spent more time on household work than fathers on a workday: 2.4 hours when the child was an infant, declining to somewhat less than 2 hours when children were older. Fathers spent about an hour on household work, and that did not vary by age of child.[22]

Fathers more or less compensate for the lower hours spent on childcare and household work by spending more hours of the day in market work. Comparing mothers and fathers who worked on the diary day, we find that men spent 9.5–10 hours on market work, and those hours did not vary much with age of youngest child. Mothers, however, somewhat increased their work time from 7.2 hours when the youngest child was an infant to 8.4 hours when the youngest child reached 13–17 years.

Primary childcare understates the total burden of childcare because responsibility for children does not end when a parent does housework or other activities. It is striking that total time spent with children for mothers is considerable even on a day when the mother worked (8.2 hours for mothers with an infant, declining to 6.2 hours when the child reached ages 6–12). Fathers spend about 4 hours of total time with children in their care on an average workday, and that time does not vary with age of child.

The ATUS data demonstrate that women continue to be responsible for a disproportionately large share of household work and childcare even when working. The burden of household responsibilities affects more than desired hours on the job. In an important extension of his work on the economics of the family, Gary Becker (1985) has developed a model of the allocation of energy.[23] Becker's analysis shows how the energy demands of childcare and housework reduce the energy available for market work. Women who are heavily engaged in childcare and other household work could be expected to choose less-demanding and consequently lower paying jobs.

Analyzing the Gender Pay Gap with NLSY79 Data

It is a challenge to estimate the determinants of the gender gap because differences in standard variables such as schooling are not likely to be important sources of the gender gap. The NLSY79 is superior to most other data sources because it provides detailed information on lifetime patterns of work participation. Although differences in lifetime work patterns have received considerable attention as a source of the gender gap, another significant source of wage differentials is what Adam Smith, in his *Wealth of Nations*, termed "Inequalities arising from the Nature of the Employments themselves." Smith observed that the "agreeableness and disagreeableness of the employments themselves" are one of the principal circumstances that make up for "small pecuniary gain in some employments and counterbalance a great one in other" (Smith, 1776).[24] Those nonpecuniary characteristics of employments surely may be evaluated differently by women and men. For example, occupations and individual firms differ in the extent to which they provide part-time work or otherwise accommodate flexible work schedules, characteristics that are likely to be more highly valued by women than by men. To the extent that these amenities are costly for employers to provide, jobs with amenities will be paid for with lower wages.

Jobs with disamenities, such as exposure to hazards or an unpleasant environment, are likely to require a pay premium. A large and growing literature in psychology, sociology, and economics has studied the risk-taking tendencies of men and women in many domains, including physical danger and financial risk.[25] The general finding is that women are more risk-averse than men, which means women may self-select into less risky lower paying jobs. In addition, men and women may differ in their attitudes toward work involving dirty or otherwise unpleasant physical conditions. Physical differences are likely to affect aptitude for certain work. For example, jobs requiring extremely heavy lifting favor physically capable men, although the proportion of jobs requiring hard physical labor has declined sharply over time.

Another source of differences in financial rewards among occupations is the extent to which skills depreciate during periods of withdrawal from work. The rate of depreciation will vary depending on the rate of technological change and obsolescence of the skills acquired. Since women are more likely than men to expect to take career breaks for child rearing, they are more likely to avoid training for occupations with a larger financial penalty for withdrawal.[26]

Although women and men are more likely than they once were to work in the same occupation, large differences still prevail in their occupational distributions. In 2010, women were 45 percent of all full-time workers.[27] Furthermore, women were 55 percent of all professional workers, but were disproportionally represented in certain fields and underrepresented in others. For example, women were 72 percent of education and library workers, 64 percent of psychologists, and 48 percent of biologists, but only 25 percent of workers in computer and mathematical occupations and 12 percent of architects and engineers. These percentages are close to women's representation in the same fields of college and graduate degrees. In nonprofessional occupations, women made up 73 percent of office and administrative support occupations and 71 percent of cashiers but made up a tiny proportion of workers in many blue-collar occupations: 2 percent of construction and extraction workers; 3.7 percent of installation, maintenance, and repair workers; and less than 1 percent of crane and tower operators.

We estimate that over the period 1994–2001, among all narrowly defined (three-digit) occupations as defined by the Bureau of the Census, 53 percent of women or men would have to change their occupation to produce gender equality in occupational distributions.[28] To assess the effect on wages of gender differences in occupational choice, we have incorporated in our wage analysis measures of the characteristics of each person's occupation based on additional information on the characteristics of each three-digit level occupation. Our analysis of the gender gap follows the same procedures used in our analysis of racial and ethnic differences. The key variables and their mean values for all men and women are given in Table 7.11.

Table 7.12 shows the effect on the gender gap of controlling for different sets of explanatory variables from a series of log wage regressions.[29] Results are shown for the full sample of male and female workers as well as for subsets of the sample disaggregated by education. Results are also given for married men and women as well as for those who never had a child and never married and can be assumed to be free of family responsibilities (an assumption corroborated by our time use data in Table 7.10).

Table 7.11 Selected characteristics of men and women (NLSY79)

	2000 (ages 35–43)		2008 (ages 43–51)	
	Female	Male	Female	Male
Hourly rate of pay[a]	15.3	19.4	16.3	21.0
% Hispanic	18.2	19.3	17.9	17.8
% Black	31.6	28.2	31.7	28.2
Education (Highest Level Attained, %)				
< High School	13.5	17.6	12.2	16.1
HS grad (diploma)	30.0	32.6	26.9	32.0
HS grad (GED)	4.5	5.6	3.9	5.1
Some college	30.8	23.2	32.6	24.2
BA or equiv. degree	15.3	15.5	16.3	16.2
MA or equiv. degree	5.3	4.1	7.5	5.1
PhD or prof. degree	0.7	1.5	0.8	1.4
AFQT percentile score	39.8	42.4	40.9	43.6
Work Experience				
Avg. years worked in civilian jobs since age 18[b]	15.6	17.2	22.1	24.2
Avg. yrs. worked in the military since 1978[b]	0.1	0.6	0.1	0.8
Proportion of total weeks worked PT since age 22 (%)	13.7	5.0	13.6	4.1
% ever out of labor force due to family responsibilities	54.9	13.0	58.6	14.3
% in gov't job	21.6	14.4	26.7	17.5
% in nonprofit job	10.0	4.9	14.1	5.2
OCC. Characteristics of Person's 3-digit OCC.				
Specific Vocation Preparation (SVP) required in occup. (months)	27.0	28.8	26.0	28.7
% in OCC. involving:				
Hazards (0,1)	1.3	8.4	1.1	10.0
Fumes (0,1)	0.4	4.3	0.6	10.2
Noise (0,1)	8.0	30.7	7.1	32.8
Strength (0,1)	9.2	21.5	8.7	17.8
Weather extreme (0,1)	3.3	18.8	2.7	22.1
% using computers	55.7	41.5	56.7	44.0
% using computer for analysis	14.3	13.9	14.9	15.2

Table 7.11 Continued

	2000 (ages 35–43)		2008 (ages 43–51)	
	Female	Male	Female	Male
% using computer for word processing	34.5	23.6	41.9	30.4
Risk of unemployment	0.8	1.1	0.8	0.9
Rate of transition to out of labor force	1.0	0.8	1.0	0.8
% female in OCC.	63.5	27.0	64.2	26.9
Sample size	2,705	2,694	2,453	2,220

[a]Hourly rate of pay in 2008 dollars (geometric mean).
[b]Years are full year equivalents based on total weeks worked divided by 52.
Note: Characteristics above are for wage and salary workers included in the regression analysis. Model also controls for age, central city, MSA, region, and occupation missing.

Source: National Longitudinal Survey of Youth (NLSY79) merged with measures of occupational characteristics (3-digit level) from the September 2001 CPS, the March CPS, the CPS ORG, and the *Dictionary of Occupational Titles* (1991).

Table 7.12 Explaining the gender wage gap: female–male hourly wage ratios (NLSY79)

	All		By schooling level (2000)	
	2000 (ages 35–43)	2008 (ages 43–51)	High school graduate or less	College graduate or more
Unadjusted hourly wage ratio (%)	79.0	77.4	79.5	75.0
Hourly wage ratio controlling for:				
1) Schooling, AFQT	79.4	77.0	79.4	78.3
2) Variables in 1) and work experience	88.6	88.2	92.8	83.4
3) Variables in 2) and labor force withdrawal due to family responsibilities and type of employer	90.9	90.7	94.2	88.7
4) Variables in 3) and occupational characteristics	92.0	91.0	93.0	92.5
5) Variables in 4) and percent female in occupation	92.4	93.4	94.7	92.5
Alternative step:				
4A) Variables in 3 and percent female in occupation	96.7	96.5	94.7	92.5

Note: All female coefficients are significant at the 10% level or lower. The log wage ratios are exponentiated log wage differentials, which are the partial regression coefficients of dummy (0, 1) variables for female from a series of OLS regressions containing the explanatory variables noted. The reference group is male. All regressions starting with stage 1 also control for age, MSA, central city, and region.

Source: National Longitudinal Survey of Youth (NLSY79) merged with measures of occupational characteristics (3-digit level) from the September 2001 CPS, the March CPS, the CPS ORG, and the *Dictionary of Occupational Titles* (1991).

We display the results as female to male hourly wage ratios.[30] The unadjusted hourly wage ratio for the full sample of men and women is 79 percent in 2000 and 77 percent in 2008 when the cohort is older. Using the 2000 data we find that the ratio is essentially unchanged after including education, AFQT score, and geographic location (stage 1). The addition of three work experience variables, however, reduces the gender gap by almost half, and the wage ratio rises to 89 percent (stage 2). The work experience variables include weeks worked in civilian jobs since age 18 (converted to years by dividing by 52), weeks worked in the military divided by 52, and the proportion part-time of total weeks worked. On average, women of the same age have worked about 2 years less than men in military and civilian jobs combined. Moreover, close to 14 percent of the weeks worked by women were part-time compared to 5 percent for men.

As a proxy for commitment to home responsibilities we add in stage 3 a variable indicating whether the worker had ever withdrawn from the labor force citing childcare or family responsibilities as the reason. Such labor force withdrawal is associated with an 8 percent reduction in the wage rate for men as well as women. However, 55 percent of women and only 13 percent of men have ever withdrawn because of family responsibilities.

We also add variables indicating whether the person's job is in government employment, the nonprofit sector, or the private sector. Nonprofit jobs offer more part-time work and are more likely to allow for flexible schedules and possibly a more relaxed ambience than work in the for-profit sector. But such amenities come at a cost to employers and are therefore associated with lower pay. As shown in Table 7.11, women are more likely than men to work in the nonprofit and government sectors. The addition of the class of worker variables combined with the labor force withdrawal variable raises the hourly wage ratio by 2.3 percentage points to 91 percent.

The final set of variables measure particular characteristics of each person's three-digit occupation. The characteristics are expected to have an effect on wages because they are associated with on-the-job investment or with particular amenities or disamenities. The occupational characteristics included in our analysis are listed in Table 7.11 along with the mean values for men and women separately. Measures of months of Specific Vocational Preparation (SVP) required for the job and other occupational characteristics were derived from the *Dictionary of Occupational Titles* (US Employment Service, 1991) and from special supplements pertaining to computer use on the job from the CPS. A variable measuring the level of transition out of the labor force and another measuring the risk of unemployment in the occupation were estimated using data from the March CPS.

A limitation of the occupational data, most of which are derived from the *Dictionary of Occupational Titles* created in 1991, is that the individual characteristics of each occupation are related to the three-digit occupations as classified at that time. The characteristics of occupations may well have changed. The coding scheme for occupations has changed significantly. Consequently the occupations of NLSY79 participants may be quite imperfectly linked to the occupational descriptions we use. To address this concern, we also use an alternative variable measuring the percent female in a three-digit occupation, contemporaneously matched with the individual's occupational code. In earlier research, occupational characteristics similar to those shown in Table 7.12 were found to explain most of the variation in the percent female across 327 three-digit occupations (Cavallo and O'Neill, 2004; O'Neill, 1983).

The hourly wage ratio rises only slightly to 92 percent when the occupational characteristics enumerated in Table 7.12 are added in stage 4. In stage 5 we add a variable that measures the percent female in the respondent's three-digit occupation. That addition barely affects the ratio, which rises to 92.4 percent. However, when we drop occupational characteristics and simply add percent female in the occupation, the female to male wage ratio increases to 97 percent (alternative, step 4A). Because of the measurement difficulties described, the occupational characteristics measure may not be able to capture occupational differences as well as the percent female variable.

Although measures of occupational dissimilarity between men and women have declined since the 1970s, the occupational distributions of women and men are still very different. As shown in Table 7.11, the women in our 2008 NLSY79 sample, on average, worked in occupations in which the percent female was 64 percent; men worked in occupations in which the percent female was 27 percent. These occupational differences are sometimes viewed as evidence of discrimination.[31] However, the occupations that women choose are strongly predicted by characteristics that are compatible with women's dual roles as workers and homemakers.[32]

The addition of the variable measuring the percent female in an occupation has only a limited additional effect on wages because it is highly correlated with the other occupational and personal characteristics that have already been accounted for in the analysis. In fact, in a log wage regression based only on the female sample, the percent female in the three-digit occupational category is not statistically significant and bears a positive sign. The variable is negative and significant only for men. The results for 2008, also shown in Table 7.12, are similar to the results for 2000 when the cohort was 8 years younger.

Table 7.12 also provides results for two subgroups of the NLSY79, differing by education level. The results for the high school group (those attaining a high school diploma or GED or with less schooling) are similar to those described earlier for all women and men. The unadjusted female-to-male ratio for this group was 80 percent in 2000. However, gender differences in work experience are more important for the high school group than for all women and men, and these alone account for two-thirds of the gender wage gap for this group. At the third stage, which also includes spells of labor force withdrawal and type of employer (government, nonprofit, or private sector), the female-to-male ratio reaches 94 percent.

The results for college graduates differ somewhat from those of the other groups. The unadjusted wage gap is larger (a ratio of 75 percent in 2000) in part because gender differences in skills among college graduates are somewhat larger. Men are more likely to receive doctoral and professional degrees, and, among college graduates, men have higher AFQT scores than women (73rd vs. 64th percentile). Although the gender difference in years worked is small at the college graduate level, the difference in part-time work is as large as for the high school group. Moreover, women who are college graduates are less likely to work in the private sector than other women or men at any education level (17 percent of female college graduates work in the nonprofit sector and 42 percent work in government compared to 8 percent of men in nonprofits and 22 percent in government). A college education appears to give women access to jobs with working conditions that allow them either to work part-time or to work full-time but under conditions more complementary with care of family, such as the long vacations of teachers.

Controlling for education, AFQT and work experience raises the ratio for college graduates to 83 percent (stage 2). But once gender differences in withdrawal for family reasons and type of employer are taken into account, the ratio among college graduates rises to 89 percent. Adding occupational characteristics brings the ratio up to 92.5 percent. Occupational characteristics are important at the college level and often reflect choice of college major. Brown and Corcoran (1997) find that adding information on field of college major to an analysis of the gender gap in pay among college graduates that also controls for work history and other factors reduces the gap to 6 percent (a female-to-male wage ratio of 94 percent).

Tables 7.13 and 7.14 further highlight the relative importance of family responsibilities versus labor market discrimination by comparing the gender gap for two groups at polar extremes: currently married men and women, and men and women who were never married and never had a child. Married women's hourly wage was about 74 percent of the wage of married men in 2000 (72 percent in 2008). Married men have somewhat higher AFQT scores and education than married women, have more years of work experience (civilian and military), and are much less likely to work part-time (Table 7.13). They are more likely to be responsible for financial support of the family, and, as shown in the ATUS data, men with children spend a much larger proportion of their time at work and have a much lower burden of home responsibilities than women with children. One might expect that married men make job and career choices that assign a higher value to pecuniary rewards than would married women who must balance the rewards of time with children against financial rewards from market work. Although we control for many variables, we have no data on time spent on household tasks and childcare in the NLSY79 data and no way to incorporate more subtle differences in preferences.

Table 7.13 Selected characteristics of men and women by marital status (NLSY79)

	Currently married				Never married and never had a child	
	2000 (ages 35–43)		2008 (ages 43–51)		2000 (ages 35–43)	
	Female	Male	Female	Male	Female	Male
Hourly rate of pay[a]	16.1	21.8	17.1	23.7	17.8	16.4
% Hispanic	19.8	19.5	17.5	18.1	15.8	17.1
% Black	20.5	21.0	21.7	21.6	35.5	29.0
Education (Highest Level Attained, %)						
< High School	11.5	14.0	8.9	13.0	5.4	16.8
HS grad (diploma)	30.9	32.4	27.6	30.9	18.7	28.7
HS grad (GED)	3.2	4.6	2.6	4.1	3.0	3.0
Some college	29.6	23.4	32.2	25.0	35.0	25.2
BA or equiv. degree	17.6	18.4	19.1	19.0	28.1	20.1
MA or equiv. degree	6.7	5.3	8.9	6.5	7.4	4.5
PhD or prof. degree	0.6	2.0	0.8	1.6	2.5	1.8
AFQT percentile score	44.2	47.3	46.0	47.7	49.2	42.6
Work Experience						
Avg. years worked in civilian jobs since age 18[b]	16.2	17.9	22.6	24.8	17.5	16.0
Avg. yrs. worked in the military since 1978[b]	0.1	0.6	0.1	0.9	0.1	0.3
Proportion of total weeks worked PT since age 22 (%)	15.8	3.9	15.7	3.3	10.5	9.5
% ever out of labor force due to family responsibilities	54.6	10.2	58.0	11.4	16.3	12.9
% in gov't job	22.2	16.9	28.5	18.9	24.1	9.0
% in nonprofit job	11.2	5.0	15.4	5.2	11.8	8.4
OCC. Characteristics of Person's 3-digit OCC						
Specific Vocation Preparation (SVP) required in occup. (months)	28.9	32.9	28.0	32.5	32.7	26.4
% in OCC. involving:						
Hazards (0,1)	1.4	7.7	0.7	9.0	0.0	6.6
Fumes (0,1)	0.3	3.8	0,4	9.2	0.5	3.3
Noise (0,1)	6.5	29.3	6.2	30.2	7.4	26.4
Strength (0,1)	8.4	18.9	6.8	15.4	4.9	21.9
Weather extreme (0,1)	2.8	17.4	2.2	20.4	3.9	18.6

(*continued*)

Table 7.13 Continued

	Currently married				Never married and never had a child	
	2000 (ages 35–43)		2008 (ages 43–51)		2000 (ages 35–43)	
	Female	Male	Female	Male	Female	Male
% using computers	58.6	46.1	59.8	48.7	62.0	41.9
% using computer for analysis	15.0	16.1	15.9	17.6	17.8	13.3
% using computer for word processing	37.3	27.2	44.8	34.4	39.0	24.3
Risk of unemployment	0.7	1.0	0.8	0.9	0.7	1.1
	65.0	27.2	65.8	27.2	63.0	32.5
Rate of transition to out of labor force	1.0	0.7	1.0	0.8	1.0	0.9
% female in OCC	65.0	27.2	65.8	27.2	63.0	32.5
Sample size	1,532	1,674	1,357	1,419	203	334

[a]Hourly rate of pay in 2008 dollars (geometric mean).
[b]Years are full year equivalents based on total weeks worked divided by 52.
Note: Characteristics above are for wage and salary workers included in the regression analysis. Model also controls for age, central city, MSA, region, and occupation missing.

Source: National Longitudinal Survey of Youth (NLSY79) merged with measures of occupational characteristics (3-digit level) from the September 2001 CPS, the March CPS, the CPS ORG, and the *Dictionary of Occupational Titles* (1991).

In 2000, the wage ratio comparing married women to married men rises to 88 percent after adjusting for all of our measured variables (stage 5); in 2008, when the group was older, the ratio rises to 91 percent with the stage 5 specifications. The variable, percent female in the occupation, has a more powerful effect when it is used alone, as in the alternative step 4A, which excludes the detailed characteristics of occupations. The ratio at model 4A was 91 percent in 2000 and 94 percent in 2008.

At the opposite pole we compare the earnings of never-married men and never-married women who never had a child. Never-married men do not the bear the responsibility for the financial support of a family as do most married men. And never-married women who never had a child do not have the responsibility for children that mothers bear, though they are more likely to be responsible for their own financial support. Never-married women without children have stronger credentials than never-married men without children with respect to education and somewhat higher AFQT scores and years of work experience. They are somewhat more likely to work part-time than never-married men. The typical occupational differences still prevail, however, as never-married women work in occupations that are 63 percent female (almost the same percent as married women) compared to 32.5 percent among never-married men. (But note that married men are much less likely to work in female-dominated occupations than never-married men.)

Table 7.14 Explaining the gender wage gap: female–male hourly wage ratios by marital status (NLSY79)

	Currently married (with or w/o children)		Never married and never had a child
	2000 (ages 35–43)	**2008** (ages 43–51)	**2000** (ages 35–43)
Unadjusted hourly wage ratio (%)	73.6	72.1	107.9^{ns}
Hourly wage ratio controlling for:			
1) Schooling, AFQT	74.1	71.4	98.1^{ns}
2) Variables in 1) and work experience	82.7	82.9	93.7^{ns}
3) Variables in 2) and labor force withdrawal due to family responsibilities and type of employer	85.6	87.3	95.9^{ns}
4) Variables in 3) and occupational characteristics	87.7	88.3	98.7^{ns}
5) Variables in 4) and percent female in occupation	87.9	91.3	97.3^{ns}
Alternative step:			
4A) Variables in 3 and percent female in occupation	91.3	93.6	101.5^{ns}

Note: All female coefficients are significant at the 10% level or lower unless indicated with "ns" (not statistically significant). The log wage ratios are exponentiated log wage differentials, which are the partial regression coefficients of dummy (0, 1) variables for female from a series of OLS regressions containing the explanatory variables noted. The reference group is male. All regressions starting with stage 1 also control for age, MSA, central city, and region.
Source: National Longitudinal Survey of Youth (NLSY79) merged with measures of occupational characteristics (3-digit level) from the September 2001 CPS, the March CPS, the CPS ORG, and the *Dictionary of Occupational Titles* (1991).

Not surprisingly, given the stronger education and work profile of never-married women, the unadjusted gender gap for this group is actually positive; the women earned about 8 percent more than their male counterparts in 2000. When we control for differences in characteristics, the gender gap in favor of women is eliminated. The wage ratio is 99 percent when we add occupational characteristics (stage 4) and rises to more than 100 percent when we measure occupation as the percent female in the worker's occupation (alternative step 4). Neither ratio is significant. (These results are for 2000; the sample for 2008 was too small to yield reliable results.)

These results lend support to the view that the factors underlying the gender gap in pay primarily reflect choices made by men and women given their different roles in the family, rather than labor market discrimination against women due to their gender. Of course, it is still possible that men who have never married have unobservable negative productivity factors that selected them into this group in the first place. The fact that they have never married could reflect personal characteristics that would also lower their productivity in the labor market. However, the same could be true of never-married women. We do not know the proportion of men or of women who are unmarried by choice, dedication to a career, or because of negative personality traits.

The comparison of male and female earnings and the interpretation of the gender gap in pay are further complicated by gender differences in the effects of certain variables on earnings. However, the variables involved are not those that have sometimes aroused suspicion of bias. As shown in separate wage regressions for women and men, the coefficients measuring the pecuniary returns to standard human capital variables, such as schooling and years of work experience, are similar for women and men. However, coefficients differ considerably by sex when the variable is one that is likely to have a different meaning for women and men. For example, the variable measuring the proportion of weeks worked part-time is negatively associated with earnings for both men and women, but the size of the effect is much larger for men. Whether one works for a nonprofit employer is negatively associated with earnings for both men and women, and again the effect is much stronger for men. The variable measuring the percent female in the individual's occupation is negatively related to earnings for both women and men, but the effect for women is weak and never statistically significant, while the effect for men is usually larger in magnitude than it is for women and is statistically significant.

How can these findings be explained? Women are likely to choose part-time work and nonprofit work because they offer more flexibility and, perhaps, in the case of nonprofit work, less stress. However, women who work part-time are more likely to have chosen part-time work as a long-term adjustment to home responsibilities. Moreover, some occupations allow for transition from full-time work to part-time work and back again (e.g., nursing and real estate sales). A smaller proportion of men work part-time than do women, and those who do are more likely to report that their part-time work is due to inability to find a full-time job. Under these circumstances men working part-time are more likely than women to accept a pay cut below their usual work. Such considerations would explain why wage data from the Bureau of Labor Statistics typically show that women working part-time earn considerably more than part-time men.[33]

When it comes to full-time work within the private for-profit sector, women may seek job situations that offer more flexibility in schedules, although we have no easy way to detect that with the available data. In that case the difference in work situations between full-time work in profit or nonprofit employment may be less stark for women than for men.

Because of gender differences in coefficients, such as those noted earlier, the adjusted wage ratio differs depending on whether male or female coefficients are used to evaluate the effect of adjusting for several of the variables. The unadjusted gap, expressed as the ratio of women's to men's hourly wage, was 79 percent in

2000. Using male regression coefficients, the ratio rises almost to 100 percent when all variables are included; using female coefficients, it rises to 92 percent.

Which are the more appropriate coefficients to use? The answer depends on the degree to which our data accurately measure differentials in personal and job characteristics and the effects of those differentials on wages. Without better data, all we can conclude is that labor market discrimination is unlikely to account for a differential of more than 5 percent, but it may not be present at all. The results of the analysis comparing men and women who never married nor had a child also suggest no differential.

Comparison to Other Studies on the Gender Wage Gap

A number of recent studies have analyzed gender differences in earnings focusing on those with higher degrees. These studies rely on unusually detailed survey instruments and take account of gender differences in life-cycle work experience. Their findings are generally consistent with the results of our analysis of the gender gap among college graduates. Bertrand, Goldin, and Katz (2010) focus on male and female MBA graduates from a top US business school. They find that, when they include all graduates, the annual earnings ratio unadjusted for any explanatory variables except for cohort and year is 75 percent.[34] Adjusting for hours worked per week raises the ratio to 84 percent. The ratio jumps to 91 percent after adding the effect of MBA grade point average (GPA) and concentration in finance courses (women have lower grades and are less likely to have taken finance courses). Once work experience and career breaks are accounted for, the wage ratio reaches 96 percent and is no longer statistically or substantively significant.

Black, Haviland, Sanders, and Taylor (2008) analyze gender wage differences comparing white non-Hispanic men with four groups of college-educated women (white non-Hispanic, Hispanic, Asian, and black). The observed unadjusted gaps are on the order of 74 percent, expressed as wage ratios. Their statistical methodology differs from the standard regression analysis in that they match men and women for comparability on certain key characteristics. After matching for age, highest degree, and field of major the ratio rises to 83 percent or to 92 percent depending on the group. When the authors further restrict the match to women with "high labor force attachment," the gender wage gap is essentially eliminated for Hispanic and Asian women and is reduced to 9 percent for white women and 12 percent for black women (implying wage ratios of 91 percent and 88 percent, respectively). Black et al. do not appear to have accounted for detailed data on hours worked on current job or measures of differences in cognitive skills (at the college level women have lower SAT scores and GPAs than men; the sizes of these female–male gaps vary by race).

The results of statistical analysis of the gender gap are clearly dependent on access to information on lifetime work patterns, measures of cognitive skills other than years of schooling completed, details of job characteristics, and personal preferences that are not available in most datasets. Bertrand, Goldin, and Katz (2010) use an unusually complete dataset and find no substantive differences in pay between male and female MBAs once differences in characteristics are taken into account. We generally find little or no difference in pay among more heterogeneous samples of men and women.

Comparable worth is a mechanism for raising women's pay directly by requiring a firm to equalize pay between occupations dominated by women and occupations dominated by men when these occupations are determined by job evaluations to be of "comparable worth." Since there is no uniform way to rank occupations by worth, a comparable-worth policy would ultimately lead to politically administered wages that would depart from a market system of wage determination. Ironically, if implemented, it would likely impede women's progress. Women have been moving into higher-paying occupations such as medicine, law, and even engineering. Apart from the gross inefficiencies it would breed, these pay distortions would discourage women and men from investing in the skills to enter these higher paying fields.

Comparable worth has been rejected in the courts, notably by the Ninth Circuit Federal Court of Appeals in 1985 (*AFSCME v. Washington*).[35] Overturning the decision of the district court in the state of Washington, the court upheld the state's right to base pay on market wages rather than on a comparable worth job evaluation. Judge Anthony Kennedy, later Supreme Court Justice, wrote, "Neither law nor logic deems the free market system a suspect enterprise."[36]

CONCLUSION

Several lessons can be drawn from this survey of group differences in earnings. One is that it can be highly misleading to use earnings differentials alone to determine the extent of labor market discrimination. Groups vary in productivity, sometimes considerably, because of their particular advantages and disadvantages with respect to such factors as educational attainment and immigrant status. In the case of the gender gap, differences in preferences for working conditions are an additional source of pay differentials. Women are more likely to assume responsibility for child rearing than men, and, as a result, they acquire less work experience in the market and are more likely to place a high value on shorter hours and flexible work situations, which usually involve a wage tradeoff. Those factors explain most and in some cases all of the variation in earnings among racial and ethnic minorities and between women and men.

Labor market discrimination is a minimal source of wage differentials. However, this does not mean that discrimination in society has been eliminated. Prejudiced individuals clearly exist, as we are sharply reminded when acts of violence occur against minorities. Some individual employers and managers are prejudiced. However, as Gary Becker (1957/1971) has shown, as long as the pool of nonprejudiced employers is large enough, those employers who would discriminate against women and minorities have little effect on their market opportunities and wages.

NOTES

1. The pervasiveness of gender differences in lifetime career paths is underscored in Bertrand, Goldin and Katz (2010). The authors find that even female graduates of Harvard, 60 percent of whom had attained at least one professional degree or doctorate, took career breaks after the birth of a child, had more total months of non-employment, and were less likely to work full-time and full-year when compared to male Harvard graduates (60 vs. 90 percent).

2. Average hourly earnings were calculated from the CPS ORG microdata. Earnings tabulations are restricted to those who worked full-time (35 hours or more per week).

3. The hourly wage ratios were derived from OLS regressions of an individual's log hourly wage on a set of explanatory variables including a binary "dummy" variable indicating the individual's race/ethnicity, with white non-Hispanic as the omitted reference category. The anti-log of the partial regression coefficients of the variable indicating race/ethnicity yields the wage ratios.

4. Average hourly earnings are derived from CPS ORG microdata. Earnings tabulations are restricted to those who worked full-time (35 hours or more per week).

5. The earnings of all persons in the sample were converted into hourly wages unless they were paid on an hourly basis. For example, a weekly salary is converted into an hourly wage by dividing by the hours worked each week. The regressions are OLS, in which the log hourly wage is regressed on a set of explanatory variables.

6. Attrition occurs because of deaths as well as because participants cannot be located or, when located, choose not to participate. The composition of the sample can also change because some participants who had dropped out rejoin the panel.

7. We use the NLSY79 version reported in 1989, which includes scores on reading comprehension, word knowledge, arithmetic reasoning, and mathematical knowledge. For a discussion of recent validation tests conducted by the National Academy of Sciences in conjunction with the Department of Defense, see Neal and Johnson (1996).

8. Herrnstein and Murray (1994) assign a causal role to genetic factors in explaining differences in the AFQT and refer to the test as an IQ test. Many analysts, however, have found that AFQT scores are significantly affected by environmental factors. See, for example, Korenman and Winship (1995), Fryer and Levitt (2004), and Heckman (2008).

9. The AFQT was administered to the NLSY79 sample just once: in 1980, when the cohort was 15–23 years of age. Test score results are affected by age and years of schooling at the time of the test, although the precise effect is difficult to quantify because we do not have readings on the AFQT for the same individual at different stages in his or her life. We hold constant age and completed education in 2000 in our analyses—an implicit adjustment. Neal and Johnson (1996) adjust scores for age but not for education at the time of the test. O'Neill (1990) holds constant both years of schooling completed at time of test and since the test.

10. The large influx of immigrants between 1979, the year in which the NLSY79 cohort was selected, and 2000, the census year, makes it difficult to compare census and NLSY79 results for Hispanics. As noted, the NLSY79 cohort is fixed as of 1979.

11. Similar findings on the return to AFQT by race were reported by O'Neill (1990) and Neal and Johnson (1996) when the cohort was younger.

12. Neal and Johnson (1996) discuss a large study of the relation between AFQT scores and performance in the military conducted by the National Academy of Sciences in conjunction with the Department of Defense. The study concluded that the AFQT predicted performance in the military as well for African Americans as for whites.

13. The lower return to military service could reflect less relevance of military skills to civilian jobs, since we exclude the active military from our wage sample. However, the subject bears further investigation into the timing of exit from the military and other circumstances of military service. For example, those who recently separated may be experiencing transitional problems.

14. In other analyses we have found that the work experience coefficients converge when we add a variable indicating jail time.

15. The statistics discussed in this paragraph are results from an analysis in which we use the difference in characteristics and evaluate them using the partial regression coefficients derived from separate log wage regressions for white, black, and Hispanic men. We refer here to the results using the minority coefficients because they presumably do not reflect an upward bias due to discrimination. Note that the analyses shown in Tables 7.5 and 7.6 are based on pooled regressions in which the coefficients are implicitly based on the average coefficients of the three groups.

16. The statistics discussed in this paragraph are results from an analysis in which we use the difference in characteristics and evaluate them using the partial regression coefficients derived from separate log wage regressions for African American and Hispanic women. We refer here to results using the minority coefficients because they presumably do not reflect an upward bias. Note that the analyses shown in Tables 7.7 and 7.8 are based on pooled

regressions in which coefficients are based on an average of the coefficients for whites, blacks, and Hispanics.

17. A growing literature has investigated how women's greater attachment to child rearing influences human capital acquisition as well as energy for work. See Mincer and Polachek (1974), Mincer and Ofek (1982), and Becker (1985). For research on the "motherhood wage penalty" see, for example, Anderson, Binder, and Krause (2003) and Waldfogel (1995).

18. These data are influenced by the recession. Data for 2006 show a similar pattern but somewhat higher employment rates for both genders.

19. See US Department of Labor, BLS (2011), *Highlights of Women's Earnings in 2010*, Report 1031, July, table 5.

20. Similar polls conducted by the Pew Center show similar results. A Gallup survey published in Newsweek (1986) also indicates similar preferences.

21. Respondents were assigned either a weekday or a weekend day for their diary day. In this table we show results for those assigned a weekday. We focus on weekday reports because work is much more likely to occur on weekdays than weekends.

22. Consistent with popular impressions, ATUS data show that the type of household work differs by gender. Women specialize more in traditional housework and food preparation, men in lawn and garden care.

23. Becker (1985).

24. Part 1 of book 1, chapter 10 of *The Wealth of Nations* by Adam Smith, 1776, is entitled "Inequalities arising from the Nature of the Employments themselves." In the text, Smith lists five principal circumstances that give rise to wage differentials, the first of which is quoted here: "the agreeableness or disagreeableness of the employments themselves." In one of the oft-cited examples from this part, he notes that "the most detestable of all employments, that of public executioner, is, in proportion to the quantity of work done, better paid than any common trade whatever."

25. For a broad survey of results from studies on gender differences in risk taking, see Byrnes, Miller, and Schafer (1999). For a study of the effect of physical risk on earnings, see DeLeire and Levy (2004), who examine the tradeoff between wages and hazards and find that married women are much more risk-averse than men, thus requiring a larger compensating differential.

26. Mincer and Ofek (1982) demonstrated that women's wages deteriorate during periods of labor force withdrawal and found that the rate of depreciation is greater for more educated women who are more likely to have acquired significant market skills before withdrawal. McDowell (1982) estimated the costs of interrupted careers in several doctoral fields and found that women were less likely to be represented in fields such as physics, where knowledge depreciates rapidly.

27. This statistic and those that follow are from the US Department of Labor, Bureau of Labor Statistics, *Highlights of Women's Earnings in 2010,* Report 1031, July 2011. Note that the occupational data refer to full-time workers.

28. This measure is usually referred to as the *Duncan index of occupational segregation.*

29. As before, the wage gap is estimated as the partial regression coefficient on a "dummy" variable indicating the gender of the worker. The gender coefficient is expressed as a wage ratio by taking the anti-log.

30. The log wage differential is converted to an hourly wage ratio by taking the anti-log of the coefficient.

31. One school of thought maintains that occupational segregation is the main mechanism through which discrimination is imposed. See the well-known work on the crowding hypothesis by Bergmann (1974).

32. Cavallo and O'Neill (2004) conduct an analysis of the determinants of the percent female in an occupation across three-digit occupations and find that variables compatible with women's constraints (such as the incidence of part-time work, a long workweek, and the extent of specific training required) explain most of the variation. Also, see O'Neill (1983) for similar findings for an earlier period.

33. The median usual weekly earnings of women working part-time was 8 percent higher than that of men working part-time in 2008. In fact, when the earnings of women and men who worked the same number of hours per week are compared, wage ratios are higher and therefore the gender gap smaller than for the overall average (unadjusted for hours). Thus, in 2008, among those working 35–39 hours per week, the wages of women were 8 percent higher than men's; at 40 hours, the female to male ratio was 87 percent, and for those working 41 hours or more a week, the ratio was 86 percent. These statistics are not adjusted for other characteristics. Similar results are reported for other years. (US Department of Labor, Bureau of Labor Statistics, *Highlights of Women's Earnings in 2008,* Report 1017, July 2009.)

34. We have expressed the log earnings differential (Bertrand, Goldin, and Katz, 2010, table 6) as a ratio by taking the anti-log.

35. *AFSCME v. Washington,* 770 F.2d 1401 (9th Cir. 1985).

36. For additional information about comparable worth, see O'Neill (1984) and O'Neill (1993).

REFERENCES

Anderson, Deborah J., Binder, Melissa, and Kate Krause. 2003. "The Motherhood Wage Penalty Revisited: Experience, Heterogeneity, Work Effort, and Work-Schedule Flexibility." *ILR Review,* 56(2): 273–294.

Becker, Gary S. 1957/1971. *The Economics of Discrimination*. Chicago: University of Chicago Press.

Becker, Gary S. 1985. "Human Capital, Effort, and the Sexual Division of Labor." *Journal of Labor Economics*, 3: 33–58.

Bergmann, Barbara. (1974). "Occupational Segregation, Wages and Profits When Employers Discriminate by Race or Sex." *Eastern Economic Journal*, 1(2): 103–110.

Bertrand, Marianne, Claudia Goldin, and Lawrence F. Katz. 2010. "Dynamics of the Gender Gap for Young Professionals in the Financial and Corporate Sectors." *American Economic Journal: Applied Economics*, 2: 228–255. doi:10.1257/app.2.3.228.

Black, Dan, Amelia Haviland, Seth Sanders, and Lowell Taylor. 2008. "Gender Wage Disparities Among the Highly Educated." *Journal of Human Resources*, 42(3): 630–659.

Bound, John, and Richard B. Freeman. 1992. "What Went Wrong? The Erosion of Relative Earnings and Employment Among Young Black Men in the 1980s." *Quarterly Journal of Economics*, 107(1): 201–232.

Brown, Charles, and Mary Corcoran. 1997. "Sex Based Differences in School Content and the Male-Female Wage Gap." *Journal of Labor Economics*, 15(3): 431–464.

Byrnes, J. P., Miller, D. C., and Schafer, W. D. 1999. "Gender differences in risk taking: A Meta-Analysis." *Psychological Bulletin*, 125(3): 367–383.

Cavallo, Alex, and June O'Neill. 2004. *Determinants of Gender Differences in Occupational Choice*. Paper presented at the annual meeting of the Society of Labor Economists, San Antonio, May 1.

DeLeire, Thomas and Helen Levy. 2004. "Worker Sorting and the Risk of Death on the Job." *Journal of Labor Economics*, 22(4): 925–954.

Fryer, Roland G., and Steven D. Levitt. 2004. "Understanding the Black-White Test Score Gap in the First Two Years of School." *Review of Economics and Statistics*, 86(2): 447–464.

Goldin, Claudia, and Lawrence F. Katz. 1997. "Swimming Upstream: Trends in the Gender Wage Differential in the 1980s." *Journal of Labor Economics*, 15(1): 1–42.

Heckman, James J. 2008. "School, Skills, and Synapses." *Economic Inquiry*, 46(3): 289–324.

Herrnstein, R. J., and Murray, C. A. (1994). *The Bell Curve: Intelligence and Class Structure in American Life*. Free Press.

Jencks, Christopher, and Meredith Phillips. 1998a. "America's Next Achievement Test: Closing the Black-White Test Score Gap." *American Prospect*, 40(September–October): 44–53.

Jencks, Christopher, and Meredith Phillips. 1998b. "The Black-White Test Score Gap: An Introduction." In *The Black-White Test Score Gap*, edited by C. Jencks and M. Phillips (pp. 1–51). Washington, D.C.: Brookings Institute.

Korenman, Sanders, and Chris Winship. 1995. A Reanalysis of The Bell Curve. National Bureau of Economic Research, Inc, NBER Working Papers.

McDowell, John M. 1982. "Obsolescence of Knowledge and Career Publication Profiles: Some Evidence of Differences Among Fields in Cost Interrupted Careers." *American Economic Review*, 72(September): 752–768.

Mincer, Jacob and Haim Ofek. 1982. "Interrupted Work Careers: Depreciation and Restoration of Human Capital." *Journal of Human Resources*, 17(1): 3–24.

Mincer, Jacob and Solomon Polachek. 1974. "Family Investment in Human Capital: Earnings of Women." *Journal of Political Economy*, 82(2): S76–S108.

Neal, Derek, and William R. Johnson. 1996. "The Role of Premarket Factors in Black-White Wage Differences." *Journal of Political Economy*, 104(5): 869–895.

O'Neill, June. March 1983. *The Determinants and Wage Effects of Occupational Segregation*. Washington, DC: The Urban Institute Working Paper.

O'Neill, June. 1983. "Comparable Worth." *The Concise Encyclopedia of Economics*. Indianapolis: Liberty Fund.

O'Neill, June. 1990. "The Role of Human Capital in Earnings Differences between Black and White Men." *Journal of Economic Perspectives*, 4(4): 25–45.

O'Neill, June and Solomon Polachek, 1993. "Why the Gender Gap in Wages Narrowed in the 1980s." *Journal of Labor Economics*, 11(1): 205–228.

Smith, Adam. 1776/1777. *The Wealth of Nations*, ed. Edwin Cannan. Chicago: University of Chicago Press.

US Employment Service. 1991. *Dictionary of Occupational Titles*. Washington, DC: U.S. Department of Commerce, Bureau of the Census.

US Department of Labor, Bureau of Labor Statistics. 2011. *Highlights of Women's Earnings in 2010*, Report 1031, July, Table 5.

US Department of Labor, Bureau of Labor Statistics. 2009. *Highlights of Women's Earnings in 2008*, Report 1017, July.

Waldfogel, Jane. 1995. "The Price of Motherhood: Family Status and Women's Pay in a Young British Cohort." *Oxford Economic Papers*, 47(4): 584–610.

8

THE DISTRIBUTION OF WEALTH IN AMERICA (1983–2013)

John C. Weicher

Wealth is one of the most important measures of economic well-being but also one of the most difficult to measure. Transactions for some types of wealth, such as stocks and bonds, occur very frequently at prices which are readily available and provide a current valuation. Transactions for other types, such as owner-occupied homes, occur much less frequently and the value of the home is not easily measured in between transactions. In addition, shares of stock in a specific corporation are identical; the sale of any 100 shares establishes the value of all shares. By contrast, homes can differ widely: the sale of one three-bedroom, two-bath home does not establish the market value of all such homes even in an area as small as a city block. Research on wealth has been limited by these and other differences, despite extensive and serious efforts by numerous economists and other analysts.

In 1983, the Federal Reserve Board began to sponsor a survey of household wealth, the Survey of Consumer Finances (SCF). The SCF has been conducted every 3 years since then. The 2013 survey is the most recently completed as of this writing. The SCF contains the most detailed information available about the wealth of American households. It consists of detailed interviews with several thousand households. Some are chosen randomly from the population, while others are selected because they are expected to be households with high wealth. Each household is asked several hundred questions about its assets and its debts, and also about its demographic and other economic attributes. The typical interview lasts about 90 minutes, but some are substantially more than 3 hours.

John C. Weicher, *The Distribution of Wealth in America (1983–2013)* In: *United States Income, Wealth, Consumption, and Inequality.* Edited by: Diana Furchtgott-Roth, Oxford University Press (2021). © Oxford University Press. DOI: 10.1093/oso/9780197518199.003.0009.

Much of the research on wealth has focused on its distribution: the extent to which wealth ownership is concentrated among a small number of households and whether it is becoming more or less concentrated over time. This has been true since the first SCF in 1983, and indeed before then using other data. The distribution of wealth in the United States is more concentrated than the distribution of income, as reported in the Current Population Survey (CPS) conducted yearly by the US Bureau of the Census. Also, the distribution of income has become increasingly more unequal since about 1967. It is natural to expect a similar change for wealth, but that need not necessarily occur.

This study uses the surveys since 1983 to analyze changes in the distribution of wealth. There are some differences between the 1983 survey and the surveys from 1989 to 2013, so part of the analysis is based on the shorter period.

WEALTH AND INCOME

The term "wealthy" is often used indiscriminately to refer to people with high incomes as well as people with high wealth. For that reason, it is essential to make clear the distinction between *wealth* and *income*. Wealth is a stock and income is a flow. For any particular household *at any particular time*, wealth is the value of the total assets it owns, minus the total amount of its debts. Wealth is synonymous with net worth. Income is the money that a household receives *over a given period of time*, reported most commonly for a calendar year.

Some assets yield income: stocks have a value and pay dividends. But some important assets do not have an income counterpart. Owner-occupied homes are the most valuable asset for many households and for all US households combined, but they do not produce income. Conversely, wages and salaries—income from working—is the most important category of income, but it does not have a wealth counterpart. It is therefore quite possible for high-wealth households to have low incomes, such as elderly homeowners who are "house poor," and similarly for doctors or lawyers or other professionals to start their careers at a good salary but have little in the way of assets—just a checking account and a car (and perhaps a loan on the car). It is also possible for the income and the wealth of a household to change in opposite directions, at least for some time.

AMERICAN WEALTH OVER THREE DECADES

Growth and Recession, 1989–2013

Wealth in the United States increased rapidly, as the SCF reports—until the Great Recession. This is clearly shown in Table 8.1. Total wealth in nominal terms

Table 8.1 Total and average wealth of American families, 1983–2013

Year	Total wealth (nominal[a])	Total wealth (real[b])	Annual inflation rate since previous survey	Mean family Wealth (real[b])	Median family Wealth (real[c])
1983	$10.2	$23.8	Not Applicable	$280,000	$80,200
1989	$17.6	$33.1	3.7%	$356,000	$85,100
1992	$17.9	$29.9	4.2%	$312,000	$80,800
1995	$21.1	$32.4	2.8%	$327,000	$87,700
1998	$29.0	$41.6	2.3%	$406,000	$102,500
2001	$42.3	$55.9	2.8%	$524,000	$113,900
2004	$50.2	$62.1	2.2%	$554,000	$114,800
2007	$64.5	$72.6	3.1%	$625,000	$135,900
2010	$58.5	$62.4	1.7%	$530,000	$82,500
2013	$64.7	$64.7	2.2%	$528,000	$81,400

[a]Measured in trillions of nominal dollars.
[b]Measured in trillions of 2013 dollars.
[c]Measured in 2013 dollars.
Note: Calculated by the author from published SCF data files.

increased sixfold between 1983 and 2007; total wealth in real terms tripled. The annual average rate of increase was about 8 percent for nominal wealth and close to 5 percent for wealth in real terms. The data for 1983 are not precisely comparable to the later years, but there is no question that both nominal and real total wealth, measured consistently, increased during the economic boom of the 1980s, as well as between 1989 and 2007.[1] Average real wealth per family more than doubled from 1983 to 2007, while median real wealth per family increased by 70 percent.

The story is quite different since 2007. During the Great Recession and immediately afterward, total wealth dropped by almost 15 percent, adjusted for inflation; average wealth per family by 15 percent; and median wealth per family by 40 percent—almost back to its level in 1983. Moreover, neither total, mean, nor median wealth recovered any of these sharp declines between 2010 and 2013; in terms of wealth, we remained at the depressed levels of the Great Recession.

This experience is unlike the aftermath of other recent recessions. Before the Great Recession, there were more typical postwar recessions during 1990–1991 and during 2001 (March to November), each lasting only 8 months. In real terms, both total wealth and mean family wealth declined somewhat less between 1989 and 1992 than between 2007 and 2010 (total wealth by 10 percent and mean wealth by 12 percent); median family wealth declined by only 6 percent. But from 1992 to 1995, total net worth rose to almost its 1989 level, mean family net worth regained about one-third of the loss, and median wealth rose above its 1989 value, while between 2010 and 2013, total net worth regained only about

20 percent of its previous decline and both mean and median family net worth continued to decline, albeit slightly.

The recovery after 2001 was similar to the recovery after 1992, but it is difficult to measure the changes over the economic cycle because the data collection period for the 2001 SCF almost perfectly coincides with the dates of the recession: May to December for the SCF interviews, March to November for the recession. Thus, some households were interviewed at or just after the cyclical peak, while others were interviewed at or just after the cyclical trough.

Measuring Household Wealth, 1983–1995

The SCF data for 1983 are not precisely comparable to the later years. The same is true for the weights originally constructed for each of the first three surveys. Consistent weighting techniques were developed in 1997 for the surveys of 1989, 1992, and 1995. These weights have been used for the subsequent surveys. The weighting techniques could not be used for 1983 because the information needed for that purpose was no longer available by 1997.[2] Thus, it is possible to describe the changes in the distribution of wealth on a consistent basis during 1989–2013, but not during 1983–2013. It is possible, however, to use the original weights for 1983, 1989, and 1992, in combination with the consistent weights for 1989, 1992, and 1995, to look at 1983–1992 separately and then use the two overlapping periods to describe, at least in general terms, what happened over the full period 1983–2013.

There is a further complication. Before the consistent weights were developed in 1997, there had been a period of active research into weighting issues, during which more than one set of weights had been constructed for each of the first three surveys. The results for 1983 to 1992 in particular depend on which sets of weights are chosen for the analysis. For the 1983 survey, weights were constructed separately by analysts at the Survey Research Center, which conducted the SCF, and by analysts at the Federal Reserve Board (FRB). The SRC weights were aligned on the basis of total households and the division between urban and rural location. The first set of FRB weights were aligned on the basis of the household totals for the four US Census regions. Subsequently, the FRB analysts constructed a second set of weights when the individual income tax data for 1982 suggested that the high-income household sample might have been weighted too heavily.

There are differences of about 7 percent in both total wealth and mean family wealth for 1983, using either set of weights. As shown in Table 8.1, which is calculated with the FRB weights, total wealth was about $23.8 trillion in 2013 dollars; calculating with the SRC weights, which is not shown, total wealth was about $25.5 trillion. Similarly, mean family net worth was about $280,000 in 2013 dollars with the FRB weights and $300,000 with the SRC weights.[3] Subsequent research by the Federal Reserve analysts typically used the FRB weights for comparison with later surveys.[4]

This difference does not materially affect most of the measures of net worth reported in Table 8.1. Nominal total wealth rose about sixfold between 1983 and 2013, and real total family wealth by about 150 percent, using either set of 1983 weights. Mean real family wealth nearly doubled over the three decades using either set of weights.[5]

For the 1989 survey, two sets of weights were created and published as part of the database for the survey: preliminary weights used by the Federal Reserve analysts for comparing 1983 to 1989 and revised weights for comparing 1989 to 1992. The difference between them was not large. The preliminary weights produced net worth estimates about 2.25 percent above the revised weights.[6] The original *Federal Reserve Bulletin* article that reported the 1989 wealth calculations and compared them to 1983 employed the preliminary weights. Total net worth was calculated as $30.5 trillion, and mean family net worth as $327,000, both in 2013 dollars.[7] This article was published in 1992.

Between 1992 and 1997, Federal Reserve analysts conducted a number of further studies in weighting, typically calculating mean family net worth in the range of $330,000 to $342,000 for 1989. This research culminated in a 1997 working paper and *Federal Reserve Bulletin* article, both of which created consistent weights for the 1989, 1992, and 1995 surveys to describe changes in net worth over that period. Most recently, the FRB has prepared tables reporting net worth for each of the surveys since 1989.

The results from these weights are shown in Table 8.2. There are some differences between the calculations for 1989, with a range of about 6 percent between the highest and lowest estimates for both total and mean family net worth, but the overall pattern is clear: there was a sharp decline between 1989 and 1992, and a partial recovery between 1992 and 1995.

Also, when 1983 is included, it is clear that there was a substantial increase in wealth during the 1983–1989 boom, but much of that gain was lost during and immediately after the 1990–1991 recession. Using the values for 1983 in Table 8.1, about 20–35 percent of the 1983–1989 increase in total wealth and about 50–67 percent of the corresponding increase in mean family wealth was lost during the next 3 years. Despite the recession, however, net worth increased dramatically between 1989 and 2007. Total real wealth more than doubled, and mean real family wealth rose by 75–90 percent.[8]

THE CHANGING COMPOSITION OF HOUSEHOLD WEALTH

The SCF disaggregates assets into financial and nonfinancial categories. Throughout the three decades, nonfinancial assets comprised the larger share of net worth, but financial assets were an increasing share. In 1983, nonfinancial

Table 8.2 Household net worth during 1989–1995

Panel A. Total net worth
(in trillions of 2013 dollars)

Source	1989	1992	1995
Kennickell, Starr-McCluer, and Sunden (1997)	$30.8	$29.4	$34.7
Kennickell and Woodburn (1997)	$32.7	$29.5	$31.4
SCF Tables (2013)	$32.9	$29.2	$32.0

Panel B. Mean family net worth
(in 2013 dollars)

Source	1989	1992	1995
Kennickell, Starr-McCluer, and Sunden (1997)	$331,200	$306,500	$314,700
Kennickell and Woodburn (1997)	$351,200	$307,700	$316,800
SCF Tables (2013)	$353,300	$303,900	$323,500

Panel C. Median family net worth
(in 2013 dollars)

Source	1989	1992	1995
Kennickell, Starr-McCluer, and Sunden (1997)	$ 86,400	$ 80,700	$ 86,200
Kennickell and Woodburn (1997)	$ 87,100	$ 80,700	$ 84,200
SCF Tables (2013)	$ 87,800	$ 80,700	$ 87,700

Source: Arthur B. Kennickell, Martha Starr-McCluer and Annika E. Sunden, "Family Finances in the US: Recent Evidence from the Survey of Consumer Finances, " *Federal Reserve Bulletin*, 83 (January 1997), pp. 1–24, available at http://www.federalreserve.gov/econresdata/scf/files/1995_bull0197.pdf;
Arthur B. Kennickell and R. Louise Woodburn, "Consistent Weight Design for the 1989, 1992 and 1995 SCFs, and the Distribution of Wealth," Revised August 1997, available at http://www.federalreserve.gov/econresdata/scf/files/wgt95.pdf;
Federal Reserve Board, "Historic Tables and Charts: Tables based on external and internal data, Excel based on public data, Estimates adjusted to 2013 dollars," available at http://www.federalreserve.gov/econresdata/scf/scfindex.htm.

assets amounted to 72 percent of net worth; by 2013, they amounted to 54 percent. Throughout the period, the most widely held assets were transaction accounts, vehicles, owner-occupied homes, and retirement accounts, in that order. More than 85 percent of households had transaction accounts (90 percent from 1998 through 2013); about 85 percent owned vehicles (rising from 84 percent in 1989 to 87 percent by 2007 and declining to 86 percent by 2013), about 65 percent owned homes (rising from 64 percent to 69 percent in 2004, then dropping to 65 percent by 2013), more than 35 percent had at least one retirement account in 1989 (rising to about 50 percent by 1998 and remaining at about that level through 2013). The most common liabilities were credit card balances, home mortgages, and car loans; the first two were held by between 38 and 48 percent of all households, the last by 30 to 35 percent. Through 2010, home equity constituted the largest share of total household wealth, privately owned businesses the second largest (proprietorships, partnerships, and closely held corporations whose stock was not widely traded), and retirement accounts a steadily growing third. In 2013, the value of unincorporated businesses slightly exceeded home equity. Home mortgage debt was by far the largest liability, between two-thirds and three-quarters of all household debt.

The growth in retirement accounts was paralleled by increasing ownership of stocks, both directly and indirectly held. In 1989, there were two major household assets, owner-occupied homes and closely held businesses, which together accounted for about half of total household wealth, even subtracting mortgage debt. By 2001, the total value of stockholdings was larger than either and amounted to almost a quarter of household net worth; together these three asset categories constituted more than 60 percent of household wealth, and they continued to do so through 2013.

MEASURES OF DISTRIBUTION

The distribution of economic well-being is commonly measured in two different ways: measures describing the entire distribution and measures describing the concentration at one end of the distribution, typically the high end. Each type of measure has strengths and limitations.

The Gini Coefficient

The most common quantitative measure of the entire distribution is the Gini coefficient. It is regularly reported as a measure of the distribution of income in the United States; the Census Bureau publishes a Gini coefficient for the distributions of household income and family income each year as part of an annual report on income and poverty and has been doing so since 1967.[9]

In calculating a Gini coefficient, households or individuals are ranked from the lowest income or wealth to the highest. The cumulative share of total income or wealth is measured against the cumulative share of the population. Figure 8.1 illustrates this ranking. The cumulative share of population is measured along the horizontal axis; the corresponding cumulative share of total income or wealth is measured along the vertical axis. The line showing these cumulative shares is the *Lorenz curve*, named for the person who first depicted it and showed its significance.[10] The Gini coefficient is measured as the ratio of the area between the diagonal line (indicating a perfectly equal distribution) and the Lorenz curve (showing the actual distribution) to the total area under the diagonal line.

The Gini coefficient has a range of 0 to 1. If the distribution of wealth is perfectly equal, the coefficient is zero; if all the wealth in the society is owned by one single household, the coefficient is unity. The greater the concentration of wealth, the closer the Gini coefficient is to unity.

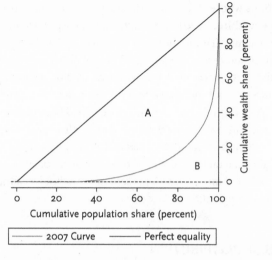

$$\text{Gini Coefficient} = \frac{\text{Area between Lorenz Curve and the Line of Perfect Equality}}{\text{Total Area under the Line of Perfect Equality}} = \frac{A}{(A+B)}$$

Figure 8.1 Lorenz curve for 2007.

The Lorenz curve in Figure 8.1 starts at the horizontal axis, which is conventional with income distributions because a household's minimum income is measured as zero. For wealth, it could be negative, in which case the Lorenz curve would start below the horizontal axis. Households with negative net worth may have outstanding student loans or credit card debt, or the balance on their mortgage or car loan may exceed the value of their home or car. In 2007, about 9 million households (7.75 percent of all households) had negative net worth; in total, their debts exceeded the value of their assets by $184 billion, about $20,000 per household. The lowest net worth for any household was about -$550,000 in 2007.

The advantage of the Gini coefficient is that it takes into account changes that occur in any part of the distribution. Its main drawback is that it has no intuitive interpretation, except at the extreme points. A Gini coefficient of 0.5, for example, does not necessarily mean that the society is "halfway between" a perfectly equal and perfectly unequal distribution of wealth, and indeed it is not clear what such a statement means. A coefficient of 0.5, or any other value between the theoretical limits, is consistent with a number of different distributions. Nor is it possible to explain the meaning of a Gini coefficient in terms of any other measure. All that can be said is that higher coefficients indicate greater inequality.[11]

Concentration Ratios

Measures of concentration have become more common in recent years for several reasons. The ownership of wealth is highly skewed compared to income or other measures of economic well-being, so the shares held by the richest 1 percent or 10 percent of all households attract attention. Such concentration ratios are easy to calculate and intuitively easy to understand.

The main limitation of concentration ratios is that they only describe part of the distribution of wealth. Changes in net worth for "the wealthy" may not correspond to changes in the opposite direction for any other particular subset of the population (e.g., "the poor"), and, conversely, changes may occur among lower wealth groups without any corresponding changes among the rich. Nor is there anything inherently significant in any particular concentration ratio: the highest 1 percent, 5 percent, 10 percent, or any other share.

The SCF provides information about all households, not only about the wealthy. It can therefore be used to measure both the overall distribution of wealth and the share held by "rich" or "poor" (however defined) American households.

CHANGES IN THE DISTRIBUTION OF WEALTH, 1989–2013

Table 8.3 reports the changes in the overall distribution of wealth and in the share held by the richest households between 1989 and 2013. The Gini coefficient declined slightly from 1989 to 1992, then increased in each 3-year period through 2013. The table also shows the standard errors for the coefficients. The largest and most statistically significant increase occurred between 2007 and 2010, covering the onset of the Great Recession through the first stages of the subsequent recovery. There were also statistically significant—but much smaller—increases in 1995–1998, 1998–2001, and 2010–2013. Otherwise, the change in inequality was smaller and not significant from one survey to the next. Over longer periods, however, the changes were significant.[12]

The table also shows the concentration of wealth among the richest households by several criteria: the richest 1 percent, the richest 5 percent, and the richest 10 percent, and also for the households between these cutoffs: between 1 and 5 percent, and between 5 and 10 percent. These all show little or no increase from 1989 to 1992. After 1992, the shares for the richest 1 percent, 5 percent, and 10 percent generally increased, with the largest increase for the richest 1 percent occurring between 1992 and 1995.

Through 2007, the share of the richest 1 percent tended to increase more than the shares of those between 1 percent and 10 percent and, for that matter, more than the share of the rest of the population. But around the end of the Great Recession, between July and December 2009, the Federal Reserve conducted a follow-up survey of those households that had been interviewed in 2007. In a report on the changes between 2007 and 2009, Kennickell noted that "the share of the wealthiest one percent of households has shown no significant change since 1995," in comparison to 2007, and added that, between 2007 and 2009, the share of total wealth owned by the richest 1 percent of households had declined by 4 percentage points, from 33 percent of total wealth to 29 percent.[13]

Table 8.3 The distribution of wealth, 1989–2013

	1989	1992	1995	1998	2001	2004	2007	2010	2013
Panel A: Gini coefficients									
Gini coefficient	0.787	0.781	0.785	0.794	0.803	0.805	0.812	0.833	0.838
(Standard error)	*.0033*	*.0025*	*.0026*	*.0026*	*.0023*	*.0023*	*.0023*	*.0021*	*.0017*
Panel B: Concentration ratios									
Richest 1%	29.9%	30.0%	34.7%	33.6%	32.1%	33.2%	33.5%	33.9%	35.3%
Richest 5%	54.1%	54.3%	55.9%	57.0%	57.4%	57.2%	60.2%	60.5%	62.5%
Richest 10%	66.8%	66.8%	67.7%	68.3%	69.5%	69.3%	71.2%	73.9%	74.5%
Between 1% & 5%	24.2%	24.3%	21.2%	23.4%	25.3%	24.0%	26.7%	26.6%	27.2%
Between 5% & 10%	12.7%	12.5%	11.8%	11.3%	12.1%	12.1%	11.1%	13.4%	12.0%
Panel C: Net worth (Measured in trillions of 2013 dollars)									
Richest 1%	$ 9.9	$ 9.0	$11.1	$14.0	$17.8	$20.6	$25.0	$21.8	$23.5
Between 1% and 5%	$ 8.0	$ 7.3	$ 6.8	$ 9.7	$14.1	$13.3	$19.9	$17.1	$18.1
Between 5% and 10%	$ 4.2	$ 3.7	$ 3.8	$ 4.7	$ 6.7	$ 6.7	$ 8.3	$ 8.6	$ 8.0

Note: Calculated by the author from SCF data files.

The rich got richer between 1992 and 2007, but the poor did not get poorer. In 1992, the total real wealth for the lower half of US families was about $860 billion; in 2007, their total real wealth was about $1.6 trillion.[14] Real mean wealth per family increased from about $18,000 to about $28,000. Their *share* did not increase, rather the reverse—they held 3.3 percent of total net worth in 1992, compared to 2.5 percent in 2007—but their *actual wealth* did.

Between 2007 and 2013, this pattern changed. The poor became poorer, but so did the rich and the people in between. The rich were less affected, however. The top 10 percent lost a smaller share of their 2007 wealth than the remainder of the population—about 7 percent of their net worth, $3.6 trillion out of $52.2 trillion. The remaining 90 percent of households lost about 22 percent of their net worth—$4.3 trillion out of $19.4 trillion. Indeed, as these figures show, the top 10 percent lost a smaller *amount*, not just a smaller *share*, than the remaining 90 percent.[15] As Panel B shows, the shares of wealth owned by the richest 1 percent, 5 percent, and 10 percent all rose during both the Great Recession and the subsequent weak recovery.

CHANGES IN THE DISTRIBUTION OF WEALTH, 1983–1992

It is not possible to construct measures of the distribution of wealth for 1983 that are fully consistent with measures for 1989 and later surveys for the same reasons that it is not possible to construct consistent measures of net worth over that period. The weights developed in the mid-1990s could be utilized for the surveys from 1989 onward, but the relevant information was not available for 1983.[16] There is still, of course, the further complication that more than one set of weights was constructed for the 1983 and 1989 surveys, when those survey results were first reported and the data files were made public.[17] Comparisons can be made for 1983 to 1992 with the original weights, which in conjunction with comparisons using the consistent weights for 1989 and the later years can provide a description of the changes in the distribution over the full 30-year period, paralleling the discussion of total net worth.

Table 8.4 summarizes the 1983–1992 results using the different weights. As the table shows, the results are quite sensitive to the choice of weights, even to the point of the direction of the change during both 1983–1989 and the full 1983–1992 period. Three of the four comparisons for 1983–1989 indicate that the distribution of wealth became more unequal and more concentrated during that period, both comparisons for 1989–1992 show that the distribution became more equal and less concentrated during that period, and the two comparisons over the full period 1983–1992 show opposite results. Only one of the Gini coefficient comparisons is statistically significant: the increase from .778 in 1983 to .805 in 1989.

It should be noted that the 1989 weights in this comparison are those intended to be comparable to 1992 rather than to 1983. The other two comparisons using the 1983 FRB weights come close to statistical significance. Similar significance tests for the share of the richest 1 percent show that two of the four 1983–1989 increases and one of the two 1989–1992 decreases were statistically significant. For the full period, one comparison shows an insignificant increase in concentration and the other shows a decrease that is almost significant.[18]

The reason for these conflicting results is that the measured changes in inequality and concentration are small. By contrast, there were substantial increases in total wealth and average household wealth between 1983 and 1992, no matter which weights are used.

It may also be worth noting that the revised weights for 1989 and 1992—the weights consistent with those for 1995 and later surveys (shown in Table 8.3)—result in much lower Gini coefficients than any of the original weights (shown in Table 8.4). This invites speculation that a revised 1983 weight would also produce a lower Gini coefficient.

Table 8.4 The distribution of wealth, 1983–1992

	1983	**1989**	**1992**
Gini coefficient	.778 or .795	.793 or .805	.787
(standard error)	(.008)	(.008)	(.006)
Share of top 1%	31.5% or 35.8%	35.3% or 36.5%	32.6%

Source: Weicher (1997), tables 6 and 7.

WEALTH INEQUALITY AND INCOME INEQUALITY

As described earlier, the SCF collects information on household income as well as household wealth. The distribution of income as reported in the SCF has followed a somewhat similar path to the distribution of wealth, but the path for income has been more erratic. The Gini coefficient for income declined sharply for three periods: between 1988 and 1991, between 2000 and 2003, and between 2006 and 2009 (see Table 8.5; the income data collected in the SCF is for the calendar year before the survey year). There are also three sharp increases: between 1997 and 2000, between 2003 and 2006, and between 2009 and 2012. Nearly all of the changes in income between survey years are statistically significant, which is not the case for the changes in wealth.[19] Overall, the Gini coefficient for income is quite a bit higher in 2012 than it was in 1988.

Unlike wealth, there is separate information on household income, on an annual basis, from the CPS conducted by the Census Bureau; Gini coefficients and other measures of income distribution have been published for each year since 1947. The Gini coefficient declined steadily from 1947 to 1967; since then, it has increased steadily.[20] Between 1988 and 2012, the Gini coefficient for income calculated from the CPS rose substantially more than the coefficient calculated from the SCF: by .051 compared to .033. Technical differences explain part of this difference. The CPS population controls are updated after each decennial Census, and in those years the change in the Gini coefficient reflects changes in the characteristics of the population as well as changes in the assets and debts of households. The difference between 1992 and 1993, for instance, is .021—an increase from .433 to .454. There are also recurring changes in the CPS sample design and occasional increases or reductions in the sample size. The Gini

Table 8.5 Gini coefficients for household wealth and household income, 1988–2012

Year	Wealth	Income (SCF)	Income (CPS)
1988	.787	.540	.426
1991	.781	.501	.428
1994	.785	.515	.456
1997	.794	.530	.459
2000	.803	.562	.462
2003	.805	.540	.464
2006	.812	.572	.470
2009	.833	.547	.468
2012	.838	.573	.477

Note: Wealth and Income (SCF): calculated by the author from SCF data files; Income CPS: Proctor, Semega, and Kollar (2016), table a-2.

coefficients calculated from the SCF are consistently higher than those from the CPS. One factor contributing to these differences is the definition of "income." The SCF definition of income includes realized capital gains, while the CPS does not. Capital gains are, by definition, increases in the value of particular assets, and they are also correlated with income.[21]

Most notably, the Gini coefficient for net worth is consistently much higher than the coefficient for income.[22] Between 1989 and 2013, the coefficient for household net worth was never below .781, and the coefficient for household income in the SCF was never above .573. Over these years, the Gini coefficient for household income published annually by the Census Bureau from the CPS was never above .477.[23]

The most important reason for this difference is the relationship between age and income or wealth. Figure 8.2 shows the pattern over the life of the household head for each SCF. The data for households are calculated for 3-year age cohorts, corresponding to the time between successive SCF surveys. A young household does not typically start with much income or wealth. As the household head ages, both income and wealth tend to increase. Wealth increases much faster than income, however, and over a longer period of time, as the figure shows. Median incomes are generally highest for households whose head is in his or her late 40s to late 50s; median wealth is generally highest for households whose head is about 10 years older. Furthermore, median incomes tend to peak at $75,000–85,000; median wealth at $225,000–300,000. For much of a typical household's life, wealth is several times as much as income. This continues into retirement, up to the point where households start to draw on their wealth for living expenses. Past the age of 80, median wealth tends to fluctuate, sometimes sharply, perhaps at least partly because the SCF samples are smaller for these households. For that reason, the charts are truncated at the age 78–80 cohort.

With these age-related differences, it is no wonder that wealth is much more unequally distributed than income. The data in Figure 8.2 are median values. There is, of course, a great deal of variability around these values for each age cohort. But even if every household in each age cohort had the median value for wealth and income for that cohort, there would be a substantial difference in the Gini coefficients. The coefficient for wealth would be about .350, the coefficient for income about .190. Certainly there is still quite a bit of variability within each cohort, but no other factor is as important for understanding the distribution of wealth.

HOW COME?

Several asset and liability categories stand out as contributors to the difference between the experience during the 1980s and the experience during the Great Recession. The category with the most notable difference, and also with

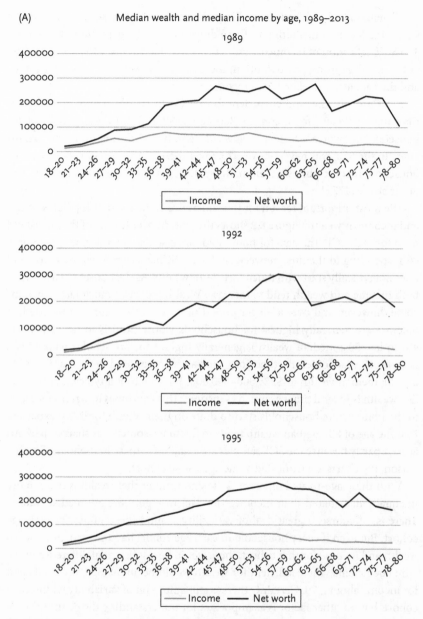

Figure 8.2 Median wealth and median income by age, 1989–2013.

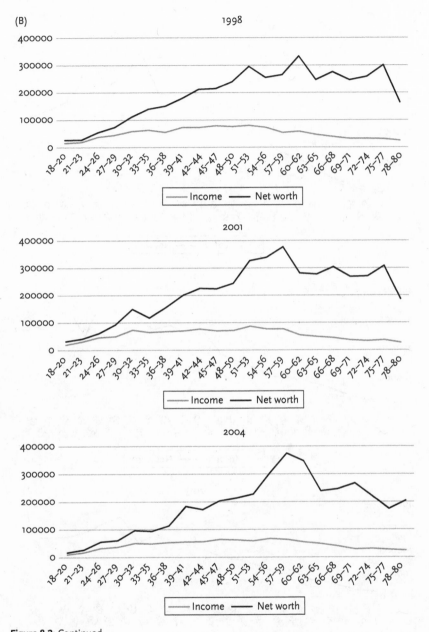

Figure 8.2 Continued

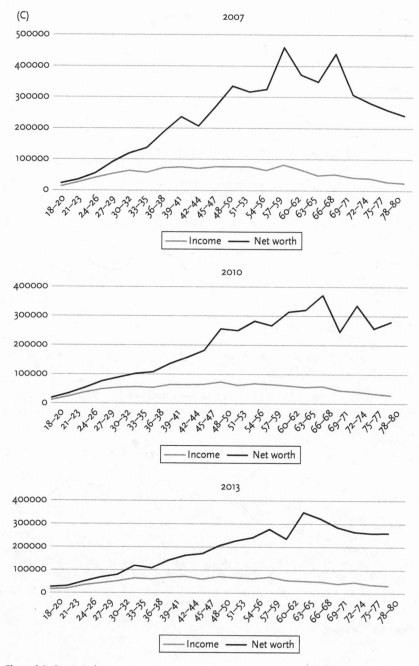

Figure 8.2 Continued

the greatest change during the recession and its aftermath, was owner-occupied housing. During the unprecedented peacetime inflation between 1965 and 1982, the real value of financial assets dropped dramatically and the demand for real assets rose sharply as households sought protection against inflation. The most widely held real asset was owner-occupied homes. The home ownership rate rose from 62.9 percent in 1965 to a then-record 65.6 percent in 1982, a very large increase by historical standards. Then, as the inflation rate dropped during the 1980s, home ownership decreased and real home prices fell. During and after the 1990–1991 recession, home ownership was stable and real house prices declined slightly. In contrast, home ownership and house prices rose strongly during the 2001–2007 expansion; whereas, since 2007, both have fallen.

Home equity is by far the most important asset for middle-wealth households, and they were hit hard after 2007. Their home ownership rate dropped by more than 10 percentage points in 6 years. For those who kept their homes, their equity fell by nearly 50 percent, and their total wealth by about 40 percent. The home ownership rate was stable for the richest 30 percent, and, while their equity dropped, the decline was less than for those in the middle. The decline in home ownership and home equity was the biggest factor in the increase in inequality.

At the same time, the market for second homes—vacation homes—was strong, particularly after 2010. There were 1 million more vacation homeowners in 2013 than 3 years earlier, and they owned 1.4 million more homes. Their vacation home equity increased by more than 50 percent. Vacation homeowners were wealthier than most households to begin with and became somewhat more so.

Student debt increased through recessions and recoveries, also contributing to a more unequal distribution of wealth. In 1989, there were 8 million households (9 percent of all households) where someone had a student loan, and their total education debt was about $82 billion. By 2007, there were 18 million households (15 percent) with a total debt of $426 billion; by 2013, there were 24 million (20 percent) with a total debt of $710 billion. In 2010, total outstanding student debt exceeded the total value of car loans and also exceeded total credit card debt. Most student debt is owed by households in the lower half of the wealth distribution, and most are relatively young; the median age for the head of household with student debt has consistently been about 35. Most have a low net worth, partly because they are young and partly because they have student debt. The Great Recession had a substantial impact on these debtors; the median wealth of households with student debt dropped from $43,000 in 2007 to $15,000 in 2013. About 20 percent had a negative net worth in 2007 because their student debt exceeded the aggregate total of all their assets and all their other debts. By 2013, the proportion was about 30 percent.

The steadily growing proportion of households with retirement accounts might be expected to promote a more equal distribution of wealth. About half of all households had retirement accounts by 1998, and that has been true ever since. The same is true for stocks; since 1998, about half of all households have owned stocks, either directly or indirectly—through mutual funds, trusts, and annuities, but most importantly through retirement accounts. As of 2013, 87 percent of households that owned stocks did so through their retirement accounts; only 28 percent owned stocks directly, and the percentages were smaller for other forms of ownership.

Although half of all households have retirement accounts, the accounts owned by the richest households have consistently had a large share of the assets, and their share increased during and after the Great Recession. Between 1992 and 2007, the retirement accounts of the richest 10 percent of households consistently held about 60 percent of the total value in all accounts. As of 2007, their share was 59 percent. By 2010, their share had risen to 65 percent, and it remained at that proportion in 2013. This was less than their share of total net worth. Retirement assets have not been as concentrated among the richest households as has total wealth, and thus it is correct to say that retirement accounts have contributed to a more equal distribution of wealth; but, since the Great Recession retirement assets have become more concentrated among the rich.

THE FAMILIES IN THE MIDDLE

The changes within these various asset and liability categories affected the families in the middle of the wealth distribution—typical American families. There has been relatively little research scrutiny given to the families in the middle. They deserve more attention. As shown in Table 8.1, real median household wealth was about $80,000 in 1983, rising to about $136,000 by 2007, and then dropping to $81,000 in 2013. There was hardly any difference between 1983 and 2013, but there was a horrendous loss of 40 percent during the Great Recession and the weak recovery.

This was essentially the experience of families around the median—the middle 10 percent, those whose net worth was between the 45th and the 55th percentile of the wealth distribution. In 2007, the wealth of these families ranged from about $105,000 to $175,000. In 2013, the range was between $59,000 and $111,000. Thirty years earlier, the range had been very similar, about $62,000 to $98,000.

The families in the middle were certainly not the same families in 2013 as they were in 1983, but they were largely the same sorts of families. They were mostly middle-aged, mostly married couples, and, if married, mostly with children living at home. The real median income of these families was about $48,000 in the earliest survey; it peaked at about $54,000 in the 2007 survey and declined to about $46,000 in 2013—much the same pattern as their wealth. In both years, their income was higher than the median for all households reported by the Census Bureau. One possible contributor to the drop in income between 2007 and 2013 may be that unemployment was higher among the families in the middle. There was no working adult in about 5 percent of the families where the head of the household was under 65 in 2007; in 2013, about 10 percent did not have a working adult.

It was not particularly noticeable to the public that typical families in 2013 were essentially no wealthier than typical families had been in 1983. Even if the families in the middle in 2013 were the children of families in the middle in 1983, it would not have been obvious to them. Actual prices more than doubled over those three decades: $35,000 in 1983 dollars had the same purchasing power as $82,000 in 2013. Also, most middle-wealth homeowners probably would have had to estimate the value of the home their parents lived in back in 1983 and perhaps also the home they owned in 2013.

But the 40 percent decline in wealth between 2007 and 2013 was certainly noticeable, and noticed. About 89 percent of the families in the middle owned a home in 2007, and their equity in their home averaged about $88,000. This was almost 60 percent of their wealth. By 2013, only about 82 percent owned a home, and their equity had been cut almost in half, to $50,000. The decline in home ownership and the drop in the value of their homes for those who continued to be owners together accounted for about 85 percent of the decline in their net worth. Something similar happened to their retirement accounts. In 2007, about 55 percent had accounts, with an average value of $40,000. In 2013, only 47 percent did, and the assets in their accounts were about $32,000, accounting for about 13 percent of the decline in their wealth.

These families were typical of a much broader group, amounting to half of all families: those between the 30th percentile and the 80th percentile of the wealth distribution. For most of these families, their most important assets were their homes and their retirement accounts, which together represented more than half of their net worth. On average, they lost 37 percent of their wealth.

In every wealth bracket, Americans were hurt by the Great Recession, but not all Americans were hurt to the same extent. The richest 10 percent saw their average wealth drop from $4.5 million to $4 million, a loss of about 11 percent. As a result of this relatively small reduction, their share of total household wealth increased from 71 percent in 2007 to 75 percent in 2013—their largest share reported in any SCF over the full three decades. The share of the 10 percent in the middle dropped from 2.1 percent to 1.6 percent. Between 2007 and 2013, the distribution of wealth became noticeably more unequal for the first time since the first SCF in 1983.

The depth of the recession, the weakness of the recovery, and the more unequal distribution of wealth may all have contributed to the dissatisfaction of Americans with the current state of America. Since the beginning of 2009, a majority have consistently said they believe America is "on the wrong track," as opposed to "going in the right direction." Typically about 60 percent have the negative view, compared to about 30 percent with the positive. Despite the COVID-19 pandemic, current opinions are somewhat less negative than they were during the time periods when the 2010 and 2013 Surveys of Consumer Finances were being conducted.[24]

ACKNOWLEDGMENT

The author thanks Jacqueline Seufurt and Azat Abdyrakhmanov for their assistance on this chapter.

NOTES

1. Unless specifically stated otherwise, all wealth measures are reported in constant dollars, using 2013 as the base. Wealth is more meaningfully calculated per family, rather than per individual, and therefore per-family values are reported unless stated otherwise.
2. Arthur B. Kennickell and R. Louise Woodburn, "Consistent Weight Design for the 1989, 1992 and 1995 SCFs and the Distribution of Wealth," Federal Reserve Board Working Paper, Revision II, August 1997: 2, https://www.federalreserve.gov/econresdata/scf/files/wgt95.pdf.
3. For more detailed discussion of these weighting issues, see John C. Weicher, "Wealth and Its Distribution, 1983–1992: Secular Growth, Cyclical Stability," Review, 79 (1) (January/February 1997): 4–5.
4. For example, Arthur B. Kennickell and Janice Shack-Marquez, "Changes in Family Finances from 1983 to 1989: Evidence from the Survey of Consumer Finances," Federal Reserve Bulletin, 78 (January 1992): 1–18; Kennickell and Woodburn, "Consistent Weight Design."
5. The original papers describing the 1983 SCF results calculated much lower values for net worth: $13.0 trillion for total net worth, $154,000 for mean family net worth, and $57,000 for median family net worth (all measured in 2013 dollars). Robert B. Avery, Gregory E. Elliehausen, Glenn B. Canner, and Thomas A. Gustafson, "Survey of Consumer Finances 1983: A Second Report," Federal Reserve Bulletin, 70 (December 1984): 857–868. The Bulletin article comparing 1983 with 1989 stated that, "The data reported here for 1983 may differ from the figures reported in the earlier articles because of revisions of the data and of the sample weights." Kennickell and Shack-Marquez, "Changes in Family Finances from 1983 to 1989," pp. 2–3. The revisions did not result in different calculations for income; 1983 median family income as calculated in Kennickell and Shack-Marquez was within 2 percent of the value calculated in Avery et al.
6. John C. Weicher, "Changes in the Distribution of Wealth: Increasing Inequality?" Review, 77(1) (January/February 1995): 8–10.

7. Kennickell and Shack-Marquez, "Changes in Family Finances from 1983 to 1989," table 1.

8. These figures are derived by comparing the values for 1989 in Tables 8.1 and 8.2 with those for 2007 in Table 8.1.

9. Carmen DeNavas-Walt and Bernadette D. Proctor, *Income and Poverty in the United States: 2014*, US Bureau of the Census, Current Population Reports No. P60-252, September 2015, https://www.census.gov/content/dam/Census/library/publications/2015/demo/p60-252.pdf. The data are collected as part of the Current Population Survey in March of the next year. The Census Bureau has been including Gini coefficients in the publication since 1967 and has calculated them back to 1947.

10. The Lorenz curve was first calculated by Lorenz in M. O. Lorenz, "Methods of Measuring the Concentration of Wealth," *Quarterly Publications of the American Statistical Association, New Series*, 70 (June 1905).

11. For a more detailed explanation of the Gini coefficient, see James N. Morgan, "The Anatomy of Income Distribution," *Review of Economics and Statistics*, 44(3) (August 1962). A very useful recent discussion is Evelyn Lamb, "Ask Gini: How to Measure Inequality," November 12, 2012, http://www.scientificamerican.com/article/ask-gini/, which includes a balanced discussion of strengths and limitations of the Gini coefficient, with examples. Peter Rosenmai, "Lorenz Curve Graphing Tool and Gini Coefficient Calculator," July 27, 2012, available at http://www.peterrosenmai.com/lorenz-curve-graphing-tool-and-gini-coefficient-calculator, allows users to create and modify their own small datasets, calculate the Gini coefficients, and perhaps to develop some intuitive sense of how to interpret Gini coefficients. A more elaborate and realistic example illustrating in detail the process of calculating a Gini coefficient, using real data from the field of team sports, has been posted by Stacey L Brook, "Guide to Calculating the Gini Coefficient," *Team Sports Analysis Blog*, December 18, 2012, http://teamsportsanalysis.blogspot.com/2012/12/guide-to-calculating-gini-coefficient.html. Brook uses actual data to measure how unequal are the payouts to universities by different football bowl games.

12. Kennickell has calculated that the change in the Gini coefficient was not statistically significant from one survey to the next between 1989 and 2007, but the cumulative increase between 1992 and 2007 was such that there was a statistically significant increase between each of the first four surveys (1989, 1992, 1995, and 1998) and the 2007 survey. Arthur B. Kennickell, "Ponds and Streams: Wealth and Income in the US, 1989 to 2007," Federal Reserve Board, Finance and Economics Discussion Series (FEDS) N. 2009-13, table 3, https://www.federalreserve.gov/pubs/feds/2009/200913/200913pap.pdf.

13. Arthur B. Kennickell, "Tossed and Turned: Wealth Dynamics of US Households 2007–2009," *FEDS Finance and Economics Discussion Series*, No.

2011-51 (May 2012): 13–15, http://www.federalreserve.gov/pubs/feds/2011/201151/201151pap.pdf.

14. Kennickell, "Ponds and Streams," figures A3a (2007) and A3f (1992).

15. The Gini coefficients in Panel A of Table 8.1 are positively correlated with each of the three concentration ratios over the period 1989–2013; the correlation coefficients are at least 0.6. With only nine observations, however, there is no point to measuring the significance of the relationships.

16. Kennickell and Woodburn, "Consistent Weight Design," p. 2, fn. 2, http://www.federalreserve.gov/econresdata/scf/files/1995_bull0197.pdf.

17. Weicher, "Wealth and Its Distribution, 1983–1992."

18. Ibid., table 4.

19. Kennickell reports that all survey-to-survey changes in income Gini coefficients between 1988 and 2006 are statistically significant except for 1988–1991 (Kennickell, "Ponds and Streams," table 3).

20. U.S. Bureau of the Census, "Historical Income Tables: Income Inequality," Table F-4. Gini Ratios of Families by Race and Hispanic Origin of Householder. https://www.census.gov/data/tables/time-series/demo/income-poverty/historical-income-inequality.html. Last revised: August 27, 2019.

21. There are terminological differences between the CPS and SCF that can be confusing but have no effect on the reported income distributions. The SCF definition of "family" is essentially the same as the CPS definition of "household," and the number of families per the SCF is the same as the number of households per the CPS. Single individuals are counted as "families" in the SCF but as "households" in the CPS.

22. As with the measures of wealth in Table 8.1, there is a positive correlation between the Gini coefficients for wealth and those for income in Table 8.5, but the nine observations are too few to draw conclusions about the statistical significance of the relationships.

23. US Bureau of the Census, "Historical Income Tables: Income Inequality," Table F-4.

24. RealClearPolitics, "Polls: Direction of Country," accessed May 4, 2020. http://www.realclearpolitics.com/epolls/other/direction_of_country-902.html.

REFERENCES

Avery, Robert B., Gregory E. Elliehausen, Glenn B. Canner, and Thomas A. Gustafson. 1984. "Survey of Consumer Finances 1983: A Second Report." *Federal Reserve Bulletin*, 70(4): 857–868. https://www.federalreserve.gov/econres/files/1983_bull1284.pdf

Brook, Stacey L. December 18, 2012. "Guide to Calculating the Gini Coefficient." *Team Sports Analysis Blog*. http://teamsportsanalysis.blogspot.com/2012/12/guide-to-calculating-gini-coefficient.html

DeNavas-Walt, Carmen, and Bernadette D. Proctor. September 2015. *Income and Poverty in the United States: 2014*. US Bureau of the Census, Current Population Report No. P60-252. https://www.census.gov/content/dam/Census/library/publications/2015/demo/p60-252.pdf

Kennickell, Arthur B. January 2009. "Ponds and Streams: Wealth and Income in the US, 1989 to 2007." *FEDS Finance and Economics Discussion Series*, No. 2009-13. http://www.federalreserve.gov/pubs/feds/2009/200913/200913pap.pdf

Kennickell, Arthur B. May 2012. "Tossed and Turned: Wealth Dynamics of US Households 2007–2009." *FEDS Finance and Economics Discussion Series*, No. 2011-51. http://www.federalreserve.gov/pubs/feds/2011/201151/201151pap.pdf

Kennickell, Arthur B., and Janice Shack-Marquez. 1992. "Changes in Family Finances from 1983 to 1989: Evidence from the Survey of Consumer Finances." *Federal Reserve Bulletin*, 78(1): 1–18. https://www.federalreserve.gov/econres/files/bull0192.pdf

Kennickell, Arthur B., Martha Starr-McCluer, and Annika E. Sunden. 1997. "Family Finances in the US: Recent Evidence from the Survey of Consumer Finances." *Federal Reserve Bulletin*, 83(1): 1–24. http://www.federalreserve.gov/econresdata/scf/files/1995_bull0197.pdf

Kennickell, Arthur B., and R. Louise Woodburn. 1997. "Consistent Weight Design for the 1989, 1992 and 1995 SCFs and the Distribution of Wealth." Federal Reserve Board Working Paper, Revision II (August 1997). http://www.federalreserve.gov/econresdata/scf/files/1995_bull0197.pdf

Lamb, Evelyn. November 12, 2012. "Ask Gini: How to Measure Inequality." *Scientific American*. http://www.scientificamerican.com/article/ask-gini/

Lorenz, M. O. 1905. "Methods of Measuring the Concentration of Wealth." *Quarterly Publications of the American Statistical Association, New Series*, 70(1905): 209–219. https://www.jstor.org/stable/2276207?origin=crossref&seq=1metadata_info_tab_contents

Morgan, James N. 1962. "The Anatomy of Income Distribution." *Review of Economics and Statistics*, 44(3): 270–283.

Proctor, Bernadette D., Jessica L. Semega, and Melissa A. Kollar. 2016. *Income and Poverty in the United States: 2015*, US Bureau of the Census, Current Population Report No. P60-256. https://www.census.gov/library/publications/2016/demo/p60-256.html., 2016

RealClearPolitics. Accessed May 4, 2020. "Polls: Direction of Country." http://www.realclearpolitics.com/epolls/other/direction_of_country-902.html

Rosenmai, Peter. July 27, 2012. "Lorenz Curve Graphing Tool and Gini Coefficient Calculator." http://www.peterrosenmai.com/lorenz-curve-graphing-tool-and-gini-coefficient-calculator

US Bureau of the Census. "Historical Income Tables: Income Inequality. Table F-4. Gini Ratios of Families by Race and Hispanic Origin of Householder." https://www.census.gov/data/tables/time-series/demo/income-poverty/historical-income-inequality.html.

Weicher, John C. January/February 1995. "Changes in the Distribution of Wealth: Increasing Inequality?" *Review of the Federal Reserve Bank of St. Louis*, 77(1): 5–23.

Weicher, John C. January/February 1997. "Wealth and Its Distribution, 1983–1992: Secular Growth, Cyclical Stability." *Review of the Federal Reserve Bank of St. Louis*, 79 (1): 3–23.

9

PUBLIC OPINION ON INEQUALITY

Karlyn Bowman and Eleanor O'Neil

INTRODUCTION

Eighty-four years ago, when the polling business was in its infancy, *Fortune* magazine, with its partner the Roper Organization, asked the first questions in the polling literature touching on inequality and what should be done about it. In the in-person *Fortune* survey conducted in 1935, people split nearly evenly about whether "the government should allow a man who has investments worth over a million dollars to keep them, subject only to present taxes," with 45 percent saying it should and 46 percent saying it should not (*Fortune*, 1935). In their 1939 poll, 15 percent said the government should "confiscate all wealth over and above what people actually need to live on decently and use it for the public good," while 76 percent said the government should not. In another question in this survey, 35 percent said our government should "redistribute wealth by heavy taxes on the rich," while 54 percent said the government should not (*Fortune*, 1939). In the decades since then, pollsters have explored the subject fitfully. On occasion, such as around the time when the protest movement Occupy Wall Street emerged in 2011, they have devoted a little more attention to the topic.

Some major survey organizations such as the National Opinion Research Center (NORC) at the University of Chicago, the Gallup Organization, and Pew Research Center regularly update a few questions on this topic, but most pollsters do not. The dearth of long trends with identically worded questions limits analysis. We should note, too, that polls are not a precise tool. Pollsters do

Karlyn Bowman and Eleanor O'Neil, *Public Opinion on Inequality* In: *United States Income, Wealth, Consumption, and Inequality.* Edited by: Diana Furchtgott-Roth, Oxford University Press (2021). © Oxford University Press. DOI: 10.1093/oso/9780197518199.003.0010.

not make distinctions between income inequality and economic inequality, for example. The polls yield general perceptions, some of which are contradictory.

We begin with a look at survey data on Americans' self-perceived social class, what they think it means to be rich, and how they view those who are. We then turn to general perceptions of inequality and opportunity in America. Finally, we look at opinions about government's role in addressing inequality.

HOW AMERICANS SEE THEMSELVES

Discussions of inequality tend to focus on the gap between the rich and the poor, but few Americans see themselves at either end of the socioeconomic spectrum. Since 1972, in its General Social Survey series, NORC has asked adults this question about their social class: "If you were asked to use one of these four names for your social class, which one would you say you belong to?" No more than 5 percent have ever identified as upper class, and fewer than 10 percent as lower class. Most people consistently say they belong somewhere in between—to either the working class or the middle class (see Figure 9.1). Figure 9.2 shows how people across family income categories described their social class in NORC's 2018 General Social Survey. Responses differ by income level, but even in the lowest and highest family income categories, a majority identified as working or middle class.

Looking at responses by educational attainment, which are simpler to compare over time than responses by income, the magnitude of difference in class identification between those with lower and higher levels of formal education

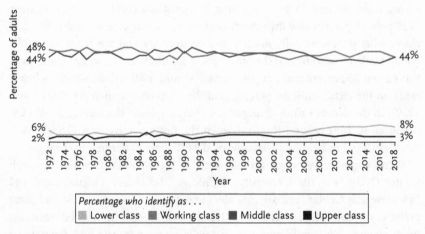

Figure 9.1 Self-identified social class. The wording of the question is "If you were asked to use one of four names for your social class, which would you say you belong in: the lower class, the working class, the middle class, or the upper class?"
Data from T. Smith et al., 2019.

Family income, 2017 dollars

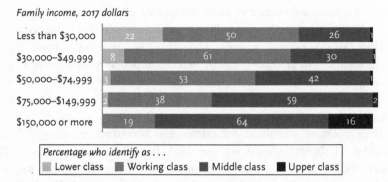

Figure 9.2 Self-Identified Social Class in 2018, by Total Family Income in Previous Year. The wording of the social class question is "If you were asked to use one of four names for your social class, which would you say you belong in: the lower class, the working class, the middle class, or the upper class?" Total family income is based on the income group in which the respondent said their total family income fell in 2017, before taxes. The authors of this essay consolidated the reported income groups into the income groups shown earlier.
Data from T. Smith et al., 2019.

has not increased notably over the past few decades (see Figure 9.3). People with a bachelor's degree or more formal education are more likely than those with less education to say they belong to one of the two higher classes (middle or upper), but again, fewer people place themselves at the extremes of the class

Percentage who identify as middle class or upper class among those with . . .

Figure 9.3 Self-identified social class by highest educational degree earned. The social class question wording is "If you were asked to use one of four names for your social class, which would you say you belong in: the lower class, the working class, the middle class, or the upper class?" The education groups are based on highest educational degree attained. "Less than a bachelor's degree" includes those with junior college degrees, high school graduates, and those who did not graduate high school.
Data from T. Smith et al., 2019.

spectrum than describe themselves as working or middle class. In 2018, more than half of people with less than a bachelor's degree said they belonged to the working class—51 percent of people who did not graduate high school, 53 percent of high school graduates, and 57 percent of people with a junior college degree gave that response. Most people with a bachelor's degree and most of those with a graduate degree identified as middle class—62 percent and 71 percent, respectively.

Other pollsters ask about subjective class identification using different categories. All show that few Americans think they are socioeconomically at the top or at the bottom. Gallup asks Americans to choose one of five names for their social class instead of four. In Gallup's latest survey from April 2018, 11 percent said they belonged in the lower class, 31 percent in the working class, 40 percent in the middle class, 15 percent in the upper middle class, and 2 percent in the upper class (Newport, 2018b). Similarly, in an October 2019 NBC News/ *Wall Street Journal* poll that asked people to describe their "economic circumstances" using a five-part response, 7 percent said poor, 24 percent working class, 47 percent middle class, 17 percent upper middle class, and 3 percent well-to-do (NBC News and *Wall Street Journal,* 2019).

In five surveys since 1990 when Gallup has asked Americans a different question about their financial situation rather than their social class, no more than 2 percent have ever said they considered themselves to be rich. In May– June 2018, 1 percent described themselves as rich, 9 percent as upper income, 51 percent as middle income, 28 percent as lower income, and 10 percent as poor.

WHAT DOES IT MEAN TO BE RICH?

If only a small number of people describe themselves as rich, how do they view those who are? And what do they think it means to be rich? The questions we have on this topic suggest that Americans have mixed feelings about the rich.

Pollsters do not ask Americans to define class in terms of income as often as they ask them about their class identification. Table 9.1 shows the results of a few polls from the 2010s that asked people about the amount of annual income needed to be rich. While the questions and responses varied somewhat, it is clear that most Americans did not think it would take a seven-figure annual salary—or even a $300,000 annual salary—to be considered rich. A 2011 Gallup survey asked people how much they would need to make per year to consider themselves rich. The survey found that those with annual household incomes of less than $50,000 tended to place the threshold lower (their median response was $100,000) than did those with household incomes of $50,000 or more (their median response was $200,000) (Jones, 2011).

Table 9.1 Opinions on amount of income needed to be rich

Gallup Organization, 2011 Q: Just thinking about your own situation, how much money per year would you need to make in order to consider yourself rich? [OPEN-ENDED]		Pew Research Center, 2012 Q: Just your best guess, how much does a family of four need to have in total annual income to be considered wealthy in your area? [OPEN-ENDED]	
Less than $60,000	18%		
$60,000–$99,999	12	Less than $50,000	6%
$100,000–$150,000	23	$50,000–$99,999	11
$150,001–$299,999	18	$100,000–$249,999	39
$300,000–$999,999	14	$250,000–$999,999	20
$1,000,000	11	$1,000,000 or more	10
More than $1,000,000	4		
Median response	$150,000	Median response	$150,000
Washington Post/Miller Center, 2013 Q: There is a lot of talk about the difference between being middle class and being rich. In your opinion, how much would someone have to make in a year in order to be considered rich? [OPEN-ENDED]		**CBS News/New York Times, 2014** Q: About how much money per year do you think the typical American family of four needs to make in order to be considered rich?	
		Less than $100,000	18%
Less than $50,000	2%	$100,000–$199,999	27
$50,000–$74,999	4	$200,000–$299,999	20
$75,000–$99,999	4	$300,000–$399,999	3
$100,000–$299,999	41	$400,000–$499,999	1
$300,000–$999,999	21	$500,000–$749,999	8
$1,000,000 or more	19	$750,000–$999,999	1
		$1,000,000 or more	7
Median response	$250,000		

Note: Income ranges shown as reported by each pollster.
Source: Data from Jones, 2011; Pew Research Center, 2012b; Washington Post and Miller Center at the University of Virginia, 2013; CBS News and New York Times, 2014.

Few Americans think they will become rich themselves, and they do not equate being rich with achieving happiness. In a 2018 Gallup survey, 32 percent of those who had said they were not rich or gave no opinion (99 percent of the sample) said it was very or somewhat likely that they would ever be rich, while 66 percent said it was not very or not at all likely. Only 12 percent of the non-rich group thought the rich were happier than they were, while 28 percent said the rich were less happy, and 56 percent thought their level of happiness was about the same (Newport, 2018a). Other surveys show that accumulating wealth does not rank high when people think about life accomplishments. A 2017 Pew survey about the American Dream that asked people about whether various things were essential, important but not essential, or not important to their own view of the American Dream found that 11 percent said becoming wealthy was essential, while 49 percent said it was important but not essential, and 40 percent said it was not important. At the top of the list of seven items Pew asked about, 77 percent said having freedom of choice in how to live was essential, followed by having a good family life (70 percent), being able to retire comfortably (60 percent), making valuable contributions to community (48 percent), owning a home, and, separately, having a successful career (43 percent each) (S. Smith, 2017a).

Polls suggest that Americans respect people who have earned their fortunes, but they are not convinced that hard work is the reason why people are rich. In eight identical questions asked by Pew between 1992 and 2012, large majorities said they completely or mostly agreed with the statement "I admire people who get rich by working hard." Eighty-nine percent gave that response in 1992, and 88 percent gave it 20 years later in 2012. Yet when a more general question that did not mention individual initiative was asked, just 27 percent in the 2012 Pew survey agreed with the statement "I admire people who are rich," while 66 percent disagreed (Pew Research Center, 2012a).

On four occasions since 2014 when Pew asked people whether hard work or personal advantages generally has more to do with why a person is rich, responses were divided. In 2018, 43 percent chose the response "because he or she worked harder than most other people," while 42 percent chose the response "because he or she had more advantages in life than most other people" (Dunn, 2018). In 2017, 45 percent and 43 percent gave those responses, respectively; in 2015, 40 percent and 49 percent did; and in 2014, 38 percent and 51 percent did (S. Smith, 2017b). Partisans differ sharply on this question. In 2018, about 7 in 10 (71 percent) of Republicans and Republican-leaning independents attributed a person's wealth to their hard work, while a majority (62 percent) of Democrats and Democratic-leaning independents gave the opposite response. Opinions also varied by gender and income level. Men were more likely than women to say someone is rich because they worked harder. Americans with annual family incomes of $75,000 or more were more likely to see wealth as the result of hard work than were those with family incomes of less than $30,000 (see Table 9.2).

For comparison, when Pew asked which of two reasons is more to blame if a person is poor—lack of effort on his or her own part or circumstances beyond his or her control—about half (52 percent) of Americans in 2018 faulted uncontrollable circumstances. Thirty-one percent said a person's lack of effort is generally more to blame.

In a question asked by Gallup in 2018, 58 percent said that the United States benefits from having a class of rich people, while 39 percent said it does not (Newport, 2018a). At the same time, other polls show that Americans see

Table 9.2 Views on why a person is rich

	Because he or she has worked harder than most other people	Because he or she has had more advantages than most other people
National response, 2018	43%	42%
Men	48	37
Women	37	47
Family income (2017 dollars)		
Less than $30,000	36	56
$30,000 to $74,999	41	43
$75,000 or more	49	37
Democrats/Lean Democratic	22	62
Republicans/Lean Republican	71	18

Note: Question wording is "In your opinion, which generally has more to do with why a person is rich—because he or she worked harder than most other people, or because he or she had more advantages in life than most other people?"
Source: Data from Dunn, 2018.

inequality as a problem and think those at the top have more opportunity to get ahead than average Americans, as we discuss in the following sections.

INEQUALITY: HOW BIG A PROBLEM?

Awareness of inequality is not new, nor is the belief that it is growing. In September 1972, when Harris pollsters asked Americans whether they felt "the rich get richer and the poor poorer," 67 percent said they felt that way. In Harris's 2016 online survey, 78 percent did (Harris Insights & Analytics, 2016). The response has never dipped below 66 percent in the more than two dozen times Harris has asked the question.

A Pew and *USA Today* survey from 2014 found that 65 percent believed the gap between the rich and everyone else had increased in the past 10 years, while 25 percent said it had stayed the same and 8 percent said it had decreased. When the people who felt it had increased were asked why it had done so, 17 percent, the top response, said it was because of the tax system. Nine percent mentioned "Congress/government policies" and 7 percent "jobs/unemployment." No other single reason was given by 5 percent or more (Pew Research Center and *USA Today,* 2014). In 2015, 67 percent told CBS News/*New York Times* pollsters that the gap between the rich and the poor in the United States was getting larger, while 25 percent said it had stayed about the same, and 5 percent said it was getting smaller (CBS News and *New York Times,* 2015a).

Since 2013, on six occasions, Pew has asked how big a problem, if at all, the gap between the rich and poor is in this country today. In June 2019, 51 percent said it was a very big problem, 30 percent a moderately big problem, 14 percent a small problem, and 5 percent not a problem at all (see Table 9.3).

People also express dissatisfaction with the way income and wealth are distributed in the United States. In Gallup's early 2019 survey, 36 percent were satisfied and 62 percent were dissatisfied with this. Again, there is stability in the responses to this question in recent years. In 2018, the responses were 32 percent satisfied, 66 percent dissatisfied. In 2017, they were 35 percent and 64 percent, respectively. In 2016, they were 29 percent and 68 percent, respectively. In 2015, they were 31 percent and 67 percent, and in 2014, 32 percent and 67 percent (Jones, 2019).

While polling evidence clearly indicates that Americans believe inequality is a big or moderately big problem and that it is growing, the issue is rarely mentioned spontaneously as a top or even middling level problem facing the country. In Gallup's 2019 monthly surveys between January and August, when people were asked to name the most important problem facing the country, dissatisfaction with the government and immigration were generally the top problems. No more than 2 percent mentioned the gap between rich and poor (Gallup Organization, 2019). When CBS News and the *New York Times* asked people in late 2015 about the most important economic problem facing the country and gave them four choices, 37 percent chose the federal budget, 23 percent jobs and unemployment, 20 percent income inequality, and 9 percent taxes (CBS News and *New York Times*, 2015b). Similarly, in an April 2016 Fox News survey of registered voters that asked which of four economic issues was the

Table 9.3 Views on inequality as a problem

The gap between the rich and the poor is . . .

	A very big problem (%)	A moderately big problem (%)	A small Problem (%)	Not a problem at all (%)
2013	47	27	14	9
2014	46	32	13	7
Aug. 2016	52	31	10	6
Oct.–Nov. 2016[a]	57	29	9	5
2018 [a]	54	28	12	5
2019 [a]	51	30	14	5

Note: Question wording from 2013 to 2016 was "Do you think the gap between the rich and the poor is a very big problem, a moderately big problem, a small problem or not a problem at all in our country?" Question wording from 2018 to 2019 was "How much of a problem do you think each of the following are in the country today . . . the gap between the rich and poor?"
[a]The October–November 2016 survey and later surveys were conducted online using the Pew Research Center's American Trends Panel.
Source: Data from Pew Research Center, 2019.

most important facing the country, 35 percent chose government spending and the deficit, 31 percent jobs and unemployment, 20 percent income inequality, and 9 percent taxes (Fox News, 2016).

OPPORTUNITY FOR AVERAGE AMERICANS

Most people do not say becoming wealthy is a top goal for them personally. But what about the more prosaic goal of just being able to get ahead, to live a comfortable life? The belief that widespread opportunity is present can dull feelings of inequality. How do Americans view opportunity today, and has that changed from the past?

In 1952, the University of Michigan's National Election Survey asked this question: "Some people say there's not much opportunity in America today— that the average person doesn't have much chance to really get ahead. Others say there's plenty of opportunity and anyone who works hard can go as far as they want." Eighty-seven percent said there was plenty of opportunity, and 8 percent said there was not much. Gallup has asked that question four times, starting in 1998. In 2016, 70 percent said there was plenty of opportunity, and 28 percent said not much (see Table 9.4).

Most polls show that most Americans think they are better off than their parents in terms of living standards, quality of life, and preparation to get ahead (Bowman et al., 2014). In a 2014 CNN poll, 54 percent said they were better off financially than their parents at the same age, while 41 percent said they were worse off (CNN, 2014). An ABC News question asked more than a dozen times between 1981 and 1996 with slightly different wording found no fewer than 64 percent saying they were better off financially (ABC News, 1996), and Gallup updates in 1998 and 2011 found 74 percent and 69 percent, respectively, saying the same thing (Mendes, 2011).

Table 9.4 Is opportunity present in America today? What Americans say

	Plenty of opportunity (%)	Not much opportunity (%)
1952	87	8
1998	81	17
2011	57	41
2013	52	43
2016	70	28

Note: 1952 data from the University of Michigan National Election Survey. 1998–2016 surveys conducted by Gallup Organization. Question wording is "Some people say there's not much opportunity in America today—that the average person doesn't have much chance to really get ahead. Others say there's plenty of opportunity and anyone who works hard can go as far as they want. Which one comes closer to the way you feel about this?"
Source: Data from Jones, 2016.

Americans hold firmly to the belief that it is possible to work hard and get ahead. On 15 occasions since 1994, Pew has asked people which of a pair of statements about opportunity comes closer to their view. In the summer of 2017, 61 percent said the view that "most people who want to get ahead can make it if they're willing to work hard," approximated their view, while 36 percent were drawn to the statement "hard work and determination are no guarantee of success for most people." A majority have chosen the former statement each time the question has been asked (Pew Research Center, 2017). In a question asked 14 times by CBS News and the *New York Times* from 1981 to 2016, no fewer than 57 percent in any survey agreed with the statement "it's still possible to start out poor in this country, work hard, and become rich." In the latest survey, 73 percent thought it was possible (CBS News, 2016). A Gallup question asked more than a dozen times since 2001 shows Americans have generally been satisfied with the opportunity for a person in this nation to get ahead by working hard. Sixty-five percent said they were satisfied in 2019, and there were no significant differences in satisfaction between those with lower and higher incomes (Jones, 2019).

Questions that ask about inequality of opportunity rather than just about ability to get ahead by working hard give a different impression, as shown by nine identically worded questions asked by CBS News and the *New York Times* since 2010. In all but two iterations, majorities have chosen the response, "in today's economy, it's mainly just a few people at the top who have a chance to get ahead," while fewer have said "everyone has a fair chance to get ahead in the long run." In the latest question from 2017, 43 percent said everyone had a fair chance to get ahead and 53 percent said just a few people at the top had a chance to get ahead (CBS News, 2017). An NBC News/*Wall Street Journal* question from 2014 found that 44 percent believed "the United States is a country where anyone, regardless of their background can work hard, succeed and be comfortable financially," while 54 percent said "the widening gap between the incomes of the wealthy and everyone else is undermining the idea that every American has the opportunity to move up to a better standard of living" (NBC News and *Wall Street Journal*, 2014). Similarly, in a 2019 Fox News survey that asked registered voters which of two statements better described their view of America, 40 percent said "people who work hard have a fair chance of getting ahead," while 56 percent said "even if people work hard, the system is rigged to favor the wealthy" (Fox News, 2019).

Surveys reveal mixed feelings about the fairness of the economic system. On two occasions, the Gallup Organization has asked people whether the "economic system in the United States is basically fair, since all Americans have an equal opportunity to succeed, or basically unfair, since all Americans do not have an equal opportunity to succeed." In 1998, 68 percent said it was basically fair, and 29 percent basically unfair. In 2013, concerns about the fairness of the system had risen. Fifty percent said it was basically fair, but 44 percent said it was unfair (Dugan and Newport, 2013). In a December 2014 survey by CBS News and the *New York Times* using identical wording, 52 percent said they thought the system was basically fair, while 45 percent said it was basically unfair (CBS News and *New York Times*, 2014). In Public Religion Research Institute surveys taken from 2012 to 2016, more than 6 in 10 completely or mostly agreed that the economic system unfairly favors the wealthy, with 68 percent saying that when the question was last asked in 2016 (Cox et al., 2017). Similar shares in Pew surveys taken from 2014 to 2019 said they thought the system unfairly favors powerful interests, with 63 percent giving that response in spring 2019, compared to 34 percent who thought the economic system is generally fair to most Americans (Pew Research Center, 2019).

Two recent questions asked by NBC and *Wall Street Journal* pollsters suggest Americans are less concerned about inequality and a rigged system than they are about opportunity for average people to get ahead. Asked which concerned them more, 68 percent in an April 2015 survey said "middle class and working class Americans not being able to get ahead financially," compared to 28 percent who said "the income gap between the wealthiest Americans and the rest of the country" (NBC News and *Wall Street Journal*, 2015a). In a December 2015 survey, 57 percent said "I am more concerned about diminishing opportunity for average people to achieve economic stability," compared to 37 percent who said "I am more concerned that the wealthy are rigging the system for the rich and leaving the rest of us behind" (NBC News and *Wall Street Journal*, 2015b).

WHAT SHOULD GOVERNMENT DO?

Questions asked in recent years about addressing inequality show variation depending on question emphasis. As a general matter, Americans want to make sure everyone has an opportunity to succeed. Large majorities at 86 percent or more in 10 questions asked by Pew between 1997 and 2012 completely or mostly agreed that our society should do what is necessary to make sure everyone has an equal opportunity to succeed (Pew Research Center, 2012a). Americans also believe money and wealth should be more evenly distributed, though the concept appears to draw support from somewhat smaller majorities. On more than a dozen occasions since 1984, Gallup has asked people whether "the distribution of money and wealth in this country today is fair," or whether "money and wealth in this country should be more evenly distributed among a larger percentage of people." Majorities (usually around 60 percent) have responded that it should be more evenly distributed. In 2016, 59 percent called for more even distribution, while 34 percent said it was fair (see Figure 9.4).

But it is not clear what precisely Americans think *government* should do about inequality. In a scale question asked by the NORC since the 1970s, most people put themselves at the midpoints on a 7-point scale when asked about government's role when it comes to income inequality. Looking at responses at either end of the scale, where 1 indicates feeling government ought to reduce

Percentage who feel . . .

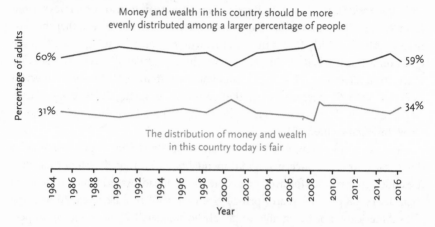

Figure 9.4 Views on the distribution of money and wealth in the United States. Wording of the question is "Do you feel that the distribution of money and wealth in this country today is fair, or do you feel that the money and wealth in this country should be more evenly distributed among a larger percentage of the people?"
Data from Newport, 2016.

income differences between the rich and the poor and 7 indicates feeling government should not concern itself with reducing income differences, the percentage of people who place themselves at points 1 and 2 has usually been higher than the percentage who put themselves at points 6 and 7 (see Figure 9.5).

Another question asked six times by NORC from 1985 to 2016 shows people have become more likely to say it should be government's responsibility to reduce income differences between the rich and poor. Fifty-four percent in 2016 said it definitely or probably should be government's responsibility, up from 35 percent the first time the question was asked in 1985. Still, in comparison, higher percentages in 2016 supported other roles for government (see Figure 9.6).

A different set of NORC questions asked several times since 1987 has generally found more opposition to than support for the idea that it is the responsibility of government to reduce income differences between people with "high incomes" and "low incomes," even if most people think the income gap is too wide. In 2018, 6 in 10 (62 percent) Americans agreed that income differences in America were too large, compared to 32 percent who agreed with the statement "It is the responsibility of the government to reduce the differences in income between people with high incomes and those with low incomes." Forty-three percent disagreed that government is responsible for reducing income differences, and 24 percent neither agreed nor disagreed (see Table 9.5).

Other surveys also give varying impressions of what Americans expect or want from their government in this area. Reason-Rupe found in 2013 that 34 percent said reducing the differences in income between people with high

Percentage who choose points _____ on a scale of 1 to 7 . . .

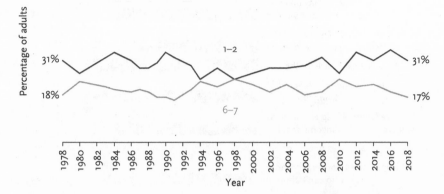

1 = Government ought to reduce income differences between rich and poor
7 = Government should not concern itself with reducing income differences

Figure 9.5 Views on government's role in reducing income differences between the rich and the poor. Wording of the question is "Some people think that the government in Washington ought to reduce the income differences between the rich and the poor, perhaps by raising the taxes of wealthy families or by giving income assistance to the poor. Others think that the government should not concern itself with reducing this income difference between the rich and the poor. Here is a card with a scale from 1 to 7. Think of a score of 1 as meaning that the government ought to reduce the income differences between rich and poor, and a score of 7 meaning that the government should not concern itself with reducing income differences. What score between 1 and 7 comes closest to the way you feel?" The percentage of people who placed themselves at points 3 to 5 is not shown on the chart.
Data from T. Smith et al., 2019.

and low incomes was a government responsibility; 61 percent said it was not (Reason-Rupe, 2013). A CBS News/*New York Times* question with a different emphasis asked for the first time in 1990 found 58 percent that year felt government should do more to reduce the gap between the rich and the average citizen in this country, while 35 percent said this was something government should not be doing. In 2015, those responses were 57 percent and 39 percent, respectively (CBS News and *New York Times*, 2015a). In a 2011 Gallup survey that asked how important it was that the federal government enact policies designed to do different things, 46 percent said it was extremely or very important for the government to reduce the income and wealth gap between the rich and the poor, compared to 70 percent who said it was important to increase the equality of opportunity for people to get ahead if they want to and 82 percent who said it was important to grow and expand the economy (Newport, 2011).

Finally, a question asked four times by Bloomberg between 2013 and 2015 found people fairly evenly divided about whether "it would be better for government to implement policies designed to shrink the gap between the rich and everyone else" or whether "it would be better for the government to stand aside

Q: Do you think it should or should not be the government's responsibility to . . . ?

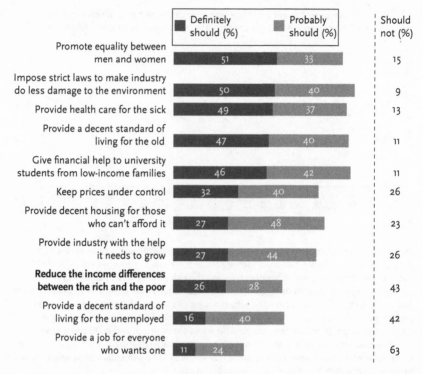

Figure 9.6 Views on government's responsibilities, 2016.
Data from T. Smith et al., 2019.

and let the market operate freely even if the gap gets wider." Those responses in 2015 were 46 percent and 47 percent, respectively (see Table 9.6).

One specific way to address inequality is to make changes in the tax system. Majorities say the rich and, separately, corporations do not pay their fair share in

Table 9.5 Views on government's role in reducing income differences between high-income and low-income groups, 2018

	Agree (%)	Neither agree nor disagree (%)	Disagree (%)
Differences in income in America are too large.	62	24	12
It is the responsibility of the government to reduce the differences in income between people with high incomes and those with low incomes.	32	24	43

Note: "Strongly agree" and "Agree" responses combined. "Strongly disagree" and "Disagree" responses combined.
Source: Data from T. Smith et al., 2019.

Table 9.6 Sentiments on addressing the gap between the rich and everyone else

	It would be better for the government to . . .	
	Implement policies designed to shrink the gap (%)	Stand aside and let the market operate freely even if the gap gets wider (%)
Dec. 2013	45	46
Mar. 2014	45	43
Jun. 2014	44	47
Apr. 2015	46	47

Note: Question wording is "In thinking about the gap between the rich and everyone else, do you think it would be better for government to implement policies designed to shrink the gap OR better for the government to stand aside and let the market operate freely even if the gap gets wider?"
Source: Data from Bloomberg, 2015.

taxes (Newport, 2017). A question in a 1939 Roper/*Fortune* poll asked whether government should or should not redistribute wealth by heavy taxes on the rich. Thirty-five percent said government should, but 54 percent said it should not. When Gallup picked up the question in 1998, 45 percent said government should do this, and 51 percent said it should not. In 2016, the responses were 52 percent and 46 percent, respectively (Newport, 2016). Recent polls show Americans also favor increasing the minimum wage (Associated Press-NORC Center for Public Affairs Research, 2016; Pew Research Center, 2016; Cox et al., 2017; Quinnipiac University, 2017). The public has long believed there should be an income floor for those who are working.

CONCLUSION

Public opinion surveys are a blunt instrument. They yield general impressions but rarely give specific guidance to policy researchers or policymakers. The polls used to examine attitudes toward inequality are no exception. Americans have long said the gap between the rich and the poor is growing. At the same time, class identification has remained fairly stable, with most people seeing themselves as somewhere in the middle. Their answers to questions about how much income it takes to be rich seem modest compared to the news accounts of vast wealth in society. It is difficult to know what level of income or wealth people think of when they respond to questions about "the rich."

Americans are clearly aware of inequality in America and believe it is a problem, but other issues rank higher when they are asked about problems facing the country. Polls provide mixed evidence on people's beliefs about opportunity to get ahead in America today. In many questions, Americans say there is opportunity for anyone to get ahead if they work hard. In others, people say there is only opportunity for a few at the top.

The polls do not give clear guidance about what Americans think should be done to address inequality. Most questions about what government should do show support in the abstract for government involvement in addressing income differences. Other questions show Americans are more concerned about increasing opportunity than they are about reducing the income gap.

The survey data we reviewed show the complexity of different perspectives on inequality and opportunity. In summary, Americans want everyone to be able to get ahead and achieve financial well-being, but it is not clear to what extent they believe that vision has been or is being realized or how they think it can best be achieved.

REFERENCES

ABC News. 1996. Distributed by Ithaca, NY: Roper Center for Public Opinion Research iPOLL Database at Cornell University. https://ropercenter.cornell.edu/

Associated Press-NORC Center for Public Affairs Research. 2016. "The Importance of Economic Issues." http://www.apnorc.org/PDFs/ImportanceEconomics/Economy_Topline.pdf

Bloomberg. 2015. Conducted by Selzer & Co. Distributed by Ithaca, NY: Roper Center for Public Opinion Research iPOLL Database at Cornell University. https://ropercenter.cornell.edu/

Bowman, Karlyn, Jennifer Marsico, and Heather Sims. 2014. *Is the American Dream Alive? Examining Americans' Attitudes.* Washington, DC: American Enterprise Institute. https://www.aei.org/research-products/report/american-dream-alive-examining-americans-attitudes/

CBS News. 2016. Conducted by Social Science Research Solutions. Distributed by Ithaca, NY: Roper Center for Public Opinion Research iPOLL Database at Cornell University. https://ropercenter.cornell.edu/

CBS News. 2017. Conducted by Social Science Research Solutions. Distributed by Ithaca, NY: Roper Center for Public Opinion Research iPOLL Database at Cornell University. https://ropercenter.cornell.edu/

CBS News and *New York Times*. 2014. Conducted by Social Science Research Solutions. Distributed by Ithaca, NY: Roper Center for Public Opinion Research iPOLL Database at Cornell University. https://ropercenter.cornell.edu/

CBS News and *New York Times*. 2015a. "Americans' Views on the Workplace and Income Inequality." https://www.scribd.com/doc/267597931/CBS-News-New-York-Times-Work-Income-Inequality-poll

CBS News and *New York Times*. 2015b. "Clinton Still Leads, Trump Seen as Toughest Challenge for Democrats." https://www.scribd.com/document/289515400/Nov-2015-CBS-News-NYT-poll-toplines

CNN. 2014. American Dream Poll. Conducted by ORC International. https://www.documentcloud.org/documents/1182928-rel6b.html

Cox, Daniel, Rachel Lienesch, and Robert P. Jones. 2017. *Beyond Economics: Fears of Cultural Displacement Pushed the White Working Class to Trump.* Washington, DC: Public Religion Research Institute and *Atlantic.* https://www.prri.org/research/white-working-class-attitudes-economy-trade-immigration-election-donald-trump/

Dugan, Andrew, and Frank Newport. 2013. "In U.S., Fewer Believe 'Plenty of Opportunity' to Get Ahead." Gallup Organization. http://news.gallup.com/poll/165584/fewer-believe-plenty-opportunity-ahead.aspx

Dunn, Amina. 2018. "Partisans Are Divided over Fairness of the U.S. Economy—and Why People Are Rich and Poor." Pew Research Center. https://www.pewresearch.org/fact-tank/2018/10/04/partisans-are-divided-over-the-fairness-of-the-u-s-economy-and-why-people-are-rich-or-poor/

Fortune. 1935. The Fortune Survey.

Fortune. 1939. The Fortune Survey. Conducted by Roper Organization. Distributed by Ithaca, NY: Roper Center for Public Opinion Research iPOLL Database at Cornell University. https://ropercenter.cornell.edu/

Fox News. 2016. Fox News Poll. Conducted by Anderson Robbins Research and Shaw & Company Research. http://www.foxnews.com/politics/interactive/2016/04/14/fox-news-poll-national-release-april-14-2016.html

Fox News.2019. Fox News Poll. Conducted by Anderson Robbins Research and Shaw & Company Research. https://www.foxnews.com/politics/fox-news-poll-3-24-2019

Gallup Organization. 2019. "Most Important Problem." https://news.gallup.com/poll/1675/Most-Important-Problem.aspx

Harris Insights & Analytics. 2016. "Americans' Sense of Alienation Remains at Record High." https://theharrispoll.com/in-the-midst-of-the-contentious-presidential-primary-elections-the-harris-poll-measured-how-alienated-americans-feel-as-part-of-a-long-term-trend-the-last-time-alienation-was-measured-was-in-novemb/

Jones, Jeffrey M. 2011. "Americans Set 'Rich' Threshold at $150,000 in Annual Income." Gallup Organization. http://news.gallup.com/poll/151427/Americans-Set-Rich-Threshold-150-000-Annual-Income.aspx

Jones, Jeffrey M. 2016. "Views of Opportunity in US Improve, but Lag the Past." Gallup Organization. http://news.gallup.com/poll/193247/views-opportunity-improve-lag-past.aspx

Jones, Jeffrey M. 2019. "Most in U.S. Satisfied with Quality of Life, Opportunity." Gallup Organization. https://news.gallup.com/poll/246236/satisfied-quality-life-opportunity.aspx

Mendes, Elizabeth. 2011. "Most Americans Still Say They Are Better Off Than Their Parents." Gallup Organization. http://news.gallup.com/poll/151772/Americans-Say-Better-Off-Parents.aspx

NBC News and *Wall Street Journal*. 2014. Conducted by Hart Research Associates and Public Opinion Strategies. Distributed by Ithaca, NY: Roper Center for Public Opinion Research iPOLL Database at Cornell University. https://ropercenter.cornell.edu/

NBC News and *Wall Street Journal*. 2015a. Study 15179. Conducted by Hart Research Associates and Public Opinion Strategies. https://online.wsj.com/public/resources/documents/WSJNBCpoll05042015.pdf

NBC News and *Wall Street Journal*. 2015b. Study 15564. Conducted by Hart Research Associates/Public Opinion Strategies. http://online.wsj.com/public/resources/documents/NBCWSJDecember2015PollFullRelease.pdf

NBC News and *Wall Street Journal*. 2019. Study 19433. Conducted by Hart Research Associates/Public Opinion Strategies. https://www.documentcloud.org/documents/6538104-19433-NBCWSJ-Late-October-Poll.html

Newport, Frank. 2011. "Americans Prioritize Economy over Reducing Wealth Gap." Gallup Organization. http://news.gallup.com/poll/151568/Americans-Prioritize-Growing-Economy-Reducing-Wealth-Gap.aspx

Newport, Frank. 2016. "Americans Still Say Upper-Income Pay Too Little in Taxes." Gallup Organization. http://news.gallup.com/poll/190775/americans-say-upper-income-pay-little-taxes.aspx

Newport, Frank. 2017. "Majority Say Wealthy Americans, Corporations Taxed Too Little." Gallup Organization. http://news.gallup.com/poll/208685/majority-say-wealthy-americans-corporations-taxed-little.aspx

Newport, Frank. 2018a. "Partisan Divide on Benefit of Having Rich People Expands." Gallup Organization. https://news.gallup.com/poll/235439/partisan-divide-benefit-having-rich-people-expands.aspx

Newport, Frank. 2018b. "Looking into What Americans Mean by 'Working Class.'" Gallup Organization. https://news.gallup.com/opinion/polling-matters/239195/looking-americans-mean-working-class.aspx

Pew Research Center. 2012a. *Partisan Polarization Surges in Bush, Obama Years*. Washington, DC. https://www.people-press.org/2012/06/04/section-3-values-about-economic-inequality-and-individual-opportunity/

Pew Research Center. 2012b. July 2012 Middle Class Update Survey. Washington, DC. Conducted by Princeton Survey Research Associates International. http://assets.pewresearch.org/wp-content/uploads/sites/3/2012/08/Middle-Class-Topline-8-2-FINAL.pdf

Pew Research Center. 2016. *Clinton, Trump Supporters Have Starkly Different Views of a Changing Nation*. Washington, DC. http://www.people-press.org/2016/08/18/clinton-trump-supporters-have-starkly-different-views-of-a-changing-nation/

Pew Research Center. 2017. *The Partisan Divide on Political Values Grows Even Wider*. Washington, DC. https://assets.pewresearch.org/wp-content/uploads/sites/5/2017/10/05162647/10-05-2017-Political-landscape-release.pdf

Pew Research Center. 2019. *Growing Partisan Divide over Fairness of the Nation's Tax System.* Washington, DC. https://www.people-press.org/2019/04/04/growing-partisan-divide-over-fairness-of-the-nations-tax-system/

Pew Research Center and *USA Today*. 2014. *Most See Inequality Growing, but Partisans Differ over Solutions.* Washington, DC. http://www.people-press.org/2014/01/23/most-see-inequality-growing-but-partisans-differ-over-solutions/

Quinnipiac University. 2017. "U.S. Voters Say 68–27% Let Transgender People Serve, Quinnipiac University National Poll Finds; Voters Disapprove 5–1 of GOP Handling of Health Care." https://poll.qu.edu/national/release-detail?ReleaseID=2477

Reason-Rupe. 2013. Conducted by Princeton Survey Research Associates International. http://reason.com/assets/db/1378949725826.pdf

Smith, Samantha. 2017a. "Most Think the 'American Dream' Is Within Reach for Them." Pew Research Center. http://www.pewresearch.org/fact-tank/2017/10/31/most-think-the-american-dream-is-within-reach-for-them/

Smith, Samantha. 2017b. "Why People Are Rich and Poor: Republicans and Democrats Have Very Different Views." Pew Research Center. http://www.pewresearch.org/fact-tank/2017/05/02/why-people-are-rich-and-poor-republicans-and-democrats-have-very-different-views/

Smith, Tom W., Peter Marsden, Michael Hout, and Jibum Kim. 2019. *General Social Survey, 1972–2018 Cumulative Datafile. Release 1 (SDA 4.0).* Chicago, IL: NORC at the University of Chicago. Distributed by El Cerrito, CA: Computer-Assisted Survey Methods Program at the Institute for Scientific Analysis. http://sda.berkeley.edu/archive.htm

Washington Post and Miller Center at the University of Virginia. 2013. "The Middle Class and the American Dream." *Washington Post.* http://apps.washingtonpost.com/g/page/politics/washington-post-miller-center-poll-september-6-12-2013/489/

10

THE ECONOMICS OF INEQUALITY IN HIGH-WAGE ECONOMIES

Edward Conard

With profits rising and productivity slowing in the face of near-zero interest rates, advocates of income redistribution have conveniently seized on the hypothesis that an increase in crony capitalism and monopoly rents have increased income inequality and slowed middle- and working-class wage growth (Barkai, 2016; De Loecker et al., 2018; Gutierrez and Philippon, 2019; Reich, 2015). If cronyism misallocates resources, theoretically, policy-makers can redistribute income without significantly slowing growth and diminishing prosperity.

By providing no alternative explanation for rising income inequality, proponents of free markets leave such claims largely unaddressed. Their beliefs that higher taxes, more regulation, diminished incentives, and growing government slow growth do not explain the outsized success of so-called superstar companies and the top 0.1 percent. Their reluctance to blame trade with low-wage economies, low-skilled immigration, or technological innovation for slowing low-skilled wage growth leaves charges of increased cronyism unanswered.

COUNTEREVIDENCE OF GROWING CRONYISM

If America's income inequality—the high-wage economy with the most income inequality—is solely the result of misallocated resources, US productivity growth should have slowed relative to other high-wage economies with more equally distributed income. Instead, America's productivity has grown faster than that

Edward Conard, *The Economics of Inequality in High-Wage Economies* In: *United States Income, Wealth, Consumption, and Inequality.* Edited by: Diana Furchtgott-Roth, Oxford University Press (2021). © Oxford University Press. DOI: 10.1093/oso/9780197518199.003.0011.

of other high-wage economies since the early 1990s—the opposite of this hypothesis' prediction (OECD "GDP per Hour Worked," 2019)— despite these economies enjoying unearned gains from the outsized contribution of American innovation, defense expenditures, and pharmaceutical pricing.

Company and industry evidence are also inconsistent with growing cronyism. Market share leaders in consolidating sectors who have invested more than competitors, chiefly in information technology, research, and development, and other intangible assets, have largely driven US productivity growth (Autor et al., 2019; Manyika et al., 2018). These leaders have gained share and are more global in scope (Autor et al., 2019; Manyika et al., 2018). Increased industry consolidation correlates with increased investment in information technology and intangible assets, greater patent intensity, faster productivity growth, and declining labor share (Autor et al., 2019; Bessen, 2019; Manyika et al., 2018). These company and industry trends are common across all high-wage economies despite different antitrust regimes and bargaining strengths of labor unions (Autor et al., 2019). Prices have not risen significantly, and output has expanded faster in increasingly consolidated sectors than in the rest of the economy (Ganapati, 2019; Peltzman, 2018; Autor, 2019). None of this evidence is indicative of oligopolistic behavior, but rather that leaders and followers are competing fiercely. Counterfactual arguments—chiefly whether companies should have borrowed and invested more when profits were high, interest rates were low, and market values exceeded replacement costs—are addressed later in this chapter.

While consolidation has occurred across all industry sectors, it has largely occurred at levels of concentration below levels that antitrust experts view as anticompetitive (Shapiro, 2017). Ironically, consolidation has largely occurred in fragmented and geographically decentralized sectors, such as retail, restaurants, and wholesale distribution, where expansion by national competitors into local markets has increased competition (Hsieh et al., 2016; Rossi-Hansberg et al., 2019). No surprise, McKinsey Global Institute finds that so-called superstar effects—the growing success of the most successful companies—account for less than 20 percent of the decline in labor's share of gross domestic product (GDP) (Manyika et al., 2019), of which only a portion would be unearned.

Rising North American profitability largely stems from the growth of idea-intensive companies with near-zero marginal costs and with profitability twice that of capital-intensive companies with emerging market competitors who have squeezed their profits (Dobbs et al., 2015). But the high-tech sector has been in turmoil, the opposite of cronyism. Excluding Microsoft, the 15 largest NASDAQ technology companies at the peak of the internet bubble have lost almost 60 percent of their market value. Meanwhile, half of today's largest 15 NASDAQ companies, with a combined market capitalization of $3.5 trillion, were worth less than $100 billion in 2000 (Moritz, 2017). With turnover like that, it is hard to see cronyism at work. Instead, competitive advantages derived from intellectual property have been surprisingly fragile and short-lived.

More broadly, nearly half of so-called superstar companies have lost their superstar status in a single business cycle over the past 30 years (Manyika et al., 2018). Nor does there appear to be any erosion in the contestability of market leadership (Manyika et al., 2018).

Were cronyism rising, we should also expect to see an increasingly entrenched status quo. We see the opposite, as Gerald Auten and David Splinter have shown in Chapter 5 of this volume. The turnover of the Fortune 500 (Foster and Kaplan, 2001), CEO tenures (Conference Board, 2013), and the Forbes 400 richest Americans (Kaplan and Rauh, 2013) have also increased. Today, the Forbes 400 richest Americans are increasingly self-made entrepreneurs, not heirs (Kaplan and Rauh, 2013). Most top 0.1 percent earners are undiversified working-age owners of closely held midmarket, skill-intensive businesses that lose almost all of their profits when the owner retires or dies (Smith et al., 2019).

Evidence of rising cronyism is lacking. The largest and most successful companies invest more, produce more innovation, grow faster, pay higher wages, and provide more spillover benefits than the rest of the economy (Atkinson and Lind, 2018; Autor et al., 2019; Babina and Howell, 2019; Moretti, 2019). We are fortunate to have them. It would be reckless for the United States, or any other economy, to dismantle its hard-won success given the lack of compelling evidence supporting rising cronyism.

CONSEQUENCES OF A CONSTRAINED SUPPLY OF PROPERLY TRAINED TALENT

Given that income inequality has risen worldwide concurrent with the commercialization of information technology, growing international trade, immigration, and other structural trends, such as the decline of marriage, hypotheses for growing inequality must address these factors. Information technology has opened a window of investment opportunities to create new technology, deploy the technology to gather better information, and use the information to make better decisions and produce innovation. With investment opportunities exceeding the supply of properly trained talent needed to capitalize on them, the 80th to 99th percentile's share of pretax income has increased modestly (Congressional Budget Office [CBO], 2019; Blau and Kahn, 2005; Benzell and Brynjolfsson, 2019). So have returns to education in America relative to other high-wage economies (Organisation for Economic Cooperation and Development (OECD) Education at a Glance, 2019).

At the same time, trade with low-wage economies and low-skilled immigration have provided an unconstrained supply of low-skilled labor. Aging demographics and slowing population growth, especially in high-wage economies, have also reduced the need to expand capacity with existing technology and, together with trade surpluses (Conard, 2016), flooded markets with risk-averse savings (Summers, 2014). A significant decline in the cost of capital goods further reduces savings constraints (Summers, 2014; International Monetary Fund [IMF], 2015). As a result, properly trained talent, rather than savings and low-skilled labor, now constrains growth. Declining research productivity (Bloom et al., 2017; Gordon, 2016), the end of one-time productivity gains from saturating high-wage populations with education, and the failure of other high-wage economies to contribute their share of innovation, exacerbate constraints on the supply of talent.

Constraints on the supply of talent are particularly acute in the United States. On an OECD-administered academic skills test, 8.5 percent of adult Americans score at the highest numeracy levels, and 28.7 percent score at the lowest skill levels. America has 0.3 high-scoring adults for every low-scoring adult. In contrast, 14.2 percent of German adults score at the highest levels and 18.4 percent score at the lowest. Astonishingly, Germany has nearly three times more high-scoring adults per low-scoring adult than the United States. Scandinavia has more than four times as many. Japan has nearly eight times as many (OECD "Survey of Adult Skills," 2019). America has half as much talent per capita as the other most successful high-wage economies and twice the supervisory needs. Cross-country comparisons that fail to account for these enormous differences— comparisons of wages and productivity as information magnifies the value of skill, for example—produce grossly distorted conclusions.

A constrained supply of properly trained talent has cascading consequences. Markets have logically dedicated a greater share of properly trained talent to increasing the productivity of constrained talent. Previously, talented workers created mass-market products produced by domestic blue-collar consumers— an allocation of talent that benefited the middle and working classes. Now they create information and information technologies, such as spreadsheets, for decision-makers and innovators. This reallocation of talent disproportionately increases the productivity of the most productive workers and consumes talent that would otherwise increase the productivity of domestic lesser-skilled workers. This slows low-skilled productivity growth and growth elsewhere in the economy.

When the supply of low-skilled labor is unconstrained, increases in high-skilled productivity disproportionately raise low-skilled employment rather than low-skilled wages. This spreads constrained talent over a greater supply of labor, which slows low-skilled productivity and wage growth further. Since the early 1980s, US employment, excluding offshore workers, has grown twice as fast as in Germany and France and three times faster than in Japan (OECD "Labour Force," 2019). Today more than 42 million foreign-born adults live in the United States (Radford, 2019). Low-skilled immigrants, offshore workers, and properly trained talent have been the chief beneficiaries of this growth.

When the window of investment opportunities exceeds the constrained supply of talent, additional high-skilled productivity disproportionately increases investment to raise high-skilled productivity rather than expanding high-skilled resources devoted to raising low-skilled productivity, especially when insights that make high-skilled workers more productive are harder for competitors to copy than innovative uses for low-skilled labor.

A constrained supply of properly trained talent not only limits the discovery of investment-worthy ideas, it also increases risk by restricting the supply of engineers and managers tasked with reducing costs and risks. The allocation of a constrained supply of talent to attractive investment opportunities created by the advent of information technology increases the risk of other investments. Higher risks consume investors' and talent's willingness and capacity to bear risk. This occurs even more when the creation of valuable information-related innovation is riskier than other investment opportunities, and even when those risks are unsystematic, since a large portion of risk-takers—entrepreneurs, for example—do not enjoy the luxury of diversification. Limits on the economy's willingness and capacity to take risk lower interest rates in the face of an unconstrained supply of risk-averse savings.

The advent of information technology has opened a window of investment opportunities that has constrained the supply of properly trained talent at a time when trade with low-wage economies, low-skilled immigration, trade deficits, and aging demographics have relieved constraints to low-skilled labor and capital. The economy has logically allocated an increasing share of talent to raising the productivity of constrained resources, namely talent. This allocation of talent slows the growth of low-skilled productivity and other endeavors not aligned with increasing high-skilled productivity.

VALUE OF RETURNS EXCEEDING THE COST OF CAPITAL

Unlike investments that expand capacity using existing technology, hard-won innovation bubbles up unpredictably from a large pool of costly failure. The prospect of returns greater than the cost of capital is the chief justification for risk-taking. If innovations were easy to copy, investors would wait for others to innovate, and the rate of innovation would grind to halt.

Fortunately, information-related innovations have captured first-mover advantages and other economies of scale that are difficult for competitors to duplicate, even more so when talent constrains growth and slows the convergence of followers to the technological frontier, which we have seen (Andrews et al., 2016; Manyika et al., 2018). Increasingly clever patenting strategies may have also slowed followers (Akcigit and Ates, 2019). Consistent with these economics, returns exceeding the cost of capital are confined to the most successful companies (Manyika et al., 2018).

A larger economy increases the value of success, which spurs increased risk-taking when success captures excess returns. As the economy grows larger relative to the individuals who compose it, success will grow larger relative to the incomes of median workers—teachers, truck drivers, and nurses—whose wages are constrained by the number of customers they can serve.

At the same time, information-derived innovation scales with less cost and investment than the capital- and low-skilled labor-intensive manufacturing of yesteryear. Successful information technology startups, such as Google and Facebook, have scaled to economy-wide success without much need for investors or labor. When the production of intangible assets requires risk-taking and success produces excess returns, lower costs and larger payoffs for success can spur increased risk-taking. This holds even if the value of innovation is declining relative to the economy and productivity growth is slowing. Consistent with the growing need to take risk, the success of companies has grown increasingly dispersed (Berlingieri et al., 2017).

Improbable success limits talent's ability to capture excess returns unless talented workers bear the cost of failure. Rather than demanding premium pay, properly trained workers have accepted less pay to gain valuable exposure to the technological frontier (Tambe et al., 2019). In addition to more interesting and prestigious work, this exposure provides invaluable on-the-job training, a network of valuable relationships with brilliant colleagues, and valuable ideas that increase the likelihood of entrepreneurial success (Babina and Howell, 2019; Moretti, 2019). Talented workers have also shared risk by accepting equity in lieu of pay, which has distorted traditional measures of labor's share of GDP (Eisfeldt et al., 2019). Uncertain returns, rising equity grants, pay-for-performance, and entrepreneurialism have concentrated returns extracted by talent in a small group of successful risk-takers. As such, rising income inequality is largely confined to the top sliver of success—the 0.1 percent or 0.01 percent (Auten and Splinter, 2018; Gold, 2017).

Successful risk-taking has gradually built institutions at the technological frontier. In turn, exposure to the technological frontier has increased the expected value of success for talented and well-trained risk-takers (Babina and Howell, 2019; Moretti, 2019). In America, fewer restrictions on creative destruction, economies of scale afforded by a larger economy and common language, and greater R&D defense spending increase the payoff and likelihood of successful risk-taking.

With higher expected payoffs, talented Americans have received better training, worked longer hours (Bowles and Park, 2005; Kuhn and Lozano, 2008; OECD "Hours Worked," 2019), and taken more entrepreneurial risk than their counterparts in Europe and Japan. A larger pool of determined risk-takers has produced a greater number of outsized successes.

The share of talented risk-takers and the productivity of America's most productive workers are far greater than many economists realize. Despite having fewer than half as many high-scorers per capita as other high-wage economies, American entrepreneurs have produced six times as many startups valued at more than $1 billion than has Europe (CB Insights, 2019)—a broad indication of risk-taking and innovativeness. Similarly, the market values of America's high-tech companies—an indication of the productivity of its workers at the technological frontier—are astonishingly high compared to German manufacturing companies ("Does Deutschland Do Digital?" 2017). Only in America have the returns been high enough to spur a substantial increase in risk-taking. Fortunately, the rest of the world benefits from America's success.

Advocates of income redistribution insist that the ongoing success of Silicon Valley in the face of a higher California tax rate indicates that higher payoffs for risk-taking do not increase risk-taking significantly (Hacker and Pierson, 2017; Krugman, 2019), despite a host of evidence to the contrary (Akcigit et al., 2015, 2018; Moretti and Wilson, 2017; Moretti and Wilson, 2019; Rauh, 2019). They disregard the amplifying effect of Silicon Valley on the expected payoff for risk-taking, which overwhelms small differences in state tax rates (Babina and Howell, 2019; Moretti, 2019) and they ignore critical long-term effects that are near-impossible to measure, such as gradual increases in training and risk-taking. Given the higher expected payoffs afforded by proximity to Silicon Valley, and the resulting increase in risk-taking and innovation that Silicon Valley and America enjoy relative to Europe and Japan, it is hard to believe after-tax payoffs do not affect the willingness of people to take risk.

The commercialization of the internet in the 1990s similarly raised expected payoffs for successful innovation far in excess of tax increases and motivated increased risk-taking, as evidenced by the rising number of internet startups. Armies of Hollywood aspirants, increased aggressiveness of World War II fighter pilots in the face of others' success (Ager et al., 2016), and swelling participation in state lotteries as payoffs rise all suggest that the value of fame and fortune spurs individuals to take risk.

When risk-taking produces success, high *ex-post* returns to success are hardly evidence of unearned profits. *Ex-ante* returns are the relevant measure of whether profits have been earned. Since 2000, venture capital—an indicator of returns to innovation more broadly—has been mediocre at best (Ivashina and Lerner, 2019), especially given the unsystematic risks faced by entrepreneurs and employees.

For the same reason, high *ex-post* rewards for successful risk-takers will not necessarily motivate increased investment or risk-taking, especially when competitors already inhabit previously unoccupied niches. Good fortune does not prove additional risks are worth taking. Expected *ex-ante* returns drive behavior. When success entails risk, we cannot conclude that the high *ex-post* stock market values relative to replacement costs should have increased investment but for rising cronyism.

As the productivity of researchers and innovators declines, expected *ex-ante* returns and risk-taking will decline unless the payoffs for success increase. With research productivity declining as investment has continued unabated, we should celebrate rising payoffs for successful risk-taking as good fortune.

There is ample evidence of the declining productivity of researchers and innovators. Not only has the growth of multifactor productivity slowed, but the productivity of researchers also appears to be declining as science grows increasingly complex (Bloom et al., 2017). Additional economy-wide productivity gains from general-purpose information technology, such as artificial intelligence, have proved difficult to create (Brynjolfsson et al., 2018; Gordon, 2016). While the growth of education in the rest of the world has increased the number of scientists, engineers, and business executives searching for and implementing innovation, so far, the United States alone—where properly trained talent is constrained—has predominately driven the technological frontier. Growing payoffs for success are critical for spurring investment in the face of declining research productivity.

While productivity growth has slowed, there appears to be no significant slowdown in the advancement of the technological frontier (Andrews et al., 2016). Instead, venture capital investment and investment by Facebook, Apple, Microsoft, Google, Amazon, and others in Silicon Valley now exceed their 2000 peak (Frothy.com, 2014; National Venture Capital Association, 2019.). Without rising payoffs for successful risk-taking, investment would decline as research productivity has declined. Fortunately, Google cannot afford to neglect investment in quantum computing because the consequences of someone else's success are too risky. Redistributing the value of success eliminates the incentive to make risky investments.

More broadly, while investment in capital goods slowed relative to GDP in the aftermath of the financial crisis, it has not slowed over the long term when economists properly adjust tangible investment for the disproportionate deflation in the price of capital goods (Summers, 2014; IMF, 2015). As the economy has shifted from capital intensity to knowledge intensity, investment has shifted from plant and equipment to salaries of properly trained talent tasked with designing a better future (Corrado et al., 2012; Haskel and Westlake, 2018). When economists account for these changes, there has been no downward trend in investment relative to GDP. Failed risk-taking also washes away accumulated investment, leaving true investment understated.

Skeptics point to declining startups as evidence of declining risk-taking (Decker et al., 2014) and slowing productivity growth, even though productivity growth can slow for a litany of unrelated reasons and investment will continue if the returns for success are large enough. While the number of startups has declined, high-potential US startups—chiefly high-tech startups—have neared their 2000 peak, a peak that was far above trend line (Guzman and Stern, 2019). Consolidation in the retail, restaurant, and distribution sectors curtailed the vast number of mom-and-pop startups that largely allocate demand between competing firms and do little to advance the technological frontier and grow productivity. With its thirst for talent, the economy gobbles up, trains, and redeploys potential "mom-and-pop" talent, leaving a vacuum of startups in its wake (US Bureau of Labor Statistics "National Business Employment Dynamics Data by Firm Size Class," 2019).

Improbable innovations bubble up unpredictably from a large pool of failure. Outsized rewards are *sine qua non* for risk-taking. As research productivity declines, we need higher returns to motive the risk-taking that produces it. We do not need outsized returns to motive success *per se*; we need them to motive a large pool of failure.

Success produces institutional capabilities—the expertise, economies of scale, and returns—needed to explore and advance the technological frontier. Exploration of the frontier produces valuable spillover that benefits the rest of the economy. Spillover raises the rewards for risk-taking, which motivates further risk-taking.

Given the failure of Europe and Japan to innovate during this time when information technology is transforming the economy and a constrained supply of talent slows growth, it would be reckless to confiscate outsized rewards for success, whether from companies or individuals. The argument that outsized returns were unexpected *ex ante* ignores the armies of American risk-takers who have followed in the wake of the success of Bill Gates, Steve Jobs, and others like them. Redistributing the ownership of future cash flows to consumers will not only demotivate risk-taking, but it will also diminish the amount of risk and investment owners demand businesses take. Less risk-taking and investment will slow growth and diminish prosperity.

RECONCILIATION WITH LOW INTEREST RATES

One of the better arguments for rising cronyism questions why profits in excess of the rental cost of capital—chiefly assets times the real interest rate—have risen since the 1980s. Leaving aside the difficulty of subtracting the unreproducible profits of successful risk-takers from the broader pool of business profits, some say that rising cronyism may have allowed increased profits.

Historical evidence, however, runs contrary to this argument. Excess profits as a share of GDP were higher in the 1950s and 1960s, when industry consolidation was lower than it is today. They reached their lowest point in the 1970s and 1980s, when real interest rates soared, and they have risen as interest rates have fallen (Karabarbounis and Neiman, 2018; Rognlie, 2018). Rather than being correlated with rising cronyism, excess profits have been inversely correlated with interest rates. Low interest rates, rather than rising cronyism, appear to give rise to excess profits. The same pattern occurred in real estate where there should be little, if any, ability to diminish competition (Karabarbounis et al., 2018).

When rates fell after the 1980s and excess profits grew, one might have expected increased borrowing to strengthen competition. An alternative version of the argument asks why business did not borrow more when real interest rates fell and profits were robust unless cronyism prevented it. A glut of savings, a constrained supply of talent, and excess returns for successful risk-taking provide a more plausible explanation than rising cronyism for why business did not borrow more.

Secular stagnation argues that aging demographics slow growth and increase savings relative to a diminished need for capacity-expanding investment (Summers, 2014). Savings in excess of investment reduce interest rates and slow growth.

Trade deficits add to the glut of savings. Manufacturing-driven economies with aging demographics and more domestic savings than their demand for investment—namely China, Germany, and Japan—deploy otherwise unneeded savings by running trade surpluses, largely with the United States, to avoid employment and wage declines.

Had the domestic demand for savings pulled offshore savings into the US economy via trade deficits, interest rates would have risen as trade deficits rose. For decades, real interest rates have fallen as trade deficits have risen (Federal Reserve Board "10-Year Treasury Constant Maturity Rate," 2019; OECD "Balance of Payments: Current Account Balance as a % of GDP," 2019). This indicates that an increase in the supply of offshore savings has fueled trade deficits.

Reluctance to displace workers catches surplus exporters in a vicious cycle. Manufacturing productivity gains—gains exporters need to remain competitive—require larger trade surpluses to achieve a given level of employment. Interest rates must fall to equilibrate the supply and demand for savings. Otherwise, rising currency exchange rates will render the price of their exports unattractive. While trade deficits have declined (OECD "Balance of Payments: Current Account Balance as a % of GDP," 2019), so far, near-zero interest rates have not fully deterred offshore savers.

Rather than export precious risk-bearing capital, surplus exporters have bought low-risk US government-guaranteed debt, displacing domestic risk-averse savers. With an increasing share of manufacturing capacity moving offshore, America has little need for risk-averse savings best suited for low-risk capacity expansion. Innovation-driven growth needs risk-bearing capital willing to suffer significant losses, which surplus exporters have been reluctant to provide.

With its constrained supply of properly trained talent preoccupied with more productive endeavors—namely, capitalizing on risky information-related opportunities—business has had limited appetite for bearing the additional risk of borrowing and investing risk-averse savings. Risk-averse savings flowed into real estate (Rognlie, 2015) and through real estate to "subprime consumption" prior to the financial crisis as homeowners borrowed against the rising value of their homes and consumed the proceeds (Mian and Sufi, 2015). At the same time, Germany financed Greek consumption. China built empty apartment buildings (Poon, 2019). Japan financed fiscal deficits. Since the crisis, US fiscal deficits and the resulting increase in low-risk government-guaranteed debt have largely consumed proceeds from the repayment of mortgage debt (Federal Reserve Board "Financial Stability Report," 2019).

Business' failure to take the risks to borrow and invest this flood of risk-averse savings is hardly evidence of rising cronyism, especially when, at every point in the economic cycle, business borrowing had already reached historical highs relative to GDP (Federal Reserve Board "Financial Stability Report," 2019). With an abundant supply of risk-averse savings relative to the demand for low-risk investment, growth has been lackluster and real interest rates have remained low while the valuation of well-positioned companies with hard-to-replicate capabilities near the technological frontier have soared.

STRUCTURAL TRENDS SLOWING LOW-SKILLED PRODUCTIVITY GROWTH

Were the success of superstar companies and the 0.1 percent not growing concurrently with the slowing growth of lesser-skilled wages, claims that the success of one comes at the expense of the other would be less persuasive. While the allocation of constrained talent to producing innovation rather than raising low-skilled productivity likely contributes to the relative slowing of low-skilled productivity growth, structural changes independent of information technology, chiefly an increase in the supply of low-skilled labor and its substitutes, have slowed the growth of lesser-skilled wages relative to GDP in high-wage economies.

The growth of information disproportionately increases high-skilled productivity. Algebraically, this slows low-skilled wage growth relative to GDP, even if low-skilled workers are better off from otherwise faster growth.

The allocation of constrained talent to endeavors other than increasing the productivity of low-skilled workers slows low-skilled productivity growth. This is especially acute in the United States given the skew of its demographics toward low-skilled workers (OECD "Survey of Adult Skills," 2019) and America's outsized success producing innovation.

As high-wage economies have automated and offshored manufacturing and shifted employment to domestic services, properly trained talent has migrated to expert-based services. Talented workers have increasingly clustered in companies largely composed of high-paid workers, such as Microsoft and Goldman Sachs (Song et al., 2018), with the know-how to magnify the productivity of the most productive workers. Meanwhile, companies such as Apple and General Motors have increasingly outsourced low-skilled labor to companies with a preponderance of low-paid workers. This sorting has produced large shifts in the allocation of skill between companies.

A large share of low-skilled workers now works in the low-skilled service sector where, aside from distribution, productivity growth has been significantly slower (Remes et al., 2018) without the capital-intensive centralized "command and control" structure of manufacturing. With less than 9 percent of the US workforce left in manufacturing, faster manufacturing productivity growth contributed less to the productivity growth of lower-skilled workers (US Bureau of Labor Statistics "All Employees: Manufacturing," 2019; US Bureau of Labor Statistics "Manufacturing Sector: Real Output," 2019).

Dividing companies that predominately produce information, such as media, finance, and information technology, with their largely white-collar workforces, from companies that predominately produce physical products, reveals large differences in productivity growth and levels of investment in information technology. The information-oriented companies have invested substantially more in information technology and grown productivity 2.7 percent per year over the past 15 years. The physical labor-oriented companies have invested less in information technology and have only improved productivity 0.7 percent per year (Mandel and Swanson, 2017). The latter group includes logistics, distribution, and manufacturing—sectors where productivity has grown substantially faster than the economy as a whole (Mandel and Swanson, 2017; Remes et al., 2018). Thus the productivity of the rest of this group—sectors that have added workers—has grown more slowly than 0.7 percent per year. These differences surely reflect differences in the productivity of high-skilled knowledge workers and low-skilled workers more broadly and are directionally consistent with other estimates of differences in high- and low-skilled productivity growth (Lazear, 2019).

At the same time, disproportionate increases in the supply of low-skilled labor from automation, trade with low-wage economies, and low-skilled immigration increase the relative supply of lower-skilled workers. An increase in the supply of low-skilled labor lowers the marginal product of labor and spreads constrained talent over a greater number of low-skilled workers, which slows low-skilled productivity growth. An increasing share of talent must be devoted to engineering and maintaining automation for example. The arrival of low-skilled immigrants spreads constrained talent, a portion of which is devoted to low-skilled supervision, over a greater number of workers. Even with balanced trade, high-wage economies largely buy low-skilled offshore labor and sell high-skilled labor to the rest of the world. This puts downward pressure on low-skilled wages and upward pressure on high-skilled wages. On net, talented engineers at companies such as Apple and Ford Motor Company increasingly design products and factories that employ offshore workers.

Low-skilled domestic workers disproportionately bear more of the cost and enjoy less of the benefits from trade with low-wage economies and low-skilled immigration. To the extent that lower priced goods offset the downward pressure that trade and immigration put on wages, low-skilled workers bear most of the cost of lower wages but capture only 40 percent of the benefits from lower prices. The top 20 percent of earners capture 40 percent of the benefits. Retirees capture 15 percent, and the non-working poor capture 5 percent of the benefits (Conard, 2016, see Figure 10.1). The disproportionate sharing of costs and benefits increases income inequality.

Trade deficits add to the supply of low-skilled labor. They also add substantially to the glut of risk-averse savings. Prior to the financial crisis, the incremental supply of offshore savings indirectly funded increased consumption through increased mortgage lending (Federal Reserve Board "Financial Stability Report," 2019; Mian and Sufi, 2015). The pressure to consume the large influx of risk-averse savings to maximize employment and wages indirectly destabilized the banking system (Conard, 2012; Reinhart and Rogoff, 2009)—a naturally unstable equilibrium—which led to the financial crisis and deep recession. Deleveraging by fearful businesses and households (Federal Reserve Board "Financial Stability Report," 2019) in the wake of the financial crisis produced the slowest recovery since the Great Depression. With employers firing marginal, easy-to-replace, low-skilled workers first and rehiring them last, no group has paid a more painful price (Aaronson et al., 2019; Benigo et al., 2015).

When properly trained talent constrains growth, and low-skilled workers are displaced by trade, high-skilled entrepreneurs may never arrive to reemploy workers at high wages, especially if the talent has moved to Silicon Valley and outsourced their blue-collar work to China. Research finds that many towns that have lost manufacturing have been slow to recover lost wages (Autor et al., 2016). The productivity of the rural economy and smaller cities is no longer converging with large cities (Ganong and Shoag, 2017; Giannone, 2017; Winship, 2019). Both are indications that the talent necessary for growth in an information-driven economy has moved away.

Trade with low-wage economies also makes it more difficult for rural Americans to ship their production competitively to faster growing urban economies. Onshore producers cannot compete without productivity gains that minimize domestic labor. Urban migration of talent and trade with low-wage economies isolates rural blue-collar Americans, leaving them with fewer benefits from trade. With less supervisory talent, rural blue-collar service sector productivity has slowed to a crawl.

Soaring real estate prices and other urban costs preclude blue-collar Americans from following high-skilled Americans who are flocking to a handful of fast growth cities—San Francisco, New York, Los Angeles, Boston, and Seattle—at the technological frontier (Erdmann, 2019; Hsieh and Moretti, 2019). Half of American employment gains since 2010 have come from just 20 cities

(Muro and Whiton, 2018). Low-skilled wages in these cities are two to three times higher than wages in the rest of the country (Moretti, 2010). But landlords have captured a large share of those gains through higher rents (Hornbeck and Moretti, 2018). For the first time, low-skilled after-rent wages are lower in larger cities than elsewhere (Hoxie et al., 2019).

Native-born middle-class workers are now moving away from coastal cities (Ganong and Shoag, 2017; Autor, 2019). Low-skilled immigrants willing to accept low after-rent wages have replaced them. Workers end up sorted by geography, with lesser-skilled Americans precluded from earning higher after-rent wages in faster growing cities filled with high-skilled workers (Clark and Cummins, 2018). We should expect workers to be less supportive of growth that excludes them.

Advocates of low-skilled immigration often ask, "Without low-skilled immigrants, who will do the jobs Americans do not want to do?" This argument ignores the effect of price on the demand for low-skilled labor or the effect of supply on the marginal product of low-skilled labor. If the supply of low-skilled labor were smaller, Chileans would grow fruit for America and, with higher low-skilled wages, the demand for low value-added tasks like landscaping would decline. Farmers might lose their investments, but these shifts would increase the marginal product of domestic low-skilled labor. In turn, low-skilled wages would rise, albeit in a smaller economy with slower growth. It is not hard to see why some workers may prefer that.

Yes, the supply of domestic labor—low-skilled immigrants in the case of America—creates its own demand, but at what marginal product of labor? An unconstrained supply of low-skilled labor will drive the shadow price of labor down to the marginal product of unskilled workers serving unskilled workers.

The value of consumer surpluses derived from an abundant supply of lower-skilled labor may be greater than the foregone wages of low-skilled workers. But, in that case, we should not blame the misallocation of resources or the success of the most productive workers for the slow growth of low-skilled wages relative to GDP. Instead, we should recognize that the productivity of high-skilled workers, especially the productivity of the most productive workers, has put upward pressure on the demand for low-skilled labor.

Other structural trends also slow low-skilled productivity growth. Governments have increased spending as a share of GDP, reduced investment, expanded income redistribution, and increased regulations. These policies slow reported productivity growth.

Onetime gains from testing, sorting, and saturating the population with productivity-enhancing education have waned. Further low-skilled productivity gains from education have been difficult to achieve (US Department of Education "Long-Term Trend Mathematics Assessments," 2019). With more women investing in higher education, men and women meet and marry through education or subsequent employment, so some children are increasingly differentiated through their parents' educational levels. (Chiappori et al., 2017; Greenwood et al., 2014).

Some proponents of income redistribution insist that the determination of upper income parents, who spend their incomes on tutoring and similar efforts to give their children advantages, blocks the rest of the population from valuable income-enhancing educational opportunities (Reeves, 2017). But this hypothesis does not square with the evidence. Rich, well-prepared students now compete more fiercely for fewer admission slots at prestigious schools (Thompson 2013). Meanwhile, less prestigious universities, where admissions have expanded to meet demand, offer curriculum at all levels of difficulty (e.g., engineering at state universities). Research shows that getting an education and earning an academic credential are akin to running a marathon: your time matters more than which marathon you run (Dale and Krueger, 2011). There is no reduction in the opportunity for any student to earn academic training and credentials at every level of difficulty.

Weakening of the family, religion, community, and respect for authority also undermines productivity growth. Today, 40 percent of American children are born out of wedlock (Winship 2017). Children raised without responsible fathers have achieved less income mobility (Chetty et al., 2014). The weakening of families disproportionately afflicts low-skilled workers.

No surprise, a recent study finds US incomes are more widely dispersed among 25-year-olds than they were in the past and that median 25-year-old incomes have drifted downward. The study also finds lifetime incomes grow similarly across the income spectrum as they have historically and concludes that the wider dispersion of 25-year-old incomes is the chief driver of lifetime income inequality (Guvenen et al., 2017).

Whether or not lower-skilled workers are net beneficiaries of trade, trade deficits, or low-skilled immigration, it seems likely that each of these factors has contributed to income inequality by slowing the growth of lower-skilled wages relative to GDP. Moreover, rising trade, trade deficits, and low-skilled immigration have occurred at a time when information technology constrained the supply of talent. Automation, trade with low-wage economies and low-skilled immigration have spread talent devoted to increasing low-skilled productivity even thinner. Structural factors, such as the saturation of education, assortative mating, the breakdown of the family, and employment shifting from manufacturing to services, have slowed low-skilled productivity growth further.

CONCLUSION AND RECOMMENDATIONS

Each economic era presents its own set of opportunities and challenges. With the advent of information technology, global trade, trade deficits, and low-skilled immigration, properly trained talent, rather than savings or lower-skilled labor, now constrains growth. To succeed, the economy must allocate resources appropriately. Where talent previously created products and jobs for lesser-skilled workers, it now creates information to increase the productivity of decision-makers and innovators.

Given the disruption to established businesses that has occurred over the past three decades, it is hard to believe that cronyism has been the predominant driver of increased income inequality. Income inequality and profits have risen across all high-wage economies concurrently with the increased use of information technology, low-skilled immigration, trade with low-wage economies, trade deficits, and structural factors that slow low-skilled productivity growth. Productivity in the United States—the country with the most income inequality—has grown faster than other high-wage economies despite a much smaller share of high-scoring workers. A growing economy relative to the workers who compose it, a reduction in the cost of achieving economy-wide success in today's information-intensive economy, and increased risk-taking to achieve lottery-like success provide a more consistent explanation for the growing success of the 0.1 percent and superstar companies than does growing cronyism.

An abundance of evidence indicates that growing inequality stems from free enterprise logically rationing constrained resources, as one should expect. Blaming cronyism and unearned rents for income inequality conveniently suggests that high-wage economies can redistribute income without slowing growth. If inequality stems from the logical allocation of resources, we should expect income redistribution to slow growth and reduce prosperity by diminishing the expected payoffs for hard work and successful risk-taking. That is a dangerous outcome given the impending cost of retiring baby boomers, workforce demographics shifting toward lesser-skilled workers, and the growing military threat of China.

Advocates of redistribution point to the competitiveness of Scandinavia to dismiss these concerns (Krugman, 2018). But an abundance of high test-scorers allows Scandinavia to remain competitive despite lower high-skilled productivity than the United States. A more homogeneous Scandinavian workforce with higher scores and greater earning potential than the US workforce also reduces redistribution's disincentives for low-potential earners to work. Scandinavia's results do not indicate that the heavy hand of income redistribution will not erode competitiveness elsewhere.

Despite having half as much talent and nearly twice as many low-skilled workers per capita as the next most successful high-wage economies, chiefly northern European economies, no other economy comes close to producing the innovation, prosperity, and demand for middle- and working-class workers as the US economy. Without benefiting from the disproportionate contribution of American-made innovation, those economies would be poorer and slower growing, even more so if they had America's demographics and resulting shortage of high-skilled supervision.

In truth, evidence supporting cronyism as the driver of inequality is lacking. Income redistribution is a riskier policy than its advocates admit, given the success of the United States relative to Europe and Japan.

To accelerate lower-skilled wage growth without slowing growth overall, economic policy must increase the expected payoff for success and raise the ratio of high- to low-skilled workers. If education is unable to produce further improvements, increasing high-skilled immigration will be the only realistic opportunity for improving the ratio of high- to low-skilled workers before the baby boomers retire. Reducing subsidies for studying curriculum where the supply of students far exceeds the demands of customers may ease constraints to properly trained talent, but the results are likely to be small and gradual. Reengineering poorly designed regulations and taxes that lower returns to successful risk-taking may gradually increase the productivity of high-skilled workers, but they will also increase income inequality. Perhaps inequality is a small price to pay for greater prosperity.

In the meantime, education, the media, and government support must prepare lesser-skilled people for success in a lightly supervised service economy that offers a wide variety of opportunities but where the safety net snares vulnerable people. While innovation and trade are essential to long-term growth and competitiveness, tax policy must recognize that low-skilled workers in high-wage economies bear a disproportionate share of the costs of trade, trade deficits, fiscal deficits, and low-skilled immigration while receiving only a portion of the benefits. Many of today's policies slow the growth of lesser-skilled wages relative to GDP. We can do better.

REFERENCES

Aaronson, Stephanie, Mary Daly, William Wascher, and David Wilcox. September 2019. "Okun Revisited: Who Benefits Most from a Strong Economy." Federal Reserve Board. https://www.federalreserve.gov/econres/feds/files/2019072pap.pdf

Ager, Philipp, Leonardo Bursztyn, and Hans-Joachim Voth. December 2016. "Killer Incentives: Status Competition and Pilot Performance during World War II." National Bureau of Economic Research (NBER). http://www.nber.org/papers/w22992

Akcigit, Ufuk, and Sina Ates. May 2019. "What Happened to US Business Dynamism?" NBER. https://www.nber.org/papers/w25756

Akcigit, Ufuk, Salome Baslandze, and, Stefanie Stantcheva. March 2015. "Taxation and the International Mobility of Inventors." NBER. http://www.nber.org/papers/w21024

Akcigit, Ufuk, John Grigsby, Tom Nicholas, and Stefanie Stantcheva. September 2018. "Taxation and Innovation in the 20th Century." NBER. http://www.nber.org/papers/w24982

Andrews, Dan, Chiara Criscuolo, and Peter Gal. September 27, 2016. "The Global Productivity Slowdown, Technology Divergence and Public Policy: A Firm Level Perspective." Brookings Papers on Economic Activity. https://www.brookings.edu/wp-content/uploads/2016/08/andrews-et-al.pdf

Atkinson, Robert, and Michael Lind. 2018. *Big Is Beautiful: Debunking the Myth of Small Business.* Cambridge and London: MIT Press.

Auten, Gerald, and David Splinter. August 23, 2018. "Income Inequality in the United States: Using Tax Data to Measure Long-term Trends." US Treasury Department and Joint Committee on Taxation. http://davidsplinter.com/AutenSplinter-Tax_Data_and_Inequality.pdf

Autor, David, David Dorn, and Gordon Hanson. January 2016. "The China Shock: Learning from Labor Market Adjustment to Large Changes in Trade." NBER. http://www.nber.org/papers/w21906

Autor, David, David Dorn, Lawrence Katz, Christina Patterson, and John Van Reenen. 2019. "The Fall of the Labor Share and the Rise of Superstar Firms." NBER. https://economics.mit.edu/files/12979

Autor, David. February 2019. "Work of the Past, Work of the Future." NBER. https://www.nber.org/papers/w25588

Babina, Tania, and Sabrina Howell. December 2019. "Entrepreneurial Spillovers from Corporate R&D." NBER. https://www.nber.org/papers/w25360

Barkai, Simcha. 2016. "Declining Labor and Capital Shares." London Business School. https://home.uchicago.edu/~barkai/doc/BarkaiDecliningLaborCapital.pdf

Benigo, Gianluca, Nathan Converse, and Luca Fornaro. 2015. "Large Capital Inflows, Sectoral Allocation, and Economic Performance." International Finance Discussion Papers. https://www.federalreserve.gov/econresdata/ifdp/2015/files/ifdp1132.pdf

Benzell, Seth, and Erik Brynjolfsson. February 2019. "Digital Abundance and Scarce Genius: Implications for Wages, Interest Rates, and Growth." NBER. https://www.nber.org/papers/w25585

Berlingieri, Giuseppe, Patrick Blanchenay, and Chiara Criscuolo. May 12, 2017. "The Great Divergence," Organisation for Economic Co-operation and Development (OECD). http://www.oecd-ilibrary.org/science-and-technology/the-great-divergence-s_953f3853-en

Bessen, James. June 2019. "Information Technology and Industry Concentration." Boston University School of Law, Law and Economics Research Paper. https://papers.ssrn.com/sol3/papers.cfm?abstract_id=3044730

Blau, Francine, and Lawrence Kahn. February 2005. "Do Cognitive Test Scores Explain Higher US Wage Inequality?" *The Review of Economics and Statistics.*

http://www2.econ.iastate.edu/classes/econ521/Orazem/Papers/Blau_Kahn_cognitive%20returns.pdf

Bloom, Nicholas, Charles Jones, John Van Reenen, and Michael Webb. September 6, 2017. "Are Ideas Getting Harder to Find?" NBER. http://www.nber.org/papers/w23782?utm_campaign=ntw&utm_medium=email&utm_source=ntw

Bloom, Nicholas, Erik Brynjolfsson, Lucia Foster, Ron Jarmin, Megha Patnaik, Itay Saporta-Eksten, and John Van Reenen. May 2019. "What Drives Differences in Management Practices?" American Economic Review. https://www.aeaweb.org/articles?id=10.1257/aer.20170491&&from=f

Bowles, Samuel, and Yongjin Park. November 2005. "Emulation, Inequality, and Work Hours: Was Thorsten Veblen Right?" The Economic Journal. http://onlinelibrary.wiley.com/doi/10.1111/j.1468-0297.2005.01042.x/abstract

Brynjolfsson, Erik, Daniel Rock, and Chad Syverson. October 2018. "The Productivity J-Curve: How Intangibles Complement General Purpose Technologies." NBER. https://www.nber.org/papers/w25148

CB Insights. Accessed October 2, 2019. "The Global Unicorn Club: Current Private Companies Valued At $1B= (including whisper valuations)." CB Insights. https://www.cbinsights.com/research-unicorn-companies

Chetty, Raj, Nathaniel Hendren, Patrick Kline, Emmanuel Saez, and Nicholas Turner. January 2014. "Is the United States Still a Land of Opportunity? Recent Trends in Intergenerational Mobility." NBER. http://www.nber.org/papers/w19844

Chiappori, Pierre-André, Bernard Salanié, and Yoram Weiss. August 2017. "Partner Choice, Investment in Children, and the Marital College Premium." American Economic Review. https://www.aeaweb.org/articles?id=10.1257/aer.20150154

Clark, Gregory, and Neil Cummins. July 29, 2018. "The Big Sort: The Decline of Northern England, 1780–2018." Center for Economic and Policy Research. https://voxeu.org/article/decline-northern-england-1780-2018

Conard, Edward. 2012. Unintended Consequences: Why Everything You've Been Told About the Economy Is Wrong. New York: Portfolio Penguin.

Conard, Edward. 2016. The Upside of Inequality: How Good Intentions Undermine the Middle Class. New York: Portfolio Penguin, figure tables, 10-1.

Conference Board. 2013. "Departing CEO Age and Tenure." The Conference Board, CEO Succession Practices. https://www.conference-board.org/retrievefile.cfm?filename=TCB-CW-019.pdf&type=subsite

Congressional Budget Office (CBO). July 9, 2019. "The Distribution of Household Income, 2016." cbo.gov/publications/55413

Corrado, Carol, Jonathan Haskel, Cecilia Jona-Lasinio, and Massimiliano Iommi. July 2012. "Intangible Capital and Growth in Advanced Economies: Measurement Methods and Comparative Results." Institute for the Study of Labor (IZA). https://www.conference-board.org/pdf_free/workingpapers/EPWP%201203.pdf

Dale, Stacy, and Alan Krueger. June 2011. "Estimating the Return to College Selectivity Over the Career Using Administrative Earnings Data." NBER. http://www.nber.org/papers/w17159

Decker, Ryan, John Haltiwanger, Ron Jarmin, and Javier Miranda. Summer 2014. "The Role of Entrepreneurship in US Job Creation and Economic Dynamism." *Journal of Economic Perspectives.* https://www.aeaweb.org/articles?id=10.1257/jep.28.3.3

De Loecker, Jan, Jan Eeckhout, and Gabriel Unger. November 22, 2018. "The Rise of Market Power and the Macroeconomic Implications." NBER. http://www.janeeckhout.com/wp-content/uploads/RMP.pdf

Dobbs, Richard, et al. September 2015. "The New Global Competition for Corporate Profits." McKinsey Global Institute. http://www.mckinsey.com/business-functions/strategy-and-corporate-finance/our-insights/the-new-global-competition-for-corporate-profits

"Does Deutschland Do Digital?" November 21, 2017. *The Economist.* https://www.economist.com/news/business/21678774-europes-biggest-economy-rightly-worried-digitisation-threat-its-industrial

Eisfeldt, Andrea, Antonio Falato, and Mindy Z. Xiaolan. July 2019. *Human Capitalists.* Stanford University. https://economics.stanford.edu/sites/g/files/sbiybj9386/f/abstract_5.pdf

Erdmann, Kevin. 2019. *Shut Out: How a Housing Shortage Caused the Great Recession and Crippled Our Economy.* Lanham, MD: Rowman & Littlefield.

Federal Reserve Board of Governors. May 2019. "Financial Stability Report." https://www.federalreserve.gov/publications/2019-may-financial-stability-report-borrowing.htm. See 2-2 Business and Household Sector Credit to GDP Ratios

Federal Reserve Board of Governors. Accessed October 8, 2019. "10-Year Treasury Constant Maturity Rate." Federal Reserve Bank of St. Louis. https://fred.stlouisfed.org/series/DGS10

Foster, Richard, and Sarah Kaplan. (2001). *Creative Destruction: Why Companies That Are Built to Last Underperform the Market—and How to Successfully Transform Them.* New York: Crown.

"Frothy.com." December 20, 2014. *The Economist.* http://www.economist.com/news/business/21636754-new-tech-bubble-seems-be-inflating-when-it-pops-it-should-cause-less-damage

Ganapati, Sharat. January 30, 2019. "Growing Oligopolies, Prices, Output, and Productivity." Georgetown University. https://papers.ssrn.com/sol3/papers.cfm?abstract_id=3030966

Ganong, Peter, and Daniel Shoag. November 2017. "Why Has Regional Income Convergence in the US Declined?" *Journal of Urban Economics.* https://www.sciencedirect.com/science/article/abs/pii/S0094119017300591

Giannone, Elisa. January 4, 2017. "Skilled-Biased Technical Change and Regional Convergence." University of Chicago. https://home.uchicago.edu/~elisagiannone/files/JMP_ElisaG.pdf

Gold, Howard. November 29, 2017. "Never Mind the 1 Percent." *Chicago Booth Review.* https://review.chicagobooth.edu/economics/2017/article/never-mind-1-percent-lets-talk-about-001-percent

Gordon, Robert. 2016. *The Rise and Fall of American Growth: The U.S. Standard of Living Since The Civil War.* Princeton, NJ: Princeton University Press.

Greenwood, Jeremy, Nezih Guner, Georgi Kocharkov, and Cezar Santos. January 2014. "Marry Your Like: Assortative Mating and Income Inequality." NBER. http://www.nber.org/papers/w19829

Gutierrez, German, and Thomas Philippon. June 2019. "How EU Markets Became More Competitive Than US Markets: A Study of Institutional Drift." NBER. http://www.nber.org/papers/w24700

Guvenen, Fatih, Greg Kaplan, Jae Song, and Justin Weidner. April 2017. "Lifetime Incomes in the United States over Six Decades." NBER. http://www.nber.org/papers/w23371

Guzman, Jorge, and Scott Stern. July 2019. "The State of American Entrepreneurship: New Estimates of the Quantity and Quality of Entrepreneurship for 15 US States, 1988-2014." NBER. https://www.nber.org/papers/w22095

Hacker, Jacob, and Paul Pierson. July 30, 2017. "The Path to Prosperity Is Blue." *New York Times.* https://www.nytimes.com/2016/07/31/opinion/campaign-stops/the-path-to-prosperity-is-blue.html?_r=0

Haskel, Jonathan, and Stian Westlake. 2018. *Capitalism Without Capital: The Rise of the Intangible Economy.* Princeton & Oxford: Princeton University Press.

Hornbeck, Richard and Enrico Moretti. May 2018. "Who Benefits from Productivity Growth? Direct and Indirect Effects of Local TFP Growth on Wages, Rents, and Inequality." NBER. http://www.nber.org/papers/w24661?sy=661

Hoxie, Philip, Daniel Shoag, and Stan Veuger. December 2019. "Moving to Density: Half a Century of Housing Costs and Wage Premia from Queens to King Salmon." American Enterprise Institute Working Paper 2019-24. https://www.aei.org/wp-content/uploads/2020/01/Hoxie-Shoag-Veuger-Moving-to-Density-WP.pdf

Hsieh, Chang-Tai, and Enrico Moretti. April 2019. "Housing Constraints and Spatial Misallocation." *American Economic Journal.*https://faculty.chicagobooth.edu/chang-tai.hsieh/research/growth.pdf

Hsieh, Chang-Tai and Esteban Rossi-Hansberg. June 2016. "The Industrial Revolution in Services." NBER. https://www.nber.org/papers/w25968

International Monetary Fund (IMF). April 2015. "IMF World Economic Outlook." http://www.imf.org/external/pubs/ft/weo/2015/01/. See figure 4.5 Shares and Relative Prices of Investment Categories

Ivashina, Victoria, and Josh Lerner. 2019. *Patient Capital: The Challenges & Promises of Long Term Investing.* Princeton & Oxford: Princeton University Press, figure 3:2.

Kaplan, Steven, and Joshua Rauh. May 2013. "Family, Education, and Sources of Wealth Among the Richest Americans, 1982–2012." *American Economic Review.*   https://www.jstor.org/stable/23469721?seq=1page_scan_tab_contents

Karabarbounis, Loukas and Brent Neiman. June 2018. "Accounting for Factorless Income." National Bureau of Economic Research. https://www.nber.org/papers/w24404

Krugman, Paul, October 27, 2018. "Are the Danes Melancholy? Are the Swedes Sad?" *The New York Times.* https://www.nytimes.com/2018/10/27/opinion/are-the-danes-melancholy-are-the-swedes-sad.html

Krugman, Paul. July 24, 2019. "Left Coast Rising." *New York Times.* https://www.nytimes.com/2014/07/25/opinion/paul-krugman-california-tax-left-coast-rising.html?mcubz=1

Kuhn, Peter, and Fernando Lozano. January 2008. "The Expanding Workweek? Understanding Trends in Long Work Hours Among U.S. Men, 1979–2006." University of California-Santa Barbara. http://econ.ucsb.edu/~pjkuhn/Research%20Papers/LongHours.pdf

Lazear, Edward P. November 2019. "Productivity and Wages: Common Factors and Idiosyncrasies Across Countries and Industries." NBER. http://www.nber.org/papers/w26428

Mandel, Michael, and Bret Swanson. March 2017. "The Coming Productivity Boom: Transforming the Physical Economy with Information." Technology CEO Council. http://entropyeconomics.com/wp-content/uploads/2017/03/The-Coming-Productivity-Boom-Transforming-the-Physical-Economy-with-Information-March-2017.pdf

Manyika, James, Jan Mischke, Jacques Bughinm, Jonathan Woetzel, Mekala Krishnan, and Samuel Cudre. May 2019. "A New Look at the Declining Labor Share of Income in the United States." McKinsey Global Institute. https://www.mckinsey.com/featured-insights/employment-and-growth/a-new-look-at-the-declining-labor-share-of-income-in-the-united-states

Manyika, James, Sree Ramaswamy, Jacques Bughin, Jonathan Woetzel, Michael Birshan, and Zubin Nagpal. October 2018. "'Superstars': The Dynamics of Firms, Sectors and Cities Leading the Global Economy." McKinsey Global Institute.   https://www.mckinsey.com/featured-insights/innovation-and-growth/superstars-the-dynamics-of-firms-sectors-and-cities-leading-the-global-economy

Mian, Atif, and Amir Sufi. 2015. *House of Debt: How They (and You) Caused the Great Recession, and How We Can Prevent It from Happening Again.* Chicago: University of Chicago Press.

Moretti, Enrico. April 2010. "Local Labor Markets." NBER. http://www.nber.org/papers/w15947.pdf

Moretti, Enrico. August 2019. "The Effect of High-Tech Clusters on the Productivity of Top Inventors." NBER. https://eml.berkeley.edu//~moretti/clusters.pdf

Moretti, Enrico, and Daniel Wilson. 2017. "The Effect of State Taxes on the Geographical Location of Top Earners: Evidence from Star Scientists." *American Economic Review.* https://eml.berkeley.edu//~moretti/taxes.pdf

Moretti, Enrico, and Daniel Wilson. October 12, 2019. "Taxing Billionaires: Estate Taxes and the Geographical Location of the Ultra-Wealthy." University of California. https://eml.berkeley.edu//~moretti/billionaires.pdf

Moritz, Michael. December 3, 2017. "The Fall and Rise of Technology Juggernauts." *Financial Times.* https://www.ft.com/content/6b859714-99ba-11e5-9228-87e603d47bdc. Author's calculations as of September 30, 2019

Muro, Mark, and Jacob Whiton. January 23, 2018. "Geographic Gaps Are Widening While US Economic Growth Increases." Brookings Institution. https://www.brookings.edu/blog/the-avenue/2018/01/22/uneven-growth/

National Venture Capital Association. 2019. "2019 Yearbook, National Venture Capital Association." https://nvca.org/wp-content/uploads/2019/08/NVCA-2019-Yearbook.pdf

Organisation for Economic Co-operation and Development. Accessed October 28, 2019. "Balance of Payments: Current Account Balance as a % of GDP." https://stats.oecd.org/index.aspx?queryid=67094

Organisation for Economic Co-operation and Development. Accessed October 2, 2019. "Education at a Glance 2019, Indicator A5 What are the financial incentives to invest in education." https://www.oecd-ilibrary.org/education/education-at-a-glance-2019_f8d7880d-en;jsessionid=Mxhc7LOBj6IVTX4tCIbqqZHd.ip-10-240-5-47

Organisation for Economic Co-operation and Development (OECD). Accessed October 2, 2019. "GDP per Hour Worked, Level of GDP per Capita and Productivity." https://stats.oecd.org/index.aspx?DataSetCode=PDB_LV

Organisation for Economic Co-operation and Development (OECD). Accessed October 25, 2019. "Hours Worked." https://data.oecd.org/emp/hours-worked.htm

Organisation for Economic Co-operation and Development (OECD). Accessed October 2, 2019. "Labour Force." https://data.oecd.org/emp/labour-force.htmindicator-chart

Organisation for Economic Co-operation and Development (OECD). Accessed October 2, 2019. "Survey of Adult Skills." http://www.oecd.org/skills/piaac/publicdataandanalysis/d.en.408927

Ottaviano, Gianmarco, and Giovanni Peri. February 1, 2012. "Rethinking the Effect of Immigration on Wages." *Journal of the European Economic Association.* https://academic.oup.com/jeea/article-abstract/10/1/152/2182016

Peltzman, Sam. May 10, 2018. "Productivity and Prices in Manufacturing During an Era of Rising Concentration." Social Science Research Network. https://papers.ssrn.com/sol3/papers.cfm?abstract_id=3168877

Poon, Linda. February 27, 2019. "China's Huge Number of Vacant Apartments Is Causing a Problem." Citilab. https://www.citylab.com/equity/2019/02/china-vacant-apartments-housing-market-bubble-ghost-cities/583528/

Radford, Jynnah. June 17, 2019. "Key Findings About US Immigrants." Pew Research Center. https://www.pewresearch.org/fact-tank/2020/04/07/education-levels-of-recent-latino-immigrants-in-the-u-s-reached-new-highs-as-of-2018/

Rauh, Joshua. October 2019. "Behavioral Responses to State Income Taxation of High Earners: Evidence from California." NBER. https://www.nber.org/papers/w26349

Reeves, Richard. 2017. *Dream Hoarders: How the American Upper Middle Class Is Leaving Everyone Else in the Dust, Why That Is a Problem, and What to Do About It*. Washington D.C.: Brookings Institution Press.

Reich, Robert. 2015. *Saving Capitalism: For the Many, Not the Few*. New York: Knopf.

Reinhart, Carmen and Kenneth Rogoff. October 2009. *This Time Is Different: Eight Centuries of Financial Folly*. Princeton, NJ: Princeton University Press.

Remes, Jaana, James Manyika, Jacques Bughin, Jonathan Woetzel, Jan Mischke, and Mekala Krishnan. February 2018. "Solving the Productivity Puzzle: The Role of Demand and the Promise of Digitization." McKinsey Global Institute. See Exhibit 12. https://www.mckinsey.com/~/media/mckinsey/featured%20insights/meeting%20societys%20expectations/solving%20the%20productivity%20puzzle/mg-solving-the-productivity-puzzle--report-february-2018.ashx

Rognlie, Matthew. 2015. "Deciphering the Fall and Rise in the Net Capital Share: Accumulation or Scarcity?" Brookings Papers on Economic Activity. https://www.brookings.edu/bpea-articles/deciphering-the-fall-and-rise-in-the-net-capital-share/

Rognlie, Matthew. August 2018. "Comment on "Accounting for Factorless Income." NBER Macroeconomics Annual 2018. http://mattrognlie.com/kn_comment_rognlie.pdf

Rossi-Hansberg, Esteban, Pierre-Daniel Sarte, and Nicholas Trachter. April 17, 2019. "Diverging Trends in National and Local Concentration." Federal Reserve Bank of Richmond. https://www.princeton.edu/~erossi/DTNLC.pdf

Shapiro, Carl. October 25, 2017. "Antitrust in a Time of Populism." Social Science Research Network. https://papers.ssrn.com/sol3/papers.cfm?abstract_id=3058345

Smith, Matthew, Danny Yagan, Owen Zidar, and Eric Zwick. January 2019. "Capitalists in the Twenty-First Century." National Bureau of Economic Research. https://www.nber.org/papers/w25442

Song, Jae, David Price, Fatih Guvenen, Nicholas Bloom, and Till von Wachter. October 25, 2018. "Firming Up Inequality." *The Quarterly Journal of Economics*. https://academic.oup.com/qje/article-abstract/134/1/1/5144785?redirectedFrom=fulltext

Summers, Lawrence. February 2014. US Economic Prospects: Secular Stagnation, Hysteresis, and the Zero Lower Bound. Business Economics. http://larrysummers.com/wp-content/uploads/2014/06/NABE-speech-Lawrence-H.-Summers1.pdf

Tambe, Prasanna, Xuan Ye, and Peter Cappelli. February 2019. "Paying to Program? Engineering Brand and High-Tech Wage." NBER. https://www.nber.org/papers/w25552?sy=552

Thompson, Derek. January 23, 2013. "How America's Top Colleges Reflect (and Massively Distort) the Country's Racial Evolution." *The Atlantic*. https://www.theatlantic.com/national/archive/2013/01/how-americas-top-colleges-reflect-and-massively-distort-the-countrys-racial-evolution/267415/

US Bureau of Labor Statistics. Accessed October 2, 2019. "All Employees: Manufacturing." Federal Reserve Bank of St. Louis. https://fred.stlouisfed.org/series/MANEMP

US Bureau of Labor Statistics. Accessed October 2, 2019. "Manufacturing Sector: Real Output." Federal Reserve Bank of St. Louis. https://fred.stlouisfed.org/series/OUTMS

US Bureau of Labor Statistics. Accessed (October 2, 2019. "National Business Employment Dynamics Data by Firm Size Class." See: Table F. Distribution of private sector employment by firm size class, not seasonally adjusted. https://www.bls.gov/web/cewbd/table_f.txt

US Department of Education. Accessed October 14, 2019. "Long Term-Trend Mathematics Assessments." National Center on Education Statistics. https://nces.ed.gov/nationsreportcard/ltt/

Winship, Scott. April 24, 2019. "Losing Our Minds: Brain Drain Across the United States." United States Congress Joint Economic Committee. https://www.jec.senate.gov/public/index.cfm/republicans/2019/4/losing-our-minds-brain-drain-across-the-united-states

Winship, Scott. December 2017. "Love, Marriage, And The Baby Carriage: The Rise In Unwed Childbearing." Joint Economic Committee. https://www.lee.senate.gov/public/_cache/files/3a6e738b-305b-4553-b03b-3c71382f102c/love-marriage-and-the-baby-carriage.pdf

INDEX

Tables and figures are indicated by an italic *t* and *f* following the page/paragraph number.